Guide to the GDPR

Guide to the GDPR

Edited by

Maciej Gawronski

Wolters Kluwer

Published by:
Kluwer Law International B.V.
PO Box 316
2400 AH Alphen aan den Rijn
The Netherlands
E-mail: international-sales@wolterskluwer.com
Website: lrus.wolterskluwer.com

Sold and distributed in North, Central and South America by:
Wolters Kluwer Legal & Regulatory U.S.
7201 McKinney Circle
Frederick, MD 21704
United States of America
Email: customer.service@wolterskluwer.com

Sold and distributed in all other countries by:
Air Business Subscriptions
Rockwood House
Haywards Heath
West Sussex
RH16 3DH
United Kingdom
Email: international-customerservice@wolterskluwer.com

ISBN 978-94-035-1414-7

e-Book: 978-94-035-1422-2
web-PDF: 978-94-035-1423-9

Editor

Maciej Gawronski is an authority in cloud computing, cybersecurity, data protection, IT and intellectual property. Maciej is a managing partner of Gawronski & Partners law firm located in Warsaw, Poland. Maciej served as European Commission Expert on Cloud Computing Contracts, Article 29 Working Party Expert on data transfers where he contributed ideas implemented in the GDPR (subprocessors liability, personal data portability). Maciej is recognised by leading international and domestic rankings as top Polish technology law expert. Maciej edited and co-authored the No 1 Polish legal bestseller 2018 '*Guide to the GDPR*'. Prior to setting up Gawroński & Piecuch, Maciej set up and for eight years managed the Polish office of an international technology and intellectual property boutique Bird & Bird. Maciej is the main contributor to Good Data Protection Standard GDPR compliance system (gdpstandard.com) as well as to other GDPR and cybersecurity compliance and management systems.

Contributors

Witold Chomiczewski LLM is a partner of 'Lubasz i Wspólnicy', an expert on data protection, e-commerce, information technology (IT) and intellectual property. Witold co-authored the bestselling '*General Data Protection Regulation (GDPR) Commentary*' (in Polish) co-edited by Dr Edyta Bielak-Jomaa – President of the Polish Data Protection Office – and Dr Dominic Lubasz, managing partner of 'Lubasz i Wspólnicy', as well as other books on data protection and e-commerce.

Aleksander P. Czarnowski is an expert in cybersecurity and information security, including standards and regulations as ISO 27000 family, ISO 29134, PCI DSS, PSD2, GDPR. Alexander is European Commission Expert on Cloud Computing Contracts, Member of Cloud Select Industry Group (CSIG) group in the European Commission, Member of the Polish Committee of Standardisation responsible for ISO 2700 family. Aleksander contributed to Good Data Protection Standard system (gdpstandard.com).

Marcin Dominiak has many years of experience in the Inspection Department of the former Polish Data Protection Authority (GIODO), and now he is serving as data protection officer (DPO) at banks and other institutions both from the private and the public sectors. Marcin participated in the works of the Article 29 Working Party; he is a member of the Information Security Forum at the Polish Banking Association.

Adrianna Gnatowska is an associate at Gawronski & Piecuch S.K.A., practising data protection and e-commerce as well as employment (including compliance and mobbing issues) and immigration. Adrianna's data protection experience includes GDPR implementations, e-privacy (direct marketing) and joint controllership structures and agreements for such sectors as energy, real estate and tobacco.

Michał Kibil is a Polish advocate, managing Kibil i Wspólnicy law firm. Michał specialises in employment, data protection and technology. Michał is an expert of the Polish Chamber of Information and Communications Technology (PIIT); he is actively involved in a number of innovative areas such as distributed ledger technology, legal automation, machine learning, work systems optimisation.

Katarzyna Kloc is a partner of Gawronski & Piecuch, an expert in privacy and data protection as well as in IT and intellectual property, responsible for GDPR implementations, operating and maintenance and for assisting clients in implementing cybersecurity framework requirements (NIS Directive). Katarzyna co-edited and co-authored the '*Guide to the Polish Cybersecurity System Act*' (Wolters Kluwer 2019). Katarzyna contributed to such GDPR compliance tools as Good Data Protection Standard system (gdpstandard.com), LEX Compliance RODO by Wolters Kluwer Polska and Actuality.pl (cybersecurity risk management). Prior to joining Gawroński & Piecuch, Katarzyna Kloc worked as a member of intellectual property and technology teams of international law firms CMS and Bird & Bird.

Katarzyna Kunda is a lawyer specializing in privacy and data protection as well as in IT and intellectual property. Katarzyna co-edited and co-authored the *Guide to the Polish Cybersecurity System Act* (Wolters Kluwer 2019). Katarzyna contributed to such GDPR compliance tools as Good Data Protection Standard system (gdpstandard.com) and LEX Compliance RODO by Wolters Kluwer Polska. Katarzyna is a general counsel at Cloud Technologies S.A. in Warsaw. She previously worked as an associate at Gawroński & Piecuch responsible for data protection, incident management, e-commerce, cybersecurity, cloud computing contracts and media law.

Dr Dominik Lubasz is a top Polish data protection expert and a managing partner of 'Lubasz i Wspólnicy'. Together with Dr Edyta Bielak-Jomaa – President of the Polish Data Protection Office – Dominic co-edited and co-authored the bestselling '*General Data Protection Regulation (GDPR) Commentary*' (in Polish). He also edited and co-authored several other books and publications on data protection, privacy, e-commerce and consumer law as well as contributed to a data protection impact assessment software tool RiskTracker.

Adrianna Michałowicz specialises in civil, data protection and intellectual property law. Adrianna works closely with Dr Dominik Lubasz on data protection matters.

Patrycja Naklicka is an associate at Gawroński & Piecuch S.K.A. where she is responsible for GDPR, cybersecurity regulations, cloud computing, IT and intellectual property matters. Patrycja's experience includes data protection and secondary data breach risk assessment. Patrycja contributed to Good Data Protection Standard GDPR compliance system (gdpstandard.com). Patrycja lectures at postgraduate studies on data protection and information security at Lazarski University in Warsaw.

Zuzanna Piotrowska is a regulatory lawyer focusing on regulatory aspects of security (data breaches management, SCA) as well as on financial regulation such as anti-money laundering (AML IV), payment services (PSD II), investment regulation (PRIPS), banking law.

Paweł Punda is a legal expert specialising in IT, banking and e-commerce sectors. He advised in IT projects, starting from initial stages, pre-implementation analysis, negotiating contracts, as well as at a stage of implementation. Paweł advised in GDPR implementations in banks and financial institutions and other sectors, including production. Paweł contributed to Good Data Protection Standard data protection compliance system (gdpstandard.com).

Michał Sztąberek is an expert in data protection and information security. Michał is an ISO 27001 lead auditor. He serves as a DPO for various entities.

Summary of Contents

Table of Contents

List of Abbreviations

Directive 95/46/EC	Directive 95/46/EC of the European Parliament and of the Council of 24 October 1995 on the protection of individuals with regard to the processing of personal data and on the free movement of such data (Official Journal EC L 281, p. 31)
Directive 2016/680	Directive (EU) of the European Parliament and of the Council of 27 April 2016 on the protection of natural persons with regard to the processing of personal data by competent authorities for the purpose of the prevention, investigation, detection or prosecution of criminal offences or the execution of criminal penalties, and on the free movement of such data, and repealing Council Framework Decision 2008/977/JHA (Official Journal EU L 119, p. 89)
C2C	Controller to Controller
CFR	EU Charter of Fundamental Rights (Official Journal EU C 202 of 2016, p. 389)
CJEU	Court of Justice of the European Union
CPHR	Convention for the Protection of Human Rights and Fundamental Freedoms, Rome 4.11.1950 r. (Journal of Laws of 1993, item 284 as amended)
CRM	Customer Relations Management
DPIA	Data Protection Impact Assessment
DPO	Data Protection Officer
EC	European Commission
EDPB	European Data Protection Board
EEA	European Economic Area

EU	European Union
GDPR	EU General Data Protection Regulation
IT	Information Technology
Judgment C-131/12 Google Spain	Judgment of 13 May 2014 in Case C-131/12, Google Spain SL and Google Inc. vs. Agencia Española de Protección de Datos (AEPD) and Mario Costeja González, EU:C:2014:317
PIO	Privacy Information Obligation
RDPA	Records of Data Processing Activities
Regulation 2016/679, GDPR	Regulation (EU) 2016/679 of the European Parliament and of the Council of 27 April 2016 on the protection of natural persons with regard to the processing of personal data and on the free movement of such data, and repealing Directive 95/46/EC (General Data Protection Regulation) (Official Journal EU L 119, p. 1)
TEU	Treaty on European Union (Official Journal EU C 202 of 2016, p. 13)
TFEU	Treaty on the Functioning of the European Union (Official Journal EU C 202 of 2016, p. 47)
TOMs	Technical and Organisational Measures of Data Security
UK	United Kingdom
UN	United Nations
US	United States

Part I GDPR Compendium

CHAPTER 1

Basic Compliance

Katarzyna Kloc, Maciej Gawronski, Marcin Dominiak, Michał Sztąberek, Patrycja Naklicka & Paweł Punda[*]

1 THE GDPR: THE EU'S 'ACT' ON PERSONAL DATA PROTECTION

1.1 The GDPR: The New 'Act' on Personal Data Protection

Put very briefly, Regulation (EU) 2016/679 of the European Parliament and of the Council of 27 April 2016 on the protection of natural persons with regard to the processing of personal data and on the free movement of such data, and repealing Directive 95/46/EC (General Data Protection Regulation) (Official Journal EU L 119, p. 1) – the GDPR – is the **new European 'act' on personal data protection**.

Protecting individuals in the context of the processing of personal data is one of the fundamental rights in the European Union (EU) (Recital 1 GDPR). This is stated in Article 8(1) of the EU Charter of Fundamental Rights (Official Journal EU C 202 of 2016, p. 389) and Article 16(1) of the Treaty on the Functioning of the EU (Official Journal EU C 202 of 2016, p. 47), under which everyone has the right to the protection of personal data concerning him or her.

To execute and guarantee the right to privacy and data protection within the EU, the EU found it necessary to establish a stable, consistent framework for personal data

* Section 1 contributed by Maciej Gawronski and Katarzyna Kloc. Section 2 contributed by Maciej Gawronski and Katarzyna Kloc. Section 3 contributed by Maciej Gawronski and Patrycja Naklicka. Section 4 contributed by Marcin Dominiak and Maciej Gawronski. Section 5 contributed by Maciej Gawronski and Michał Sztąberek. Section 6 contributed by Maciej Gawronski and Michał Sztąberek. Section 7 contributed by Maciej Gawronski. Section 8 contributed by Maciej Gawronski and Katarzyna Kloc. Section 9 contributed by Maciej Gawronski. Section 10 contributed by Katarzyna Kloc. Section 11 contributed by Maciej Gawronski. Section 12 contributed by Maciej Gawronski. Section 13 contributed by Maciej Gawronski. Section 14 contributed by Paweł Punda and Maciej Gawronski.

protection and to **enforce** it in a decisive manner. Until GDPR the main problem with personal data protection was in fact enforcement (forcing compliance).

1.2 The Subject Matter and the Objective of the GDPR

1.2.1 Preliminary Remarks

Officially, the GDPR keeps in place the personal data protection rules applicable up to now in the EU as set in Directive 95/46/EC (so-called Personal Data Protection Directive) and implemented in national legislation by all EU Member States, but is a more detailed version, giving natural persons material and enforcement rights and introducing severe penalties, direct liability of subcontractors (data processors) and obligation to report data breaches.

Despite reassurances given by supervisory authorities, in practice, the GDPR revolutionises data protection not only due to penalties and new obligations of companies and other bodies that process personal data but also due to a complete shift of approach concerning liability and interpretation of law. This is due to the so-called risk-based approach, which is the obligation of everyone to evaluate risk connected with personal data processing and match data compliance and data protection measures to that risk, and also due to introduction of the principle of accountability – the obligation to demonstrate compliance on the part of a person subject to an obligation. One hundred per cent compliance is a myth in relation to any law, but in the first years of application of the GDPR, a data protection compliance will be like the Schrödinger's Cat mixed with Heisenberg's uncertainty principle.

Under Article 1 GDPR:

(1) The Regulation lays down **rules relating to the protection of natural persons with regard to the processing of personal data and rules relating to the free movement of personal data**.
(2) The Regulation protects fundamental rights and freedoms of natural persons and in particular their **right to the protection of personal data**.
(3) The free movement of personal data within the Union shall be neither restricted nor prohibited for reasons connected with the protection of natural persons with regard to the processing of personal data.

1.2.2 Protection of Natural Persons

The GDPR is comprehensive. It covers protection of privacy and personal data (of natural persons) in a broad manner and also addresses the issue of free movement of personal data within the EU. According to Recital 14, the GDPR does not cover the processing of personal data which concerns legal persons and in particular undertakings established as legal persons, including the name and the form of the legal person and the contact details of the legal person. The above is enigmatic, and it is the only reference to 'personal data of legal persons'. In particular, it is hard to tell straight from the GDPR if an employee's professional email (john.smith@corporation.eu) is a personal data or personal data of an institution. Treating a professional email as personal data in communication with an institution leads to nonsensical consequences. In each business to business or more widely institution to institution communication we would have to check if an information obligation has been completed.[1] In addition simple communication with non-EU entities would amount to regulated transfer of data. From the other perspective a professional email can be used to reach a particular individual and may contain data on the occupation and employer of an individual. So john.smith@corporation.eu can be used as personal data of an institution or as 'regular' personal data. That is why post-GDPR personal data protection is getting close to quantum physics, and we sometimes call GDPR a quantum minefield.

1.2.3 Direct Applicability

While the GDPR is legislation passed at EU level, it is directly applicable to any organisation that processes personal data as the controller or processor in an EU Member State. In certain cases (when you are addressing EU residents with your offer or monitoring EU residents' behaviour) you may become subject to the GDPR even if you are not in the EU.

This direct applicability and resulting function of an 'act' on personal data protection are features that distinguish the GDPR from Directive 95/46/EC of the European Parliament and of the Council of 24 October 1995 on the protection of individuals with regard to the processing of personal data and on the free movement of such data (Official Journal EC L 281, p. 31) (Personal Data Protection Directive). Directive 95/46/EC was intended to harmonise rules on personal data protection within the EU, but in practice, due to considerable differences in the national provisions implementing that directive, the level of personal data protection and approaches to this question varied greatly from Member State to Member State.

As a new, common 'act' on data protection, the GDPR is intended to provide a high and uniform level of data protection across the entire EU. Due to being general in nature and effective at a high level, at the same time the GDPR allows extensive freedom of approach, broad scope for interpretation, and development of practice in individual Member States. In reality, it creates immense room for administrative discretion as well as the need for dozens of procedures and formalities, being a perfect example of so-called Brussels law.

1.2.4 What the GDPR Means for Businesses?

As of 25 May 2018, EU businesses and other businesses addressing their offer to EU residents first have to directly consult the GDPR, and not, as was the case up to now,

1. In practice this issue is sometimes circumvented based on the assumption that a person who communicates with an institution in the name of another institution already knows her/his rights under GDPR as a trained professional (Arts 13.3 and 14.5.a GDPR). But it does not solve the issue of communicating with non-EU entities.

the national legislation of particular EU Member States. Which, in principle, is good news.

Bad news is that the GDPR is not at all specific on how to achieve compliance.

Meanwhile, EU Member States are enacting legislation helping to link GDPR with the local law and adapting local laws to GDPR. The process is still in progress in December 2018. At the same time, European Data Protection Board (EDPB) (formerly Article 29 Working Party) continues to issue more or rather less helpful guidelines on the interpretation of EU data protection rules.

In result, again we are facing a dynamic patchwork of regulations and interpretations, this time however accompanied by a set of new obligations and a perspective of severe administrative fines for non-compliance.

1.3 Three Pillars, Two Foundations, One Turtle

The objective of the GDPR is to construct a new, uniform personal data protection system at EU level, based on three pillars:

(I) **Lawfulness** - rules that organisations are required to implement and comply with continuously.

(II) **Rights** - a number of rights of data subjects concerning the processing of their personal data, from the organisation's point of view - specific processes to be effected.

(III) **Security** - the process of continuously ensuring security, meaning a set of measures taken by organisations to ensure confidentiality, integrity, and accessibility of the processed personal data, and protection against threats.

Each of these GDPR pillars constitutes rules to be understood and implemented, obligations to be met, processes to be executed, documentation to be drawn up and adopted within an organisation, information technology (IT) functionalities to be implemented, and any other measures enabling an organisation to affirm and demonstrate that it processes personal data in line with the intention of and in compliance with the GDPR. In practice, each pillar presents a separate challenge.

However, the pillars of the GDPR rely on the foundations of accountability and risk-based approach.

Accountability

The principle of **accountability** is fundamental to the GDPR. In practice, this means that a business and any other organisation has to be able to account for how they comply with and implement particular GDPR provisions. This is no easy task because the provisions are very general and do not give specific and practical guidelines as to how to understand and apply a particular rule.

This approach is, in fact, a presumption of liability. The cynical and primitive way (still the most effective) to deal with accountability is documenting - designing documentation of compliance, documenting procedures, documenting compliance with procedures.

Risk-Based Approach

In theory, the GDPR is built around a so-called risk-based approach. The risk-based approach basically corresponds to what I call the 'Spiderman rule', i.e. 'with great power comes great responsibility'. A data processing entity (controller or processor) should understand and assess the risk of data processing and apply measures corresponding to that risk.

'Risk' is repeated seventy-five times in the GDPR. The two main provisions directly concerning 'risk-based approach principle' are Article 24(1) GDPR, according to which:

> Taking into account the nature, scope, context and purposes of processing as well as **the risks of varying likelihood and severity for the rights and freedoms of natural persons**, the controller shall implement appropriate technical and organisational measures **to ensure and to be able to demonstrate that processing is performed in accordance with this Regulation.**

and Article 32(1) GDPR, according to which:

> Taking into account the state of the art, the costs of implementation and the nature, scope, context and purposes of processing as well as the risk of varying likelihood and severity for the rights and freedoms of natural persons, the controller and the processor shall implement appropriate technical and organisational measures to ensure a level of security appropriate to the risk … .

According to the GDPR you should calculate the risk of processing of personal data and then adopt measures (technical and organisational) appropriate to the risk, which would normally be measures bringing the residual risk to low level (unless, according to Article 36 GDPR, you really wish to contact your supervisory authority to ask what to do with 'high-risk data processing').

There is an important difference between Article 24(1) and Article 32(1) GDPR partly quoted above. Article 32 GDPR concerns the risk of data security, i.e. in fact risk of a personal data breach and its adverse consequences to data subjects (persons whose data are affected by a breach). It requires you to adopt technical and organisational measures of data security 'appropriate' to that risk.

However, Article 24(1) GDPR goes even further – it requires you (controllers and processors) to 'implement appropriate […] measures to [first] **ensure** and [second] **be able to demonstrate** that **processing is performed in accordance with this Regulation**'. It means that you should scale your whole personal data protection system (budget, compliance tools, procedures, staffing, technology & security), up to the risk your data processing is causing for persons whose data you process. Moreover, it is up to you to prove that you are compliant appropriately to the risk you are generating (principle of accountability).

What does a 'risk-based approach' mean in practice can be easily manifested by quoting the current Head of the EDPB – Mrs Andreas Jelinek. In response to a request for more guidance from the EDPB she said. 'It's a question of which side of the table you're sitting on', Jelinek answered. 'As a regulator, we have tasks too. You don't have to fulfill my tasks, so don't expect me to fulfill yours.'[2]

In brief, you are processing personal data at your own risk and the supervisory authorities will not tell you the rules until you break them.

The Giant Turtle Underneath

Finally, the two principles of accountability and risk-based approach underlying the three pillars of the GDPR (legality, data subjects rights, security) rely themselves on the shell of the Giant Star Turtle named A'Tuin[3] who carries the GDPR across the galaxy. No, there is no turtle in the European data protection law. We are just kidding to check your focus.

Example 1

Accountability for implementing the GDPR

A controller implements and documents each element and step of that process, from the board resolution launching the implementation of the GDPR to documenting training sessions and meetings, breaking down the GDPR into particular obligations, and drawing up the relevant documentation. Implementation and maintaining that GDPR implementation documentation and compliance documentation are means by which a controller can account for how it implements the GDPR.

Example 2

Failure to account for marketing consent

A customer requests access to data and a copy of data, including a copy of the marketing consent given to the controller. The controller is not able to locate the consent, and therefore only states that consent was given, and the supposed scope. The customer lodges a complaint with the Data Protection Office, saying that they did not give that consent, and the Data Protection Office begins to investigate. The investigation reveals that the controller did not take care to keep marketing consent records in order. The controller is fined and is also ordered to stop direct marketing until new consents are obtained or the consents in its possession are catalogued.

---

2. https://iapp.org/news/a/new-wp29-chair-talks-enforcement-role-of-the-dpo/# (last accessed on 9 March 2019).
3. The Great A'Tuin is a creation of mind of Terry Pratchett, from his Discworld fantasy novels. https://en.wikipedia.org/wiki/Discworld_(world) (last accessed on 3 March 2019).

1.4 GDPR Requirements

In the past, there has not been any act of law in the legislation of EU Member States or EU legal system that imposes such high penalties for failure to comply with such unclear provisions on practically every organisation. It is tempting to say that the GDPR is difficult, intelligent, severe, and incomprehensible, but upon further analysis based on the pillars of privacy, rights of individuals, security, and the fundamental principle of accountability, the general and high-level GDPR is revealed to be simply **demanding**.

The GDPR is characterised by:

(a) generality,
(b) measurability,
(c) direct applicability,
(d) severity,
(e) a presumption of responsibility.

1.4.1 Generality

Under Article 5 GDPR, the GDPR should be approached according to the following principles:

(1) legal compliance (lawfulness, action based on legal grounds, fulfilling other obligations);
(2) fairness (not misleading, loyalty, honesty, good faith);
(3) transparency (legibility, comprehensibility);
(4) specificity of purposes (purpose limitation);
(5) necessity for the purpose of processing ('data minimisation');
(6) ensuring data accuracy and actuality (accuracy);
(7) kept no longer than necessary (storage limitation);
(8) security (called by the GDPR as 'integrity and confidentiality'[4]).

In the manner described above, the GDPR formulates the basic personal data protection principles. In subsequent provisions it only gives general guidelines as to how they should be effected. It does not say what is meant by 'large-scale' processing, even though it makes certain obligations dependent on this. Even with regard to the issue of security, apart from the examples of vague terms encryption and pseudonymisation, the GDPR does not provide any specific answers as regards to means of secure processing personal data. For this reason, the GDPR **requires** significant intellectual and organisational effort on the part of controllers and processors in order to analyse these rules that are so general in nature and produce on that basis specific documents, technologies, processes, and measures suited to the organisation in question.

4. Article 5(1)(f) GDPR.

1.4.2 *Measurability*

On the one hand the lack of specificity and on the other strict time limits for executing certain processes are the next challenges that the GDPR presents for organisations. Where individuals' requests (so-called subject access requests) are processed (execution of an individual's rights) a business has a month to respond to a request from a data subject (e.g., a request for erasure of data or provision of a report on the kind of data the business processes and for what purpose). This time limit can be extended by a maximum of two months, but information that the time limit has been extended and the grounds for this extension have to be provided within one month.

Where reporting breach of data to a supervisory authority is compulsory (this is a new development in relation to the old rules) organisations have to do this within seventy-two hours of learning of the breach.

Specific, measurable time limits for complying with obligations of controllers mean that the processes subject to time limits imposed by law have to be properly and carefully planned in advance. Measurability **requires** that the appropriate resources be provided and personnel trained and that the appropriate means and procedures are put in place, including cooperation with subcontractors.

1.4.3 *Direct Applicability*

The GDPR applies directly throughout the EU. Direct applicability means that in practice, as of 25 May 2018, all controllers or processors face the risk of prosecution. For this reason, the provisions in the GDPR **have** to be analysed in a detailed way and the GDPR has to be implemented with precision by every business.

1.4.4 *Severity*

Despite most of the provisions in the GDPR being general in nature, it is highly specific with regard to penalties. It introduces an exorbitant upper limit for administrative fines for breach of the GDPR. Fines are set on a case-by-case basis for each business according to a minimum of eighteen criteria. Fines should be 'effective, proportionate, and dissuasive' (Article 83(1) GDPR).

Under the GDPR there are two ranges for fines:

(1) up to EUR 10 million, or up to 2 % of the undertaking's total worldwide annual turnover in the preceding financial year, whichever is higher (i.e., when the undertaking's turnover or turnover of a group of undertakings exceeds EUR 500 million);
(2) up to EUR 20 million, or up to 4 % of the undertaking's total worldwide annual turnover in the preceding financial year, whichever is higher (i.e., when the undertaking's turnover or turnover of a group of undertakings exceeds EUR 500 million).

Therefore, the GDPR **requires** a serious approach on the part of an organisation to the issue of personal data protection, which was trivialised in the past due to being unenforceable. The severity and probably the inevitability of penalties, which we will be able to observe as of 25 May 2018, means that this area of activity of businesses cannot be treated lightly and throws an entirely new light on the question of protection of privacy and personal data.

1.4.5 Presumption of Guilt

As mentioned, the principle of accountability is fundamental to the GDPR. It creates a practical presumption of guilt (liability). This presumption of guilt **requires** an organisation to be able to demonstrate, account for, and prove that it complies with personal data protection, while at the same time it does not have a simple checklist of tasks or organisational and technical measures to take or implement. Presumption of responsibility follows from the following provisions in the GDPR:

Under Article 5(2) GDPR:

> The controller shall be responsible for, and **be able to demonstrate compliance with** paragraph 1 ('accountability').

Under Article 24 (1) first sentence GDPR:

> Taking into account the nature, scope, context and purposes of processing as well as the risks of varying likelihood and severity for the rights and freedoms of natural persons, the controller shall implement appropriate technical and organisational measures **to ensure and to be able to demonstrate** that processing is performed in accordance with this Regulation.

Under Article 82(3) GDPR:

> A controller or processor shall be exempt from liability under paragraph 2 **if it proves that it is not in any way responsible** for the event giving rise to the damage.

To summarise, all of the elements described above mean that the new personal data protection system requires and in fact forces organisations to make a significant effort to adapt their personal data processing procedures to comply with the GDPR. This effort has to be made at multiple levels and comprehensively throughout the organisation, not only with regard to the law and documentation but also with regard to organisational, procedural, awareness, and technological issues.

As a rule, in order to implement the GDPR properly, specialist knowledge is needed of personal data protection law, IT, cybersecurity, and organisation and project management. Hopefully, however, in the next few years, suitable templates will emerge that can be used to ensure GDPR compliance without the need for specialist knowledge in all of these fields.

1.5 How the GDPR Is Divided from a Functional Point of View?

The GDPR has a typical layout for EU legal acts and comprises the recitals (140 points which take up approximately 35% of the GDPR total contents) and the following chapters:

(I) General Provisions
(II) Principles
(III) Rights of the Data Subject
(IV) Controller and Processor
(V) Transfers of Personal Data to Third Countries or International Organisations
(VI) Independent Supervisory Authorities
(VII) Cooperation and Consistency
(VIII) Legal Remedies, Liability and Penalties
(IX) Provisions Relating to Specific Processing Situations
(X) Delegated Acts and Implementing Acts
(XI) Final Provisions.

From the point of view of organisations which have to understand the GDPR and translate it into specific measures feasible in their business enterprise, the GDPR can be divided according to function by grouping the individual issues in logical **streams** according to subject matter. By this way of thinking, the GDPR is divided into the following streams, in which certain distinct issues can be identified:

Basic Compliance:

- basic data processing principles (lawfulness, fairness, transparency, specificity, being up-to-date, processing on a temporary basis, retention, period of storage) (Article 5 GDPR);
- consent and notification, other grounds for processing data (Article 6 GDPR);
- privacy by default (Article 25(2) GDPR);
- privacy by design, i.e., incorporating privacy into plans for changes to activity, in particular technological and organisational changes (Article 25(1) GDPR);
- processing of special categories of personal data (Article 9 GDPR) and data relating to criminal convictions and offences (Article 10 GDPR);
- processing which does not require identification (Article 11 GDPR);
- records of processing activities (Article 30 GDPR);
- profiling (Article 13(2).f, Article 14(2).g, Article 22, Article 35 GDPR).

Rights of Individuals:

- right to be informed that data is collected (Articles 13–14 GDPR);
- right of access to data and copies of data (Article 15 GDPR);
- right of rectification and to have incomplete data completed (Article 16 GDPR);
- right to erasure (‘right to be forgotten’) (Article 17 GDPR);

- right to restriction of processing (Article 18 GDPR);
- right to data portability (Article 20 GDPR);
- right to object to processing (Article 21 GDPR);
- right to human intervention in cases of automated processing (Article 22 GDPR), as well as other requirements that give rise to obligations for businesses and other organisations, such as:
  - right to have a request processed (ignoring communication prohibited) (Article 12(3) GDPR);
  - right to 'legibility'(Article 12(1) GDPR);
  - right to facilitation (e.g., in the form of a handbook, 'guide to your rights', bookmark on a website) (Article 12(2) GDPR);
  - right to timeliness of action (Article 12(3) GDPR);
  - right to be informed of rights (Article 13(2) and 14(2) GDPR);
  - right to withdraw consent (Article 7(3) GDPR);
  - right of withdrawing being 'as easy' as giving consent (Article 7(3) GDPR);
  - right to be informed of recipients of rectified/erased/restricted data (Article 19 GDPR);
  - right to be notified of a breach likely to result in a high risk to the rights and freedoms of a person (Article 34(1) GDPR);
  - right to lodge a complaint and to appeal (Articles 77 and 78 GDPR);
  - right to compensation (Article 82 GDPR);
  - right to support from a not-for-profit organisation.

Security:

- security of data as a basic principle of personal data processing (Article 5(1)(f), Recital 39);
- assessing the risk of processing data and adopting security measures that are adequate to that risk (Articles 24, 32 GDPR);
- designing privacy (privacy by design) and minimisation (privacy by default) (Article 25 GDPR);
- data protection impact assessment (DPIA) (Article 35 GDPR);
- prior consultation with a supervisory authority if DPIA returns high residual risk of processing (Article 36 GDPR).

Processor:

- detailed regulation of a data processing agreement between a controller and processor (Article 28 GDPR);
- processors' liability;
- principles and standards for selecting a processor (Article 28(1) GDPR);
- subprocessing – engaging another processor by the main processor (Article 28(2) and (4) GDPR).

Managing Operational Incidents and Reporting Breaches:

- understanding and specifying within the organisation what is meant by personal data breach – classification of incidents (Article 4(12) GDPR);
- reporting personal data breaches to the supervisory authority within seventy-two hours of becoming aware of the breach (Article 33(1) GDPR);
- procedure and management of determining a breach;
- reporting to the controller by the processor of personal data breaches (Article 33(2) GDPR);
- notifying the data subject of personal data breaches (Article 34 GDPR).

Data Protection Officer:

- analysis of whether there is an obligation to designate a data protection officer (DPO) in the organisation (Article 37 GDPR);
- status of a DPO (Article 38 GDPR);
- duties of a DPO (Article 39 GDPR);
- scope of responsibility of a DPO.

Regulator:

- status, independence, general conditions, competence, tasks, and powers of the supervisory authority (Articles 51–59 GDPR).

Export of Data (To Outside of the EU):

- rules for data transfers to third countries.

Cross-Border Processing:

- identifying cross-border processing (i.e., in multiple EU Member States) within an organisation;
- determining the lead supervisory authority;
- determining the main establishment.

Codes of Conduct and Certification:

- option for sectoral codes of conduct relating to processing of personal data (Article 40 GDPR);
- monitoring approved codes of conduct (Article 41 GDPR);
- certification (Article 42 GDPR);
- certification bodies (Article 43 GDPR).

Penalties and Liability:

- right to lodge a complaint with a supervisory authority (Article 77 GDPR);
- right to an effective judicial remedy against a supervisory authority (Article 78 GDPR);
- right to an effective judicial remedy against a controller or processor (Article 79 GDPR);
- right to compensation (Article 82 GDPR);
- imposing administrative fines (Article 83 GDPR);
- option for criminal law provisions – derogated to national laws.

2 MATERIAL AND TERRITORIAL SCOPE OF THE GDPR

2.1 Applicability of the GDPR

The material and territorial scope of the GDPR is provided for in Articles 2 and 3.

2.1.1 Material Scope

Under Article 2(1), the GDPR applies to processing of personal data (a) wholly or partly by automated means and to (b) other processing (e.g., in paper files) of personal data which form part of a filing system or are intended to form part of a filing system (i.e., if the data are catalogued in a manner allowing to find particular persons, e.g. alphabetical files of individual clients).

To understand the provision on the material scope of the GDPR, Article 1, which states the subject matter and objective of the GDPR, Article 3, which states the territorial scope and the section on definitions need to be consulted. To determine whether the GDPR applies to a particular business (an organisation of any kind) or a particular process, an understanding is needed of the individual elements of the provision stipulating the material scope of the GDPR, i.e.:

(a) data processing – any operations (activities) performed on personal data, for example the mere storage of personal data;
(b) personal data – any information relating to an identified (specific) or identifiable natural person, such as first name, surname, official individual identification number, and telephone number;
(c) data processing wholly or partly by automated means – data processing using IT systems, for example in Outlook or Customer Relation Management (CRM) databases but also data recorded using video cameras (closed-circuit television, building security services). The term 'processing by automated means' has been left undefined in the GDPR deliberately to ensure that the regulations remain technologically neutral. Due to the fact that processing by automated means does not necessarily refer to data in a database (structured), the GDPR

also applies to unstructured data, for example personal data in emails between employees;

(d) processing personal data which form part of a filing system or are intended to form part of a filing system by other means – manual processing of personal data that in this case must form part of a filing system or an organised set of such data (e.g., arranged alphabetically).

Example

A business operating on a small scale that holds details of its customers or employees and performs operations of any kind on those data, even correspondence and keeping the data on a computer, regardless of the volume of the data, has to process those data as required under the GDPR. Even if the customers are capital companies, the GDPR must be applied, because people are employed in companies of this kind and a business communicates with specific individuals, and in general processes various information about them, even if this is only their email address and mobile telephone number.

However, at the end of 2018 when we are writing this book, not everything about processing data 'by automated means' is clear. In particular scope of applicability of the GDPR to so-called unstructured data is unclear. Is a lawyer writing a pleading in a text editor on her laptop processing data of persons mentioned in that pleading 'by automated means'? Is a general file server or Sharepoint like resource or other common computer space for an organisation an automated means of processing even if filing and sharing are not governed by any centralised filing system based on personal data? Does a personal address book created and kept by an employee amount to processing data of contacts by automated means by her employer? Is a practice of identifying and indexing of all personal data in an organisation's systems (as promoted by certain IT vendors) a good or bad thing? To a certain extent Article 11 GDPR treating about processing personal data for which identification is not needed (called by us 'unidentified data') and Article 14(5) GDPR describing exemptions from informing a person (data subject) about processing her personal data help to reconcile duties of data controllers and rights of data subject with specific situations, without claiming that the GDPR does not apply at all. In any case, breaking the GDPR Code is not easy.

2.1.2 Exclusion of Applicability of the GDPR

There are certain cases in which the GDPR does not apply even though an organisation performs operations on personal data that fall within the material scope specified in Article 2(1):

(1) activity which falls outside of EU law – activities over which EU authorities do not have jurisdiction, for example national security, defence, and official registration of births, marriages, and deaths;
(2) actions of Member States which fall under title V Chapter 2 of the Treaty on EU – common foreign and security policy;
(3) activity of natural persons in the course of a purely personal or household activity – activity which is unrelated to professional or commercial activity, for example a guest list for a wedding or a list of addresses of friends;
(4) activity of competent authorities for the prevention, investigation, detection or prosecution of criminal offences or the execution of criminal penalties, including the safeguarding against and the prevention of threats to public security – activities of this kind are governed by a special legal act – the Police Directive, Directive (EU) 2016/680 of the European Parliament and of the Council of 27 April 2016 on the protection of natural persons with regard to the processing of personal data by competent authorities for the purposes of the prevention, investigation, detection or prosecution of criminal offences or the execution of criminal penalties and on the free movement of such data, and repealing Council Framework Decision 2008/977/JHA. The GDPR does apply however to judicial bodies. It applies also to law enforcement agencies with regard to internal matters (e.g., personnel matters);
(5) journalistic, academic, artistic, and literary statements – the GDPR has limited applicability to statements of this kind in order to reconcile the right to personal data protection and freedom of expression and information. Unfortunately, the relevant derogations are enacted at national level, so their details may differ from a Member State to a Member State.

2.1.3 Territorial Scope

Article 3(1) GDPR specifies the territorial scope:

> This Regulation applies to the processing of personal data **in the context of the activities** of an establishment of a controller or a processor **in the Union, regardless of whether the processing takes place in the Union or not**.

The territorial scope is formulated in a very broad way, and this is intended to ensure the greatest personal data protection possible regardless of where the technical means used to process data are in fact located.

First, if you are located in the EU. the GDPR applies to you whether you are a controller or you act as a processor, even if you are processing personal data of non-EU residents.

The processing alone may be performed outside of the EU, which is a significant departure from the old rules.

A notion of 'establishment in the Union' refers to any type of organisational presence on the territory of the EU, not necessarily a subsidiary or a branch, representative office. For example it may cover having agents in the EU.[5]

Processing data 'in the context of the activities of an establishment' does not need to take place in the establishment of a particular economic organism.[6] In a decision imposing an administrative fine on Google LLC,[7] CNIL found that Google Ireland Limited is not a main establishment of Google in the meaning of Recital 36 GDPR as decisions relating to processing do not take place in Ireland but in Google LLC's headquarters in Mountain View, California, United States (US). Though the CNIL's decision tackles directly another issue – competence of supervisory authorities – and waters down the so-called one-stop-shop principle (Article 56 GDPR), it is not a bad example of processing and deciding outside of the EU while having an EU establishment.

Under Article 3(2) GDPR, the territorial scope of the GDPR is also extended to cover the following cases:

> The processing of personal data of **data subjects who are in the Union** by a controller or a processor not established in the Union, where the processing activities are related to:
>
> a) the offering of goods or services irrespective of whether a payment of the data subject is required, to subjects in the Union; or
> b) the monitoring of subjects' behaviour as far as it takes place within the Union.

This means that even entities located outside of the EU may have to apply European personal data protection laws when processing data of EU residents. This is a major departure from the former regulations. Under the former regulations, entities established in a third country and which processed personal data outside of the European Economic Area (EEA) or used technical means located in the EU solely to transfer data to a third country would not have been subject to the data protection rules.

The offering, in any form, of goods or services to persons in the EU, even at no charge, regardless of the location of the registered office of the controller and place of data processing, must be in compliance with the GDPR. Offering of goods or services 'irrespective of whether a payment of the data subject is required' is a particularly puzzling expression, knowing that EU regards just having a website as offering an electronic service. Therefore an actual target audience of a particular offer, service or electronic service will decide on whether the GDPR applies or not. If your site has an

5. Guidelines 3/2018 on the territorial scope of the GDPR (Article 3) – Version for public consultation Adopted on 16 November 2018, European Data Protection Board, p. 5.
6. Guidelines 3/2018 on the territorial scope of the GDPR (Article 3) – Version for public consultation Adopted on 16 November 2018, European Data Protection Board, p. 5.
7. Commission Nationale de l'Informatique et des Libertés, Délibération de la formation restreinte n° SAN – 2019-001 du 21 janvier 2019 prononçant une sanction pécuniaire à l'encontre de la société Google LLC, https://www.legifrance.gouv.fr/affichCnil.do?oldAction=rechExpCnil&id=CNILTEXT000038032552&fastReqId=2103387945&fastPos=1 (last accessed on 9 March 2019).

EU language version (beware of using 's' instead of 'z' when writing in English [a joke]) or it offers delivery to the EU, the GDPR) may apply to your business. But moving from scaring to caring, 'offering of goods or services to data subjects in the Union' concerns truly addressing your offer to EU residents. If you are addressing your offer to the whole world (e.g., you provide an app or a web service useful in any place on Earth and you place it on a global marketplace platform such as App store or Google Play or like you are subject to the GDPR). In contrast if you are operating a website offering fishing equipment and you ship only to the US and Canada (with the exception for fishing rods, which you do not ship to Canada) you are not subject to the GDPR and you do not need to implement geofencing, even if an EU resident while visiting the US decides to go fishing and buys equipment through your website.

Seemingly the most intriguing is a premise of say 'monitoring EU behaviour of EU residents' (Article 3(2)(b) GDPR). In cases where the behaviour of persons within the EU is monitored by third-country organisations, these organisations have to conduct this process in accordance with the GDPR. In the age of cookies, Google Analytics, affiliate marketing, and retargeting, it is hard to say we are not monitoring our website guest base. Would a simple use of web traffic analysis tools amount to monitoring EU residents? We do not think so. However, the more we are interested in the geographical analysis of our traffic and preferences of our EU-based guests the more likely we fall under the GDPR. The EDPB guidelines on the territorial scope of the GDPR are here (as usual in problematic situations) rather useless. Let us try to be more practical.

The EDPB theoretically agrees that not all 'online collection or analysis of personal data of individuals in the EU would automatically count as "monitoring"'. Though immediately after that statement it is getting strange.[8] The EDPB lists probably all possible marketing uses of online data (behavioural advertisement, geo-localisation, online tracking in particular through cookies) going even farther to include closed circuit television (CCTV).[9] We end up between dimming and pure nonsense – making the whole world subject to the GDPR if they are using behavioural online advertising or just marketing cookies. Here goes to the EDPB the same 'facepalm' as the 'facepalm' for Facebook relying on consent[10] to suck up all data on our online behaviour in exchange for allowing us to use our Facebook profile (with a slight difference that Facebook is slightly more effective than the EDPB).

In our opinion, simple retargeting does not amount to monitoring as the goal is to display an advertisement or another message to a user wherever s/he/neutral goes and not to register and analyse what other websites she visits, etc. Affiliate marketing – likewise. However, if you are analysing your individual website guests' behaviours online, you are probably monitoring them even if you do not know their identity. If you apply also a location criterion, you might fall under the GDPR even if you refrain from further analysing data gathered on EU residents. In practice only when your activity is,

8. Guidelines 3/2018 on the territorial scope of the GDPR (Art. 3) – Version for public consultation Adopted on 16 November 2018, European Data Protection Board, p. 18.
9. What exactly CCTV is doing there is not easy to guess. The EDPB probably has in mind a global security centre located in Bangalore, as a part of shared services 'follow the sun' approach. As obvious as useless example.
10. Which by no means can be 'informed', nor it is very freely given.

to say, 'EU significant' (e.g., you do not sell to the EU, but if you help to sell to the EU, you are a data analytics factory) you might fall under the 'monitoring extension'. Otherwise our US fishing equipment start-up delivering to the US and Canada is in serious trouble.

> **Example**
>
> A company based in the US which operates a global online store that includes France and Poland has to operate the online store in compliance with the GDPR even if it has no servers and no team in the EU.

Paragraph 3(3) GDPR says meanwhile that the GDPR also applies to the processing of personal data by a controller which is not established in the EU but in a location in which the laws of a Member State apply under international public law, such as embassies, consulates, seagoing vessels, and aircraft.

3 GDPR GLOSSARY: NOTES ON BASIC GDPR TERMS, WITH EXAMPLES

3.1 Preliminary Remarks

This chapter describes selected terms that will help to understand and apply the GDPR - Regulation (EU) 2016/679 of the European Parliament and of the Council of 27 April 2016 on the protection of natural persons with regard to the processing of personal data and on the free movement of such data, and repealing Directive 95/46/EC.

3.2 Controller

Under Article 4(7) GDPR:

> 'Controller' means a natural person or legal person, public authority, agency, or other body which, alone or jointly with others, determines the purposes and means of the processing of personal data; where the purposes and means of such processing are determined by EU or member state law, the controller or the specific criteria for its nomination may be provided for by EU or member state law.

A controller determines by itself (or jointly with others) (i) the purposes and (ii) means of data processing. A controller can be a natural person or legal person operating in any legal form, public authorities, an agency, or other authority.

As a rule, with regard to personal data, an institution can only act in two ways – as a controller (using data for its own purposes) or a processor (processing data for a different entity).

Examples of Status of a Controller:

(1) **organisations** such as banks, investment funds, insurance companies, and online stores are controllers with regard to their customers' data;

(2) **an employer** is a controller in relation to an employee's[11] personal data;

(3) **associations, political parties, and religious communities** are controllers with regard to the data of their members, former members, supporters, and opponents;

(4) **a website operator** which collects user data for its own purposes, for example an IP address, user profile, location;

(5) **a housing association** is a controller with regard to the data of the residents;

(6) **an internet search engine operator** with regard to information containing personal data which the operator locates and indexes;[12]

(7) **a lawyer** with regard to a client - an individual - represented in court;[13]

(8) **organisations** when cooperating with other organisations (e.g., contracting) with regards to personal data of their personnel involved in such cooperation.

Controllers and processors are discussed further in a separate section.

3.3 Risk Analysis

The GDPR requires risk analysis (risk is discussed here separately), in particular in order to employ the appropriate data protection measures and to make processing-related decisions. Risk analysis for an intended change in activity or new plan may reveal a high data processing risk. In such a case, a DPIA will be necessary. As a result, any entities that are required to apply the GDPR now have to devise their own risk

11. Article 29 Working Party, Opinion 1/2010 on the concepts of controller and processor adopted 16 February 2010 (WP 169), p. 12, http://www.giodo.gov.pl/pl/file/1939 (last accessed on 31 December 2017).
12. Court of Justice judgment of 13 May 2014, C-131/12, Google Spain SL and Google Inc. vs. Agencia Española de Protección de Datos (AEPD) and Mario Costes González, EU:C:2014:317.
13. Article 29 Working Party, Opinion 1/2010, p. 31.

analysis methods. Assessment of risk analysis performed by an entity subject to the obligation is one of the items on a supervisory authorities' inspection checklist.

Risk analysis and impact assessment are discussed further in a separate section.

3.4 Anonymisation

The GDPR does not define 'anonymisation' or 'anonymising'.

We use the term 'anonymising' to describe stripping sets of personal data (records) of such attributes (certain personal data) which allow identifying persons (data subjects) these sets of data (records) concern – permanently.

In other words, anonymisation means replacing identification data with some not meaningful values. 'Identification data' include usually family name, different personal identification numbers (personal ID, tax ID, social security ID, client ID, user unique identification number, numbers of other personal documents). But pending on circumstances erasing (or overwriting) of other data might be needed (car licence plate numbers, mobile phone IMEI number, etc.).

Anonymisation techniques are often used to erase (delete) personal data from databases. Instead of deleting the whole record (which you can imagine as a single row in a spreadsheet), the content of specific entries (cells) is overwritten with meaningless data (or blacked out in case of paper records). Why not delete the whole record (row) instead? Because the integrity of a whole database may be compromised, the other records may be affected, and data in your database may become shuffled like a pack of cards (which would amount to a personal data breach). The problem is easy to imagine to anyone who tried to segregate a spreadsheet where someone merged cells before.

For data to be considered anonymised there should be no risk of reidentification.[14] It means that anonymisation should be real. It sounds obvious, but in practice IT departments have a tendency to pretend anonymisation or to 'overlook' specific identification data (e.g., unique insurance policy number), often for purely convenience reasons.

3.5 Data Processing Activities

There is no definition of 'processing activity' in the GDPR, even though this is a fundamental term from the point of view of the new personal data protection rules.

Processing activity is a larger or smaller (or longer or shorter) segment of a 'business' process/data processing process performed for a specific purpose. Businesses are free to 'chop up' their processes as they wish into individual data processing activities, provided that consistency with a specific purpose is maintained and the list of activities in the records of data processing activity is manageable.

Data processing activities consist of data processing operations. (Un)Surprisingly there is no definition of 'data processing operations' either. Not very useful examples

14. *See* Art. 29 Working Party, Opinion 5/2014 on anonymisation techniques, adopted 10 April 2014 (WP 216), http://www.giodo.gov.pl/pl/file/6338 (last accessed on 26 January 2018).

of data processing operations are given in the definition of 'processing' (collection, recording, organisation, structuring, storage, adaptation or alteration, retrieval, consultation, use, disclosure by transmission, dissemination or otherwise making available, alignment or combination, restriction, erasure or destruction).

Both of these terms are used in a vague manner in the GDPR; for example, a detailed risk analysis, the DPIA, is conducted as required under Article 35 GDPR with regard to a processing operation, and not a data processing activity. A review of examples of situations in which a DPIA should be conducted reveals, however, that this is more a question of a sequence of operations (which could be considered to be activities). Unfortunately, the GDPR cannot be interpreted without semantics of this kind.

3.6 Personal Data

Under Article 4(1) GDPR:

> 'personal data' means any data relating to an identified or identifiable natural person ('data subject'); an identifiable natural person is someone who can be identified, directly or indirectly, in particular by reference to an identifier such as a name, an identification number, location data, or an online identifier, or to one or more factors specific to the physical, physiological, genetic, mental, economic, cultural or social identity of that natural person.

Personal data are: (1) information (any information) concerning (2) an identified or identifiable (3) natural person.[15]

Personal data are: (i) disclosed – anything that somebody reveals about themselves or which other sources reveal about that person (e.g., public registers); (ii) observed – anything that we observe about an individual (e.g., their behaviour, when they come home and switch on the television, their movements, whom they make cash transfers to, where and when they make cash machine withdrawals); (iii) concluded – anything we deduce about an individual and the kind of person we consider them to be, for example when we classify a person as being in an automobile accident high-risk group due to their style of driving.

(i) information – personal data are information about specific individuals, while we do not need to know their first name and surname.[16] In each instance, a test must be carried out to determine whether particular information constitutes personal data in the case in question. Information constituting personal data may be subjective, does not have to be true and does not have to be universally comprehensible.

15. Article 29 Working Party, Opinion 4/2007 on the concept of personal data, adopted 20 June 2007 (WP 136), http://ec.europa.eu/justice/policies/privacy/docs/wpdocs/2007/wp136_pl.pdf (last accessed on 20 January 2018).
16. A telephone number is personal data even if it is now known who the call is made to. The practice of unsolicited calls by sales personnel is against the law and a breach of the principle of fairness.

Example

Date of birth, residential address, sex, eye colour, weight, height, or other biometric data, data of a physiological nature, and data about opinion or world view, statements or wishes; operational data relating to use of a website, browsing history, name and details of a device used by a user, photographs of an individual, a recording from a closed circuit video camera, drawings, or voice recordings.

(ii) identified or identifiable natural persons – identification is a situation in which we can determine someone's identity. According to the Article 29 Working Party, a natural person is deemed to be 'identified' if that person can be distinctly identified within a group from all of the other people in the group.[17]

Example

Telephone number, official individual identification number, email address, IP address, first name and surname, and username in a system.

(iii) natural persons – information is considered personal data only when it relates to a **natural person**. The GDPR does not apply to data of people who are deceased, foetuses, or legal persons.

At the moment, data of **persons conducting business activity** are subject to general protection under the GDPR.

3.7 Categories of Personal Data

Categories of data. The notion of 'categories of data' has not been defined in the GDPR. A 'category' is a generic notion, which could have different levels (division, family, species, genus – these are all categories). For example, 'information' is a higher category than 'personal data', and 'personal data' is a higher category than 'special categories of personal data', and 'special categories of personal data' is a higher category than 'personal data' or 'ethnic origin data'.

Dividing 'personal data' into lower categories might be problematic. There are at least the following approaches to dividing personal data into categories:

(1) **Division resulting from the GDPR.** The GDPR refers to the following categories:
  (a) Special categories of personal data (Article 9 GDPR):
    (i) data revealing racial origin,
    (ii) data revealing ethnic origin,

17. Article 29 Working Party, Opinion 4/2007, p. 12.

(iii) data revealing political opinions,
(iv) data revealing religious beliefs,
(v) data revealing philosophical beliefs,
(vi) data revealing union membership,
(vii) genetic data,
(viii) biometric data for the purpose of uniquely identifying a natural person,
(ix) data concerning health,
(x) data concerning a natural person's sex life,
(xi) data concerning sexual orientation.

(b) personal data relating to criminal convictions and offences (Article 10 GDPR);
(c) 'ordinary personal data' (Article 6 GDPR);
(d) children's data (Article 8 GDPR);
(e) other (than children) vulnerable person data (Recital 75 GDPR);
(f) personal data of persons for which identification is not needed (Article 11 GDPR) (called by us 'unidentified data').

The division of categories of data contained directly in the GDPR is not sufficient especially for assessing risks associated with processing data and risks resulting from data breaches. 'Simple data' (despite that term is not defined in the GDPR) is an extremely capacious category and contain very different subcategories of data such as different identification data, state register number, data about alcohol consumption, family data, financial data, indebtedness data, and what is more the GDPR requires additional divides categories in a number of provisions.

(2) That is why we look into the division proposed by the Belgian supervisory authority – la Commission de la protection de la vie privée (currently Autorité de protection des données),[18] which identifies about ninety-five categories of personal data:

Absenteeism and discipline
Academic curriculum
Agreements and settlements
Assets in possession of the employee
Biometrical identification data
Career
Categories of legal data
Compensation
Complaints, incidents, or accidents
Composition of the family

18. Recommendation No. 06/2017 14 June 2017 https://www.autoriteprotectiondonnees.be/sites/privacycommission/files/documents/recommandation_06_2017_0.pdf (last accessed on 28 February 2019).

Consumption habits
Current employment
Data about the sex life
Data regarding risk situations and risk behaviour
Debts and expenditures
Details regarding other family or household members
Distinctions
Education and training
Electronic identification data
Electronic localisation data
Financial assistance
Financial identification data
Financial means
Financial overview of studies
Financial transactions
Genetic data related to population studies, genetic research, etc.
Habits
Health data
Identification data
Identification information assigned by government institutions, other than the social security number
Images
Immigrant status
Insurance policy details
Legal data regarding administrative penalties
Legal data regarding convictions and sentences
Legal data regarding DNA
Legal data regarding judicial actions
Legal data related to suspicions
Leisure activities and interests
Leisure pursuits and interests
Lending data
Lifestyle
Loans, mortgages, lines of credit
Marital history
Marriage or current form of cohabitation
Media use
Membership and/or participation in professional organisations
Membership in a trade union
Membership in an interest group or militant organisation
Memberships
Memberships (other than professional, political, or in trade unions)
Mental health data
Military details
Occupational medicine

Pension plan details
Permits
Personal characteristics
Personal details
Philosophical or religious beliefs
Physical description
Physical details
Physical health data
Political affiliation
Political opinions
Political tendency
Possessions
Private habits
Profession and employment
Professional activities
Professional experience
Professional qualifications
Psychological descriptions
Psychological details
Public mandates
Publications
Racial or ethnic data
Recruitment
Recuperation data
Rental data
Residence data
Review
Security
Social contacts
Social Security Number
Solvency
Sound recordings
Special financial data
Surveillance images
Training for the position
Travel and movement details
Use of technology
Video recordings
Wages
Work organisation
Work termination.

(3) You may also categorise personal data yourself, remembering to fit into the general categories dividing from the RODO.

3.8 Type of Data

'Type of data' is an another mysterious GDPR concept. The GDPR seems to use 'type of data' and 'category of data' synonymously. Intuitively we would say that 'type of data' is a narrower notion to 'category of data' as 'type' is one of the types of category. That subtle difference does not seem, however, to have any practical meaning.

GDPR refers to the 'types of data' in Article 6(3) 2 and in Article 28. Article 6(3) 2 GDPR requires statutes to specify 'types of data' which are processed on the legal basis laid by Union's or Member State's law. Article 28 GDPR regarding the entrusting of data processing states that the data processing agreement should specify 'type of data' entrusted to processing.

3.9 Data Export/Data Transfer

Data export is a phrase used in jargon to mean the transfer of data to a third country (a country outside the EEA) or international organisation (not to be confused with data portability - the right to transfer data from a controller (provider) to a controller (provider)). This form of transfer of data to outside of the EU is subject to additional regulation, and a data subject whose data are to be moved to outside of the EEA has at least to be notified of this.

Data transfer is a transfer of data to a third country (a country outside the EEA) or an international organisation. Data export in data protection jargon means the same as data transfer. Data transfer/data export should not be confused with data portability - the right to transfer data from a controller (provider) to a controller (provider). Transfer of data outside of the EU is subject to additional requirements; for example, data subjects whose data are to be moved to outside of the EEA have at least to be notified of this. We discuss transferring data out of EU in Chapter 5 (Articles 44-50 GDPR).

Example

A company with its registered office in Estonia has subsidiaries in the United Arab Emirates, Vietnam, and the US. These companies share IT infrastructure and a mailing list and send each other customer and customer representative lists. Employees go on business trips and are seconded to work for long periods in branches.

Example

A company uses cloud computing services of a popular file storage provider with its registered office in the US. The provider states that it participates in the Privacy Shield scheme.

Data export (transfer of data to third countries and international organisations) is discussed further in a separate section.

3.10 Supervisory Authority

Authority in the Member States that control compliance with personal data protection laws, as defined in the GDPR.

3.11 European Data Protection Board and Article 29 Working Party

The Article 29 Working Party was a team of representatives of the national supervisory authorities set up by the European Commission (EC) (plus representatives of the European Data Protection Supervisor and the EC itself) to help to develop harmonised personal data protection rules.

Now the Article 29 Working Party is replaced with the formal authority created under the GDPR - the EDPB. Formally the EDPB is composed of the head of one supervisory authority of each Member State and the European Data Protection Supervisor, or their respective representatives. Technically the EDPB consists mostly of the same people the Article 29 Working Party consisted of. However the EDPB has much more power thanks to the GDPR.

3.12 Data Protection Officer

DPO is a formal function defined in Articles 37–39 GDPR. The GDPR in Article 37 (1) GDPR defines situations designating a DPO is mandatory. DPO is a 'watchman' who is responsible for helping the organisation to maintain data protection compliance. DPO is obligated to inform, advise and monitor compliance with the GDPR, but (contrary to the popular misconception) the DPO is not responsible for the organisation's compliance with the GDPR and data protection in general.

The DPO is an integral part of the organisation, and s/he could be an employee or an external specialist. Nevertheless, DPO should be able to perform their duties independently and needs to be protected from being dismissed or penalised for performing DPO tasks by the controller or the processor.

The DPO is discussed further in a separate section.

3.13 Personal Data Breach

Under Article 4(12) GDPR:

> 'personal data breach' means a breach of security leading to the accidental or unlawful destruction, loss, alteration, unauthorised disclosure of, or access to, personal data transmitted, stored, or otherwise processed.

A personal data breach occurs when information security is compromised, and this leads to loss of control of the data due to the data becoming corrupt or being destroyed, the data becoming inaccessible, unauthorised access being gained to the data, the data being made public, etc.

Personal data breach is in fact a violation of information security resulting in consequences (leak, unauthorised access, alteration, destruction, inaccessibility of data).

Example

Data leaks, failure to conceal email addresses in group emails, loss of data carriers, incorrect erasure of data.

Data breaches and data security are discussed further in a separate section.

3.14 Data Protection Impact Assessment

DPIA is a formalised impact and risk assessment of a planned change to the way personal data are processed. It is a new obligation imposed on the controller by Article 35 GDPR. DPIA is a formalised analysis to help the controller to ascertain where processing operations are likely to result in a high risk to the rights and freedoms of data subjects and subsequently minimise the data protection risk to an accepted (low) level. You may look at a DPIA as a mini GDPR implementation, as it requires describing the processing and scope, verifying legality of processing, verifying that/how data subject rights are served, identifying technical and operational security measures, assessing risk to the rights and freedoms of data subjects, adding more risk controls (security measures or others such as limiting scope of processing) and reassessing the risk – all that documented.

The EDPB broadens the interpretation of Article 35 GDPR, requesting DPIA for a variety of situations which would not fall under a literal interpretation of Article 35 GDPR.

DPIAs are discussed further in a separate section.

3.15 Recipient

Under Article 4(9) GDPR:

> 'recipient' means a natural or legal person, public authority, agency or another body to which the personal data are disclosed, whether a third party or not. However, public authorities which may receive personal data in the framework of a particular enquiry in accordance with EU or member state law shall not be regarded as recipients; the processing of those data by those public authorities shall be in compliance with the applicable data protection rules according to the purposes of the processing.

A recipient is a natural or legal person, public authority, agency or other body to which personal data are disclosed regardless of whether it is a third party. Public authorities that receive data in connection with proceedings in a specific case on a legal basis do not fall under the definition of a recipient.

Example

A different controller (such as a parent company, where a decision to made to transfer data concerning personnel to that company when there is a legitimate interest), a processor, a data subject, other controller, entities affiliated to the controller, consultants to the data subject, persons close to the data subject, and companies trading in personal data are 'recipients'. There is a special type of recipient, which is a 'recipient in a third country or in an international organisation' because a data subject has to be informed of this recipient separately.

Under Article 4(9) GDPR:

> 'recipient' means a natural or legal person, public authority, agency or another body, to which the personal data are disclosed, whether a third party or not (GDPR provides the definition of third party in Art. 4 (12)). To become a 'recipient' of personal data you just need to receive data. From that definition public authorities are excluded when they receive data for the purpose of specific proceedings.

Contrary to the Data Protection Directive, under the GDPR a data processor may be a 'recipient' as well. It complicates interpretation and application of the GDPR, especially that you have the duty to inform data subjects about 'recipients' or 'categories of recipients' (the first too specific at least in relation to subcontractors, the second too vague and not helpful at all).

Example

Recipient is: controller, a different controller (such as a parent company, where a decision to made to transfer data concerning personnel to that company when there is a legitimate interest), processor, subprocessor, a data subject, entities affiliated to the controller, consultants to the data subject, family of the data subject, companies trading in personal data are 'recipients'. There is a special type of recipient, which is a 'recipient in a third country or in an international organisation' because a data subject has to be informed of this recipient separately.

3.16 Restriction of Processing

Under Article 4(3) GDPR:

> ‘restriction of processing’ means the marking of stored personal data with the aim of limiting their processing in future.

This legal definition of restriction of processing does not tell us anything, but there is its another element in Article 18(2) GDPR, which says that where processing has been restricted, personal data shall, with the exception of storage, only be processed with the data subject’s consent or for the establishment, exercise or defence of legal claims or for the protection of the rights of another natural or legal person or for reasons of important public interest of the EU or of a Member State.

In view of the principle of restriction of processing, a data controller may possess (store) data and perform only operations (i) consented to by the data subject and, independently, data (ii) needed for a dispute or to protect another entity’s rights or where there is an important public interest.

Restriction of processing is not automatically granted though. A data controller may reject a data subject request for restricting of processing.

Example

The debt recovery department of a telecommunications operator has been calling me. I have concluded that they are not entitled to do that because I have paid, and in any case, it is not my debt. I therefore demand restriction of processing and that they do not call me about such claims until they have investigated the matter internally.

A person requests a copy of a CCTV recording documenting alleged pickpocket in action. But a data controller is not sure if the footage is clear enough, and moreover there are other people’s faces. So the data controller rejects the request for a copy of data (based on rights of others) but instead advises the person that she may request the restriction of processing to preserve the recording as a piece of evidence in case the Police decides to open an investigation.

Restriction of processing is discussed further in a separate section.

3.17 Processing Operations

> ‘Processing operations’ is an another misleading GDPR term of significant importance. Article 4 (2) GDPR defining what is ‘processing of personal data’, explains processing operations as ‘any operation or set of operations which is performed on personal data: such as collection, recording, organization, structuring, storage, adaptation or alteration, retrieval, consultation, use, disclosure by transmission, dissemination or otherwise making available, alignment or combination, restric tion, erasure or destruction’.

GDPR refers to ‘processing operations’ about 60 times. Sometimes GDPR under the term of ‘operations of processing data’ means ‘if’ data are processed, but mainly GDPR means ‘how’ data are processed.

The GDPR refers directly to the operations of processing data in two provisions: in Article 6(3) paragraph 2 sentence 2 GDPR in the rules regarding requirements as to the law entitling the processing of the personal data and in Article 35 referring to the obligation to carry out DPIA if the operations of processing data (or set of operations) are likely to result in a high risk to the rights and freedoms of natural persons.

3.18 Data Subject

A data subject is an identified or identifiable natural person and is always a specific person.

The protection conferred by the GDPR applies to alive natural persons, i.e. people. The GDPR makes the general assumption that as computerisation and surveillance are constantly becoming more advanced, each person should be afforded control over their personal data regardless of who processes the data and for what purpose. The personal data protection system was established to assist people and protect fundamental human rights and freedoms.

3.19 Personnel

The GDPR does not expressly define 'personnel' even though it refers to this term (Article 47(2)n GDPR). It needs to be understood that a controller, processor, supervisory authority, third party, and law enforcement institutions make use of personnel.

In practice, the definition of personnel is contained within the definition of a third party (Article 4(10) GDPR). This mentions the following persons classified as 'personnel' – 'persons who, under the direct authority of the controller or processor, are authorised to process personal data'.

3.20 Processor

Under Article 4(8) GDPR:

> 'processor' means a natural or legal person, public authority, agency, or other body which processes personal data on behalf of the controller.

A processor must be a separate legal entity. It must perform processing operations on the documented instructions of the controller on behalf of the controller. Data processing is of fundamental importance with regard to creating an outsourcing chain and any resulting further outsourcing activity.

In French, the processor is the *sous traitant*, i.e. subcontractor.

Example

Typical functions of processors include external marketing services, IT services, HR and payroll services, accounting services, tax services, hosting services, customer service, document destruction services, data archiving, data processing (cloud computing).

'Processor' is the name given to a role which can be performed by any organisation when it is entrusted with personal data by another organisation. At the same time, the GDPR uses the term 'processor' for organisations whose core business activity is data processing for other entities (e.g., a cloud computing provider, outsourcing centre). A 'processor' in the second sense also means at the same time, of course, a controller of its own personal data. This mixing of categories does not help understand the data protection system.

Controllers and processors are discussed further in a separate section.

3.21 Processing

Under Article 4(2) GDPR:

> 'processing' means any operation or set of operations which is performed on personal data or on sets of personal data, whether or not by automated means, such as collection, recording, organisation, structuring, storage, adaptation or alteration, retrieval, consultation, use, disclosure by transmission, dissemination or otherwise making available, alignment or combination, restriction, erasure, or destruction.

The notion of 'processing' consists of two elements: (i) a general definition and (ii) an open-ended list of examples of 'processing'. An activity is processing if the following occur cumulatively: (i) an operation or set of operations (ii) performed on personal data or sets of personal data (iii) whether or not by automated means.

Actions Which Constitute Processing:

1. **Collection** of personal data;

Example

Obtaining filled in forms on paper containing personal data, or an electronic form on a website.

2. **Recording** data should be understood as saving data on a permanent, material, data carrier.

Example

Noting down on paper, saving on a disc, printing of a document. Data collected may be recorded many times on different data carriers.

3. Organisation and structuring are operations that do not result in alterations to the content of the data.

> **Example**
>
> Putting first names into alphabetical order, putting photographs in order according to eye colour, sorting patient record charts according to the street where they live.

4. Storage is the keeping of data on a data carrier. This can be a data carrier of any kind, but the data must be kept in a manner enabling them to be read. Legal title to the carrier is immaterial.

> **Example**
>
> Storing on paper, a hard disk, USB memory stick, memory card, or in a cloud.

5. Adaptation or **alteration** is a broader operation and is a change to the content of personal data.

> **Example**
>
> Execution of the right to rectify data and provide additional information.

6. Retrieval means producing copies of personal data on a data carrier using a telecommunications network and also the actual reading of information on the specific data carrier.

> **Example**
>
> Downloading an attachment from an email message.

7. Review of data.

> **Example**
>
> Performing a search for data in an internet search engine. Verifying data accuracy (e.g., if your contact list is up-to-date – btw. practically not doable unless you subscribe to LinkedIn and Facebook).

8. Erasure and destruction – both serve the same purpose, which is making it impossible to process the data further. Erasure is deletion of data from a data carrier, while destruction leads to the physical destruction of a data carrier.

> **Example**
>
> Removal of files from a computer, shredding a document, blacking out certain data in a document, dissolving a hard disk, destroying a laptop with a hammer or submerging it in water.

3.22 Pseudonymisation

Under Article 4(5) GDPR:

> 'pseudonymisation' means personal data processing in such a manner that the personal data can no longer be attributed to a specific data subject without the use of additional information, provided that such additional information is kept separately and is subject to technical and organisational measures to ensure that the personal data are not attributed to an identified or identifiable natural person.

The pseudonymisation should be irreversible.

Pseudonymisation is replacement of identifiers (e.g., first name, surname, official individual identification number, telephone number, email address) with pseudonyms, i.e. codes, numbers, or images (and here there is a certain amount of freedom) unique to a particular individual which do not have any real connection to the person in question. In other words, this is a separation of personal data in such a way that the data revealing the identity of specific individuals is replaced[19] with data that has no meaning (pseudonyms or usually numbers connecting a concealed identity data file with descriptions of features of the individuals in question).[20]

Pseudonymisation is a means of data protection as well as a means of minimising access. The GDPR mentions pseudonymisation fifteen times.

Pseudonymisation is discussed further in a separate section.

3.23 Records of Data Processing Activities

Records of data processing activities (RDPAs) are a form of documenting of data processing activities, serve as a data processing map, and are a crucial element of execution of the fundamental principle on which the entire personal data protection system is based, which is the principle of accountability. They also play an informative

19. Screen, print, etc.
20. A simple means of pseudonymisation is moving columns containing the first name and surname to another sheet (provided that lines and columns are numbered and the numbers are moved as well).

role and are a source of information about data processing procedures in the organisation in question for a supervisory authority.

Most of the data controllers and data processors have to maintain RDPAs. Article 30(5) GDPR theoretically relieves some entities employing less than 250 employees from that obligation. However, first, exemptions from the exemption of having an RDPA are illusive; second, it makes no sense not to have an RDPA. RDPAs are discussed further in a separate section.

3.24 Risk

The GDPR uses the word 'risk' seventy-six times, and it is said that the GDPR forces applying and is based upon a risk-based approach to data processing and data protection. Recital 75 GDPR states, and it is stated in twenty-seven other places in which this wording is used, that this is about a 'risk to the freedoms and rights of natural persons' (data subjects). This does not refer to the risk of a penalty or direct damage to a business when personal data is lost or leaked. It is a question of the harm that can be done to the data subjects. Data protection measures as well as other measures taken to comply and prove compliance with the GDPR (Article 24(1) GDPR) have to be adapted to suit the risk to the rights and freedoms of natural persons.

At this point the simplest solution is to quote the entire Recital 75 GDPR in full:

> The risk to the rights and freedoms of natural persons, of varying likelihood and severity, may result from personal data processing which could lead to physical, material or non-material damage, in particular: where the processing may give rise to discrimination, identity theft or fraud, financial loss, damage to the reputation, loss of confidentiality of personal data protected by professional secrecy, unauthorised reversal of pseudonymisation, or any other significant economic or social disadvantage; Where data subjects might be deprived of their rights and freedoms or prevented from exercising control over their personal data; where personal data are processed which reveal racial or ethnic origin, political opinions, religion or philosophical beliefs, trade union membership, and the processing of genetic data, data concerning health or data concerning sex life or criminal convictions, and offences or related security measures; where personal aspects are evaluated, in particular analysing or predicting aspects concerning performance at work, economic situation, health, personal references or interests, reliability or behaviour, location or movements, in order to create or use personal profiles; where personal data of vulnerable natural persons, in particular of children, are processed; or where processing involves a large amount of personal data and affects a large number of data subjects.

3.25 Joint Controllership

'Joint controllership' has been first described by the Article 29 Working Party, before being introduced to the EU legislation in the GDPR.[21] According to Article 26 (1) GDPR

21. *Opinion 1/2010 on the concepts of 'controller' and 'processor'* https://www.pdpjournals.com/docs/88016.pdf (last accessed on 28 February 2019).

first sentence 'joint controllership' means where two or more controllers jointly determine the purposes and means of processing. The operator 'AND' points that two or more organisations should jointly agree on BOTH the purposes of the processing AND the means of its implementation (means of processing) to be able to recognise them as joint controllers.

'Joint controllership' differs from what the authors of this book call 'parallel controllership'.[22] Joint controllership should be considered in a situation **where at least two controllers jointly set purposes and means of processing.**

Joint controllership should be regulated by an agreement reflecting primarily the responsibilities and relationships of the joint controllers vis-à-vis the data subjects.

Examples of situations where personal is in joint controllership:

- there is one CRM system in a group of companies;
- cooperating entities implement the same IT solution for their client;
- real estate company sets up several unstaffed special purpose vehicle companies for specific development projects;
- a consortium agreement for the implementation of a joint project;
- a purchase group.

The Court of Justice of the European Union (CJEU) in the case of the signature of C-210/16[2] decided that a Facebook fan page operator may be responsible for how Facebook uses personal data of that fan page guests. Many commentators assumed that it means the CJEU decided a fan page operator co-controls data with Facebook. We believe it is a nonsense. Facebook is neither a processor of fan page guests' data nor a fan page operator and Facebook jointly control a fan page guests data. Facebook and a fan page operator are controlling data in parallel. Likewise, we would not say a tank and a bicycle jointly control a road while they are riding alongside.

4 PERSONAL DATA PROCESSING PRINCIPLES

4.1 Preliminary Remarks

Article 5 GDPR lays down the fundamental personal data processing principles. This makes direct reference to Article 5 of Convention 108 of the Council of Europe on Protection of Individuals with regard to Automatic Processing of Personal Data,

22. 'Parallel controllership' is not defined by the GDPR. It is just a term we use to describe a situation when two or more controllers process the data of the same person at the same time within the same process but for their own different purposes and without control over how the others use those data.

    [1] *Opinion 1/2010 on the concepts of 'controller' and 'processor'* https://www.pdpjournals.com/docs/88016.pdf (last accessed on 28 February 2019).

    [2] Judgment of the Court of Justice of the European Union of 5 of June 2018 r. in the case of signature C-210/16 *Unabhängiges* Landeszentrum für Datenschutz Schleswig-Holstein vs. Wirtschaftsakademie Schleswig-Holstein GmbH, ECLI:EU:C:2018:388. Judgment available: http://curia.europa.eu/juris/document/document.jsf?docid=202543&doclang=EN (last accessed on 28 February 2019.

Strasbourg, 28 January 1981 (Journal of Laws of 2003, item 25), and to Article 6 of Directive 95/46/EC of the European Parliament and of the Council of 24 October 1995 on the protection of individuals with regard to the processing of personal data and on the free movement of such data.

The direct specification in the GDPR of the main personal data protection principles is the basis for new data protection standards, illustrates the areas in which protection of privacy is developing, and creates a framework for the remaining, detailed GDPR provisions. In addition, inclusion in the personal data protection system of a uniform catalogue of principles gives rise to new obligations for processors. These rules are fundamental to the entire regulation and lay down a framework for personal data protection.

The fact that these are overriding principles is demonstrated among other things by the fact that in many cases they cannot be modified, even with the consent of the data subject. For instance, in many situations the maximum permissible scope of data that can be collected in a particular case (principle of proportionality and minimisation) may not be extended, even on the basis of a consent of the data subject.[23]

4.1.1 Material Principles

Article 5(1) GDPR provides for eight personal data processing principles contained in six points, and these are:

(1) the principle of lawfulness, fairness, and transparency (legal compliance);
(2) the principle that processing shall be for a specific purpose (purpose limitation);
(3) the principle of data minimisation (proportionality);
(4) the principle of accuracy (correctness);
(5) the principle of limitation in time (temporary basis); and
(6) the principle of appropriate security (integrity and confidentiality).

4.1.2 Formal Principle: Accountability

The burden of proof that the controller and the processor meet all GDPR obligations when processing data lies with the controller and processor themselves. This is due to the **principle of accountability** provided for in Article 5(2) GDPR.

'Accountability' means not only the obligation to comply with the principles described above but also to demonstrate that actions and the methods employed comply with the GDPR and achieve the desired effect. Compliance with the GDPR has to be **accounted for**.

Observance of the principle of accountability requires that the appropriate procedures be introduced and accurate documentation be maintained describing both

23. M. Krzysztofek, *Ochrona danych osobowych w Unii Europejskiej po reformie. Komentarz do rozporządzenia Parlamentu Europejskiego i Rady (UE) 2016/679*, Warsaw 2016, p. 54.

the guarantees that have been put in place to ensure that data processing is lawful[24] and the method by which they are put in place.

In practice, the only known method of accounting for anything is documentation. Therefore it will be difficult to account for compliance with the GDPR without the appropriate documentation, in particular internal by-laws, even if a specific obligation to have these rules is not expressly provided for in the GDPR. By the same token, the principle of accountability requires active measures and initiative on the part of the controller and the processor.[25]

4.1.3 More about Data Protection Principles

Individual data processing principles are related and interdependent in various ways, and these include conflict, and for this reason none of them can be analysed without reference to the others.[26]

4.2 The Principles of Lawfulness, Fairness, and Transparency (Legal Compliance)

Essentially, the principles of lawfulness, fairness, and transparency are three principles in one.

4.2.1 Lawfulness

Lawfulness means that personal data have to be processed in compliance with the law and the GDPR above all.

The obligation of lawfulness of data processing means above all that there have to be grounds for the processing (legal basis for processing). These grounds, depending on the data category, are defined in Articles 6 and 9 GDPR. For data on criminal convictions and offences, the grounds are practically laid down in Article 10 though formally Article 10 GDPR just adds extra requirements to Article 6 GDPR.

Also, lawfulness means compliance with the other provisions in the GDPR (such as conditions for consent – Article 7 GDPR) and acts currently in force, and the acts passed to implement them.

For example, if no preparations have been made to execute an individual's rights and as a result there is no technical capacity or resources to execute requests from individuals in a timely and effective way, this is a breach of the principle of lawfulness. A similar situation exists if the kind of security measures (data protection) to be employed is not determined, or they are not employed.

24. *See* Art. 29 Working Party (established under Art. 29 of Directive 95/46/EC) opinion 3/2010 on the principle of accountability, adopted 13 July 2010, http://ec.europa.eu/justice/policies/privacy/docs/wpdocs/2010/wp173_pl.pdf (last accessed on 11 January 2018).
25. *See*. M. Krzysztofek, *Ochrona danych …*, p. 55.
26. P. Drobek [in:] *RODO. Ogólne rozporządzenie o ochronie danych. Komentarz*, ed. E. Bielak-Jomaa, D. Lubasz, Warsaw 2017, p. 326.

4.2.2 Fairness

The principle of fairness means that personal data must be used in an honest and fair way and requires loyalty in relationships with data subjects.

For example, it would not be fair and honest to call on the phone people we do not know and state that no personal data processing takes place because we do not know the person called and it was not known whether the number dialled would be answered.

The simplest way in which the principle of fairness can be explained is in colloquial, everyday language. The processor is not permitted to 'con' the data subject.

4.2.3 Transparency

Processing must be transparent for data subjects, and communication must be legible and comprehensible.

Transparency of processing means, for example, that if a controller asks a data subject to provide the serial number and number of their personal identification card or their official individual identification number, the data subject is entitled to request that the grounds for that request be specified clearly, and the party requesting the data has to comply with the request.

Legibility means that communication with the data subject (e.g., a consent clause, information clause) should be in plain and legible language, i.e. comprehensible to the individual whose data is processed. Complicated, vague, and overly complex forms can prove to be defective, and consent given on that basis will not be considered effective.

Communication must be simple and legible, and not contain legalese. If a typical recipient of particular information in connection with GDPR obligations does not understand the message conveyed, this means that the legibility test has been failed. Of course, there is a clear conflict between the principle of legibility and the amount of notification obligations. This leaves a great deal of discretion for an administrative supervisory authority. The EDPB responds recommending a so-called layered approach to the information obligation.

4.3 Principle of Purpose Limitation

Next principle for lawfulness of data processing is the principle of purpose limitation/specific purpose provided for in Article 5(1)(b) GDPR. **The concept of specific purpose is that collection of personal data must be for purposes that are identified and lawful, and further processing cannot take place for other purposes** ... unless pre-informed and legal.

For a controller, this means among other things that it cannot omit or conceal any purpose for which it intends to use the data. The purpose of data processing cannot be specified in a general way. This would be a breach of both the principle of specific purpose (specificity) and the principle of fairness. Data processing for unspecified purposes or purposes specified in such an imprecise way that the purposes are unrestricted or unclear renders the processing unlawful.[27] In practice, trying to implement GDPR, organisations learn for how many purposes personal data are being processed. This is an interesting exercise.

The principle of collection of data for strictly defined purposes is directly connected with the notification obligation provided for in Articles 12–14 GDPR, because a controller is required to inform an individual of the purposes for which their data are processed.

At this point, the principle of accountability comes into play because it has to be proven that the individual was informed of the purposes of data processing.

The principle that the purpose is binding means that data cannot be processed for purposes other than those for which they were originally collected. However, this has to be interpreted reasonably. First, data can be processed for purposes that are aligned with the original purpose – collection of data for the purpose of concluding a contract enables the performance of that contract and payment to be claimed for performance of the contract. Second, it is allowed to amend or add a purpose of data processing, provided the data subject is informed of this new purpose and there is a legal basis for this new type of processing (e.g., consent to the marketing of third-party products[28]).

EU lawmakers determined first that data must be collected for lawful purposes, and second that data collected for one purpose cannot be used for a different purpose unless additional requirements are fulfilled, in particular notification is given of the intended new purpose of processing.

For example, an applicant for a position as business analyst for an international financial corporation cannot receive a newsletter the day after she applies, unless she has freely given separate and informed consent to use of their data for marketing or information (e.g., as a minimum by ticking a corrected formulated checkbox).

4.4 Principle of Data Minimisation (Proportionality)

According to the principle of data minimisation, **data must be proportional, appropriate, and limited to that essential for the purposes for which the data are processed. A controller can only process data, and the data can only be of content, necessary in view of the purpose for which the data is collected**. The relevance of data must be assessed no later than the moment they are collected. This means that the controller is required to conduct an assessment and analysis of whether the data processed data are excessive. Data processing other than that essential to achieve the purpose will be a breach of the GDPR.

The principle of data minimisation is woven into the GDPR in a number of forms, in a number of places, under a number of names, and this can be deceiving. The GDPR

27. M. Krzysztofek, *Ochrona danych ...*, p. 60.
28. The view is that marketing third-party product ranges falls under the grounds of legitimate purposes of a controller and consequently does not require prior consent to personal data processing. Even in this situation, however, the data subject has to be informed of the new intended purpose of data processing and of the right to object to processing.

requires minimisation of the volume and scope of data, of the period of storage (principle of limitation in time), and of access to data (privacy by default). It thus adopts the position that the less you know about a citizen, the better.

The principle of data minimisation is closely linked to the purpose of processing (the principle of purpose limitation). Depending on the purpose defined by the controller, the scope of data will have to be aligned with that purpose. For this reason, the collection of data that are not necessary now but maybe might prove useful in the future is not permitted. A review of the personal data collected may reveal that a large amount of the data is held unlawfully. We only need to ask ourselves the simple question 'what do we need the data for?'

To avoid the problem of an excessive amount of data, internal procedures and methods providing for periodical review of the current practices (in particular forms) have to be devised. It is also necessary to define the procedure and specify the individuals involved in the process of drawing up and assessing new documents in terms of proportionality and the specific purpose of data processing.

Example

In banking, an entirely different scope of data will be obtained for the conclusion of an agreement for a fixed-term savings account or current account than for conclusion of a loan agreement. Apart from personal details, a loan agreement requires the collection of information concerning the financial standing and family situation of the applicant. This is because this information is necessary and indispensable for assessing the risk and credit rating of the data subject. Data of this kind are not necessary however to open a bank account.

Example

Processing official individual identification numbers of potential customers in order to identify them to offer those persons products and services and tax identification numbers of customers to provide financial consultancy by offering, selling and servicing financial products and services on the basis of an analysis of a customer's financial standing, and free-of-charge investment advice,[29] for example, is considered processing of personal data in a manner disproportionate to the purpose.

Obtaining data about qualifications and marital status when concluding third-party insurance agreements for owners of vehicles, collection by a bank of customers' personal data regarding former registered addresses, the category and date of issue of

29. Report on the activities of the Inspector General for the Protection of Personal Data in 2011, pp. 20–21, http://www.giodo.gov.pl/data/filemanager_pl/sprawozdaniaroczne/2011.pdf (last accessed on 11 January 2018).

a driving licence, and data on an employment certificate concerning a bank's customer's employment history may also be considered disproportionate.

4.5 Principle of Accuracy

According to the principle of accuracy, **data must be correct and, where appropriate, up-to-date. All reasonable measures must be taken to ensure that personal data that are inaccurate in view of the purposes of processing are promptly erased or rectified. By the same token, the processed data must be up-to-date and true.**

Accuracy of data requires implementation of data quality verification procedures and attention to quality of personal data. The possibility of execution of the right to have data rectified and updated must also be assured (Article 16 GDPR).

Accuracy of data presents a practical problem, which is that data become outdated. When combined with disregard for requests that data be updated or lack of skill in processing data, data becoming outdated can lead to a serious breach of the GDPR.

Example

If marketing data files are not updated for a period of eight years, this is a breach of the principle of accuracy. If messages from email accounts saying that the address no longer exists are disregarded, the marketing department does not update its central database according to information received from the rest of the firm, or if call centre operators do not place new data in the system – this is a breach of the principle of accuracy.

Updating data can also cause problems related to the correctness of data. For this reason, procedures need to be applied to limit discrepancies, for example verification via two channels (information about a change of an email contact address can be sent to the old and new email address or mobile telephone number in order to rectify an error where necessary or prevent a deliberate attempt at identity theft).

4.6 Principle of Storage Limitation

Personal data must be **stored in a form enabling identification of the data subject for a period not exceeding that necessary for the purpose for which the data are processed.**

A controller is required to determine in advance the period for which it will store personal data and as a minimum the manner in which it verifies whether the data continues to be useful. The controller is required to inform the data subject of this (Articles 13 and 14 GDPR).

The limitation in time of storage, or 'retention time', is essentially another form of the principle of data minimisation – in this case, minimisation of the period for which personal data are stored.[30]

A controller has an obligation to analyse, internally, the data processing purposes and the storage periods corresponding to them. Determining the period of storage of personal data or the criteria for further need of the data is not a simple task, as more and more organisations implementing the GDPR are finding.

Even if the maximum retention (storage) period is specified by currently applicable law (usually a prescription period), this is not obvious. First, provisions specifying retention/prescription periods are spread across various legal acts. Second, the prescription period does not necessarily mean the appropriate period; for example, storage of information for a period longer than the prescription period set by law might be necessary to protect the vital interests of an individual,[31] and at the same time storing personal data for the whole prescription period may help to secure evidence for rare cases started at the end of a prescription period, but at the same time it generates a risk for confidentiality of data of all people whose data are till stored.

Example

When a loan agreement with a bank expires and the grounds for processing under Article 6(1)(b) GDPR, for data processing for the purpose of performance of an agreement, cease to exist, this does not give rise to an automatic obligation on the part of the bank to cease processing and erase the data. The bank has an obligation to continue to process the data under Article 6(1)(c) GDPR, i.e., separate provisions, for instance the Act of 9 October 2015 on the Agreement between the Government of the United States of America and the Government of the Republic of Poland to Improve International Tax Compliance and to Implement FATCA.

It is even more difficult to determine the data storage period if the purposes for which personal data are processed are not regulated by law. In such a case, a controller has to determine by itself the periods of personal data storage, while maintaining the correct balance between the rights of an individual under currently applicable law and its own needs with regard to data processing and achieving the defined purposes for which processing takes place. Moreover, where there are multiple purposes for which processing takes place, theoretically has to be an individual storage period, or at least

30. There is a distinction in the GDPR between data of an identified and unidentified person. At the same time, it states that personal data can be stored for longer than necessary if processed solely for archiving purposes in the public interest, for scientific or historical research purposes or for statistical purposes provided that appropriate technical and organisational measures are implemented to protect the rights and freedoms of the data subjects. These are special, exceptional cases and probably irrelevant to the average business. For this reason they are disregarded when discussing this principle.
31. For example my father cannot obtain documentation affecting the level of his pension from a bank investment fund.

criteria for verifying it, for each of them. We believe that practical problems with managing many different retention periods for different kind or purposes of processing of personal data allow for unifying retention periods to some limited number of those, say three or four general situations.

When the GDPR comes into force, the practice of many bodies, for instance international law firms, of indefinite storage of data and information (e.g., eternal storage of email correspondence) will probably no longer be possible. For this reason, the purposes for which processing takes place and legal provisions will have to be analysed, and procedures for data storage, monitoring periodical data usefulness, and scheduled erasure of data will have to be developed.

Finally, for the sake of thoroughness, we need to mention that Article 5(1)(e) GDPR provides for a derogation from the principle of limitation in time for storage of data in a form enabling identification. Data in a form enabling identification may be stored for longer than necessary for the purposes for which those data are processed, provided that they are furthered stored and processed solely for archiving purposes in the public interest, for scientific or historical research purposes or for statistical purposes, provided that appropriate technical and organisational measures are implemented to protect the rights and freedoms of the data subjects. The security measures described in the preceding sentence should take the form of implementation of technical and organisational measures ensuring in particular compliance with the principle of data minimisation. Further data processing for archiving purposes in the public interest for the sake of scientific or historical research or for statistical purposes is possible if the controller concludes that these purposes cannot be attained by processing personal data that from the outset, or at that point no longer, enable identification of data subjects, provided that the appropriate safeguards are in place (such as pseudonymisation of personal data, which is discussed separately in greater detail below).

4.7 Principle of Security (Data Integrity and Confidentiality)

Data must be processed in a manner that ensures appropriate security, including, for instance, protection against unauthorised or unlawful processing and accidental loss, destruction or damage, by appropriate technical or organisational means. The principle of security is linked to Articles 24, 28, 32 and 39 GDPR.

The GDPR requires that the appropriate level of security of personal data be provided, including integrity and confidentiality of personal data.

Personal data protection laws incorporate into the legal system terms and requirements known in information security. This occurs in fragmentary fashion, and therefore to explain them some backtracking is needed. Typically, information security has three attributes, which can be remembered by using the abbreviation CIA (confidentiality, integrity, availability). There is another, which is accountability, which is the possibility of attributing a specific task to a specific person with regard to particular information. Confidentiality means the prevention of unauthorised access to information. Integrity means prevention of unauthorised change to the information, including damage. Availability means that the information can be accessed by authorised persons.

4.7.1 *Confidentiality*

Confidentiality is intuitive. This is ensuring that unauthorised persons do not gain access to data, i.e. that the data are not leaked (e.g., by loss of a mobile telephone on which there is a file containing two thousand business contacts and one year's worth of emails) and that no unauthorised person gains access to the data in their normal location (e.g., by peaking at telephone records on a computer monitor of a telecommunications operator employee).

4.7.2 *Integrity*

Put simply: The GDPR requires measures to ensure that data are not changed or damaged deliberately or by accident.

4.7.3 *Availability*

As mentioned, availability means that the data can be accessed at any given time (by authorised persons). Lack of availability occurs when the data are destroyed (erased) or when they cannot be accessed (e.g., they are on a hard disk on a computer on which the processor has burnt out; there is a breakdown of the customer service system; production system computers have been destroyed, for example by a NotPetya virus; and opening a backup copy requires lengthy repairs to the system because someone has taken the files home with them and is currently away).

For reasons that are not entirely clear, stress has been placed as a rule only on confidentiality and integrity, and accessibility of information is not mentioned in the name of the rule.[32] This is detrimental to legibility and consistency of the GDPR because the problem of not ensuring availability of personal data is subsequently also treated as a breach of personal data security[33] (the typical example given in various guidelines is lack of access to medical records before and during an operation), while naturally, under Article 32 GDPR, ensuring continuity and resilience of systems is an element of data security. This eventually leads to recurrence of an error and the principle of security being referred to as the 'principle of integrity and confidentiality', instead of possibly the 'principle of information security'.

32. The definition of breach of personal data also does not mention availability. This terminology error might be due to a wish to exclude temporary downtime of IT systems from the obligation to notify the supervisory authority.
33. *See* Art. 29 Working Party Guidelines on Personal Data breach notification under Regulation 2016/679, http://ec.europa.eu/newsroom/document.cfm?doc_id=47741 (last accessed on 12 January 2018).

Unlike the personal data protection laws still in force, the GDPR does not define a strict information security framework. A closer description of the functional requirements and conditions that IT systems are required to fulfil to protect processed data from unauthorised disclosure, change, or destruction is sought in vain. EU lawmakers intended to produce rules that would remain relevant for a long period and a framework into which other content could be inserted at any time, as times required.

4.7.4 Appropriate

Another keyword is the word 'appropriate'. Security and compliance measures should be 'appropriate'. An analysis of the recitals and provisions within the GDPR shows that (i) data security measures should be appropriate to the risk for the rights and freedoms of data subjects (Article 32(1) GDPR) and (ii) measures (technical and organisational) taken to ensure data protection compliance and to demonstrate data protection compliance should be 'appropriate' to the risk for the rights and freedoms of data subjects. This means that the level of security as well of compliance procedures and other measures should be suited to the damage or harm that can be done to individuals due to (i) breach of security of their data and (ii) risk generated by mere processing (e.g., if legality of processing is questionable or scope of data is broad).

Observing the principle of an appropriate level of security and compliance is therefore closely linked to assessment of the risk related to data processing. Depending on the type of data held, the manner in which they are processed, or the size of the business being the controller, the appropriate security and compliance measures will have to be employed to minimise the risk of loss of control over the processed data. For the reasons described above, the measures employed following the risk analysis by one controller are not necessarily effective for another controller. Yet, in the end, for micro and small and medium businesses risk analysis is repetitive and can be standardised.

The principle of appropriate level of security, combined with the principle of accountability, means that if the risk of breach is not analysed and classified, and this does not include assessing the risk and consequences of breach of individuals' rights and freedoms, then it cannot be demonstrated that the appropriate security measures were applied. As the measures must be appropriate in relation to risk, the risk has to be assessed for the appropriate measures to be taken.

A controller (as well as processor) has to concentrate on security issues, having regard for the threat presented both from outside and inside the organisation. The crucial factor is analysis of and increasing the level of security. Digitisation of resources and universal use of modern technology means that attaining business objectives efficiently depends upon information and services, and information and communication technology infrastructure enabling use of cyberspace, being secure. Use by controllers of data leak prevention systems (so-called DLP systems) to secure data which could expose an organisation to criminal or civil liability or loss of some other kind if disclosed is becoming more and more common. Technology of this kind is not cheap. Unfortunately, a business' financial capabilities as regards implementing appropriate security measures are of secondary importance, and thus this will not constitute mitigating circumstances and will not be considered, should a supervisory authority have cause to set a penalty in cases of incidents caused due to inadequate security measures. To complicate the matter further, the principle of security sometimes has to be reconciled with the principles of lawfulness and minimisation. The issue of erasure of data from backup copies is a typical example, which is discussed when describing the right to have data erased and is mentioned in the context of the right to have data rectified.

4.8 Principle of Accountability

As mentioned, the principle of accountability provided for in Article 5(2) GDPR means that a controller is responsible for demonstrating compliance with data protection rules with regard to substantive issues. The principle of accountability transfers the burden of proof that the GDPR is complied with to controllers. The principle of accountability, being in practice a presumption of guilt, is incorporated throughout the GDPR, in various provisions. It is mentioned in Article 24, requiring a controller to implement the appropriate technical and organisational measures to ensure, and be able to demonstrate, that processing complies with the GDPR. Under Article 82(3) GDPR, a controller or a processor is exempt from liability for damage caused by processing contrary to the GDPR '**if it proves** that it is **not in any way** responsible' for the event giving rise to the damage.

Considering that the primary substantive principle is that data processing has to be lawful, the principle of accountability means that a controller is required to account for the performance of all obligations under the GDPR, which is no easy task.

5 LEGAL BASIS FOR PERSONAL DATA PROCESSING

5.1 Preliminary Remarks

First of all, let us divide personal data into broad categories. The GDPR recognises the following types of data:

(1) **'ordinary' personal data,** i.e. all data other than (2) and (3) below, for which the grounds for processing are provided for in Article 6 GDPR, while Articles 7 and 8 GDPR lay down more specific conditions for consent, including a child's consent;
(2) **special categories of personal data**, which in general cannot be processed except when an exception provided for in Article 9 GDPR applies;
(3) **so-called criminal data, i.e. personal data 'relating to criminal convictions and offences'** (convictions, breaches of law and security measures), which as a rule cannot be processed either, unless authorised under separate laws or under the control of an official authority (Article 10 GDPR).

5.2 'Ordinary' Personal Data: Articles 6–8 GDPR

A list of grounds for processing 'ordinary' personal data is given in Article 6(1) GDPR, under which data processing is permitted on the basis of:

(1) **consent** – 'the data subject has given consent to the processing of his or her personal data for one or more specific purposes' (Article 6(1)(a) GDPR);
(2) **performance of or entering into a contract** – 'processing is necessary for the performance of a contract to which the data subject is party or in order to take steps at the request of the data subject prior to entering into a contract' (Article 6(1)(b) GDPR);
(3) **legal obligation** – 'processing is necessary for compliance with a legal obligation to which the controller is subject' (Article 6(1)(c) GDPR);
(4) **vital interests** – 'processing is necessary in order to protect the vital interests of the data subject or of another natural person' (Article 6(1)(d) GDPR);
(5) **public task, exercise of official authority** – 'processing is necessary for the performance of a task carried out in the public interest or in the exercise of official authority vested in the controller' (Article 6(1)(e) GDPR);
(6) **legitimate interests pursued by the controller or by a third party** – 'processing is necessary for the purposes of the legitimate interests pursued by the controller or by a third party, except where such interests are overridden by the interests or fundamental rights and freedoms of the data subject which require protection of personal data, in particular where the data subject is a child' (Article 6(1)(f) GDPR).

Although literature on this subject has stressed for a long time that the grounds listed above are completely autonomous, independent, and unrelated, there are still firms and even administrative authorities that treat data processing as being the equivalent to having consent to data processing. The following clause is a typical example of an error in this regard. It can frequently be found on online shopping websites: 'I give consent to personal data processing to XYZ sp. z o.o. with its registered office in Milan, Via Monte Napoleone 90210, for purposes related to processing of an order'. It is clear even upon a brief glance at the list of grounds given above that in such a case, where data are necessary to perform a contract, the fact alone that the contract is entered into authorises to process data, of course only for purposes related to performance of the contract. Therefore there is no need to obtain consent for this purpose, and this clause is even misleading because it wrongly suggests that the party concerned can withdraw that consent.

Supervisory bodies usually recommend to pick one appropriate lawful basis for processing if more than one is available.[34] In our opinion, controller can specify

34. ICO: 'Take care to get it [determine your lawful basis] right first time – you should not swap to a different lawful basis at a later date without good reason' https://ico.org.uk/for-organisations/guide-to-the-general-data-protection-regulation-gdpr/lawful-basis-for-processing/ (last accessed on 29 November 2018).

multiple lawful basis for processing data. In practice this can even be a frequent occurrence (especially when performance of a contract mixes with legitimate interest or some scope of data is processed under 'entering into contract' basis, but some other requires consent[35]), but nevertheless, from the point of view of lawfulness of data processing, one lawful basis is sufficient and preferred to many.

The most important issue is that the controller is responsible for selecting the appropriate grounds.

5.2.1 *Consent of a Data Subject as Basis for Processing*

Consent is probably the most often used legal basis for personal data processing. However, it is overused. It is also treacherous as at any time it can be withdrawn, and when it is not freely given or informed, it is not valid. The 'recourse to consent' results often from reluctance to rely on legitimate interest of a data controller or legitimate interest of a third party.[36] It may also result from poor understanding or just disregarding of the EU data protection law, where a forced consent comes into play. Consent is not a viable ground for a business process requiring transfer of personal data out of EU as there need to be an intra-EU subsidiary process in place for all who decide to reject or withdraw their consent.

Processing of personal data is allowed when, according to Article 6(1)(a) GDPR:

> the data subject has given consent to the processing of his or her personal data for one or more specific purposes.

or According to Article 9(2):

> the data subject has given explicit consent to the processing of those personal data for one or more specified purposes... .

We describe requirements for consent to be effective a few paragraphs below, in a separate chapter specifically discussing consent.

5.2.2 *Entering into and Performance of a Contract*

The grounds described in Article 6(1)(b) GDPR can be cited by a controller in two situations, and these are:

35. For example draft Art. 22[1]. § 1 of the Polish Labour Code sets a closed list of data an employer can request from a candidate – there lawful base for processing is Art. 6(1)b GDPR – entering into contract. If a candidate provides a broader scope of data in her resume, apparently she gives consent to processing such extra data – the lawful basis for processing is Art. 6(1)a GDPR – consent, allowed by the draft Art. 22[1a]. § 1 of the Polish Labour Code under certain conditions. That makes choosing a right lawful basis for processing not an obvious task even for basic processes.
36. Legitimate interest of a third party has been introduced as a legal basis of personal data processing by GDPR.

(1) when the data processing is necessary for performance of a contract, or
(2) when the data processing is necessary for the taking of steps before a contract is entered into, while this must be at the request of the data subject (pre-contractual exchange of information).

5.2.2.1 *Actions Before a Contract Is Entered into (Pre-contractious)*

Let us start with exchange of information for the purpose of entering into a contract. We are allowed to process personal information of a person wishing to enter into a contract with us. If the person states that intention, this is a basis for processing their data without which the contract cannot be entered into in the form expected by that person. Therefore, if a person contacts us with an intention to enter into a contract with us, we do not need to request her consent to process related personal data of that person.

5.2.2.2 *Performance of a Contract*

It is possible to process the personal data necessary for the contract to be performed. This applies to performance of the contract by either party, i.e. the elements of the contract not only pertaining to themselves but also causing performance of the contract by the other party. Processing a client's data in order to enforce remuneration for performing a contract from that client constitutes processing for performance of that contract. At the same time, it is processing based on a legitimate interest of the controller (Article 6(1)(f) GDPR). When a data controller decides to sell receivables, passing personal data of debtors to a purchaser will be based solely on a legitimate interest of the controller.

5.2.2.3 *Processing Third-Party Data*

Technically entering into or performing a contract can serve as a legal basis for data processing only for data of a party to the contract.

If, in the context of the contract, we acquire knowledge about another person than a party to a contract (insured, a beneficiary, person who receives flowers on their birthday) we need to rely on grounds other than entering into or performing of a contract. This will usually be the legitimate interest of the controller or a party to a contract (grounds under Article 6(1)(f) GDPR). Performance of a contract with the party that entered into the contract with the controller will constitute this legitimate interest of the controller.

According to a literal interpretation of the GDPR, as a rule, in such a situation that third party should be informed that their data has been obtained and processed.[37] There are exemptions from this obligation, for instance, where the law clearly lays

37. For details consult the text on the notification obligation under Art. 14 GDPR.

down the rules for obtaining that information, or where the information constitutes professional secrets (e.g., privileged insurance information or information subject to attorney-client privilege).

The purpose of data processing in order to enter into/perform a contract is also narrow, because it is limited to that necessary for the parties to meet obligations under the contract. As regards the scope of data that can be processed on that basis, the principle of adequacy formulated in Article 5(1)(c) GDPR applies fully in this case.

5.2.3 Legal Obligation

Data processing is permitted where this is 'necessary for compliance with a legal obligation to which the controller is subject' (Article 6(1)(c) GDPR).

The grounds under Article 6(1)(c) GDPR are independent of the other types of grounds listed in the GDPR, but these grounds are incomplete. For grounds for a legal obligation to be complete, it is important to be linked to the relevant national or EU law which gives rise to a specific legal obligation to which the controller is subject (as in the case of the grounds for a legitimate interest of the controller, which also require that interest to be identified).

A legal obligation can be cited as grounds where two conditions are fulfilled jointly: there must be a provision in law that places a legal obligation on the controller, and at the same time data processing must be necessary to perform that legal obligation.[38]

The grounds for the legal obligation resemble the grounds specified in Article 6(1)(e) GDPR, which states that data processing is permitted when 'processing is necessary for the performance of a task carried out in the public interest **[public task]** or in the exercise of official authority **[official powers]** vested in the controller'.

When considering the wording of a national or EU provision, the guidelines on this subject in Recital 45 GDPR have to be taken into consideration. The Regulation does not require a specific law for each individual processing. It is sufficient for a law to be a basis for several processing operations based on a legal obligation to which the controller is subject or where processing is necessary for the performance of a task carried out in the public interest or in the exercise of official authority. The act of law does not have to break down a legal obligation into multiple data processing operations (collection, transmission, storage, transmission, enrichment, etc.) or define a specific catalogue of data that it is permitted to process. It is sufficient for the legal obligation to be described. This obligation cannot be performed without carrying out particular operations on personal data. The criterion of a logical link between the legal obligation and processing should, therefore, be applied.

The grounds for a legal obligation will apply not only to public authorities but also to any person who has a specific legal obligation which processing of specific

38. P. Litwiński, P. Barta, M. Kawecki [in:] *Rozporządzenie UE w sprawie ochrony osób fizycznych w związku z przetwarzaniem danych osobowych i swobodnym przepływem takich danych. Komentarz*, ed. P. Litwiński, Warsaw 2017, p. 297.

personal data of a particular group is needed to perform, for example laws regulating obligations of road users.

5.2.4 *Protection of Vital Interests*

Under Article 6(1)(d) GDPR, data processing is permitted where 'necessary to protect the vital interests of the data subject or of another natural person'.

As the name suggests, and as provided for in Recital 46 GDPR, a data subject's vital interests are those that have a major impact on a particular person's life, such as the saving of life, health, or property (e.g., if somebody's wallet is found in an office). This also applies in cases of disasters affecting a large number of people, for example epidemics or natural disasters.

Importantly, this is not solely a question of the personal data of a person in danger. To protect the vital interests of one individual, it is permitted to process the personal data of other persons.

On the grounds of and to protect vital interests, it is permitted to process 'ordinary' data, for example contact details and information about family and friend relationships.

It is permitted to process special categories of data (usually in matters concerning health) on the grounds of protection of vital interests only where the data subject is physically or legally incapable of giving consent' (Article 9(2)(c) GDPR).

For example details concerning state of health of an accident victim can be processed if that person is unconscious or if it is a question of a child's health and the child's legal guardian is not present.

Recital 46 GDPR also states:

> 'Processing of personal data based on the vital interest of another natural person should in principle take place only where the processing cannot be manifestly based on another legal basis' – i.e. grounds specified in Art. 6(1) GDPR other than those discussed here. This is therefore 'standby' grounds for personal data processing.

5.2.5 *Tasks Carried out in the Public Interest or in the Exercise of Official Authority*

Under Article 6(1)(e) GDPR, personal data processing is permitted when 'necessary for the performance of a task carried out in the public interest or in the exercise of official authority vested in the controller'.

This relates to two different types of grounds for data processing, which are:

(1) performance of a task carried out in the public interest, and
(2) the exercise of official authority vested in the controller.

In both of these cases, both a public task and exercise of public authority have to be described in greater detail in the law, whether national or EU law, and therefore knowledge is required of specific legal grounds for a public task or official authority, and these specific legal grounds have to be cited.

A task carried out in the public interest means in particular public utility works such as supplying water, electricity, gas and heat for the population, maintaining roads and communication, providing education, healthcare, social welfare, etc.

Bodies entitled to cite grounds of performance of a public task are public authorities, and natural and legal persons as well, who have been given public tasks (such as running the Family Welfare Centre in a municipality).

As in the case of grounds being an exercise of public authority, public authorities and other bodies as well can cite these grounds if they have been given public authority powers.

5.2.6 *Legitimate Interest of a Controller or Third Party*

The grounds of legitimate interest of a controller or third party as provided for in Article 6(1)(f) GDPR is one of the most useful types of grounds, and despite this is not fully appreciated by controllers so far. This is probably due to the wording and the need to find a balance between the interests of the controller or other entity on the one hand, and the interests of the data subject on the other.

To cite the grounds of legitimate interest effectively, both of the following requirements have to be fulfilled:

(1) processing has to be necessary for the performance of a specific purpose arising from legitimate interests of a controller or third party, and
(2) the interests or fundamental rights and freedoms of the data subject that require personal data protection do not override in the case in question the interests of a particular entity that requires processing of data of the individual. A balance must be found between these interests in particular in cases of processing of a child's data. It should not be assumed automatically that the interest or rights of a child will be an obstacle to processing of their data in order to perform a legitimate interest of a different entity.

For data processing to be determined to be necessary, a situation has to arise in which a controller's interest cannot be realised without processing specific data (i.e., data processing is a condition for realising that interest).

These interests must be legitimate in legal terms. The term 'legal' should not be considered to mean the same as the need to demonstrate a specific legal basis under some statute, because in such a case these grounds would overlap with the grounds provided for in Article 6(1) (c) GDPR. The established view is that a legitimate purpose for data processing is one that follows, for example, from the scope of business activity of a business, or pursuit of statutory goals by a foundation.[39] This is therefore an interest that the organisation in question is authorised to pursue (it is not prohibited).

39. A. Drozd, *Ustawa* ..., p. 135.

As regards the fundamental rights and freedoms of a data subject, this should be interpreted as rights and freedoms of every person under the EU or national legislature.

Under Recital 69 GDPR, but also in line with the accountability principle, it is the controller who is responsible for demonstrating that the legitimate interests of an organisation (controller or third party) override the legitimate interests or fundamental rights and freedoms of the data subject.

According to Article 6(1) paragraph 2 GDPR, public authorities cannot cite legitimate interest to justify processing personal data for the performance of their duties. Authorities should seek grounds for processing among those provided for in Article 6(1)(c) and (e) GDPR. We believe that for 'internal' goals such as physical security, even authorities may rely on legitimate interest. Others invoke the relation between statutory goals and internal processes to legitimise data processing for internal purposes based on statutory goals. That, however, seems more like a prosthesis of a legal grounds and goes beyond the wording of art. Article 6(1) paragraph 2 GDPR.

The GDPR provides for quite a large number of situations in which the grounds for personal data processing are in fact the legitimate interest of a controller (*see* Recitals 47–49 GDPR). These include:

(1) prevention of fraud, for example personal data processing to identify suspicious payments;
(2) direct marketing; interestingly, Recital 47 does not specify that this relates to an organisation's own direct marketing. This may mean that marketing of products of a different entity, for example affiliates in a capital group, is possible based on legitimate interest, but it needs to be borne in mind that for this purpose, for marketing in electronic form and by telephone (sending commercial information electronically or using telecommunications terminal devices) to be valid, the appropriate consent to communication under the Act on Electronic Services and the Telecommunications Law, and soon probably the planned e-privacy regulation should be obtained;
(3) data transmission within a capital group, i.e. 'for internal administrative purposes, including the processing of clients' or employees' personal data' (Recital 48 GDPR);
(4) cybersecurity, i.e. for 'ensuring the ability of a network or an information system to resist, at a given level of confidence, accidental events or unlawful or malicious actions that compromise the availability, authenticity, integrity and confidentiality of stored or transmitted personal data, and the security of the related services offered by, or accessible via, those networks and systems, by public authorities, by computer emergency response teams (CERTs), computer security incident response teams(CSIRTs), by providers of electronic communications networks and services and by providers of security technologies and services', for example 'preventing unauthorised access to electronic communications networks and malicious code distribution and stopping "denial of service" attacks and damage to computer and electronic communication systems' (Recital 49 GDPR);
(5) pursuit of claims.

Other practical examples can be included in the catalogue given above:

(6) keeping records of incoming and outgoing correspondence,
(7) keeping records of entry and exit of office premises,
(8) review of complaints by private entities,
(9) transfer of receivables.

According to supervisory bodies and experts, relying on legitimate interests should be preceded by a 'balancing test'[40,41] or a more exhaustive 'legitimate interest analysis'.[42] With the growth of data protection awareness, recourse to legitimate interest and therefore performing a balancing test becomes more and more common. For instance it can be very helpful to define proper direct marketing practices, which can then be coded by a particular business in a sustainable direct marketing policy or similar document.

5.3 Choice of the Legal Basis for Processing

According to supervisory bodies a controller should choose only one legal basis for processing data if more than one is available.

Subsequent changing of a legal basis for processing during processing is, as a rule, not allowed. The reasoning behind that conclusion is, though, not straightforward. It seems that supervisory bodies are afraid of circumventing the law through juggling with legal basis for processing (e.g., moving from consent to legitimate interest in case consent is withdrawn) as well as of overcomplicating things for consumers (as if data protection was not overcomplicated for businesses and other organisations). However, such issues can be solved without such formal restrictions. Probably it would be better to say that if you are changing a legal basis for processing we will look closer at what it really means.

Anyway an organisation should choose their legal basis for processing wisely, bearing in mind that a mistake may lead to illegal processing, which is a major data protection 'offence'.

The authors of this book are fans of relying on legitimate interest of a controller or third party as provided for in Article 6(1)(f) GDPR, considering it as one of the most useful types of grounds for personal data processing. Legitimate interest is not fully appreciated by controllers so far. This is probably due to the fact it is not 'mechanical', and it requires thinking, balancing interest, documenting and therefore it contains elements of knowledge, decision and personal responsibility because the need to find

40. Balancing legitimate interest of a controller against legitimate interests of a data subject.
41. Article 29 Data Protection Working Party Opinion 06/2014 on the notion of legitimate interests of the data controller under Art. 7 of Directive 95/46/EC, 844/14/EN WP 217.
42. https://ico.org.uk/for-organisations/guide-to-data-protection/guide-to-the-general-data-protection-regulation-gdpr/lawful-basis-for-processing/legitimate-interests/ (last accessed on 22 December 2018).

a balance between the interests of the controller or other entity on the one hand and the interests of the data subject on the other. Still 'legitimate interest' corresponds to 'common sense, documented', and in applying data protection relying on common sense is often inevitable.

6 ARTICLES 9 AND 10 GDPR: SPECIAL CATEGORIES OF DATA AND DATA ON CRIMINAL CONVICTIONS

Article 9(1) GDPR specifies the kinds of personal data that are subject to special protection (corresponding in general to so-called under the old Data Protection Directive 'sensitive data'[43]) and emphasises at the same time that by default, processing of these data is prohibited. In turn, point 2 of this provision gives a set of exceptional situations in which processing of special categories of personal data is permitted. In other words, the rule prohibiting the processing of special categories of data is not absolute.

The list of types of personal data given in Article 9(1) GDPR is a closed list, and therefore only the types of data listed can be considered special categories of data. This is less obvious than it may seem because data commonly called 'sensitive data' often refer to an official identification number, bank account number, information about salary or more widely even to personal data as a whole. It has to be stressed that these are not sensitive data in the meaning of the GDPR. Coming back to the list in the provision in question, the following are mentioned distinctly among special categories of data:

(1) data revealing racial or ethnic origin;
(2) data revealing political opinions, or religious or philosophical beliefs;
(3) data revealing trade union membership;
(4) genetic data;
(5) biometric data **for the purpose of uniquely identifying a natural person;**[44]
(6) data concerning health or sex life or sexual orientation.

Some types of data among those listed are clearly defined in Article 4 GDPR. Under this provision, genetic data should be understood to mean 'personal data relating to the inherited or acquired genetic characteristics of a natural person which give unique information about the physiology or the health of that natural person and which result, in particular, from an analysis of a biological sample from the natural person in question' (Recital 13). Meanwhile, biometric data are defined as 'personal data resulting from specific technical processing relating to the physical, physiological or behavioural characteristics of a natural person, which allow or confirm the unique identification of that natural person, such as facial images or dactyloscopic data' (Recital 14). Data concerning health should be understood to be information 'related to

43. Together with data relating to crimes and convictions.
44. Under the GDPR, biometric data processed at each step, for example face or voice. This is why there are special restrictions only when they are to be used for identification.

the physical or mental health of a natural person, including the provision of health care services, which reveal information about his or her health status' (Recital 15).

The exceptions to the rule prohibiting the processing of sensitive data are as follows (Article 9(2) GDPR):

(1) [**consent**] the data subject has given explicit consent to the processing of those data;
(2) [**employment law**] processing of data of this type is provided for in an existing employment relationship so far as it is authorised by EU or Member State law or a collective agreement pursuant to Member State law providing for appropriate safeguards for the fundamental rights and the interests of the data subject;
(3) **[vital interests of those who are unable to consent]** processing is necessary to protect the vital interests of the data subject or another natural person, where the data subject is physically or legally incapable of giving consent;
(4) **[not-for-profit body]** processing is carried out in the course of its legitimate activities by a foundation, association, or any other not-for-profit body with a political, philosophical, religious or trade union aim and on condition that the processing relates solely to the members or to former members of the body or to persons who have regular contact with it in connection with its purposes;
(5) **['self-disclosure']** processing relates to personal data which are manifestly made public by the data subject;
(6) **[legal claims]** processing is necessary for the establishment, exercise or defence of legal claims or whenever courts are acting in their judicial capacity;
(7) **[statutory law]** processing is necessary for reasons of substantial public interest on the basis of EU or Member State law;
(8) **[healthcare]** processing is necessary for the purposes of preventive or occupational medicine, for the assessment of the working capacity of the employee, medical diagnosis, the provision of health or social care or treatment or the management of health or social care systems and services on the basis of EU law or Member State or pursuant to contract with a health professional;
(9) **[public health]** processing is necessary for reasons of public interest in the area of public health;
(10) **[public archiving, science, history, statistics]** processing is necessary for archiving purposes in the public interest, scientific or historic research purposes or statistical purposes in accordance with Article 89(1) GDPR based on EU law or Member State law.

6.1 'Explicit' Consent for Processing Special Category Data

Article 9(2)(a) GDPR requires a consent for processing special category data to be 'explicit'. As consent should consist of 'a clear affirmative act establishing a freely given, specific, informed and unambiguous' act of a data subject (Recital 32 GDPR), what more 'explicit' means? Trying to differentiate 'a clear affirmative act' from 'explicit' we may demand that a data subject should explicitly state they are consenting to the processing their particular special category data – so a formal question should be asked, e.g. 'Do you consent to processing by us the XXX Bank data relating to your health you provided us with for the purpose of granting you loan repayment vacation or partial relieve based on our discretionary decision?'. Of course, a reasonable man could ask: 'For what other sake a bank's debtor would send the bank her/his tumour diagnosis and treatment documentation accompanied by pictures of her/his three children if not to get loan repayment vacation?'. But in case a debtor sends the bank his spouse's tumour diagnosis and treatment documentation even a reasonable man would agree that a documented explicit consent of that spouse should be required.

We discuss consent and its requirements in more detail in the following chapter about consent.

6.2 Processing in Connection with an Employment Relationship Is Lawful

The law or a collective bargaining agreement may allow special category data processing (e.g., detailed data about the state of health of persons working in the foodstuff sector) when required under the employment relationship. It is assumed that this applies both to employees on employment contracts and persons working under civil law agreements (according to the method of classification of employees and service providers adopted by the Belgian Commission de la protection de la vie privée for the purpose of RDPAs).

6.3 Protection of Vital Interests

As mentioned when describing similar grounds for processing ordinary data under Article 6(1)(d) GDPR, the grounds for processing special category data to protect vital interests require that the data subject be physically or legally incapable of giving consent to personal data processing. Such a situation may arise, for example, due to a particular state of health (state of unconsciousness) as a result of legal incapacitation, or in the case of a child. Formally it narrows a catalogue of events when you may justify processing special categories of personal data to protect the vital interest of a person. Inability to consent may result from unconsciousness or being a person formally not allowed to decide on her/himself (e.g., a minor). In practice, this gap might not be as big as it seems as it may be narrowed to a situation when you are processing personal data of a person against a will of a data subject – allowed for ordinary data, not allowed for special category data.

6.4 Membership of an Association

Associations of various kinds are authorised to process sensitive data of their members, former members and supporters if those data are related to the association's activities. This relates to not-for-profit organisations such as political parties, foundations, and associations. For example, a political party is authorised to process data about its members' political views. The wording of Article 9(2)(d) GDPR is interesting. It stems from it that an organisation is allowed to process special categories data of its opponents who are actively communicating with that organisation. It is not the conclusion that is surprising but the fact that you really need to speculate to get to the real meaning of that rule.

6.5 Data Made Public/Self-Disclosure

It is permitted to process sensitive data if it is obvious that the person concerned made the data public themselves. These grounds could be called 'celebrity exemption' because they are based on the assumption that it is permitted to process sensitive personal data of the person concerned if that person manifestly makes them public, for example during an interview for the glossy press or television. However, we would not rely on this ground when citing information from celebrity gossip sites.

6.6 Court Cases

It is permitted to process special data in order to establish, exercise or defend legal claims. In a similar way, under the GDPR, it is possible for courts to process such data when acting in their judicial capacity.

6.7 Important Public Interest in Reality Just: 'Based on Law'

The notion of relying on important public interest appears in the context of the grounds provided for in Article 6(1)(e) GDPR, and thus the comments made above apply here. In turn, a reference is also made to public interest, but in the context of public health, in Article 9(2)(i) GDPR. A similar situation arises with regard to the grounds in Article 9(2)(j) GDPR, but in this case the public interest arises due to scientific or historical research or for statistical purposes as provided for in Article 89(1) GDPR or under EU law or Member State law.

Organisations operating in the healthcare sector also have grounds for processing sensitive data. The provision in question lists numerous data processing purposes, and these include preventive or occupational medicine, assessment of the working capacity of the employee, medical diagnosis, the provision of health or social care or treatment or the management of health or social care systems and services. Processing of special category data on these grounds must be necessary to achieve the purposes defined above and provided for in EU or national law or under a contract with a health professional (this should be a professional who is subject to an obligation of secrecy or a person for whom that professional is responsible, or other person subject to a professional obligation of secrecy).

But let us get back to Earth. A reader will not find out in Article 9 GDPR any exemption directly allowing to process special categories of data based on a Member State's law. But yes, Article 9(2)(g) GDPR in reality constitutes such basis. The trick is not for businesses or any other normal organisations. It is for the EU bodies and Member States to dispute if a particular Member State law is compatible with Article 9(2)(g) GDPR or not. 'Lay' businesses and organisations should just rely on the local EU Member State law and Article 9(2)(g) GDPR when the processing of special category data is allowed or required under that Member State law.

6.8 Data on Criminal Convictions

Data on convictions, breaches of law and related security measures (safeguards) are not included in the catalogue of special category data under the GDPR personal data protection system. Nevertheless, the processing of such data continues to be regulated and it is possible only if a specific provision of a Member State's or EU's law exists or when 'under the control of official authority' (Article 10 GDPR) and subject to existence of a legal basis of processing defined in Article 6 GDPR. Rules on the processing of data on criminal convictions are laid down in more detail in the so-called Police Directive,[45] which was passed at the same time as the GDPR.

7 CONSENT AS BASIS FOR PROCESSING PERSONAL DATA

Consent is a valid legal basis for processing both 'ordinary' personal data (Article 6 GDPR) and special categories data (Article 9 GDPR).

Surprisingly, the wording of Article 10 GDPR suggests that consent would not be sufficient to process 'criminal' data as Article 10 GDPR on top of legal basis for processing from Article 6(1) GDPR requests either 'control of official authority' or specific 'Union or Member State law'. We are not sure how deliberate is that limitation. In practice, however, processing 'criminal' data based on consent (or contract) should be allowed. Very prudent controllers intending to commence such processing could pre-inform their local Prosecution about their intentions, pointing to laws allowing for such activity. For example, they may refer to local regulations allowing to publish name and face of a suspect or convict based on their consent, as an argument that if consent justifies 'public' processing, then consent is enough for a 'non-public' processing as well.

45. Directive (EU) 2016/680 of the European Parliament and of the Council of 27 April 2016 on the protection of natural persons with regard to the processing of personal data by competent authorities for the purposes of the prevention, investigation, detection or prosecution of criminal offences or the execution of criminal penalties and on the free movement of such data, and repealing Council Framework Decision 2008/977/JHA (Official Journal of the European Union, L 119, p. 89).

7.1 Consent: Most Important GDPR Quotations

According to Article 7 of GDPR:

(1) 'Where processing is based on consent, the controller will be able to demonstrate that data subject has consented to processing of their personal data' [principle of accountability].
(2) 'If the data subject's consent is given in a written declaration which also concerns other matters, the request for consent will be presented in a manner which is clearly distinguishable from the other matters, in an intelligible and easily accessible form, using clear and plain language. Any part of such a declaration which constitutes an infringement of this Regulation will not be binding' [principle of transparency].
(3) 'The data subject will have the right to withdraw their consent at any time. The withdrawal of consent will not affect the lawfulness of processing based on consent before its withdrawal. Prior to giving consent, the data subject will be informed. Consent will be as easy to withdraw as it was to give consent' [principle of freedom to grant consent].
(4) 'When assessing whether consent is freely given, utmost account will be taken of whether the performance of a contract, including the provision of a service, is conditional on consent to the processing of personal data that is not necessary for the performance of that contract' [principle of freedom to grant consent] [proper choice of legal basis of processing].

According to the definition in Article 4(11) GDPR, consent of a data subject means:

> freely given, specific, informed and unambiguous indication of the data subject's wishes by which he or she, by a statement or by a clear affirmative action, signifies agreement to the processing of personal data relating to him or her.

According to Recital 32 GDPR:

> Consent should be given by a clear affirmative act establishing a freely given, specific, informed and unambiguous. ... [conditions for consent]

According to Recital 42 first sentence:

> the controller should be able to demonstrate that the data subject has given consent to the processing operation. [principle of accountability]

According to Recital 42 fourth sentence:

> For consent to be informed, the data subject should be aware at least of the identity of the controller and the purposes of the processing for which the personal data are intended. [informed consent] [layered approach]

7.2 Conditions for Consent

From the definition given above as well as from the revised Guidelines on Consent adopted by the EDPB (Article 29 Working Party) on 10/04/2018 (17/EN WP259 rev.01), consent to be considered a valid basis for data processing, the following conditions apply:

(1) Consent is freely given.
(2) Consent is specific.
(3) Consent is informed.
(4) Consent is unambiguous.

7.2.1 Freely Given Consent

Freely given. Consent is considered free if it is given freely and willingly by the data subject. 'Freely given consent' means that the person concerned has to have true freedom of choice. Consent of this kind cannot be given under pressure, and moreover, refusal to make the relevant statement or withdrawing consent cannot have adverse consequences for the data subject. Consent is not considered to be freely given if lack of consent results in negative consequences for the data subject. In this respect, we should concur with the views contained in the WP259 guidelines.

Another words consent is freely given if it depends on a free will of a data subject. Consent is not freely given if lack of consent results in adverse consequences to a data subject.[46]

According to Article 7(4) GDPR quoted above, if 'the performance of a contract, including the provision of a service, is conditional on consent to the processing that is not necessary for the performance of that contract' then consent is not considered freely given. Two interesting conclusions stem from this provision. First, that bundling consent with contract is not allowed (we talk more about bundling below). Second, that a data controller should not mistake consent with contract as they are separate legal basis legitimising personal data processing.

Imbalance of power. If there is an imbalance of power between data subject and an institution, the consent is not deemed freely given.

Under Recital 43 GDPR:

> In order to ensure that consent is freely given, consent should not provide a valid legal ground for the processing of personal data in a specific case where there is a clear imbalance between the data subject and the controller.

In case there is a clear imbalance of power between a data subject and a controller, a consent might not be considered freely given. When it comes to operations performed in relation to all employees, employers generally cannot rely on the consent.

46. EDPB 259rev01 Guidelines on Consent under Regulation 2016/679.

Interestingly, the GDPR permits an employer to process an employee's personal data on the basis of consent in cases defined in detailed provisions of law or collective bargaining agreements. This is stated in Recital 155.

Conditionality. In order for a consent to be considered freely given, it should not be conditional. While it happens fairly often, a consent should not be required if data are needed for the performance of a contract. This is a common mistake. Conclusion and performance of a contract are independent (Article 6, section 1, letter b of GDPR).

The distinction is blurred if a customer is offered add-on services which, should s/he wishes to take advantage of them, s/he needs to consent to (by sending a text message about an incoming email or a money transfer or using double authentication feature – customer needs to provide their mobile phone number so they need to agree that it is used). According to the EDPB (Article 29 Working Party), such 'consents' are deemed freely given and justifiably obtained. Contrary to the view of the EDPB, we see such actions as a mere entering into a contract for add-on services even.

(Dis)bundling/detailing. A consent is not considered to be freely given if it cannot be expressed separately for each type of (data processing) activity. The Article 29 Working Party uses the example of consent to an email communication combined with a consent to transfer of data to another company within the same group of companies. This example is misleading though because it mixes a consent for personal data with a consent for direct marketing communication (electronic communication consent). It ignores controller's justified interest in direct marketing and transferring data. The problem lies in law which creates two parallel regimes – data protection regime and electronic communications regime with separate rules for consents (and, even more misleading, soon redirecting from e-communication to data protection when the e-Privacy Regulation is finally adopted). In practice, consents for different activities (processing data for different purposes) should be given on separate forms or by ticking individual checkboxes.

The price of no consent. If consent is bundled up as a non-negotiable part of terms and conditions of an agreement, it is presumed not to have been given freely. Should this happen, and in case of an audit, offering significant benefits in exchange for the consent will be subject to closer evaluation.

Example

A cable TV operator offers a discount of 1 EUR a month in exchange for a consent or a financial institution reduces their margin by 0.5% in exchange for a consent to process customer's data for marketing purposes. Customers who refuse to take up the offer will pay PLN 60 and PLN 1500 more per year respectively. Lack of consent or its withdrawal will have negative financial consequences for the customers.

On the other hand, both the consent itself and the data acquired are a 'commodity' and may be paid for in various benefits. From this point of view, it is about the 'unconditional aspect' and 'not bundling' with any other benefits (bundling of non-related services is additionally banned under the EU consumer law).

The consent should be given independently and separately from any other 'transaction' between the data subject and the controller. It is not so much about the 'maths' as it is about economics and psychology. We are not in a situation of acting 'freely' when we apply for a bank loan, instead we are driven by a need. The data are being processed in order to enter into an agreement and not on the basis of a consent given.

Offering vouchers or other incentives in exchange for consent should be allowed. It should also be allowed to pay for the consent but preferably not in the form of an adjustment of price for the requested service. The problem lies in financial conditions more than in a legal structure.

For example, we are finding ourselves in an 'economic need' of borrowing money and the necessity to pay for it, but we do not want to overpay. This is why, in our opinion, in the context of GDPR, the idea of offering a lower interest rate in exchange for a consent takes the 'free' aspect away. Of course, we may say that instead of asking for a consent a bank may offer to their customers a contract for 'acceptance of e-marketing'. This could, however, lead to circumventing GDPR and e-privacy regulations and as such be considered as unfair consumer practice.

Paid consent or a contract? Eventually if we were to be rigorous about principles of consent, a remunerated consent is not freely given as a non-consenting party loses an opportunity. Therefore, more broadly, a paid consent should rather be considered as a contract where a data subject allows for processing of their personal data in remuneration for a specific consideration. Such contract would in many cases be under scrutiny of consumer protection authorities as in many cases it would be bundled with a primary contract, and the question would be asked if a 'consent contract' is an independent contract or it is just a 'primary contract' bundled with an unrelated contract which is generally considered an abusive clause.

7.2.1.1 Withdrawing Consent

Under Article 7(3) GDPR the person can withdraw consent at any time. For many organisations, it will be a true challenge to introduce simple mechanisms to handle that procedure efficiently. This is crucial because it must be as easy to withdraw consent as it is to give consent. If, for example, consent is given by ticking a checkbox online, then it is not permitted to require that a data subject withdraw consent by sending notice to this effect in writing. Withdrawal of consent means that the controller is no longer able to process personal data on those grounds. Naturally, withdrawal of consent does not affect the lawfulness of processing operations performed up until that time.[47]

47. However, authors of the GDPR require data controllers to inform data subjects that time travels are still impossible, because according to Arts 13(2)c and 14(2)d GDPR, a data controller is obliged to inform a data subject that withdrawing consent does not affect 'the lawfulness of processing based on consent before its withdrawal'.

The prerequisite that consent be given is also provided for in other acts of law, in particular a prior consent to use of automated communication (automated calling machines, fax, electronic mail) for direct marketing is required by Article 13 of the so-called e-Privacy Directive.[48] The GDPR does not change anything in this respect.

However, we need to be aware that consent for digital direct marketing communication is often mistaken with consent for data processing, even by supervisory authorities. In result often two or three separate consents are being required. In reality, if a person consents to use a particular communication channel for direct marketing (text message, email, telephone, a particular internet communicator) then that person usually expects getting some sort of direct marketing messages through agreed channels. Therefore as you do not plan to market unexpected goods or services (e.g., offering cooking books to gamers) to those who consented to receive direct marketing messages from you, you may rely on legitimate interest (Article 6(1)f GDPR) instead of requiring a separate consent for data processing.

Finally, the burden of proof that consent has been given rests with the controller, and therefore as a fundamental rule consent must be documented.

7.2.1.2 Easy Withdrawal

According to Article 7(3) fourth sentence, consent has to be as easy to withdraw as it was to give. This right and process must be handled by the controller.

In practice, withdrawal should be available through the same communication channels which were available for the consent to be given. Controller's systems and processes must make note of the consent withdrawal. In practice, where consent was given via electronic interface by filling in an online form, the same website should give an option of an easy retrieval, withdrawal or unclicking.

Most of the electronic services are built clearly against the easy withdrawal principle. Opt-out or terminate options are hidden as deep as possible. When consents are collected through any channel possible, withdrawal is often available only through call centre, emailing human operator and hoping it works, etc. Taking into consideration the privacy by design principle (Article 25(1) GDPR), imposing or staying with such practices after 25 May 2018 may and should result in severe administrative fines when reviewed by supervisory bodies.

7.2.1.3 Click Fatigue

According to Recital 32 fifth sentence GDPR:

> If the data subject's consent is to be given following a request by electronic means, the request must be clear, concise and not unnecessarily disruptive to the use of the service for which it is provided.

48. Directive 2002/58/EC of the European Parliament and of the Council of 12 July 2002 concerning the processing of personal data and the protection of privacy in the electronic communications sector (Directive on privacy and electronic communications).

Based on the above Article 29 Working Party we believe that it is necessary to make sure that data subjects do not get 'tired' when clicking and reading, that they remain vigilant and do not simply, mechanically, without understanding continue to consent.

There are practical problems with the above righteous approach. One is that there are online guidelines how to make user consent and they are based on disturbing user enough to force her/him to take action.[49] Second is that according to GDPR, consent should not be predefined (default option); therefore, consenting should by default be more exhausting than doing nothing (hence UX guidelines how to make 'non-consent' at least equally disturbing as consenting). Third, that the whole programmatic or ad-tech business model is based on multidirectional hundred partner traffic of data, which one could compare to a simultaneous intercourse between hundreds or thousands of those who the online advertising industry calls 'trusted partners'. It is beyond human perception and performance to freely and in an informed manner agree to be a subject of a traffic for two or seven hundred 'trusted partners' at a time. And this is exactly what happens with our data when we enter popular internet portals. Our personal data are being trafficked to hundreds of third parties of which we know nothing, and we have no human ability to learn about. That is why the burden of responsibility for choosing partners for such interchange of our data should rely on our data controllers and not on us. That is, our consent is not a valid legal basis for such processing of our data, a legitimate interest of controllers based on a properly performed legitimate interest analysis (Article 1.f GDPR) could be.

7.2.2 Consent Which Is Specific

Specific consent means consent that reasonably precisely defines the purpose for which data is processed. It is not possible to obtain abstract or blanket consents; for example, 'I consent to personal data processing as provided for in the GDPR.' Information related to consent must be distinctly separate from information concerning other issues, for example connected with a contract.

Specific consent corresponds to the principle of specific purpose of data processing. As the purpose should be specific, it should be formulated using specific wording.

As usual with the GDPR the key word is 'reasonably'. The requirement of precision of consent and the requirement that consent should be informed (as briefly explained below) contradicts the requirement of conciseness, transparency and intelligibility (Articles 5(1)a and 12(1) GDPR). To sort out of this contradiction, the EDPB came up with the concept of 'layered' information duty, which we describe below.

However, the requirement that consent should be specific should not result in demanding a data controller to know the future or the unknown. Therefore a consent should be goal/purpose oriented. According to Recital 32 fourth sentence, 'Consent should cover all processing activities carried out for the same purpose or purposes.' We

49. For example https://www.iabeurope.eu/category/policy/gdpr-implementation/ enforces consent to cookies and 'processing of the (personal) data' to access their site – which is an example of a controversial 'cookie wall' practice.

should tell a data subject 'what for' we are going to use the data, but not necessarily describe 'what we will do' with the data (as long as they stay within the EU and no automated decision-making resulting in legal or similar effects is involved, *see* Articles 13.1.f & 14.1.f and 13.2.f & 14.1.g GDPR).

7.2.3 Informed Consent

Informed consent means providing a data subject with vital information enabling an informed decision to be made so that the individual understands what they are consenting to. In this context, the clause itself also has to be worded in plain and simple language (principle of transparency contained in Article 5(1)(a) and expanded in Article 12(1) GDPR).

Informed consent follows from the principle of fairness (Article 5(1)(a) GDPR), which is the obligatory approach for a controller in their relationship with the data subject.

In order to determine that a consent is informed, a person (data subject) needs to know the consequences of such a consent in the context of their rights. This way we will fulfil the duty to inform as per Article 13 or 14 GDPR. If we request consent to use data which have already been in our possession, having previously fulfilled our duty to inform about it, we need to at least provide the missing information (listed in the WP259 guidelines on consent). The WP260 guidelines recommend however that the full set of information is requested again. Such an approach (requesting full set of information again) might be easier to process.

Transparency/Plain/intelligible language. Consent forms and other communications related to requesting and obtaining of consent should be clear and intelligible for data subject. Remarks referred to in the context of Article 12 GDPR – rights of the data subject – apply. The WP259 guidelines go as far as even recommending voluntary test panels. Such test panel could be recruited from staff or a group of friends (referred to in Article 12 GDPR).

Layered approach. According to Recital 42 fourth sentence:

> For consent to be informed, the data subject should be aware at least of the identity of the controller and the purposes of the processing for which the personal data are intended.

Based on the above minimum requirement for consent and taking into consideration the vast scope of information obligation contained in Articles 13 and 14 GDPR, the EDPB (Article 29 Working Party) proposed in their Guidelines on Consent,[50] a so-called layered approach to consent and information obligations.

The layered approach means providing immediate essential information (who and for what) associated with a reference to a more detailed, complete explanation (most often a link to an internet place where an appropriate privacy policy resides). Though the Guidelines on consent refer to situations where it is needed 'to accommo

50. Article 29 Working Party Guidelines on consent under Regulation 2016/679 Adopted on 28 November 2017 as last Revised and Adopted on 10 April 2018, 17/EN WP259 rev.01.

date for small screens or situations with restricted room for information', the Guidelines on transparency (WP260 rev.01) refer to it more broadly. In practice the layered approach works best for any situations.

7.2.4 Unambiguous Consent

Lack of ambiguity is the last of the listed criteria and means that consent must be given unambiguously in the form of a statement or explicit action confirming consent, for example subscription to a newsletter and confirming this by clicking on an activation link sent in an email stating that an email address has been added to the database (double opt-in).

Consent has to be unambiguous and demonstrated with a clear action of data subject: signature, ticking a box by a mouse click, sending an email, responding to a text message or otherwise saying 'I agree', registering or clicking 'I agree' button. Article 29 Working Party even refers to turning a smartphone in a figure of eight.[51]

7.2.5 'Internet Consent'

Let us be realistic; a very popular e-commerce practice of requiring consent to be able to use an electronic service (a social media platform, a news portal, a mobile application) usually by no means meets the described above requirements for consent to be valid. Most of the time it is not freely given – if the use of the service depends on consent it is not a consent – it is more like consideration, so the user and the provider enter into a contract. Most of the time it is not informed – you are humanly unable to give an informed consent to a data controller for sharing your data with two or seven hundred so-called trusted partners. Neither it is specific. We are ignorant of what our data are used for, and if we were presented with the scope of use of our data, it would be too long and too complicated to read for most of the people.

Data controllers should consider using legitimate interest instead and to make it truly legitimate, they should perform and document the so-called legitimate interest analysis we are writing about above. At the same time, supervisory bodies should become more welcoming to legitimate interest though it requires a legitimate judgment call not only from controllers but also from supervisory bodies. Opportunistic reliance on consent undermines sustainability of the whole, still fragile system of data protection.

7.3 Conflict of Principles

All of the above principles (freedom of granting, specificity, being informed, unambiguity, transparency, intelligibility) taken separately might seem reasonable and feasible. Unfortunately, when mixed together, they create an unattainable level of smart

51. Which, according to authors, works provided the phone has an accelerometer and provided it is not weekend after 8pm in a country where consumption of alcohol is allowed.

communication requiring telling everything in a few words. To make consent or consents specific, informed and unambiguous, you would have to provide detailed explanations of what specifically you are going to do with the data – i.e., what the data subject is consenting to. Add to it an information obligation from Articles 13 and 14 GDPR and you are ending up in a bureaucratic heaven or hell (pending from which perspective you look at it) ideal for regulators and big corporations but particularly hostile for micro, small and medium enterprises.

As we have mentioned above, the EDPB (Article 29 Working Party) tried to camouflage a little this immovable conflict in their Guidelines on Consent,[52] where they proposed the so-called layered approach to consent and information obligations which we have already briefly described.

7.4 Form of Consent

Theoretically consent can be given in any form, as the GDPR does not impose any rules directly in this respect. Though, the principle of accountability continues to apply, and thus consent can be given in any form, but the controller is required to prove that consent was given. For this reason, as a rule, consent must be documented.

This does not necessarily mean in writing, as the ticking of a checkbox, selection of technical settings, or a recording of a telephone call, for example, is sufficient. Let us remember that inaction on the part of a data subject, for example lack of response to an email requesting consent, even if it can be deemed to be silent consent (tacit acceptance), is not effective under the GDPR. Tacit acceptance does not meet the minimum unambiguity requirement, and it does not meet 'affirmative action' requirement.

Documenting that consent has been given does not always require recording a mere act of consenting. For example, a technical (e.g., IT) process may be designed in such a manner that you are not able to advance without confirming your consent. Yet, two issues arise. First, you need to relate a process to data, so you need to register either entering data to a system or consenting to use them. Second, you need to consider if a process conditioning certain actions on consent meets previously described criteria of validity of consent and in particular a requirement of freedom of consent.

According to Recital 32 GDPR, 'consent should be given by a clear affirmative act'. EDPB in an interesting view which allows such act to be even waiving a mobile device. Authors of that view probably do not drink alcohol.

A situation in which a statement giving consent is part of a different statement is not permissible either. For example, a controller cannot effectively cite consent if it takes the form of acceptance of service terms and conditions in which a statement of that kind is one of the provisions. This will not meet the criterion of freely given consent.

52. Article 29 Working Party Guidelines on consent under Regulation 2016/679 Adopted on 28 November 2017 As last Revised and Adopted on 10 April 2018, 17/EN WP259 rev.01.

7.4.1 Explicit Consent

'Explicit consent' is a category specified by GDPR for the purpose of consent for processing special categories of data, for automated decision-making and special data transfer outside the EEA. This relates to a more formalised consent than 'regular' though setting a difference taking into consideration the requirements for an 'regular' consent is not that easy.

Under Recital 32 GDPR:

> Consent should be given by a clear affirmative act establishing a freely given, specific, informed and unambiguous indication of the data subject's agreement to the processing of personal data relating to him or her such as by a written statement, including by electronic means, or an oral statement.

This essentially means that each consent must be explicit because otherwise it is not unambiguous. Therefore 'explicit consent' in the meaning of GDPR should be understood in a more explicit way.

The logical explanation to this question is that a data subject should explicitly state they are consenting to processing their data when the FGDPR requests so. A formal question should be asked, e.g. 'Do you consent to processing by us the XXX Bank data relating to your health you provided us with for the purpose of granting you loan repayment vacation or partial relieve based on our discretionary decision?' (an example used to illustrate explicit consent in a chapter about special categories data). Answer to that question should be explicit and directly associated with the question (i.e., why at the elementary school we are requested to answer with the 'whole sentence').

Apart from requesting a full documented sentence 'I agree to processing my health/sexual/political/etc. data/to automated processing my data for the purpose of/to transferring my data to your Dubai branch,' Article 29 Working Party proposes a two-tiered consent (a consent with additional confirmation). It seems as though the consent not only has to meet all the basic requirements but also be given in a way that cannot be performed only mechanically (without thinking), for instance 'yes, I agree for my medical records about my fractured arm to be sent to (X) Medical Clinic in the US' – signature' (which basically consumes the first possible method of obtaining an 'explicit consent').

7.5 Accountability

Controller has to demonstrate that consent was given.

As we have mentioned in a precedent point, it is, therefore, necessary either to record consents and be able to find/reference them in a different way or to prove that a business or technical process is organised in such a manner that consent is a prerequisite for advancing. Recording consents seems to be quite an archiving task, particularly in relation to consents given orally. As a rule, it is unacceptable to call for witnesses to prove that consent was given, although it may be done under special circumstances (if consent was granted in emergency). Proving that a business process does not allow for circumventing a consent may be quite a challenge as well, especially against experienced supervisory bodies.

7.6 Retention (Consent Validity Period)

There is no time limitation for the consent validity. Article 29 Working Party recommends that consents are 'refreshed' at 'appropriate intervals', e.g. annually.

In our view, a controller should use their judgment to decide in what circumstances consent should be deemed 'no longer valid' and document it accordingly. If controller handles the right for consent withdrawal, there is no point in disrupting the privacy of data subjects with unnecessary communication.

In case a controller communicates periodically with data subjects based on consent, it may just add to each communicate a brief information about an option to withdraw consent. That seems least invasive.

If processing data based on consent by a controller does not require communicating with data subjects responding to a question if and how often to remind about the possibility to withdraw consent should depend on risk analysis. A controller should ask themselves a question what risk to rights and freedoms of data subjects such processing generates and based on an answer decide if and how often remind data subjects about their ability to withdraw consent and about potential adverse consequences of the consent remaining in place (has anybody ever done it?!).

7.7 Child's Consent to Information Society Services (Social Media, Electronic Services, Etc)

Article 8 GDPR introduces additional rules on consent to the processing of personal data of a child of below 16 years of age when the child is offered information society services.

According to Article 8, section 1 GDPR, offering information society services directly to a child can be based on a consent of that child if they are at least 16 years old.[53] Where the child is below the age of 16 such processing will be lawful on the basis of a consent given by their parent or legal guardian.

Information society services are services provided electronically, which in fact are access to various content and functionalities online or thanks to online enablers/'platforms' – websites, applications, even tangible things such as cars,[54] etc. – not necessarily for a charge,[55] especially as very often (and practically in every case)

53. Some EU Member States lowered this threshold as Art. 8.1 second paragraph GDPR allowed to lower it down to 13 years old.
54. The fact that the European Court of Justice, in a judgment of 20 December 2017 Case C-434/15, decided Uber to be a 'service in the field of transport' and not 'information society service' does not change the rule that application and services connecting people electronically would usually fall under 'information society services' category.
55. D. Lubasz [in:] *RODO. Ogólne rozporządzenie ...*, p. 431, points out that this is a 'normal' [...] service for a fee, but a service provided electronically does not necessarily entail a fee, and the

payment in the digital word takes the form of provision of information.[56] This relates in particular to popular social networking sites on which people can post text, photographs, and films, or a combination of these forms.

As we point out when discussing right for information, the Article 29 Working Party Guidelines on Transparency (WP260 rev. 01) stipulate that the responsibility to adapt communication for children rests not only on the controllers who target children but also on those who should be aware that their products and services are used particularly by children (e.g., social media for posting short video messages which disappear after viewing, etc). The same guidelines suggest the possibility of using the language and rhetoric of the United Nations (UN) Convention on the Rights of the Child. In the WP259 guidelines on Consent, the Article 29 Working Party lays out Article 8 GDPR in a narrower way, referring to the controller's intention (that they do not address their website to children, because the content is 'adult', because the controller does not intend to derive profits from children). Though the same guidelines wrongly refer to the age limit of 18 (instead of 16 as stated in Article 8(1) GDPR) which may suggest that whoever wrote it had either not familiarised themselves with Article 8 GDPR or had only skim-read it.

To protect children against the consequences of posting their personal data online (not even necessarily when this is done irrationally), the GDPR requires the consent of a child's legal guardians to the child's use of electronic services offered to the child (e.g., setting up an account on a popular social networking site and then posting photos and film clips for fun). Under Article 8(2) GDPR, this means an obligation for a controller to take reasonable measures to determine whether the guardian has given consent. As a minimum, this requires certain mechanisms to verify the age of a guardian but also probably the relationship to the child who wishes to make use of specific services.

The issue of a consent of a child's guardian to use of an internet site is not new. Certain international corporations that offer services to children have introduced systems to solve the problem. Systems of this kind are also known in the 'adults only' industry – as a general rule they require identification using a credit card; that is, an instrument rarely made available to minors. Even the largest social networking sites balance on the edge of the law and officially offer their services to adults or persons aged over 13, for example in the US (Children's Online Privacy Protection Act), relying on waivers of liability.

The offering by a website of services to a child directly does not mean, despite appearances, that it is a store with toys or software for children. This term should be interpreted broadly, to include situations in which the controller is aware that the products it offers are attractive to children as well, which it attracts as users of the service.

aim of the provision is not to protect the parents' wallet but children's privacy. For this reason the question of a fee for the service is not discussed.

56. M. Macenaite, *Consent for Processing Children's Personal Data in the EU: Following in US Footsteps?*, 'Information & Communications Technology Law' 2017/2, http://www.tandfonline.com/doi/full/10.1080/13600834.2017.1321096 (last accessed on 22 January 2018).

What are the reasonable steps that need to be taken to ensure that the guardian has given consent? The GDPR does not provide an answer to this interesting question, to ensure technological neutrality. This is a difficult question and may depend on the type of e-service offered. Even the issue of identification of a user of electronic services is a sensitive subject by itself. It seems that age verification requires either identification or prediction (based on a kind of test or artificial intelligence). It is possible to imagine a situation in which a controller introduces user age profiling mechanisms that are based on a user's behaviour on the site or in which it profiles a user's age according to data that it collects in any case (i.e., without collecting additional data). In such a case, it can identify minors and require them to produce proof of their age or consent from their guardian. Any parent knows that at a popular video streaming service age verification mechanisms and content control tools for parents are fiction.

Finally, it only needs to be said that the argument that once a child reaches their majority for personal data purposes their consent to processing of their data posted in the past will have to be obtained again is not practically reasonable. For this reason we will not be addressing this issue. If it transpires that the supervisory authority wishes to examine this aspect, we will conduct a more thorough analysis or update our assessment.

8 THE CONTROLLER AND PROCESSOR

8.1 Preliminary Remarks

A relation between personal data and an organisation can be described as either controlling data (data controller) or processing data (data processor) for someone else (data controller).

A controller processes data for their own purposes, while a processor processes data for the purposes of the controller, and is engaged to do this by the controller.

Each organisation is a controller of some personal data, primarily of their staff and of contact persons of their business partners.

An organisation becomes a processor when another organisation gives them certain personal data asking to do something with those data.

8.2 A Controller: Definition, Characteristics, Obligations

8.2.1 Definition

Under Article 4(7) GDPR:

> A '**controller**' means a **[1]** natural or legal person, public authority, agency or other body which, **[2]** alone or jointly with others, determines **[3]** the purposes and means of the processing of personal data; **[4]** where the purposes and means of such processing are determined by EU or member state law, the controller or the specific criteria for its nomination may be provided for by EU or member state law.

8.2.2 *Every Organisation Is a Controller*

Anyone who makes use of personal data for their own purposes is a controller. Everyone makes use of personal data of some kind for their own purposes. There are always subcontractors and suppliers of some kind, and when doing business there is always contact with natural persons. This means that everyone acts as a controller of personal data of some kind. Being a controller is an organisation's role. This same entity usually acts as a controller, a processor, a data recipient and sometimes as a third party, and if it is a natural person, as a data subject as well. This does not help those who are not well practised in this area to become accustomed to GDPR terminology.

The only practical exception is provided for in Article 2(2)(c) GDPR. This states that the GDPR:

> does not apply to the processing of personal data by a natural person in the course of a purely personal or household activity.

Therefore, apart from ordinary consumers, almost everybody is a controller. Controllers might therefore be:

- legal persons: joint-stock companies, limited liability companies, limited liability partnerships, partnerships, cooperatives, foundations, associations, state-owned enterprises, faiths, research institutes, political parties, trade unions, church legal persons;
- public authorities;
- units or other entities, for example organisational units that do not have legal personality, that are afforded capacity to perform legal transactions by law;
- natural persons who run their own business (microenterprises);
- other natural persons existing in a public space, e.g. bloggers, influencers.

8.2.3 *What Determines That a Particular Entity Is a Controller?*

You are a controller if acting individually or with others, you:

- determine the purposes and
- means of personal data processing.

Under the GDPR, the purposes and means of processing can be determined by an organisation individually or with others, in cases relating to **joint control of personal data**.

8.2.4 *Determining the Purposes and Means of Processing*

If a number of organisations are actively involved in data processing, it has to be determined which of them, in fact, determines the purposes and means of processing. This organisation will be considered the controller responsible for all elements of data processing under the GDPR, such as legality, responding to data subject requests, data security, and controlling a data processing supply chain.

Determining who is a controller has to be functional and thus reflect who in fact specifies the purposes and means of data processing. Deciding the purposes and means corresponds to deciding on one's own behalf and for oneself as to the purpose for which and the means by which personal data are processed.[57]

Example

A company that has employees is a controller with respect to those employees' personal data. It is the company that determines the system in which it processes its employees' data and the security measures used.

Example

A Company A collects personal data through its website for the purpose of online marketing activities. Company A processes personal data collected through the website and then sends a newsletter to its potential clients – i.e., website's users. Company A is a controller of personal data collected and used for marketing purposes.

However, regardless of the above process, Company A uses services of a marketing agency (a Company B) for a part of data of its potential clients. Company B also sends the newsletter of Company A to its potential clients acting on behalf of Company A, so Company B is a typical processor of personal data entrusted by Company A.

8.2.5 Are We a Data Controller: Practical Test

If someone is not a household or a person that processes data for household purposes, then they are definitely a controller of personal data of some kind. And if you are a processor (you process data for someone else 'on hire' being an organisation, including sole proprietorship), then you are for sure a controller for some other data (e.g., data of your personnel). So, each processor is a controller, which does not facilitate understanding the EU data protection system.

57. M. Sakowska-Baryła, *Prawo do ochrony danych osobowych*, Wrocław 2015, p. 143.

8.2.6 Role of a Controller

The GDPR is chiefly intended for controllers, and controllers are the main parties obligated under the GDPR. A controller is responsible for data processing as a whole, including data entrusted to a processor. A controller is the subject of all GDPR obligations except for Member State, supervisory authority, accreditation bodies and certification bodies' obligations. A controller is subject to obligations provided for directly and indirectly in the GDPR – the controller is in fact also the subject of provisions applicable to the processor, as a controller is also responsible for a processor. If a number of organisations are involved in the processing, then the key issue is which organisation in fact determines the purposes and means of processing. In the event of an inspection, it is the controller that is required to prove that it processes data in accordance with the GDPR.

8.2.7 A Controller's Obligations

More than half of ninety-nine provisions of the GDPR (fifty-seven provisions) provide for obligations of the controller. They are presented in Table 1.1.

Table 1.1 Controller's Obligations

No	*Obligation*	*Article in the GDPR*	*A Controller Is Obliged To*
1.	**General principles**	Article 5	observe the general rules, such as: – lawfulness, fairness, transparency; – purpose limitation; – data minimisation; – accuracy; – storage limitation; – integrity and confidentiality; and – accountability.
2.	**Lawfulness of processing**	Article 6 Article 9	ensure legal grounds for the processing in accordance with Article 6 ('regular'/'ordinary' personal data) or Article 9 (special categories) or Article 6 + Article 10 ('criminal' data)
3.	**Valid consent**	Article 7	if the processing of data is based on a data subject's consent – ensure that the consent is informed, voluntary, specific, unambiguous or explicit (in case of special category data) and possible to demonstrate
4.	**Children's data**	Article 8	if processing children's data via the internet (information society services) – obtain parental consent

No	*Obligation*	*Article in the GDPR*	*A Controller Is Obliged To*
5.	**Criminal data**	Article 10	if processing of data relating to criminal convictions and offences – process such data only under the control of official authority, or when such processing data is authorised by the law – ensure appropriate safeguards for the rights and freedoms of data subjects
6.	**Processing which does not require identification** (we like to call them: 'unidentified data' or 'UFO data')	Article 11	meet the requirements provided by Article 11 when processing data of unidentified persons
7.	**Execution of rights of data subjects**	Articles 12 to 22	ensure the execution of individual's rights provided by Articles 12–22
8.	**Security**	Articles 24 and 32	ensure data security as required under Articles 24 and 32 implement technical and organisational security measures that are appropriate to the risk to the rights and freedoms of data subjects, identified by the controller
9.	**Privacy by design**	Article 25(1)	meet the obligations to ensure 'privacy by design' (taking into account data protection issues when introducing new services, new projects, etc.)
10.	**Privacy by default**	Article 25(2)	ensure 'privacy by default' (minimising processing)
11.	**Joint controllers**	Article 26	enter into a joint controller arrangement when the data is processed jointly by two or more controllers
12.	**Representative in the EU**	Article 27	designate a representative in the EU if not established in the EU
13.	**Entrustment of data processing**	Article 28	if the controller engages a processor, enter into a detailed agreement with the processor, engage in the process only trustworthy processors
14.	**Records of processing activities**	Article 30	keep records of processing activities of the controller's data (very important obligation to manage the data and ensure accountability for the organisation!)

No	*Obligation*	*Article in the GDPR*	*A Controller Is Obliged To*
16.	**Supervisory authority**	Article 31	cooperate with the supervisory authority
17.	**Data breach notification**	Article 33	notify the supervisory authority of personal data breach (leak, destruction, damage, amendment, including critical cases of lack of access)
18.	**Data breach communication**	Article 34	inform data subjects affected of a breach of their data when there is high risk to their rights or freedoms
19.	**Data protection impact assessment**	Article 35	conduct a formal data protection impact assessment when a high risk to the rights and freedoms of persons whose data are processed is likely
20.	**Prior consultations**	Article 36	consult the supervisory authority prior to processing data if the data protection impact assessment reveals a high risk and a controller is not sure what measures can mitigate that risk
21.	**Data protection officer – analysis**	Article 37 to 39	examine whether a data protection officer needs to be designated and designate the data protection officer where required by law
22.	**Transfer of data outside of the EEA**	Articles 44–47 and 49	ensure that an out of EU transfer of data is legal, when transferring data outside of the EEA (EU + Norway, Iceland, Liechtenstein) (third country), employ the measures described in Articles 44–47 or 49
23.	**Cross-border processing**	Article 56	in the case of cross-border processing, determine the lead supervisory authority described in Article 56

Meeting all of the above obligations must be accountable, in practice: documented.

8.3 A Processor: Definition, Characteristics, Role, and Obligations

8.3.1 Definition

The definition of a processor is given in Article 4(8) GDPR and states that a '**processor**' means a natural or legal person, public authority, agency or other body which processes personal data on behalf of the controller.

8.3.2 *Role of the Processor*

A processor acts on behalf of a controller. A processor's task is to process personal data in accordance with the GDPR for and on behalf of a controller and in accordance with the agreement on entrusting the processing of data (data processing agreement) concluded with the controller. Thus, a processor's obligations result from two sources:

(1) an agreement with the controller and
(2) the GDPR directly.

8.3.3 *Credibility and Sufficient Guarantees*

As demonstrated by the obligations of a controller, where processing is to be performed on the controller's behalf, the controller:

> 'shall use only processors providing sufficient guarantees to implement appropriate technical and organisational measures in such a manner that processing will meet the requirements of this regulation and ensure the protection of the rights of the data subject' (Art. 28(1) GDPR).

A processor must be a professional entity. But according to the accountability rule as a logical consequence of a controller's role in the data processing, **the controller has to demonstrate upon the request of the supervisory authority that the processor of its choice meets the requirements provided by the GDPR for processors.**

8.3.4 *Agreement with the Processor or Subprocessor*

A processor processes personal data on the basis of an agreement or other legal instrument governed by EU law or Member State law.

A processor processes personal data on the basis of an agreement or other legal instrument governed by EU law or Member State law. This agreement is concluded with the controller and must meet all the requirement and include all elements required by Article 28.

A processor may engage another organisations based on the general consent of the controller, i.e. consent for the processor to engage other organisations, provided that the controller is given sufficient notice of that intention, enabling it to object to the specific processor. The GDPR also provides for specific consent, which means that the processor is required to inform the controller on a case-by-case basis whenever it wishes to engage a particular further processor and seek the controller's consent (or at least allow them to object). **The processor is fully liable by law towards the controller for the processors it engages.**

8.3.5 *Contractual Obligations: Under the Agreement with the Controller*

According to Article 28, the agreement on engaging a processor must contain the following:

- a description of the guarantees by which the processor ensures data security (in the recitals, representations and covenants, or references or other documents demonstrating the credibility of the processor as applicable, as appendices to the agreement);
- an undertaking to process personal data only upon the documented instructions of the controller;
- an undertaking to obtain non-disclosure obligations from personnel unless that personnel is under the statutory duty of confidentiality;
- an undertaking to employ adequate security measures required under Article 32 GDPR (consultations to agree on the level of adequacy between the controller and the processor);
- an undertaking to comply with the rules described above for engaging **another processor** (subcontractor, entity engaged by the processor to perform processing) (consent/objection, transfer of obligations, adequacy of security measures);
- an undertaking to limit engagement of other processors to specific activities (not being an 'empty shell' under Article 28(4) GDPR);
- rules on execution of an individual's rights – assisting the controller in the performance of obligations towards data subjects 'insofar as this is possible, by employing the appropriate technical and organisational means, for the fulfilment of the controller's obligation to respond to requests for exercising the data subject's rights laid down in chapter III' (Article 28(3)(e) GDPR);
- rules on notification of data breach, including assisting with notification of data breach;
- rules for participation in the DPIA, including assisting the controller in consultations with the supervisory authority;
- an undertaking to assist the controller in the performance of other obligations – 'assists the controller in ensuring compliance with the obligations pursuant to Articles 32 to 36, taking into account the nature of processing and the information available to the processor' (Article 28(3)(f) GDPR);
- an undertaking to delete and return, once the agreement expires, data and data copies – 'at the choice of the controller, deletes or returns all the personal data to the controller after the end of the provision of services relating to processing and deletes existing copies unless EU or Member State law requires storage of the personal data' (Article 28(3)(g) GDPR);
- an undertaking to document the activities of the processor and grant the controller access in order to comply with the principle of accountability;
- rules on assisting with the execution of inspections by the supervisory authority and other auditors, including notification of the inspection and determining the lead supervisory authority;

- an undertaking to give notification of the risk of the lawfulness of instructions being compromised; the processor must be required to give prior notice of concerns as to lawfulness of the controller's instructions, and otherwise face consequences such as loss of recourse towards the controller in case of liability;
- rules on the procedure in the case of concerns as to lawfulness of instructions;
- an undertaking to provide the controller with all information necessary to demonstrate fulfilment of obligations and enable the controller or auditor authorised by the controller to conduct audits, including inspections, and making a contribution towards them.

List of processor's obligations is impressive which does not make personal data processing entrustment agreement short. But a cautious controller will approach the data entrustment taking into account all possible obligations of a processor to ensure the highest standard and security level of data managed by the controller.

8.3.6 *Practical Problems*

Issues that may arise *between a controller and a processor* are for example:

(1) **scope and understanding** of the obligations of the processor under the GDPR - if the processor is not properly aware of its obligations under the GDPR or has no understanding at all of its role as a processor, there might be a lot of discussion, for example on its responsibility;
(2) **the 'one-size-fits-all' list of questions for potential processors** - applying the same monitoring requirements and tools to a major processor and minor processors;
(3) **the question of contractual power** - a small-scale controller will be in a weaker position in a relationship with a large processor as well as a strong controller will try to contractually transfer their responsibilities onto their weaker processors;
(4) **responsibility of another processors** - under the GDPR both the controller and the processor are liable (with respect to data security, lawfulness and compliance with the controller's instructions). While all processors[58] engaged in the data processing are also liable towards the supervisory authority and data subject for the GDPR incompliance, large-scale suppliers, for example cloud computing providers, may be tempted to act 'in the third line' (as another processor, formerly 'subcontractors') believing that it will protect them against direct penalties from supervisory authorities and legal action from data subjects.

58. Referred to in Art. 28 GDPR as 'another processor'.

8.3.7 *Obligations under the GDPR*

The obligations of the processor under the agreement with the controller include:

- personal data processing only on the documented instructions of the controller (Article 28(3)(a) GDPR);
- ensuring the appropriate level of security of the processed personal data by implementing the appropriate technical and organisational measures, at the same time taking into account 'the state of the art, the cost of implementation and the nature, scope, context and purposes of processing as well as the risks of varying likelihood and severity for rights and freedoms of natural persons' (Article 32(1) GDPR);
- keeping records of categories of processing activities performed on behalf of the controller (Article 30(2) GDPR);
- making the records available to the supervisory authority upon request (Article 30(4) GDPR);
- cooperation with the supervisory authority in the performance of its tasks (Article 31 GDPR);
- designating a representative in the EU where Article 3(2) GDPR applies (Article 27(1) GDPR);
- notifying the controller without undue delay of personal data breach (Article 33(2) GDPR);
- designating a DPO where required by law (Article 37(1) GDPR).

8.4 Comparison of the Roles and Obligations of the Controller and Processor

The analysis performed above of the obligations of the controller and processor leads to the conclusion that some of these obligations are the same, for example obligations provided for in Article 30(4), Article 31, Article 32(1), and Article 37(1) GDPR, to name a few. Not all obligations are common to both, and it is this difference that determines the separate roles of each of these entities with respect to personal data protection.

The controller is the 'superior' of the processor because the processor is entitled to process personal data upon the controller's instructions.

9 DATA PROCESSING WHICH DOES NOT REQUIRE IDENTIFICATION

9.1 Preliminary Remarks

Upon the first reading of **Article 11 GDPR**, it may seem unintelligible and pointless. **However, Article 11 GDPR plays an important role in the personal data protection system.** It reconciles data protection and processing of unstructured data such as video surveillance, email, and even file servers, as well as the use of personal data for data analysis – creating profiles.

Article 11 concerns cases in which a particular activity at any given time does not require knowledge about whose personal data is processed. Situations of this kind arise when it can only be surmised that information for which an organisation is responsible contains personal data or in cases where it is certain that data of this kind are held, but it is not known precisely whose data these are or where exactly they are. Similarly, when we have anonymised data or if we received pseudonymised data without a key required for reidentification, we know we process personal data, but we cannot know whom they concern.

In practice, the processing of personal data which 'we do not know' (which we call here as 'unidentified data') occurs frequently, despite it was not addressed in any manner by the Data Protection Directive. Video surveillance (closed-circuit television) of public space consists of processing personal data (faces and behaviours) of unknown individuals. Content of a company's electronic correspondence (stored on mail servers but also in specific mailboxes) contains personal data, but it is not known whose or how they are connected with a company's activity. The same applies to file servers and any system in which 'unstructured' data, generally referred to as 'content', can be inserted. As a rule, visitors to websites are not identified by hosts[59] even if cookies are placed in their browsers and they can be tracked further.

Particular individuals who place data in a company's resources (save a file in a catalogue, send emails or even only place it in a company computer) may know (but do not necessarily know) what kind of data they are placing in a company's resources. Does this mean that the organisation now has that information at its disposal? In practice the organisation does not control data of that kind.

A different situation arises when a company knows the identity of a person whose data are processed, but this information will not be needed in future. In this case, Article 11 GDPR supplements anonymisation. If a data controller seeks only general trends or profiles or statistics and is not interested in specific individuals, then anonymising data allows to rely on Article 11 to avoid unnecessary onerous duties otherwise resulting from GDPR.

Article 11 GDPR applies to situations of this kind.

9.2 No Need to Identify

Under Article 11(1) GDPR:

> If the **[1]** purposes for which a controller processes personal data **[2]** do not or **[3]** no longer require identification of the data subject by the controller, the controller **[4]** shall not be obliged to maintain, acquire, or process additional information **[5]** in order to identify the data subject for the sole purpose of complying with this regulation.

Article 11(1) GDPR, therefore, states that GDPR does not oblige a data controller to identify persons whose data that controller processes. A controller does not have to

59. Does not apply to omniscient Facebook and Google of course.

take measures to identify 'unidentified' persons just to satisfy GDPR. That is actually in line with the 'necessary knowledge' principle, i.e. principle of minimisation.

Example: email

An email can contain a large amount of personal data. A controller has information about which user, when, and to which address a user sends correspondence. Meanwhile, the controller does not monitor the entire correspondence on the presents and contents of personal data, that controller is not aware of what specific data are in the correspondence, and does not need to know that. Moreover, a proactive semantic monitoring of the content of all email correspondence of an organisation goes against the principle of privacy by default (Article 25(2) GDPR), which in fact is a principle of multidimensional minimisation of knowledge about data subjects.

The purpose of data processing in email is to enable communication between users and between users and the outer world. Only a particular email might become important for a certain data processing purpose due to its content. In such a situation, the content should be accordingly catalogued or printed, and placed in a binder for the case, or copied into the case folder, or marked in the document management system (DMS). Of course, the DMS can be integrated with email system, and then an analysis of the purposes of data processing within email becomes more complex.

Example

As a rule, a controller will not know about emails exchanged between two employees using company email accounts regarding another employee's private life or an office love affair that employee is having.

The situation regarding the storing of data on company computers, in shared resources and on private devices used for business, is similar. Even if the controller's systems automatically index the content in those resources, this does not mean that the controller knows the identity of the persons mentioned in those resources. Only the posing of a specific question (search) regarding specific identifying data of a particular individual can provide it with that information.

The controller is required however to be aware of the structure of shared resources. If that structure relates to personal data, for example it mentions the case files of a particular natural person, then the content of that catalogue will, as a rule, be normal personal data relating to that person, and the controller will of course be able to identify them.

9.3 No Need to Monitor Unstructured Data

Article 11(1) GDPR states that if no information about whose data is processed is needed for the data processing purposes, their identity does not have to be determined. Therefore, there is no need to proactively monitor content that passes through controller's systems solely to detect any personal data, in particular data concerning the identity of particular individuals.

As there is no obligation to identify individuals unless the data controller needs it, there is no need to monitor information resources solely to find out everything there is to know about particular individuals by analysing all of the information in a company's resources. In general we may have a lot of material allowing us to learn a lot about specific individuals. Meanwhile, there is no obligation to analyse that material solely in order to ascertain the level of potential knowledge. Moreover, as we have mentioned above, from the point of view of privacy and the principle of minimisation, proactive monitoring of this kind could be considered excessive, and unlawful violation of privacy. This has major implications for the scope of data processing obligations.

9.4 Notification Obligations

Under Article 11(2) GDPR:[60]

> Where, in cases referred to in paragraph 1 of this Article, the controller is able to demonstrate that it is not in a position to identify the data subject, the controller shall inform the data subject accordingly, if possible. In such cases, Articles 15 to 20 shall not apply except where the data subject, for the purpose of exercising his or her rights under those articles, provides additional information enabling his or her identification.

Under Article 11(2) GDPR there are two notification obligations:

(1) an obligation to inform a data subject that they cannot be identified, where possible;
(2) an information obligation under Article 13 GDPR – if a data controller is able to inform a data subject that they cannot be identified, the data controller can provide other information as well.

Consequently, a controller does not have to ensure execution of other individual's rights (data subject requests), except notification of processing (Articles 13 and 14 GDPR).

60. It is hard not to comment on this legislative gem.

9.4.1 *Obligation to Inform 'Unidentified' Persons That They Cannot Be Identified: Where Possible*

A controller has an obligation 'where possible' to inform an individual that they cannot be identified if the controller 'is able to demonstrate that it is not in a position to identify the data subject'. This is enigmatic, as first there is the question of demonstrating that someone cannot be identified and second there is the question of how to inform somebody, if they cannot be identified. This might not be that complicated, however.

Example

Some thirty years ago my friend was on his way home in the morning after a party in Kraków when he heard this conversation about the problem of providing unidentified persons with information. 'John, when are you going to finally sign up with Alcoholics Anonymous?' 'How am I supposed to find them if they are anonymous?' was the reply.

In the case of video surveillance, it is sufficient to display a notice stating that video surveillance is used in the area, of the wording required for the notification obligation under Article 13 GDPR, also stating that identification is not possible.

In internal conference call systems, information notices or messages screened before the call starts can also be used.[61]

Where an anonymised or pseudonymised database is purchased for the purpose of research, creating profiles, etc. one can imagine that a controller might stipulate in the agreement with the seller of the database that the seller will inform the persons whose data are in the database of the data required under Article 14 GDPR and of the fact that they cannot be identified.

Similarly, where an electronic marketing services provider enables an online seller to send an offer to the email address of a visitor to that seller's website, after verifying (e.g., using cookies) that the person gave a different entity consent to direct marketing of third-party products,[62] in the same email the addressee can be informed of 'unidentified' processing of their data.

In the case of email, a controller that does not filter sent content is not able to determine en masse what is written and about whom. Under Article 11(1) GDPR, a controller is not required to filter content from the point of view of personal data. For this reason, it is not possible to communicate with people whose data are featured in the email.

61. Electronic communication will be further regulated and harmonised with the proposed EU e-Privacy Regulation and with the Directive (EU) 2018/1972 of the European Parliament and of the Council of 11 December 2018 establishing the European Electronic Communications Code.
62. A true case described on the website niebezpiecznik.pl, where a provider of a service of 'identification of the email address of a visitor' explained the mechanics of the service. Hopefully, it was not in fact based on exploitation of the vulnerability of websites to direct disclosure of email addresses of visitors to websites.

The situation with regard to email addressees is different. A controller is not required to know whom the email is addressed to, but the recipient's address will be retained in the email system. Therefore we may have a situation of processing 'unidentified data'. The addressee may, however, be reached out (in the same email) to be informed about their data processing. What to do? Probably the easiest solution would be to assume all email addresses are identifiable (to avoid differentiating between emails such as isomuchlikelarrypage@gmail.com and satya.nadella@microsoft.com) and apply the layered approach to information obligation, described in the previous chapter, providing in an email footnote a basic info that XYZ Incorporate is a data controller of personal data consisting of sender's and addressee's email addresses and contained in the body of an email, that data are processed primarily to allow email communication and that more information can be found at www.privacypolicy.XYZ.com.

9.4.2 Enabling Execution of an Individual's Rights

The last of the obligations of specific nature relating to 'unidentified' data is a return of the obligation to accommodate rights of individuals (Articles 15–20 GDPR), when the individual enables themselves to be identified. A situation of this kind might arise where somebody wishes to access data from video surveillance, to determine who scraped a car in a shopping centre car park. There might also be other circumstances. The important issue is that providing 'additional information enabling identification' of the person making the request does not mean presenting a personal identification card but giving details allowing specific information about the person making the request to be 'tracked down' in the files.

Example

Coming back to the example of company gossip, if an employee who is the subject of gossip among colleagues using company email accounts is appropriately identified, it will probably be necessary to assess how to execute their rights of an individual with respect to the problematic email. What would the procedure be for identification of this kind? For example 'I saw Kowalski send Malinowska on 26 May 2018 a photograph of me taken at the office party, when I felt ill due to interaction of medicine. I demand that the material be deleted from the company resources, but first I demand restriction of the processing of that email, because I will be seeking satisfaction against Kowalski.' Lessons in life may suggest that in practice this would have the opposite effect to that intended, but this is possible under the law.

9.4.3 Security

When processing 'unidentified' data, the same security obligations apply as in other cases. The risk to the rights and freedoms of persons whose data is processed needs to be analysed and appropriate security measures adopted. To achieve this, information about the identity of data subjects is not needed. One of the easiest organisational security measures in this respect might be to inform and require users who might place those 'unidentified' data in the controller's resources to do this sensibly (e.g., not use company email for private purposes, not send material that violates people's personal rights unless there is a legitimate reason).

9.4.4 Minimisation (Of Access and Retention)

Minimisation of unauthorised access to 'unidentified data' also has to be ensured. For example, conference calls should not be accessible by third parties (preventing unauthorised access is a security matter), and shared resources (intranet, Sharepoint, file servers) should be divided into zones according to needs and powers.

Example

At a meeting at a consultancy firm, the conference call monitor suddenly came on and we could see ourselves on it. In fact it was not clear who could see and hear us at that point. Apparently, in the TOR network, for a small fee it is possible to buy access for a short time to hundreds of thousands of unsecured webcams. It is possible to block webcams physically by taping over them, but this is not usually done, and this is hard to do effectively for microphones. For this reason, it is important to take care of the security of video and audio means of transmission. This example comes from the area of e-Privacy/electronic communication, you may say. However, processing of personal data understood in a traditional way (at endpoints) and transfer of voice, video and data (telecommunications and internet) become more and more convergent, both technologically and legally.

'Unidentified' data must also only be stored as long as necessary for the processing purposes. From this point of view, the practice of storing emails indefinitely, which happens in many companies, including some law firms seems unlawful. However long the period for which they are necessary might be, an indefinite period will exceed it.

10 RECORD OF DATA PROCESSING ACTIVITIES

10.1 A Company's Own Record Instead of Registration with a Supervisory Body

One of the fundamental obligations of organisations that process data, whether controllers or processors, is an obligation under Article 30 GDPR – to keep a record of all data processing activities.

Under Article 30(1) GDPR:

> Each controller and, where applicable, the controller's representative, shall maintain a record of processing activities under its responsibility.

Article 30(2) GDPR provides for a comparable obligation for processors.

The obligation to keep a record of personal data processing activities is a new data processing obligation. In the past, controllers were required to register their data filing systems with local supervisory bodies. During work on the reform of the EU personal data protection system, it was correctly concluded that this obligation led to 'administrative and financial burdens and did not always help to improve personal data protection' and was replaced with 'effective procedures and mechanisms focused instead on those types of processing operations which are likely to result in a high risk to the rights and freedoms of natural persons by virtue of their nature, context and purposes' (Recital 89 GDPR), i.e. among other things with a personal data impact assessment.

In order to keep a record of and organise in some way the kind of personal data that organisations process, and for what purpose and on what grounds, it is no longer necessary to register data filing systems with the supervisory authority, instead RDPAs do have to be maintained.

10.2 Records of Data Processing Activities: Foundation for Accountability

The purpose of keeping a record of data processing activities is ensuring compliance with the GDPR. This is stated clearly in Recital 82 GDPR. A record of data processing activities is a form of documenting of data processing activities, acts as a data processing map and is one of the key elements enabling execution of the fundamental principle on which the entire personal data protection system is based, which is the principle of accountability.[63] It also plays an informative role, for instance by providing the supervisory authority with information about data processing processes in a particular organisation.

63. Confirmed among other things in the Art. 29 Working Party document *Core topics in the view of trilogue*, http://www.giodo.gov.pl/pl/file/9537(last accessed on 26 September 2017).

10.3 Data Processing Activities

In order to understand how a record of data processing activities should be approached from a practical point of view, first, it needs to be determined what a data processing activity is under the GDPR.

A 'data processing activity' is not a term defined in the GDPR, and this causes practical problems when trying to grasp what should be specifically referred to in the record of data processing activities and what should be recorded. Considering the legal definitions in the GDPR, a data processing activity is a separate term from general term 'data processing' or a 'data filing system' and 'data processing operations'.

10.4 Activities Performed for the Same Purpose

All of the commentaries and publications released to date on the subject of RDPAs emphasise that processing activities are: **[1] operations performed on data**, which have in common **[2] pursuit of the same processing purpose**.[64] Therefore a distinction has to be made between activities according to shared, specific data processing purposes connected with those activities.

This approach is feasible in practice. The notion of an activity can be so multifaceted that if activities are not grouped according to their purposes, the number of processes identified can be between several hundred and several thousand (some organisations in fact do this). RDPAs of this level of detail cease to be intelligible, useful, and manageable for both the organisation and the supervisory authorities. Records of several thousand activities are questionable from the perspective of the fundamental principle of the GDPR – the principle of accountability.

According to a recommendation published in June 2017 by the Belgian personal data protection authority on keeping RDPAs in connection with Article 30 GDPR,[65] activities recorded in RDPAs or – put another way – data processing procedures have to be identified and grouped according to data processing purposes. Depending on the complexity of data processing procedures, if various data processing activities are performed for the same purpose, then a single entry may (but does not have to) be kept. In the case of large organisations and complex business processes, a number of distinct data processing activities performed for the same purpose can be identified in separate entries, for example in the form of steps in the process in question, to ensure that a record of data processing activities continues to be intelligible.

64. D. Lubasz [in:] *RODO. Ogólne rozporządzenie …*, p. 668.
65. Commission de la protection de la vie privée/Commissie voor de bescherming van de persoonlijke levenssfeer, *Aanbeveling betreffende het Register van de verwerkingsactiviteiten (artikel 30 van de AVG) (CO-AR-2017-011)*, 2017, https://www.privacycommission.be/sites/privacycommission/files/documents/aanbeveling_06_2017_0.pdf (last accessed on 12 January 2018).

Example

A small organisation (e.g., a small online store intended for a specific group of people) collects and saves in a system and analyses personal data for one purpose – managing customer relationships. In such a case a single entry may be kept for the entire customer relationship management process, and not three separate entries, such as 'collecting customer data', 'placing in the customer data system', and 'customer data analysis'.

A larger organisation that manages customer data at several levels and processes them in a number of organisational units can divide those customer relationship management activities into a number of separate activities (entries) even if they are performed for the same purpose.

Examples of data processing activities:[66]

(1) **personnel and service provider administration** – recruitment and selection of personnel and intermediaries (brokers, independent representatives, etc.); administration of remuneration, extras, commissions and payroll; applying social provisions;
(2) **personnel and service provider management** – personnel and intermediary evaluation and monitoring; training and career planning;
(3) **work organisation** – planning and monitoring tasks, work input, and productivity;
(4) **monitoring the workplace** – monitoring job-related activity in the workplace using video cameras or computer systems (reviewing email, use of telephones and the internet);
(5) **client relationships** – managing customers, managing orders, deliveries, invoicing tangible and intangible services; monitoring solvency; personalisation of marketing and advertising; registration of the firm's customers and profiling on the basis of purchasing habits;
(6) **combating fraud and breach by customers** – preventive measures and detection;
(7) **dispute management** – including repayment of receivables;
(8) **supplier relationships** – order management, payments to suppliers; finding and evaluating potential suppliers;

66. Appendix to recommendation issued by the Belgian personal data protection authority on records of data processing activities in connection with Art. 30 GDPR – 'Excerpt from notes on ordinary notification of processing described in Art. 17 of the Belgian personal data protection act'; *Uittreksel uit de toelichting bij de gewone aangifte van een verwerking bedoeld onder artikel 17 van de WVP*, https://www.privacycommission.be/sites/privacycommission/files/documents/aanbeveling_06_2017_0.pdf (last accessed on 12 January 2018).

(9) **accounting;**
(10) **public relations.**

10.5 Activities Classified in Other Ways

Due to the fact that making distinctions between and registering personal data processing activities according to the purposes they have in common is not an obligation provided for expressly in the GDPR, but only a practical recommendation for organisations required to maintain RDPAs, there is no reason why processing activities cannot be classified in a different way, provided that the record fulfils its function and the principle of accountability is observed.

This means that data can also be divided according to data subject categories (e.g., activities relating to processing of employees' data), the data scope (e.g., activities relating to basic contact details, and to data concerning employees' state of health) or the security measures employed (e.g., activities on data locked away in the archives).

10.6 Record of Data Processing Activities for Small and Large Firms: Differences

The data controller's challenge is to classify and record data processing activities so that the record is intelligible and fulfil its fundamental functions of (1) enabling the principle of accountability and (2) being informative. The size and complexity of an organisation and the number of business processes it performs in which personal data are processed are also important factors.

As practices to apply the GDPR are developed, smaller businesses need to consider using record-keeping services available on the market, which incorporate the typical, standard data processing activities and specific categories of measures. A business will only be required to specify which options are relevant to their organisation and regularly update the record.

Larger businesses have to take a more individual approach to the record of data processing activities - according to the principle that the larger the organisation, the more categories of particular activities will have to be differentiated due to the volume and diversity of business processes involving personal data processing. Usually, a record in a large organisation has to take account of the division into individual organisational cells within the company so that it corresponds to the steps and elements of the organisation's business processes.

This is due to the fact that while in a sole proprietorship everything is done by the 'boss' and the criterion for division of activities only according to purpose (direct marketing, accounting, suppliers, customers, disputes) is sufficient, in larger companies in which particular organisational units (divisions, departments) are not responsible for the entire process, in the record of data processing activities a distinction will have to be made between recruiting and management of personnel and activities relating to payment of remuneration (even though the purpose of data processing can be listed collectively, as general personnel matters).

10.6.1 *Does Every Organisation Have to Keep a Record of Data Processing Activities? Yes*

Formally not every organisation has an obligation under the GDPR to keep RDPAs, but it is recommended that every organisation do so.

Under Article 30(5) GDPR:

> The obligations referred to in paragraphs 1 and 2 shall not apply to an enterprise or an organisation **employing fewer than 250 persons**, **[1]** unless the processing it carries out is likely to result in a risk to the rights and freedoms of data subjects, **[2]** the processing is not occasional, or **[3]** the processing includes special categories of data as referred to in Article 9(1) **[sensitive data]**, or personal data relating to criminal convictions and offences referred to in Article 10.

As a result, under Article 30(1) in conjunction with Article 30(5) GDPR, a business (organisation) has to maintain a record of data processing activities if:

- it employs 250 or more people, or
- it processes data and it is likely to result in a risk to rights and freedoms of data subjects, and this processing is not only occasional, or
- even if it only occasionally processes data, and this gives rise to a risk to rights and freedoms of data subjects, and this processing relates to special data or data concerning convictions.

10.6.2 *A Headcount of 250*

If an organisation employs 250 people, RDPAs have to be drawn up and maintained. The headcount covers both employees and individual contractors.

10.6.3 *High-Risk Processing*

Where an organisation has a headcount of less than 250, it needs to conduct a data processing risk assessment to determine whether it performs long-term or regular data processing giving rise to a high risk to the rights and freedoms of individuals or even occasionally processes special data or data relating to convictions, and this gives rise to a high risk to the rights and freedoms of individuals.

In practice, the obligation to keep a record of data processing activities applies in almost every case (who does not process data concerning the health of employees, service providers or their families?). Experts recommend that every organisation keep RDPAs for the following reasons:

- every organisation has to assess whether it has an obligation to keep RDPAs, and an exemption applies if it is determined that processing does not result in risk to the rights and freedoms of data subjects. This assessment is burdensome in itself and should be documented, and moreover any activity concerning personal data generates risks to their subjects;
- RDPAs are an aid that shows that small businesses comply with the GDPR. RDPAs enable accountability, ensure mapping of data processing operations and enable identification of measures that need to be taken to comply properly with personal data protection principles;
- RDPAs are a tool for an organisation to control its own data and information which are business secrets, which is beneficial in the age of the information society and information economy.

10.7 Scope of Information in RDPAs: Controllers

Article 30(1) GDPR specifies the scope of information that has to be included in the record of data processing activities kept by a controller (or controller's representative):

Each controller, and where applicable, the controller's representative, shall maintain a record of the data processing activities under its responsibility. That record shall contain all of the following information:

(a) the name and contact details of the controller and, where applicable, the joint controller, the controller's representative and the DPO;
(b) the purposes of the processing;
(c) a description of the categories of data subjects and the categories of personal data;
(d) the categories of recipients to whom the personal data have been or will be disclosed including recipients in third countries or international organisations;
(e) where applicable, transfers of personal data to a third country or an international organisation, including the identification of that third country or international organisation and, in the case of transfers referred to in the second subparagraph of Article 49(1), the documentation of suitable safeguards;
(f) where possible, the envisaged time limits for erasure of the different categories of data;
(g) where possible, a general description of the technical and organisational security measures referred to in Article 32(1).

As a result, individual, **compulsory** elements of RDPAs (e.g., columns, if the RDPAs are in a spreadsheet format, or screens, if maintained in the form of an IT tool developed for that purpose or paper files) are as follows:

(a) the name and contact details of the controller, for example company X, established in Y, contact details: telephone number: Z; email: W; website: AA;

(b) data security officer: John Smith, telephone number: ZZ; email: WW (these details can be put at the top of the document as collective information for all of the other sections of RDPAs);
(c) the title of the data processing activity (or business process, as the case may be), for example recruitment, customer service, complaint procedure, human resources management;
(d) the purpose of data processing within a particular procedure;
(e) categories of data subjects, for example employees, job applicants, customers, suppliers;
(f) data categories, for example ordinary data, sensitive data (particular items to be marked or entered manually);
(g) categories of recipients, for example divided according to (1) processors, (2) other recipients, i.e. organisations granted access to data in order for them to administer the data, for example a parent company, and (3) third-country recipients (e.g., a processor in India, parent company recipient in the US);
(h) information on data processing in a third country and the name of the country and description of data security measures;
(i) the data retention period;
(j) security measures, for example information about the use of antivirus software, encoding (if that description is possible, this is difficult for complex security systems).

The catalogue of information that may be included in the RDPAs is open. As a tool for ensuring accountability and notification, RDPAs may also contain additional information that the controller (or processor, as the case may be) considers useful as part of their own business activity. The following are examples of non-compulsory elements that can be included in RDPAs:

(a) the legal grounds for data processing, for example consent;
(b) information about the location of the consent of the data subject, if it is the ground for data processing, for example information that the consent is recorded in system X;
(c) information about the manner in which data is collected – whether or not directly from the data subject;
(d) brief information about whether the notification obligation is complied with, and in what way, for example by email or normal post;
(e) the name of the system used for data processing;
(f) the name of the person or department responsible for a particular activity (process).

10.8 Scope of Information in RDPAs: Processors

Processors are also required to keep records of categories of processing activities carried out on behalf of controllers.

The scope of information that should be contained in a record of data processing categories of a processor is specified in Article 30(2) GDPR, which states:

> Each processor, and, where applicable, the processor's representative shall maintain a record of all categories of processing activities carried out on behalf of a controller, containing:
>
> a) the name and contact details of the processor or processors and each controller, and, where applicable, of the controller's or the processor's representative, and the data protection officer;
> b) the categories of processing carried out on behalf of each controller;
> c) where applicable, transfers of personal data to a third country or an international organisation, including the identification of that third country or international organisation, and, in the case of transfers referred to in the second subparagraph of Article 49(1), the documentation of suitable safeguards;
> d) where possible, a general description of the technical and organisational security measures referred to in Art. 32(1).

The scope of compulsory information in the record of data processing activities of the processor is therefore somewhat reduced in relation to RDPAs of controllers. Like controllers, processors are required to record their full name and contact details, details of the data security officer, information about data processing in a third country, and, where possible give a general description of the security measures.

In the RDPAs, processors have to specify the categories of processing performed on behalf of each controller. The GDPR does not state precisely the categories of processing. Because the range of detail in processors' RDPAs is less than controllers' RDPAs, and there is no obligation to specify particular data processing activities performed on data entrusted by particular controllers, 'processing categories' is a broader and more general notion. This is a question of business functions, for example keeping accounts, calculating remuneration and costs (payroll), data storage, building security, including video surveillance.

10.9 Form of RDPAs

Under Article 30(3) GDPR:

> The records referred to in paragraphs 1 and 2 shall be in, including in electronic form.

There is a general consensus that there is no obligation to maintain RDPAs in paper form, because this would be of no use from a practical point of view. RDPAs may therefore be kept in electronic form, for example in a spreadsheet or in a special software developed for that purpose.

10.10 Person Responsible for Keeping RDPAs

Keeping a data processing activities record is a general obligation of the controller and processor. In practice, a person has to be designated to be responsible for keeping, updating, and where necessary allowing the supervisory authority access to a record of data processing activities. This person may be a personal data protection expert or data security officer. The obligation to keep the record of data processing activities is not among the data security officer obligations listed in Article 39(1) GDPR, but this task does not affect the independence of the data security officer and does not cause a conflict of interest with the data security officer's other obligations. On the contrary, the keeping of a record of data processing activities by a data security officer is closely aligned with the data security officer's other tasks and function.

11 TRANSFER OF DATA TO THIRD COUNTRIES OR AN INTERNATIONAL ORGANISATION (DATA EXPORT)

11.1 Regulation of Data Export

Under Article 44 GDPR, transfer of personal data to outside of the EEA (EU and Norway, Iceland, and Liechtenstein[67]), known as 'data export', is only permitted if a level of protection is assured equal to that required under the GDPR, including specific provisions in Chapter V of the GDPR. It is not only transfer of data outside of the EEA that is considered data export. Transfer to an international organisation (the UN, Arab League, International Red Cross, etc.) is also data export.

Data can be moved freely within the EU and even with the EEA. The EU is even considering introducing additional regulations to this end. On the other hand, transfer of personal data outside of the EEA is regulated and will be regulated even further under the GDPR.

11.2 Practical Obstacles to Data Export

The fundamental difference and true restriction in relation to the previous data export regulations cannot be found in Chapter V of the GDPR. A practical restriction is the obligation to inform the subjects whose data is to be exported, provided for under Article 13(1)(f) and Article (14)(1)(f) GDPR. At the same time, recipients of data outside of the EEA have to be listed in the RDPAs, but this is less of a burden than informing the individuals whose data is processed of the intention to send the data somewhere 'unknown'. From this point of view, anyone who currently 'legally' exports data will have an unpleasant surprise when they realise that they have to start informing individuals that data are sent outside of the EEA. This surprise will be even

67. Article 44 GDPR only applies in the EU, but as up to now the other EEA countries, which are Norway, Iceland and Liechtenstein, are covered by 'free movement of personal data'.

more unpleasant when it frequently becomes clear that their processors or further engaged processors (subprocessors) export data.

11.3 Lawfulness of Data Export

The requirements for permissibility of data export are extra in relation to the general requirements for the permissibility of data processing (legal grounds, notification, etc.).

11.4 Grounds for Data Export

It is permitted to send data outside of the EEA in the following cases:

(1) on the basis of a EC decision; under Article 45 GDPR, the Commission may decide that certain countries provide an adequate level of protection of personal data. On the day on which this article was written, at the top of the list in a search in Google for a 'list of third countries that provide an adequate level of personal data protection' was the website of the GIODO, http://www.giodo.gov.pl/163/id_art/1519/j/pl, listing nine countries: Andorra, Argentina, Australia, Guernsey, Israel, Jersey, Canada, and New Zealand, and with regard to self-certifying companies, the US;

(2) data 'subject to appropriate safeguards', which means, under Article 46 GDPR, on the grounds of the following special legal instruments:
   - (a) a legal instrument between public authorities or bodies (e.g., an administrative agreement between an EU member authority and an authority in a non-EU country);
   - (b) binding corporate rules – agreements within a capital group (corporate group);
   - (c) standard data protection clauses – templates for contractual terms:
     - adopted by the EC – the most common method up to now (referred to as standard contractual clauses under the 'old system') and
     - adopted by a national supervisory authority and approved by the EC (one wonders whether it makes sense to make exceptions to the EC template if the EC has to approve the template anyway: if an exception is intended to tighten up a rule, it is better not to make use of it, and if it is intended to undermine it, it should not be approved by the EC).
   - (d) an approved code of conduct combined with enforceable commitments of a third-country data recipient to apply the 'appropriate safeguards' – a new, untested legal instrument; at the moment there are no codes of conduct of this kind;
   - (e) an approved certification mechanism combined with enforceable commitments of a third-country data recipient to apply the 'appropriate safeguards' – this is also a new, as yet not fully developed solution;

(f) a contract or administrative agreement approved by the supervisory authority, i.e., exceptions:
   - when the standard data protection clauses cannot be relied upon and consent is needed from the supervisory authority;
   - where there is not enough time to sign a formal international agreement between public authorities, and they wish to exchange information.

11.5 Other Grounds for Transfer

Under Article 49 GDPR, in addition to 'general' grounds, the following 'special' grounds are possible for data export:

(a) consent based on information about the risk;
(b) performance of an agreement or to conclude an agreement at an individual's request;
(c) conclusion or performance of an agreement where this is in the interest of a data subject who is not a party to the agreement;
(d) public interest;
(e) pursuit of legal claims;
(f) protection of vital interests of the data subject if they are incapable of giving consent:
   - physically (they are unconscious or dazed) or;
   - legally (incapacitated or a child; in the latter case there is usually a guardian, and therefore it is not clear whether EU lawmakers mean circumventing the guardian or the problem of lack of contact with the guardian, or there is some other logical interpretation of this provision).
(g) transfer from a public register according to the normal requirements for access.

11.6 Transfer in 'Truly Exceptional Cases'

Under Article 49(2) GDPR, in addition to the general grounds and additional grounds, in exceptional cases data can be transferred on special grounds, which are **valid and legitimate interests of the controller**.

These grounds can be used where the transfer:

- is not a recurring transfer (this does not mean that it cannot occur multiple times; but in each instance, it must be connected with a new event and one that in fact is hard to predict);
- affects a limited number of people (the question of the threshold for a limited number of people might depend, for example, on the means of transport and the number of survivors, because the deceased do not have personal data; a

pleasure boat can accommodate several thousand people, and an aeroplane a few hundred at the most);

- is necessary for the controller's legitimate interests ('compelling' is the word used in the GDPR; the word *imperieux* in the French version suggests the 'vital' interests of the controller);

and where:

(1) there are no overriding interests, rights or freedoms of the data subject;
(2) the controller performs a comprehensive assessment of the situation and as a result:
  - ensures appropriate personal data security measures,
  - informs the supervisory authority.
(3) informs the data subject.

11.7 Recording Transfer in Exceptional Cases

Article 49(6) GDPR requires anyone who performs data export in exceptional cases (controller or processor) to document the export in the records of data transfer activities. The question is what to do if there is no obligation to keep records of data transfer activities: Do these records have to be created, or can the obligation to keep records be deemed to serve no purpose? Without delving into systemic issues, it would be advisable as a minimum to document the transfer itself, and it is best to also draw up records of data transfer activities straightaway.

11.8 'Long Arm Disclosure'

Under Article 48 GDPR, it is not permitted to transfer or disclose personal data at the request of courts or administrative authorities outside of the EU other than under a mutual legal assistance treaty. This is intended to stop attempts at compulsion by judicial authorities, which US courts typically try to do.

11.9 Summary

The most practical grounds for transfer of data outside of the EU are either standard data protection clauses (in case of established business to business relations) or a contract (in case of business to employee relations, business to customer or similar).

Consent is an inconvenient form of grounds for data export because it can be revoked at any time. They are grounds which are not permanent and require unified management of data and require that an alternative be in place within the EU for the process that is to be normally operated using resources located outside of the EEA. In our opinion a common practice to 'require' consent for data processing or data export in return for allowing to use a free application is questionable. If the essence of the service depends on the consent, such consent is not freely given. It is a contract where there is a service and consideration in the form of providing access to one's data.

Anyway, neither adequacy decisions nor standard data protection clauses provide a defence against the obligation to inform individuals that their data are transferred outside of the EU.[68] Still there are organisations such as the guardian who water this obligation down to that extent that a data subject has no real knowledge what is happening to their data, at least according to the guardian's privacy policy in place on 26 December 2018.[69]

It is debatable whether this notification obligation applies in the case of individuals whose data are already held, but with respect to people whose data will be obtained subsequent to 25 May 2018, there is no doubt. These individuals must be informed whether there are plans to transfer their data outside the EEA. The GDPR also requires at the same time that this be done in a clearly legible and comprehensive manner. For this reason, where possible, it is best to avoid personal data transfer outside of the EU regardless of whether an organisation is a controller or processor.

Enquiries also need to be made with subcontractors to find out whether they make use of cloud computing outside of the EU or transfer data within their capital group, for example to India or even to the US, to self-certifying companies under the Privacy Shield scheme.

In fact, users in an organisation have to be monitored regularly to check whether they circumvent the company systems and security rules and use, 'on the side' for company purposes, publicly available online services that do not guarantee restriction of processing to within the EEA (shadow IT), such as services from leading firms in the Silicon Valley.

---

68. To be precise – outside of the EEA.
69. https://www.theguardian.com/help/privacy-policy International data transfers:

> Data we collect may be transferred to, stored and processed in any country or territory where one or more of our guardian group companies or service providers are based or have facilities. While other countries or territories may not have the same standards of data protection as those in your home country, we will continue to protect personal data that we transfer in line with this privacy policy.
>
> Whenever we transfer your personal data out of the European Economic Area (EEA), we ensure similar protection and put in place at least one of these safeguards:
>
> - We will only transfer your personal data to countries that have been found to provide an adequate level of protection for personal data.
> - We may also use specific approved contracts with our service providers that are based in countries outside the EEA. These contracts give your personal data the same protection it has in the EEA.
> - Where we use service providers in the United States, we may transfer personal data to them if they are part of the Privacy Shield scheme, which requires them to provide a similar level of protection of your personal data to what is required in the EEA.
>
> If you are located in the EEA, you may contact us for a copy of the safeguards which we have put in place for the transfer of your personal data outside the EEA.

12 CROSS-BORDER PROCESSING, I.E. COMPETENCE OF THE LEAD SUPERVISORY AUTHORITY (ARTICLE 4(16) AND (23), ARTICLE 56 RODO)

12.1 Preliminary Remarks

Under Article 4(23) GDPR:

> **'cross-border processing' means:**
>
> a) processing of personal data which takes place **[1]** in the context of the activities **[2]** of establishments in **[3]** more than one member state **[4]** of a controller or **[5]** processor in the EU where the controller or processor is established in more than one member state, or
> b) processing of personal data which takes place **[1a]** in the context of the activities **[2a]** of a single establishment of a controller or **[3a]** processor in the EU but which **[4a]** substantially affects or is likely to substantially affect data subjects in more than one member state.

Therefore it appears that EU law is a result of a number of compromises.

12.2 One-Stop-Shop

Cross-border processing is a notion that is relevant to companies and capital groups active in more than one EU Member State. For activity spanning multiple Member States, GDPR provides that the supervisory authority competent for the main establishment has jurisdiction (one-stop-shop).

In practice, the one-stop-shop rule means that when an organisation operates in a number of EU countries at one time, in principle the authority competent for the main establishment can impose penalties for the manner of conducting business or monitor an organisation in some other way.

Therefore, if business activity is only conducted in Slovakia or only in France, cross-border processing does not apply. If a Polish company has branches in the Czech Republic, Slovakia, and the United Kingdom (UK) (for the time being still an EU member), essentially the Polish authority, the Personal Data Protection Office, will have jurisdiction with respect to its activity. A branch of a French company will be subject to the jurisdiction of the CNIL.

If various types of business activity are conducted, there may be separate lead supervisory authorities for the individual types of business activity.

12.3 Processor

There are no exceptions for processors, i.e. companies whose activity is processing of (personal) data for other organisations, to the rule of jurisdiction of the supervisory authority competent for the main establishment (parent company).[70] There is a major exception, however, which is not provided for expressly in the GDPR. If a matter concerns a processor and controller at the same time (which usually seems to be the case), then the lead supervisory authority is the supervisory authority for the controller and not the processor.

12.4 Controllers

There is a certain exception for controllers to the rule that the main establishment is subject to the jurisdiction of the supervisory authority (at this point this means companies that need to process data mainly for their own purposes).

Under Article 4(16)(a) GDPR:

> As regards a controller with establishments in more than one member state, the main establishment is the place of its central administration in the EU, unless the decisions on the purposes and means of the processing of personal data are taken in another establishment of the controller in the EU and the latter establishment has the power to have such decisions implemented, in which case the establishment having taken such decisions is to be considered to be the main establishment.

This means that if the decision-making centre of a business, including the specifying of data processing procedures, is in an office other than the capital group's central office, the competent supervisory authority is determined according to that other office.

Example

If a German business person mostly spends time in a country other than Germany (e.g., in the Canary Islands, on the Côte d'Azur, or in London) and has opened a branch and has decision-making personnel there, then the supervisory authority in that country will be competent to monitor and determine personal data protection compliance of that business' capital group. If however a French business chooses Switzerland, the competent supervisory authority will be CNIL because Switzerland is not in the EU.

In practice, the one-stop-shop can be used to protect 'our own' and this is probably the purpose for which it was introduced. It increases legal certainty if only

70. This is an opportunity to point out an inconsistency – two meanings of the term 'processor' are used in the GDPR. 'Processor' is the title given to a role that may be performed by any organisation when it is entrusted with personal data by another organisation, but it is also the title given to an organisation whose core business activity is processing data for other organisations (e.g., a provider of cloud computing services, an outsourcing centre). According to this second meaning, a processor is a controller of its own personal data at the same time.

because it overcomes the language barrier. It also gives controllers room for manoeuvre, but there are exceptions to the rule of monitoring by the lead supervisory authority.

12.4.1 Local Processing

Above all, processing must be cross-border.

To give an example, processing of employee data is almost always local, and therefore with respect to protection of employee data supervision will be performed by the authority that is competent according to geographical territory (although this may involve transferring employee data to the central office, citing the legitimate interest of a corporate group, and then it becomes cross-border processing).

12.4.2 Local Coverage

A local authority may come to the conclusion that a case does not only concern its jurisdiction (i.e., that country). In such a case it has to give the lead authority an opportunity to take charge of the case.

12.5 Article 29 Working Party Guidelines

On 13 December 2016, the Data Protection Working Party established on the basis of Article 29 of Directive 95/46/EC adopted guidelines on determining the lead supervisory authority for a controller or processor.[71]

12.6 Conclusions

If it is possible to select the supervisory authority because a business has operations in multiple EEA countries, it is worth evaluating where the business will be best treated and deciding where to locate the decision-making centre. With regard to the core area of business activity, it will probably be difficult to move the decision-making centre. When developing new areas of business operations which are vulnerable from the point of view of data protection, the 'friendliness' of the supervisory policy of a authority in a particular country can be taken into account. In turn, when providing services that constitute data processing in the meaning of the GDPR, it is important to be aware of the supervisory policy of all of the countries in which a business has customers.

At the same time, when opening establishments in various EU countries, you should consider that for the internal matters of those establishments (in particular employee matters), the supervisory authorities in individual countries will be competent.

71. *See* http://www.giodo.gov.pl/pl/file/12381 (last accessed on 12 January 2018).

12.7 Leaving One-Stop-Shop

The one-stop-shop rule is a political compromise.

Unsurprisingly it now looks like not everybody understood it in the same way. CNIL in their decision imposing an EUR 50 million fine on Google[72] found themselves competent to decide despite Google formally operates in the EU through Google Limited Ireland.

The breach CNIL makes with their Google decision to the one-stop-shop does not come as a surprise though. Problems with fair application of the one-stop-shop rule have hit the fan in March 2019, with the leak of internal Facebook's correspondence proving that Facebook has been extensively trying to lobby the GDPR legislative works and proving that they were quite successful with the Irish government: 'Most revealingly, it includes details of the company's "great relationship" with Enda Kenny, the Irish prime minister at the time, one of a number of people it describes as "friends of Facebook".'[73,74]

The logic behind the CNIL's Google decision is simple and compelling. If your data decision centre is not in the EU, the one-stop-shop principle does not apply, as there is no 'main establishment' in the meaning of Recital 36 second sentence GDPR.

13 JOINT CONTROLLERS

13.1 Introduction

An organisation usually acts as a controller (using data for its own purposes) or a processor (a contractor that processes data for the controller's purposes).

Article 26 GDPR **acknowledges situations in which two organisations are joint controllers**, i.e. use the data for shared purposes and jointly decide how the data will be processed.

13.2 Examples of Situations in Which There Are Joint Controllers

Organisations might act as joint controllers in capital groups, where companies manage talent jointly (this might give rise to certain challenges in terms of employment law) or where they are practically unified despite being separate legal entities, sharing staff and processes, where a business operates through number of special purpose

72. Commission Nationale de l'Informatique et des Libertés, Délibération de la formation restreinte n° SAN – 2019-001 du 21 janvier 2019 prononçant une sanction pécuniaire à l'encontre de la société Google LLC, https://www.legifrance.gouv.fr/affichCnil.do?oldAction=rechExpCnil&id=CNILTEXT000038032552&fastReqId=2103387945&fastPos=1 (last accessed on 9 March 2019).
73. https://www.theguardian.com/technology/2019/mar/02/facebook-global-lobbying-campaign-against-data-privacy-laws-investment (last accessed 10 March 2019).
74. https://www.irishtimes.com/business/technology/the-world-will-be-watching-our-dealings-with-multinationals-1.3816789 (last accessed 10 March 2019).

vehicles (e.g., developers setting up separate companies for separate projects (so-called SPVs from 'special purpose vehicle') but operating them through single head-quarters); in a relationship between insurance agencies and insurance companies, in which an agent has its own customer/marketing database;[75] where a number of organisations enter into a joint venture at least for the period before it becomes a capital company; and also in the case of bancassurance, i.e. when banks sell insurance products, in procurement procedures where two or more entities enter into a consortium to bid together.

In 2010, the Article 29 Working Party adopted an opinion[76] on the subject of the terms 'controller' and 'processor', in which there were also examples of joint controller situations. The opinion is, however, questionable, and especially examples given may be qualified differently. An example of video surveillance of a building in which the owner of the building is the controller and the security firm is only the processor. If the security firm provides services for multiple organisations and its emergency response centre has a view of various premises, it might act either as a processor for a number of controllers or as a separate controller, if, for example, it uses personal data obtained from one customer to assist another customer, for example having at its disposal face recognition software.

Another example given by the Working Party is cooperation between a bank and a 'financial messaging provider' (something like a clearing chamber). The Article 29 Working Party stated that those entities are joint controllers with regard to the personal data in the messages (money transfers)[77] which is not necessarily in line with regulations and views on outsourcing in the financial sector and on regulations on bank secrecy and other types of financial secrecy.

The opinion issued by the Article 29 Working Party also mentions a social networking site as an example of a situation in which the site operator and site user (except for 'household' use) are joint controllers. Caution is also advised with respect to this example. There are probably many people who would like to decide jointly, for example with Facebook, the purposes and means of data processing. For this reason, a company operating a fan page on Facebook, or even Maciej Gawronski, maintaining the profile of Gawroński & Partners S.K.A. on LinkedIn, are not joint controllers with Mark Zuckerberg (CEO of Facebook) or Satya Nadella (CEO of Microsoft). These are simply independent controllers to the extent made possible by social networking services, which in turn make use of data for their own purposes. Even in the case of social networking sites within a group, there are distinct controllers. This is because in reality, situations in which there are joint controllers are quite rare. They require a balance in bargaining power or co-dependency.

Parallel controlling. The European Court of Justice in a judgment in Case C-210/16 Unabhängiges Landeszentrum für Datenschutz Schleswig-Holstein vs. Wirtschaftsakademie Schleswig-Holstein GmbH pronounced that an operator of a

75. Though such situations may also be seen as 'parallel' controlling which we discuss further below.
76. Opinion 1/2010 on the notions 'controller' and 'processor'.
77. The 'communications' described in the opinion are, for example, money transfers.

Facebook fan page is a controller of personal data of users visiting that fan page. ECJ considers fan page operators as jointly responsible with Facebook (Ireland) for processing personal data of the personal data of Facebook users and persons visiting the fan pages hosted on Facebook. The judgment concerns a situation before 25 May 2018; therefore, it relates to the Data Protection Directive and not GDPR. In our opinion that judgment should not be interpreted under GDPR as 'enforcing' joint controllership between Facebook and every organisation operating a Facebook fan page. Facebook has different purposes and means of processing users and other fan page visitors data than an operator of a fan page. Calling their relation joint controlling is like claiming that riding on a bicycle alongside a tank is like co-controlling the road.

At the same time, under GDPR there is no need to search for joint controllership to find joint liability. First sentence of Article 82(2) GDPR states that: 'any controller involved in processing shall be liable for the damage caused by processing which infringes' GDPR. In the case of a fan page, both Facebook and a fan page operator are involved in processing, so they may be directly liable to a data subject. Each of them may be also fined by a supervisory body based on Article 83 GDPR.

Therefore we prefer to describe situations when two or more entities in a same situation/'in the same data processing' separately and differently profit of that processing for their own separate purposes as 'parallel controlling'.

13.3 Should You Avoid Being a Joint Controller?

Usually, for practical reasons, it is better not to classify relationships between two or more organisations as a situation in which there are joint controllers. It is better to seek separate areas in which some parties are controllers and others are processors. There are however exceptions from that rule.

When organisations share data but each of them wants to keep control over them – e.g., if an agent shares his contact base with a principal (e.g., an insurance company). Though, another option for such situation is just consider it a 'parallel controlling'.[78] In highly integrated capital groups joint controllership may be a better option for processing than multiplying information obligations and other procedures and duties required by GDPR. Sometimes joint controllership may result directly from the law, for example, if the law requires employee's representatives in a supervisory board of a holding company to be chosen by employees of the whole group. An in-company social networking site in a capital group, where personnel can discuss a free range of subjects, is an interesting example. This can be classified both as a joint controller situation and mutual 'controller-to-controller' disclosure on the basis of legitimate interest.

78. Let us see that in our agent-insurer example, the agent's contact base remains in control of the agent despite contacts are transferred to the insurer and despite that subsequently the insurer may entrust the agent with further processing as a data processor.

13.4 Joint Controller Obligations

Article 26(1) of Regulation (EU) 2016/679 of the European Parliament and of the Council of 27 April 2016 on the protection of natural persons with regard to the processing of personal data and on the free movement of such data, and repealing Directive 95/46/EC states that joint controllers **[1]** 'jointly determine'**[2]** 'in a transparent manner', 'their respective' **[3]** 'responsibilities for compliance with the obligations under this regulation', **[4]** 'in particular as regards the exercising of the rights of the data subject'.

13.5 Joint Controller Agreement

This therefore means that an agreement has to be concluded and must be documented. Oral consultation to agree on the joint controller rules is not possible in light of the principle of accountability.

The joint controller agreement has to state how obligations are allocated and who is responsible for the notification of collection of data, who ensures execution of an individual's rights, how the level of security is established, etc. Responsibility towards data subjects cannot be limited in the agreement, however, because each of the joint controllers can be held responsible without limitation (joint and several responsibility).

13.6 Wording of the Agreement: Comparison with the Entrusting of Data

The GDPR does not state the specific wording of the joint controller agreement. In general, the requirements regarding the agreement between the controller and processor which are provided for in Article 28 GDPR may be referred to, taking into account that at least two joint decision-makers are parties to the agreement. These requirements include specifying the purpose, scope, and duration of the joint controller situation, the categories of the persons whose data are processed, and categories of data, the allocation of responsibility for the controller's obligations, the fact that arrangements are reached in writing, non-disclosure obligations, arrangements reached regarding processors, arrangements reached regarding security, procedures for working together to ensure execution of an individual's rights and to give notification of breach of personal data, arrangements reached regarding ending the joint controller situation, arrangements reached regarding recourse for responsibility and cooperation in the event of claims and inspection, the content of information about collection of data, and the scope and content of information as to the fundamental wording of the joint controller agreement to be disclosed to third parties, with information about the means of disclosure (as a rule at the moment of collection of data or moment of transfer of data between joint controllers).

13.7 Disclosure to Data Subjects

The fundamental nature of the arrangements reached concerning a joint controller situation has to be disclosed to data subjects for which there are joint controllers. The GDPR does not directly state when this has to be done. In line with Article 13 and Article 14 GDPR, this should occur when data are obtained for joint controller purposes and when data are shared that were previously in the possession of one of the controllers.

13.8 Cross-Border Joint Controller Situation

If processing in a joint controller situation is cross-border processing (i.e., it affects more than one country in the EEA (EU + Norway, Iceland, and Liechtenstein), the joint controller agreement should also state the lead joint controller (in order to designate the lead supervisory authority).

13.9 Conclusions

A joint controller situation is similar to the joint management of a project or joint running of a company or a country. It gives rise in practice to a number of risks relating to transfer of responsibility. For this reason, these situations should be avoided unless it is really the case. At the same time, a joint controller situation could be a solution serving such needs as: to avoid forfeiting the right to a company's own data while sharing them for business purposes (e.g., the relationship between an agent and insurance company), to limit formal duties and deduplicate procedures, to respond to requirements of law, when a group of companies truly operates as one operation, when you are setting up a number of SPV (special purpose vehicle) unstaffed companies.

In real life, there is usually some room for a decision whether a situation should be qualified as joint controlling, 'parallel' controlling or a mix of parallel controlling and data processing, as these things might be quite elusive.

14 CODES OF CONDUCT AND CERTIFICATION (ARTICLE 40 ONWARDS OF THE GDPR)

14.1 Preliminary Remarks

GDPR provides legal grounds for industry organisations to devise, in the form of codes of practice, common rules for personal data processing in their business activity. **The GDPR sees introduction of codes of conduct as a means of correct application of the GDPR, taking account of the specific nature of various sectors in which processing takes place and special needs of microenterprises and small and medium-sized enterprises.** In turn, introducing certification, and consequently quality labels with respect to personal data protection, is meant to show that the certified businesses process personal data in compliance with the GDPR.

Certification processes have been known for a long time, and not only with regard to security. The obvious examples are of course ISO standards, for instance ISO 9000 and ISO 27000 standards families.

Self-regulation in different forms, including industry codes of practice, works better or worse in EU Member States. However, the option of creating industry codes of practice and certifying controllers and processors is a new development in data protection law.

This is a major change not only for data controllers and processors, i.e. entities subject to inspection, but also for the supervisory authorities themselves, which in addition to an inspection role might also be a certifying body.

14.2 Codes of Conduct

14.2.1 Drafting Codes of Conduct

Codes of conduct can be drawn up by business associations and 'other bodies representing categories of controllers or processors'. For instance, these can be business associations, associations, chambers of commerce, and craftsmen associations.

Codes of conduct should be based on data protection best practice. There are certain practical issues with industry codes of conduct. First is that either they become an industry's wish list hard to approve for a supervisory body or they are not touching real issues in order to facilitate acceptance. Second that they require to establish an effective monitoring body. Third that national codes of conduct are not automatically recognised in other Member States unless positively opined by the EDPB (or further adopted for the whole EU in a decision of the EC).

We are not getting into detail with code of conducts in this book. The EDPB issued in February 2019 guidelines for codes of conducts[79] which give some basic insight allowing for building a checklist for a particular code of conduct mechanism. Though the GDPR is silent on the use of ISO standards in relation to codes of conduct, one may think of reaching to ISO quality management system rules (ISO 9000 family).

14.2.2 Approval

A code of conduct is approved by a supervisory authority of a Member State. When a code of conduct is approved, it is published by the supervisory authority.

79. Guidelines 1/2019 on Codes of Conduct and Monitoring Bodies under Regulation 2016/679 Adopted on 12 February 2019 (version for public consultation).

14.3 Certification

14.3.1 Certification Schemes

The GDPR allows for creating certification schemes in which supervisory authorities or other professional bodies can certify controllers and processors as personal data protection compliant and award the appropriate quality labels.

Certification means submitting to an audit of an external body to establish whether a personal data protection standard set by that body is complied with. If this test is passed, the organisation is authorised to use the specified quality label certifying that the specific data protection standard is met.

Therefore certification is a means of obtaining external confirmation of data protection compliance and obtaining recommendations on how to implement data protection.

The GDPR's certification approach is built entirely on ISO 17000 standards family concerning conformity assessment. An accreditation standard EN-ISO/IEC 17065/2012 is directly named in Article 43(1)(b) GDPR. EDPB's guidelines on accreditation[80] and certification[81] are based on the same as well.

14.4 Benefits

Observance of an approved code of conduct or approved certification mechanism has many advantages. The benefits are not insignificant and are explained below, and this is an argument for treating certification and observance of codes of conduct seriously. They make it possible to demonstrate the appropriate level of security and that an organisation gives sufficient guarantees of implementation of the appropriate personal data protection measures. They make processing risk assessment and DPIA easier, constitute exonerating or mitigating circumstances for administrative fines, and simplify lawful data export (when the recipient has an approved code of conduct in place).

Under Article 32 GDPR:

> Taking into account the state of the art, the cost of implementation and the nature, scope, context and purposes of processing as well as the risks of varying likelihood and severity for rights and freedoms of natural persons, the controller and the processor shall **implement appropriate technical and organisational measures** to ensure a level of security appropriate to the risk [...].

Implementation of appropriate technical and organisational measures has a direct impact on responsibility of the controller in the event of a leak of data or inspection by the authority regulating personal data processing. Observance of an approved code of conduct or certification mechanism helps to prove that requirements

80. Guidelines 4/2018 on the accreditation of certification bodies under Art. 43 of the General Data Protection Regulation (2016/679) – adopted on 4 December 2018.
81. Guidelines 1/2018 on certification and identifying certification criteria in accordance with Arts 42 and 43 of the Regulation 2016/679 adopted on 23 January 2019.

are met with respect to use of the appropriate technical and organisation measures. In practice, this means the possibility of repudiating a potential fin in the millions.

Due to certification, it is also possible to demonstrate compliance with the principles of privacy by design and privacy by default.

Use of a graphic symbol confirming that personal data processing complies with the GDPR will be a factor that helps directly to build credibility and trust among customers, and this will certainly also be a contributing factor in good financial results of the organisation in question. For this reason, compliance with the GDPR should not be treated as compliance with yet another tiresome obligation (series of obligations). The necessity of compliance with the GDPR can be forged into something of financial benefit and beneficial for an organisation's image.

We see also the following benefits:

- it is easier to share personal data under agreements on entrusting personal data processing – the signatories to the code of conduct will have the same security requirements and therefore meeting them means fulfilling requirements of all of the other organisations that apply the industry code of conduct in question;
- organisations do not hinder each other due to various, sometimes conflicting, security requirements – as in the preceding point, organisations that observe the code of conduct will have probably common requirements. This will mean significantly lower costs of implementing the security measures required under the GDPR;
- there is no need to reinvent the wheel – instead of devising your own best practices, which, for various reasons, not every organisation can afford to do, it is easier to obtain them from a trustworthy supplier.

These benefits described are arguments for observing industry codes of conduct and becoming certified.

14.5 Private Certification

Using a recognised private certification mechanism, before the appropriate state authority or accredited certification systems are available, should also have substantial benefits. Certification is affirmation by a trustworthy organisation that a set of practices is employed that meets the standard. Using recognised certification is proof of due diligence because an additional verification mechanism has been used and also provides access to data protection know-how developed by experts, of course, if the certification scheme in question encompasses this.

14.6 SMEs and Self-Certification

Current certification schemes are based on external audits requiring a lot of manpower. Therefore they are rather not available to micro, small or even medium enterprises, due to financial and organisational cost associated. There is however interesting far-reaching exception to the rule that a physical third party audit is required for certification. The Privacy Shield allowing US businesses to declare compliance with the EU data protection rules is a so-called self-certification scheme. So, if self-certification is available to Americans of all sizes, why should not it be available to small local EU organisations? Self-certification for small and medium enterprises (SMEs) should consist not only on asking questions but also on providing default answers, as they do not have resources for studying and debating the GDPR intricacies for weeks or months. If left with questions only SMEs usually just take the risk and carry on their business as usual (maybe except for changing their privacy policies and information obligation forms). That is why we are fans of developing self-certification mechanisms for SMEs even if they would not be accredited by supervisory authorities.

CHAPTER 2

Data Subject's Rights

Aleksander P. Czarnowski, Katarzyna Kunda, Maciej Gawronski, Michał Kibil, Michał Sztąberek & Paweł Punda[*]

1 PROCESSING DATA SUBJECT'S RIGHTS AND REQUESTS (ARTICLE 12 OF THE GDPR)

1.1 Introduction

The standard required for actions enabling exercise of an individual's rights is laid down in Article 12 of Regulation (EU) 2016/679 of the European Parliament and of the Council of 27 April 2016 on the protection of natural persons with regard to the processing of personal data and on the free movement of such data, and repealing Directive 95/46/EC. This article provides for the following requirements and issues:

(1) legibility in communication,
(2) documenting authentication,
(3) more thorough authentication,
(4) documenting communication,
(5) facilitating exercise of rights,
(6) operations carried out on unidentified data,
(7) a one-month time for first response[1],
(8) a one-month time limit for refusal to take action,

* Section 1 contributed by Maciej Gawronski and Michał Kibil. Section 2 contributed by Maciej Gawronski. Section 3 contributed by Maciej Gawronski and Michał Sztąberek. Section 4 contributed by Maciej Gawronski and Michał Sztąberek. Section 5 contributed by Maciej Gawronski and Katarzyna Kunda. Section 6 contributed by Maciej Gawronski and Michał Sztąberek. Section 7 contributed by Aleksander P. Czarnowski, Maciej Gawronski and Paweł Punda. Section 8 Maciej Gawronski and Michał Sztąberek. Section 9 contributed by Michał Kibil.

1. 'Response Time' in IT jargon.

(9) a three-month time limit for final response,[2]
(10) refusal to act on excessive requests,
(11) fees for excessive requests,
(12) icons,[3]

while there is also a fundamental principle for actions enabling exercise of an individual's rights and communication with an individual:

(13) the accountability principle.

1.2 Legibility When Communicating

1.2.1 Legibly and Concisely

Under Article 12(1) GDPR, communication with a data subject must be 'in a concise, transparent, intelligible and easily accessible form, using clear and plain language, in particular for any information addressed to a child'.

The requirement for transparent and intelligible communication reflects the fundamental principle expressed in Article 5(1)(a) GDPR – lawfulness, fairness and transparency or more specifically reflects fairness and transparency.

1.2.2 Comprehensiveness

The General Data Protection Regulation (GDPR) does not provide for a direct requirement for communication with data subjects to be comprehensive in this case, but we should not be fooled by this, as failure to observe one of the compulsory elements of communication of any kind with data subjects will constitute a breach of data protection laws.

To patch somehow the obvious conflict between being concise and legible and being precise and providing complete information, the European Data Protection Board (Article 29 Working Party) came up with something which is called 'a layered approach' (to information duty).[4] We have discussed it in the chapter about consent, but let us repeat it here for the sake of legibility (though against conciseness). The minimum scope of information duty is set in Recital 42 GDPR fourth sentence:

2. 'Solution Time' in IT jargon.
3. EU legislators have provided for the option of use of icons (images) to denote certain standard sets of conditions or information. The EC is gradually beginning to realise that the surge of disclosure obligations cannot be discharged using text, because this is beyond human powers of perception. For this reason, the new concept uses symbols (graphics, icons) which are to be standardised (by the EC). Unfortunately, under Art. 12(7) GDPR, these icons 'must be machine-readable' if presented electronically, which in practice means that until the EC proposes its own set of graphic symbols, ideas developed individually will be ineffective because they will not be 'machine-readable'.
4. Article 29 Working Party Guidelines on consent under Regulation 2016/679 Adopted on 28 November 2017 As last Revised and Adopted on 10 April 2018, 17/EN WP259 rev.01.

For consent to be informed, the data subject should be aware at least of the identity of the controller and the purposes of the processing for which the personal data are intended.

The layered approach means providing immediate essential information (who and for what) accompanied by a reference to a more detailed, complete explanation (most often a link to an internet place where an appropriate privacy policy resides). Though the Guidelines on consent refer to situations where it is needed 'to accommodate for small screens or situations with restricted room for information', the Guidelines on transparency (WP260 rev.01) refer to it more broadly. In practice the layered approach works best for any situations.

1.2.3 Non-quoting of Legal Provisions

The requirement for legibility means that using legal jargon and citing legal provisions is not permitted. The lawyers who wrote this book (ten lawyers of total of twelve authors) were moderately successful in sticking to these requirements in their first attempts to draft information clauses and consents. However, the market practice seems to go into the right direction (except for telemarketing which remains Wild Wild West at the end of 2018, at least in Poland). The best approach to the full information obligation is probably by styling headers as questions and content as responses like in the following example (it does not cover automated decision-making nor indirect collection of data):

- Who we are?[5]
- What personal data we use, why, and how do we use them?
- Who we may pass your data to?
- How long we store your data?
- Do we send your data out of EU?
- What rights do you have?
- How to reach us?

1.2.4 Children

Any information directed at children whose data are processed by a data controller should be especially clear and plain. The language used, method of communicating and form in which information is conveyed should be suitable for the age of the child receiving the information, and be the language that the child can understand (Recital 59 GDPR). In order to demonstrate that due diligence has been exercised in formulating communication of this kind, it might be advisable to consult a child psychologist.

As we have mentioned in the chapter about consent, the Article 29 Working Party Guidelines on Transparency (WP260 rev. 01) suggest the possibility of using the

5. Inversion intentionally omitted.

language and rhetoric of the United Nations (UN) Convention on the Rights of the Child.

1.2.5 Average Joe Test

When preparing a collection of templates for information and messages, the main focus should be on how the message in question might be understood by the addressee, as the burden of demonstrating that the message was formulated in objectively clear and plain language rests with us (accountability principle). It is good practice to ask third parties who do not come into contact with personal data protection provisions to review the devised texts (the 'average reader' test) and simplify the message conveyed until none of the persons consulted has any doubt as to the meaning of the message or until only unavoidable doubts remain. It needs to be borne in mind that the same test subjects cannot be used continuously for the 'average reader' test because they will eventually become more aware and no longer be useful.

In case you reach to such testing, in the name of the principle of accountability remember to note and file your findings and especially your Test Joes observations for future use. In practice, it is impossible to achieve unambiguity and comprehensibility in a communication addressed to consumers (or in any other). And if you combine this task with legibility and conciseness, it does not get simpler. Not even the layered approach will help you. So at least what you can do when questioned by a supervisory authority or a court is to prove that you tried until you got into a no progress loop.

1.3 Authentication

Authentication of a person making a request, and subsequently of the addressee of a response to a request, is a fundamental issue.

According to Article 12(1) GDPR third sentence:

> When requested by the data subject, the information may be provided orally, provided that the identity of the data subject is proven by other means.

Therefore a data controller is required to confirm the identity of a person making a request by means other than oral means.[6] The data controller is entitled to request additional information (more thorough authentication) in case of doubts.

1.3.1 Confirming Identity

It can be difficult to understand what is meant by confirmation of identity by means other than oral means due to the lack of precision of this phrase. Means other than oral means can be electronic, documented, or biometric form. The three typical options currently used for authentication are information known to the person concerned (a

6. Where communication is by telephone authenticating by other means than orally is complicated.

password, personal information such as their mother's maiden name), something the person possesses (a token), or a personal feature (biometrics). Each of these methods can be employed over the telephone. The 'other than oral means' stipulation should thus probably be understood to mean 'other than aural means', i.e. not based solely on the opinion of a service provider – the addressee of oral communication.

Oral means of authentication can be questions concerning various kinds of information, such as 'do you hold an account with us in British pounds', or 'what was the amount of the money transfer you made through us yesterday?' – which are typical questions asked when a call is made to a bank's call centre. Typing a PIN on a telephone keyboard should probably be considered today to be an electronic form of verification, even though it is done via a telephone. The 'spoken password' method used via a telephone is an oral form of authentication and therefore is not permissible despite this being a more secure method than verification by way of 'ordinary' information about the person making the request.

Authentication of a person who has an electronic profile with our firm should not cause any difficulty – ordinary methods of verification of identity should also be used in order to act to realise an individual's rights.

Authentication of an 'unknown' person will, however, require more work and would probably meaning resort to the use of personal identification documents or third-party trust providers.

The requirement of 'other than oral authentication', i.e. a pure test of knowledge about a person whom we are claiming to be, has become a real issue and obstacle in day-to-day serving client requests by many institutions. We have responded to that problem by considering Article 12(1) GDPR third sentence as a rule literally applying only to data subject requests, so when someone making a request relies on the GDPR's rights of data subject and not on a contract. It is not exactly a systemic approach to law but seems only one practical available at the moment. The GDPR is simply non-coherent here; identification and authentication for data subject requests should be a matter of risk assessment as technical and organisational measures of security of personal data (Article 32(1) GDPR).

1.3.2 More Thorough Authentication

The GDPR does not tell us at what point we should become concerned with respect to the identity of a person making a request, and this is reasonable as in case of doubt it enables us to request additional proof that the person making the request is who they claim to be. Internal procedures should provide examples of such situations, which should be constantly updated according to an organisation's growing experience especially based on risk analysis and known attempts of identity theft.

1.4 Form of Communication

As a rule, communication must be in writing or electronic form; that is, it must be documented. It complies with the accountability principle.

In special cases, upon request, information may be provided orally, but in this case as well, the identity of the person making the request must be confirmed beforehand by 'means other than oral means', and even if a response to a data subject is oral, it should be internally documented (e.g., in an internal note) especially in the light one-month response time and three-month solution time deadlines required by Article 12 GDPR (accountability principle).

Taking into account the requirements described above, communication must be in a form convenient to the person making the request. The form of communication cannot be disruptive. As a rule of a thumb – if a data controller communicates with a data subject through a specific communication channel/method, that data controller should allow a data subject respond through the same channel (or at least provide info how to reach them another way).

With regard to the question of confirmation of identity, as data must be kept confidential, the data controller is required to exercise particular diligence to ensure that the identity of the person is confirmed in a manner that leaves no room for doubt before the information is provided. From the other side, deciding on the level of scrutiny of identity verification risk of unauthorised data disclosure should be weighed against the risk of depriving an authorised person (data subject) access to their data and rights as the increase of security mostly decreases the availability of information.

1.5 Facilitation of Exercise of Rights

A data controller is required to facilitate the exercise of data subject rights, and this means being able to answer the following question: what are we doing to facilitate data subject access to their rights? Or how this is achieved.

The methods of facilitation may vary: a special tab on a website, with a guide containing information about the individual's rights and information about how to exercise those rights in our organisation, designating a special team of 'guides' and internal 'ombudsmen for a person's rights' in the organisation (whom does not need to be a DPO), ensuring legibility of communication and introducing key performance indicators for the process of serving an individual's rights (timeliness, comprehensive, level of satisfaction, etc.), outsourcing the process, implementing integrated solutions, etc.

1.6 Serving Requests Concerning 'Unidentified Data'

As explained in the chapter about Article 11 GDPR, a data controller is not required to identify the individuals whose data that data controller processes solely for the purpose of enabling exercise of rights of those individuals. For instance, there is no obligation to identify all individuals recorded on a building's security cameras, and no obligation to review all email correspondence in order to ascertain what information is sent and about whom.

On the other hand, if an 'unknown' person says that we process their data, and enables us to identify them and their details, we are required to act on that request. In such a case we can proceed in two possible ways: (i) determine where and in what way we process the data of that 'unidentified person making a request' (person X) or (ii) demonstrate that we are unable to identify person X.

In both of these cases, we are required to take measures of some kind to determine whether we can identify that person or more accurately the data requested. Our actions must be determined by the nature of the 'unidentified data' concerned (e.g., a video recording) and by additional data provided by the individual making the request. If the individual gives a specific day and time in the previous week, in which our cameras are thought to have recorded the event concerning the individual, we should be able to retrieve that data. If the individual's request covers an entire week, it might not be possible to process that volume of data in order to find a specific scene.[7]

We discuss the question of 'unidentified' data in the text on the subject of Article 11 the GDPR, where we also tackle the issue of searching through corporate emails.

1.7 Response Time and Time for Processing a Request

A data controller is required to respond promptly to any request made to it.

The GDPR specifies two main time limits, which are one month for responding and three months (one month extended by a further two months) where necessary for processing the request.

The individual must be provided with a response within a month, stating the action taken regarding their request:

(1) the individual's data are not processed, or
(2) the request will not be processed (in which case the individual must be informed of their right to file a complaint and to seek judicial remedy), or
(3) the request will be processed, or
(4) the time needed to process the request will be extended by (a maximum of) two months due to the complex nature of the request or the number of requests.

Interestingly, the wording used in Article 12(3) GDPR is 'provide [...] information on **action taken on a request**', which, according to the literal meaning, does not mean that the request has to be processed within a month or three months but that we have to provide information about the progress made in processing the request. We should not rely too much on this semantic interpretation, however, because the generally established interpretation of Article 12 GDPR is that a three-month time limit (one month extended by a further two months where necessary) is the time limit for the action taken on a request.

7. Practical solutions might involve: predefining required precision of describing requested time and cameras to review – e.g., up to six hours from one camera or three hour from more cameras. Pricing extras as excessive requests plus suggesting requesting data processing restriction of records in a form of securing them for the Police or other justice or enforcement agency for a reasonable time required to initiate appropriate legal proceedings.

The GDPR uses the wording 'within one month of receipt of the request', and therefore the question arises whether this time limit starts the moment the request is received or the moment the identity of the individual making the request is confirmed. There is some room for interpretation here; the request can be considered to have been received as of the moment of confirmation of who submitted it. To use an extreme example, if we receive an anonymous request by mail (because someone forgot to give the sender's address) we are not able to respond to the request. Objections can probably be made regarding this example, but the concept that a time limit for processing a request starts the moment the individual's identity is confirmed seems to be rational and in compliance with the GDPR. At the same time, if the individual's manner of communication enables a response, then any information or materials missing from the request rendering action impossible, for example inadequate authentication, mean that we can resolve the matter quickly by refusing the request. As we are required to facilitate the exercise of the individual's rights, the refusal must state the action needed for the request to be acted upon when it is resubmitted.

1.8 Unfounded or Excessive Requests

The main concern when a data controller has more extensive obligations as regards response to requests from subjects of data processing is that a significant number of unfounded or frequently recurring requests will be received.

To limit situations of this kind, a data controller has the following rights under the GDPR:

(1) to charge a reasonable fee for performing the actions requested, taking into account the administrative costs of providing the information, communication, or performing the requested actions; or
(2) to refuse the request – if a data controller receives requests which are manifestly unfounded or excessive, in particular because of their repetitive character.

These rights of a data controller are alternatives, though, of course, a fee can only be charged if the data controller acts on the submitted request.

The general principle under the GDPR is that individuals whose data are processed cannot be charged fees for communication with the data controller. The right to charge a fee for processing excessive requests (and providing further copies of data) is an exception to this rule (not the only one as a data controller can charge also for other than the first request for a copy of data).

Where a data controller decides to charge the individual making the request a fee, the fee should be 'reasonable' and 'take into account the administrative costs of providing the information or communication or taking the action requested'. The fundamental question remains of what can be classified as costs related to the preparation of a response. These costs are any true costs incurred by the data controller for which there is an adequate causal link with the submitted request. According to this interpretation, a fee can be charged not only for costs of materials but also for the true costs of labour and external assistance needed to provide the response. To what extent can investments on systems for realising an individual's rights be included in these costs? The proportion of unfounded and excessive request to justified requests should be one of the factors allowing to allocate investment costs related to serving data subject requests to costs of serving excessive (and unfounded) requests.

Initially, it may be difficult to find the correct proportion. Depending on the situation, an assumption can be made as to. Over time the true figures can be collected and the fee adjusted accordingly.

1.8.1 An Unfounded Request

The burden of proof regarding the demonstration that a request is manifestly unfounded or excessive lies with the data controller. A request can be considered to be unfounded if it indicates that there is no actual connection between the person making the request and the data controller, for example where the person making the request has decided to send queries about their data to several hundred large data controllers in a blanket fashion. What happens if there is no context to the query? This does not definitively mean that the request is manifestly unfounded.

Under Recital 63 of the GDPR:

> Where a controller processes a large quantity of information concerning the data subject, the controller should be able to request that, before the information is delivered, the data subject specify the information or processing activities to which the request relates.

Similarly, a data controller could ask the person making the request to provide more precise context or more details about the relationship between the person making the request and the data controller. A lack of response to this request for further information could indicate that the request was manifestly unfounded if supervisory authorities took a sympathetic view.

1.8.2 An Excessive Request

It is not easy to determine in general what requests can be considered excessive under the GDPR as it may very much depend on specific situation and usually be contextual. Moreover, in many cases, it will require [human] judgment, which is costly and subjective.

The only hint GDPR gives in that regard is in Recital 63 GDPR, stating that:

> Where the controller processes a large quantity of information concerning the data subject, the controller should be able to request that, before the information is delivered, the data subject specify the information or processing activities to which the request relates.

Based on the above wording, we could try to justify claiming that a request without basic justification why it is filed might be excessive; that is, data subject requests 'out of pure curiosity' are considered excessive. Asking 'why' could also help to deal with a 'nightmare letter subject access request' which is a request requiring execution of all data subject rights in one letter.[8]

A data controller should probably start with requesting a context of request – minimum justification allowing to assume that there is any link between a data controller and a data subject. Second, a data controller may define a default time interval between same type requests under which a subsequent request would be considered excessive unless a data subject provides a specific reason for repeating a request. Third, in case of a number of repetitive requests, a data controller may define conditions under which (e.g., sending documents) a presumed excessive request may be reviewed for processing. The problem with all that is that at the moment serving such processes requires human time and competence.

1.9 Data Controller Action Plan

An action plan for requests submitted by data subjects can be created on the basis of this provision. The plan should comprise the following steps, as a minimum:

(1) **confirmation of the identity of the person making the request** – if this is not possible, a response is given advising that the request cannot be reviewed, stating reasons (one-month time limit);
(2) **determining the fee/decision to refuse action** - review to determine whether the request is excessive or manifestly unfounded (one-month time limit), or whether the request is for further copies of data;
(3) **determining whether we process the data of the person making the request** – if it is not established that we process the individual's data, sending a response saying that we do not process the individual's data (one-month time limit);
(4) **analysis of request based on the merits of the case** in terms of whether the request is justified and precise;
(5) **request for more precise information**, if necessary;
(6) **review of the individual's request** – if there is a delay in review of the request, advising the individual that the time limit has been extended, giving the reasons for the delay and envisaged time when a response will be provided; if the data controller does not take action, the individual is informed of the reasons for action not being taken and their related rights;
(7) **providing the individual with a substantive response.**

8. https://www.linkedin.com/pulse/nightmare-letter-subject-access-request-under-gdpr-karbaliotis/ (last accessed on 30 December 2018).

2 RIGHT TO BE INFORMED AND PRIVACY INFORMATION OBLIGATION (ARTICLES 13 AND 14 GDPR)

2.1 Preliminary Remarks

The right to information about what happens to somebody's personal data is a fundamental right under the GDPR. This right is represented by specific information obligations on the part of the controller. The information obligation is nothing new – it applied earlier, under the Data Protection Directive, but the GDPR expands and modifies the notification obligation towards data subjects.

The controller has an obligation to inform an individual that their data are processed in four main situations:

(1) when data are collected directly from that person (Article 13 GDPR);
(2) when data are collected about the individual from sources other than the individual (Article 14 GDPR);
(3) when the purpose of processing changes or a new purpose is added (Article 13(3) and Article 14(4) GDPR);
(4) in the execution of a request for access to data (Article 15 GDPR).

We will call here those information obligations collectively as privacy information obligation or 'PIO'.

2.2 Scope of Information

2.2.1 Data Obtained Directly from an Individual

Where data are obtained directly from the data subject, the controller is required to provide the following information (Article 13(1) and (2) GDPR):

Basic information:

(1) the identity and the contact details of the controller;
(2) the contact details of the DPO, if designated, but not necessarily that person's identity;
(3) the purposes of the processing of personal data and the legal basis for the processing for each of those purposes;
(4) the legitimate interests pursued by the controller or a third party where they wish to process data on the basis of legitimate interest (one of the possible bases);
(5) information about the recipients or categories of recipients of personal data;
(6) information about intended 'export to third countries' with the details listed in Article 13(1)(f) GDPR if it wishes to export data;

(7) the time period for which the data will be stored, or the criteria used to determine that period.

Information about the data subject's rights, i.e.:

(8) access to data,
(9) rectification,
(10) erasure,
(11) limitation of processing,
(12) objection,
(13) transfer of data,
(14) complaint to the supervisory authority,
(15) withdrawal of consent if processed on the basis of consent.

Information about whether provision of data is:

(16) a statutory or contractual requirement, or requirement for entering into an agreement;
(17) mandatory;
(18) the consequences of not providing the data.

Where the controller makes decisions producing legal effects or similar effects (e.g., refusal to enter into an agreement) based on automated decision-making or profiling (Article 22 GDPR):

(19) information about cases of automated decision-making of that kind,
(20) important information about the rules of that automated decision-making,
(21) information about the significance and predictable implications for the data subject.

As can be seen, the list of information that the controller has to provide is impressive.

2.2.2 Data Not Obtained Directly from an Individual

If the controller obtains data from other sources than the data subject, then on top of the information listed above the controller has to inform the individual of:

(22) the categories of data it obtained,
(23) sources of data, including detailed information about publicly accessible sources, if applicable.

2.2.3 *Change of Purpose*

Where the controller intends to change or add a purpose for which data are processed it is required to inform the individual of:

(24) the new purpose and provide any information mentioned on the list above, which the individual does not have.

In particular when the controller intends to use data possessed due to the performance of a contract for marketing purposes, adequate information is necessary. Interestingly, PIO can be used as a good faith reason to reach to persons we would like to serve marketing through email or other electronic or telecommunications channels telling them about our intent and asking if they consent to receive such content.

2.2.4 *Right of Access*

Where the controller receives a request for access to data, when executing that request the controller also has to provide the individual with a large amount of information from the list above. In reality, the controller repeats the whole information obligation from Article 13 or 14, respectively. A specific list is provided in Article 15(1) and (2) GDPR.

2.3 Details of the Information

Below is a brief description of the information that has to be provided in practice with respect to elements of the notification obligation which might cause concern.

2.3.1 *Legal Basis*

If we rely on law as the basis for processing (under Article 6(1)(c) and (e), Article 9(2)(b), (g)–(j) GDPR), a specific provision of law has to be given.

2.3.2 *Categories of Recipient and Recipients*

The recipients or categories of recipients have to be stated. This is rather a question of the recipients on the side of the controller because, in functional terms, the recipient might be the data subject themselves or their relatives (e.g., for medical documentation) or so. Within the group of 'usual suspects', such as accountants, lawyers, IT personnel, and document archiving companies, it would probably be possible to limit this to stating the category, especially if the service provider structure is widely spread.

Let us see that if someone exercises a right to have their data rectified or erased, or processing restricted, then under Article 19 GDPR that individual is entitled to request information as to the identity of all of the recipients. In such a case it is not enough to state the categories, a data controller should indicate specific entities, however.

However, the definition given in Article 4(9) GDPR of 'recipients' is unusually broad. Once again, it seems that the GDPR is inconsistent in this regard, as the same words are used in different senses in various provisions. The 'recipients' referred to in Article 19 GDPR are, to be reasonable, entities other than processors and other than personnel of the controller and of the processor. This seems to be obvious, but if a specific line of reasoning does have to be formulated, then providing information about a company's own personnel and processors is like providing information about oneself. Any other interpretation would be difficult to reconcile with the generally applicable rules of civil and economic law and rules on combating unfair competition (business secrets). Nevertheless, prudent controllers prefer to list categories of usual external support functions.

As a result, only information about organisations that have been provided with data on a controller-to-controller (C2C) basis and about 'external' natural persons (e.g., an individual's relatives) should be provided. Those, according to the definition of the 'recipient' do not include the request of the Police and other law enforcement bodies (courts, etc.) based on specific provisions of law.

2.3.3 Data Export

If a company has plans to send data to a third country, a particular recipient has to be specified. Information also has to be provided about whether the recipient's country is deemed by the European Commission (EC) to ensure an adequate level of personal data protection, mention the safeguards under GDPR provisions on data export, and state how documents confirming proper data protection can be accessed.

Unfortunately, practical application of the PIO relating to the export of data in many cases is not in line with the working and spirit of Articles 13 and 14 GDPR. Apart from those controllers who have just formally realised that 'their data' are being exported because their data processors use out of European Union (EU) resources, there are those who apply a freestyle approach just telling their data subjects that everything will be all right. As an example one of the United Kingdom (UK) leading newspapers and news portals provides the users with the following notice on data export[9] (we have substituted the real name with 'NEWSPAPER'):

> Data we collect may be transferred to, stored and processed in any country or territory where one or more of our 'NEWSPAPER' group companies or service providers are based or have facilities. While other countries or territories may not have the same standards of data protection as those in your home country, we will continue to protect personal data that we transfer in line with this privacy policy. Whenever we transfer your personal data out of the European Economic Area (EEA), we ensure similar protection and put in place at least one of these safeguards:

9. https://www.NEWSPAPER.com/help/privacy -policy (dostęp 28.08.2018).

- We will only transfer your personal data to countries that have been found to provide an adequate level of protection for personal data.
- We may also use specific approved contracts with our service providers that are based in countries outside the EEA. These contracts give your personal data the same protection it has in the EEA.
- Where we use service providers in the United States, we may transfer personal data to them if they are part of the Privacy Shield scheme, which requires them to provide a similar level of protection of your personal data to what is required in the EEA.

  If you are located in the EEA, you may contact us for a copy of the safeguards which we have put in place for the transfer of your personal data outside the EEA'

Such notice does not really say if data are exported or who receives them or where to look for documents constituting appropriate safeguards.

2.3.4 *Profiling? No, Making Automated Decisions Having Legal or Similar Effect*

If the decision-making process has been automated and decisions are made that have legal consequences or a similar effect (e.g., refusal to provide a service) on an individual and are made fully automatically (but even if applied by a human), including on the basis of profiling (Article 22 GDPR), the individual must be informed. The policy regarding those decisions and what lies behind the policy, or what effect this might have on the individual, have to be explained. The Article 29 Working Party Guidelines state that at the same time it is not possible to show only one side of the story[10] (i.e., not only benefits but also risks).

We discuss automated decision-making in a specific chapter below.

2.4 When to Notify and by What Means

The notification obligation regarding such a broad range of issues as those provided for in the GDPR may lead to practical and technical difficulties. This is due to the fact that it is simply not clear how and when the data subject should be provided with the complete set of information required so that on the one hand it is possible to demonstrate that this obligation has been complied with and that on the other it fulfils its fundamental task, which is to truly give individuals information about the processing of their data. This is why it is important to know, and have established in the company, by way of the appropriate procedures, who, when, and by what means provides information about data processing.

10. Article 29 Working Party, Guidelines on transparency under Regulations 2016/679 (WP260), http://ec.europa.eu/newsroom/just/document.cfm?doc_id=48850 (last accessed on 26 January 2018).

2.4.1 When to Notify

2.4.1.1 The Moment Data Are Obtained from an Individual

When data are obtained from an individual, the individual has to be informed at the time the data are obtained. In view of the volume of information to be provided, doing so by telephone may be a problem. This is discussed further in the section on availability.

2.4.1.2 Within One Month: Indirect Collection of Data

When data are obtained from other sources, an individual has to be informed as soon as possible: within one month or at the moment of the first contact, or when the data are disclosed to the recipient. Read literally, the provision suggests that the individual also has to be informed at once when the processor is provided with data, without waiting until the end of the one-month time limit. However, according to functional logic, a recipient referred to in Article 14(3)(c) GDPR is not a processor. Otherwise, any organisation which outsources their IT functions would have to inform immediately. Anyway, one month is not a long time anyway and so perhaps the problem is not such a practical one.

2.4.1.3 Updating Information

Where specific data covered by a notification obligation will change or have changed, the Article 29 Working Party states that an update is required. Active methods on the part of the controller (email, pop-up windows, banners, etc.) are preferable.

2.4.1.4 Informing Unidentified Persons (Article 11(2) GDPR)

Even if we do not know the identity of persons whose data we process, we should provide those persons with PIO, if this is possible. Situations of this kind do arise, for example processing data concerning traffic on a website, closed-circuit television, purchase of a pseudonymised marketing database from an entity that holds these contact details, geolocation, tracking, and geo-targeting in large-scale stores and elsewhere. The processing of 'unidentified' data is discussed in greater detail separately.

2.4.2 How to Notify

2.4.2.1 Transparency

Information must be provided in legible fashion. It is better to address the data subject on first-name terms in writing because this form is shorter and involves the least options. When speaking, however, more formal register is advised. Instead of 'the controller/the company' it is possible to write 'we'. The form used should be assertive and simple language, without legalese. From the point of view of legibility, providing information verbally is not the optimal solution. The 'Average Joe Test' can be applied (this is also recommended by the Article 29 Working Party).

A controller whose product or service is intended for children or popular among children faces a particular challenge. In its guidelines on transparency, the Article 29 Working Party states that it is not only controllers who have a product range aimed at children but also those who should be aware that their products or services are used by children in particular (e.g., a social networking site for brief film clips that disappear) that have an obligation to adapt a message to make it suitable for children. The same guidelines also state that the language in the UN Convention on the rights of the child in child-friendly language[11] can be used. In its guidelines on consent,[12] the Article 29 Working Party interprets Article 8 GDPR more narrowly, citing the controller's intent (that its website is not intentionally aimed at children, because the content is for adults, as it does not envisage revenue from children), but the same guidelines mention an age limit of 18, indicating that the architect of that section did not read, or read only superficially and quickly, Article 8 GDPR, as the age limit given in Article 8 is 16, not 18.

Where a product or service is aimed at or is popular among children, according to the Article 29 Working Party, a controller is required to ensure that messages are in a medium suitable for a child's level of perception. In practice, it may prove difficult to formulate a single version of notification clauses for both children and adults and devise a method for the correct selection of the 'clause'. This is a challenge faced, for example, by social networking sites and providers of content on demand.[13]

2.4.2.2 Availability

Information must be available.

It should be easy for an individual to notice information and reach for that information. The information must be placed in full view of the data subject (but not necessarily at once in its entirety) and in such a manner that it is not combined with other messages, for example marketing content. The Article 29 Working Party stated that a full set of information on a website may be no more than two clicks away from the home page and that the home page must contain a noticeable link.

If data is obtained by telephone, in line with the 'layered approach' we see no reason why an email cannot be sent during the conversation containing all of the information, or why a text message or other message cannot be sent containing a link

11. Convention on the rights of the child in child-friendly language, https://www.unicef.pl/content/download/11357/93111/file/konwencja_dla_dzieci.pdf (last accessed on 26 January 2018).
12. Article 29 Working Party, Guidelines on consent under Regulation 2016/679, adopted 28 November 2017 (WP259), http://www.giodo.gov.pl/pl/file/12955 (last accessed on 26 January 2018).
13. Content.

to the full set of information, provided that a data controller starts with telling why they are calling and identifies themselves, if the individual consents to use of that solution. An individual cannot be denied the provision of required information orally,[14] but leaving an individual with only this means of communication when executing the full information obligation would be counterproductive. Some organisations decided to make the whole information obligation their welcome message. This should be forbidden due to being a form of emotional abuse and brief imprisonment. Or, to be specific, it is against the requirement of facilitating the execution of data subject's rights (Article 12(2) GDPR). In reality such practice is intended to discourage clients and other interested parties from disturbing a data controller.

In line with the 'layered approach', Transparency Guidelines state that full information can be provided, for example, in a product user manual containing personal data, especially if it has a small screen or no screen (e.g., a patient's armband) or by posting a QR[15] code or links to websites, etc., where there are no other options.

2.4.2.3 Specificity

Information about the purposes of data processing, for example, must be specific. It is not sufficient to say that 'we use your data to develop new products, optimise services, for analyses, and to offer personalised services and products' (examples from the Transparency Guidelines). It has to be stated specifically for what purpose the data will be processed.

A more detailed describing what we are going to do with the data may sometimes be complicated, especially that it requires different organisational units to communicate with those responsible for privacy and data protection.

2.5 Exceptions to the Information Obligation (When Not to Inform about Processing)

Data subjects do not have to be informed of the processing elements required under the GDPR in the following cases:

(1) when the individual has already been informed. To give an example, a person decides to make use of a functionality requiring that a telephone number be given, for example authentication featuring two components. The Working Party encourages repeating the entire information every now and then as part of good practice. It is advisable however only to give supplementary information, with reference information about where the full set can be found. The Article 29 Working Party (European Data Protection Board) consistently

14. The Guidelines on transparency also mention, for example, redirecting an individual to an automated message system.
15. To be honest, QR codes seem to us risky. Where links at list allow to see how the web address looks like, a QR code is totally not transparent, allowing much room for cyber fraud.

disregards the extent of the information buzz to which we are subjected and proposes maximising rather than minimising communication;

(2) where this is not possible, for example, there are no contact details (although in such cases a general announcement can be posted on the website) or when we purchase video surveillance recordings to study pedestrian movement in a city;
(3) where this would require disproportionate effort (the Article 29 Working Party gives an example of a large volume of data concerning the distant past processed for archiving or historical research purposes in the public interest, when it is difficult to inform everyone because it is not known where letters should be sent and the risk to someone's rights or freedoms is minimal);
(4) where providing the information would prevent or put at serious risk the purpose of the processing (e.g., informing someone that their data are processed in order to detect money laundering would go against the purpose of processing, though this is usually regulated, or in compliance procedures passing an identity of a whistle-blower to a person they report);
(5) where provisions of law state detailed requirements for obtaining or disclosing information. This, for example, includes different court rules of procedure;
(6) where data are classified or subject to professional privilege under national or EU law (e.g., a lawyer does not have to inform the adverse party, the lawyer's client, or a witness that their personal data are processed).

3 RIGHT OF ACCESS TO DATA AND TO A COPY OF DATA (ARTICLE 15 GDPR)

3.1 Preliminary Remarks

Under **Article 15 GDPR**, a controller has an obligation to inform a data subject whether their personal data are processed, grant access to the personal data, and provide a large amount of information corresponding to the notification obligation when collecting data, and also release a copy of the data.

All of this has to be performed promptly and within no more than one month, or at least, within this time limit, a response must be given as to whether the individual's data are processed. The time limit for a full response may be extended by two months, and the reason for the extension must be given.

In functional terms, the right of access to data comprises the following elements:

(1) confirmation that the individual's data are or are not processed,
(2) providing a set of information corresponding to the PIO,
(3) granting access to the data,
(4) releasing a copy of the data.

3.2 Time Limits

Confirmation that the individual's data are or are not processed or refusal to act to execute the right of access to data must be given within one month of receipt of a request. Access must be granted and a copy of data released also within one month, but where necessary the time limit can be extended by a further two months. Notice of the extension must be given before the first time limit expires, with reasons for the postponement (e.g., the complex nature of the request, a queue to review files in an archive).

3.3 Types of Information

Where data are processed, an individual has to be provided with a set of the information that has to be provided when collecting data and that means:

(a) the purposes of the processing;
(b) the data categories;
(c) information about the recipients or categories of recipients;
(d) the envisaged period for which the data will be stored or the criteria used to determine that period;
(e) information about the right to have data erased or rectified, to have the processing restricted, or object to the processing;
(f) information about the right to lodge a complaint with a supervisory authority;
(g) available information about data sources;
(h) information about automated decision-making and profiling;
(i) information about transfer of data to a third country,[16] the safeguards in place in this regard, and of recipients in third countries.

3.4 Access

Access must be granted to data. This access can be provided by making files or a computer terminal available in an archive. Recital 63 GDPR states clearly that this can be done using 'remote access to a secure system', i.e. a kind of electronic self-service option. Solutions of this type are being opted for by companies that have tens of thousands of customers and that do not have the resources to manually operate a data access procedure, not to mention act within the 'statutory' time limits in such cases.

There is no reason not to release a copy of the data in execution of the right of access. The only practical problem is that the right of access *sensu stricto* is free of charge, while a fee may be charged for copies of data to cover the cost of the service (except the first).

16. Transfer of data outside of the EEA, i.e. third countries or international organisations.

3.5 Copy of Data

The first copy of data is free of charge. A fee may be charged for further copies which is 'a reasonable fee based on administrative costs'. The more detailed the calculation and reasons given for the fee, the easier it will be to submit supporting arguments to supervisory authorities and consumer protection authorities. Charging a fee for subsequent copies of data should reduce the number of excessive requests.

3.6 Request for More Specific Information

Under Recital 63 GDPR, a controller can request that the individual specify the activities to which the request relates. We analyse its implications a few paragraphs above when discussing excessive requests.

3.7 Refusal

Action to execute an individual's right of access or to copies of data can be refused where the request is excessive, for example where it requires action at unreasonable intervals (too often, to paraphrase Recital 63 GDPR). Release of copies of data should be refused or copies of data limited in cases where the release of certain data could result in breach of rights of others, as discussed below.

3.8 Rights of Others

The right to copies of data cannot have an adverse effect on the rights and freedoms of others. Release of copies of data must be refused therefore if they also include third-party data release of which would breach regulations; data concerning judicial, disciplinary, or criminal proceedings if release of the copies of data would disrupt those proceedings; information covered by exclusive rights – copyright, related rights, patents – if release of copies of data would breach these rights; information subject to professional privilege, trade secrets, or other legally protected secrets of a third party, if release of copies of these data would be a breach of those secrets.[17]

Of course, the problem arises of how the controller is supposed to determine that such circumstances exist and how it is supposed to be aware of the problem. In such a case, the solutions developed in application of the E-Commerce Directive[18] can be referred to, i.e. the notice and takedown procedure, which says that action must be taken when 'credible information' comes to light of a conflict of rights.

17. J. Łuczak [in:] *RODO. Ogólne rozporządzenie o ochronie danych. Komentarz*, ed. E. Bielak-Jomaa, D. Lubasz, Warsaw 2017, p. 513. Recital 63 GDPR, Recital 68 GDPR.
18. Directive 2000/31/EC of 8 June 2000 on certain legal aspects of information society services, in particular electronic commerce in the internal market (E-Commerce Directive) (Official Journal EC L 178, p. 1), modelled in turn on the US Digital Millennium Copyright Act.

It should be noted that the GDPR uses the phrase 'rights and freedoms of others', and not 'rights and freedoms of third parties'. Persons 'other' than the data subject might also be the controller. Therefore, GDPR recognises that certain rights of the controller also cannot justify rejection to accommodate the right to copies of data. In particular, a controller's trade secret can sometimes justify rejecting a request of a data copy.

When discussing the conflict between the rights of an individual and the 'rights and freedoms of others', it is hard not to make comparisons and enter the territory of the Act on Electronic Services, the E-Commerce Directive, and the Digital Millennium Copyright Act. Formally, the GDPR concerns only personal data, but in practice, this term can be very diluted and at times also cover content or other information that falls outside of the typical understanding of features of an individual. This is particularly evident in the context of the right of transfer of data, which was 'inserted' into the GDPR even though it originates from the discussion generally concerning the right of transfer of any kind of data and not personal data.[19]

GDPR provides a certain solution to such conflicting situations. According to Article 18 GDPR, data subject may request restricting of data processing. If a data controller rejects a data copy request based on 'rights of others' exception, a data controller may (and often should) offer instead to keep the requested data for a reasonable time allowing a data subject to initiate legal proceedings and make a court, the Police, or other authorised bodies to request such data from a controller as evidence.

3.9 Authentication and Communication

An important element of the process – as in the case of all rights of individuals – is determining the identity of the person making the enquiry.

The GDPR prefers communication with the person making the request by electronic means, and this method seems to be more efficient. This does not mean however that execution of a right requested, for example, by letter can be refused. Controllers have to determine for themselves how to ensure that every communication channel is convenient and credible. It only has to be remembered that authentication of the person making the request cannot be performed orally.

A copy of data can be released in various ways: on paper, in electronic form in formats that can be read by most users (this cannot be limited to closed formats, even the most popular; the most widely used will probably be PDF format).

3.10 Terms of Service and Procedures

Due to the number of variables, as well as formalities, it makes sense to adopt terms of service for execution of the right of access – or more broadly conditions for execution

19. In the European Commission Expert Group on Cloud Computing Contracts in 2014 I was Co-leader in work on the data portability right.

of data subjects rights in which a data subject's rights, the procedure whereby they are executed, the authentication requirements, and issues relating to third-party rights are laid down. It makes sense as well to draw up internal procedures for processing requests for access and copies of data and other rights.

As a feedback mechanism it makes sense to reconcile the Record of Processing Activities with findings from the processing of data subject rights.

3.11 Data Mapping, Data Mining, Ticketing Tools

Of course, the basis of execution of an individual's rights is good data mapping in an organisation, and in most organisations it is also having IT tools that can be used to execute particular requests that automate a process, facilitate financial settlement of the process, and also – and perhaps above all – facilitate retrieval of data.

3.12 Summary

Action to execute data subject rights might prove to be a major challenge for an organisation. This has to be well prepared for at the organisation at procedural, data mapping, technology, and legal levels. The right of access to data and copies of data will probably be the most commonly exercised right because it will be exercised at the same time as or before other rights requiring action on the part of the controller are exercised, and failure to observe an individual's rights can lead to a higher penalty.

Interestingly, a proper serving of the right to access and copy of data may lead to increased knowledge of a data controller about persons whose data it processes. Most organisations of any size tend to develop 'silos', which are internal departments or business lines. Those silos do not talk to each other that leads to problems with managing corporate know-how. In result, each silo has a fragmented knowledge about a particular person whose data it processes. In result, a data controller may have a number of unrelated 'client profiles' concerning the same person.

A smart data controller might use GDPR as an opportunity to increase internal knowledge about their clients, linking a process of serving subject access requests with customer relationship management processes and data wholesale solutions.

4 RIGHT TO RECTIFICATION OF DATA (ARTICLE 16 GDPR)

4.1 Preliminary Remarks

Formally speaking, the right to rectification of data is nothing new as it existed also under the Data Protection Directive.

Under Article 16 GDPR:

> A data subject is entitled to obtain from the controller without undue delay **[1]** the rectification of inaccurate personal data concerning him or her **[2]**. Taking into account the purposes of the processing, the data subject shall have the right to

have **[3]** incomplete personal data completed, including by means of providing a **[4]** supplementary statement.

In connection with the right to have data rectified, an individual essentially has two separate rights:

(1) to have inaccurate data rectified,
(2) to have incomplete data completed.

Rectification of data is one of the control mechanisms for the principle of data accuracy provided for in Article 5 GDPR.

4.2 General Issues: The Procedure for Authentication and Communication

As in the case of other rights of an individual, it is important to determine the manner in which the controller conducts authentication of an individual (this cannot be done orally), the channel of communication with that person, and the kinds of channels of communication it makes available (letter, proxy, electronic means, telephone, etc.). This topic is discussed mainly in the text on the execution of a data subject rights. Inaccurate data have to be rectified promptly once a request is made.

4.2.1 Contentious Element

A dispute may arise between the controller and the person making the request as to which data are accurate – the data in the controller's possession or the data provided by the person making the request. It cannot be ruled out that a particular person making a request will wish to exercise the right to have data rectified in order to mislead the controller. At the same time, an inflexible approach to evaluating the credibility of the data being rectified could have serious consequences for the person making the request or that person's relationship with the controller. The controller needs to consider implementing an internal procedure for resolving disputes concerning rectification (it can be called the escalation or complaint review procedure).

The first example that comes to our mind in relation to data accuracy is a delivery address. A wrong delivery address may result in severe negative consequences for a data subject (and in result for a data controller) starting from a personal data breach by mere delivering of a correspondence to a wrong addressee. For example, if an energy provider inaccurately delivers bills to an address of residence of a husband instead of the address indicated for delivery, a wife may learn that her husband rents another apartment, drawing conclusions from that fact.

4.2.2 Right to Lodge a Complaint

When processing the right to have data rectified, the data controller should be prepared for a dispute with the person making the request.

4.2.3 *Style*

The emotional factor on the part of the person making the request (and to some extent on the part of a data controller's personnel who will be responsible for executing the requests) might play an important role in managing data subject satisfaction and therefore decreasing costs of compliance related to serving data subjects complaints to supervisory authorities. The style in which we approach data subject's requests can have a major impact on both the organisation's reputation and the risk of penalties and in fact the actual costs and burdens connected with executing an individual's rights.

4.2.4 *Demonstrating That Data Are Inaccurate*

The simplest approach to rectify inaccurate data is to rely on the same type of evidence as that received when collecting the data, allowing of course for a separate judgment in special circumstances.

A recourse to a decision of 'somebody knowledgeable and empowered' is also required in the case of automated processing. In fact, the right to human decision-making may coincide with the right to have data rectified, for example in the typical situation in which the error relates to data that have been authenticated. The above means that popular sites such as Facebook or PayPal or any other information society service or just any service must have the capacity for recovery of lost identity, i.e. access to a profile, through contact with a human being.

4.2.5 *Outdated or Inaccurate Data*

Data being out of date will probably not mean that the data are completely inaccurate. The question of whether data that are out of date have to be erased under the rectification procedure, or whether up-to-date data have to be added, and the previous data considered archived data, is determined by the context and the purpose of the personal data processing.

4.2.6 *The Scope of Correction of Data*

Rectification of data rises problems similar to those related to erasing data: should the data in backup copies or archive copies or only data in 'production' systems be rectified? The answer seems to be in the function of the right to rectification. This is not a question of erasing data but using accurate data and making sure mistakes do not recur (mistakes can exist for many years and be very troublesome, for example when identity is changed by mistake). It is therefore important to devise a mechanism ensuring that production data (data the organisation uses in its day-to-day operations) remain up-to-date. This should mean correcting production data, ensuring that a correction mechanism is in place and updating data recovered from backup copies, as well as a mechanism or procedure for alignment of archived data with the corrected data, for example records of corrected data. This shows that once again it is possible to get lost in the details and variations of problems, especially in a large organisation.

4.3 Completing Incomplete Data

Completing incomplete data means, for instance, adding a mobile telephone number or email address, or residential address to a customer's profile or adding an address for delivery, or adding any other information about an individual, provided that the information is necessary from the point of view of the purpose of data processing.

4.3.1 Adequacy of Data

A controller is not required to collect all information about an individual, and in fact this would be contrary to the principles of purpose limitation and minimisation(Article 5(1)(b) and 5(1)(c) GDPR). For this reason, only the types of data that are useful for data processing purposes may be completed.

4.3.2 Basis for Updating

Under Article 16 GDPR second sentence, the person making the request can base completion of incomplete data on their own declaration ('supplementary statement'), taking into consideration the purposes of data processing. Data are frequently collected on the basis of a declaration, and therefore completion of data in this way should be possible. It is important meanwhile to consider the purpose of the processing when determining the permitted bases for updating data. In this case as well, the principle of proportionality is particularly important. Methods of authentication by telephone employed by banks often had the drawback of the possibility of a customer's identity being falsely assumed. If someone changes the contact details by this means on the basis of a declaration, this could lead to identity theft. At the moment, organisations deal with this issue through authentication and confirmation through multiple channels (logging in, changing one's details, and receipt of information about the change using the old and the new data).

Having said the above, it is still not clear to us why a specific rule has been enacted to confirm a data subject's and controller's right to rely on 'a supplementary statement' of a data subject 'taking into account the purposes of the processing'. It looks like the same conclusions ('you may rely on a statement but not always') result from general risk-based approach required by the GDPR (in particular Article 24 and Article 32 GDPR). In any case, good reasons must be given for refusal to act on a declaration made by the person making the request. It makes sense to establish an internal appeal procedure apart from a duty to inform about a right to complain to a supervisory authority and include in the terms of service – or more generally in the terms of execution of an individual's rights – a description of the procedure concerning the right to rectify data.

4.4 Information Obligations

Finally, the controller has to remember the obligation provided for in Article 19 GDPR, under which a controller is required to inform each recipient to whom personal data have been disclosed about the rectification of data according to the procedure laid down in that provision unless this proves impossible or involves a disproportionate effort. The controller also has an obligation to inform the person making the request of the recipients with whom they provided the rectified data if the data subject makes such a request.

Article 19 GDPR provides for an obligation of a special nature to 'track' data – the controller is expected to know whom the data were disclosed to so that information can be provided about the rectification and so that the person making the request can be informed about who received the inaccurate or incomplete data.

Again the question arises of who in this case is 'recipient' of data. It seems that the term 'recipient' is used inconsistently in the GDPR (like most of the basic terms). The definition of a recipient suggests that it also includes the processor. The Belgian Commission de Protection de la Vie Privée takes the view that persons close to and advisors of the data subject, and the individual themselves, are also recipients. Informing a controller's own processors that the data have been rectified is like informing oneself, and informing the data subject serves no purpose (although formally this occurs in connection with the notification that the request has been accepted). For this reason, we believe that, in the meaning of Article 19 GDPR, 'recipients' means organisations that have been provided with data on a C2C basis or similar basis, for example controller to relatives of the data subject.

Interestingly, a definition of 'recipient' excludes a public authority to which the data were submitted under 'a particular enquiry' as part of that authority's proceedings (e.g., the Police during an investigation). To be formally consistent with the definition of 'data recipient', a data controller would not have to inform the police (or other public authority) about rectifying previously disclosed data. That is why we say, do not embed contract clauses in definitions because you will get to illogical results. Another argument supporting the view that a processor is not 'a recipient' in the meaning of Article 19 GDPR is that disclosing the specific identity of a data controller's suppliers would breach the controller's trade secret. Any other interpretation of Article 19 GDPR would open the way to requests for disclosure of the controller's supply chain. There is no functional justification for this, and no systemic or literal interpretation leads to any coherent conclusions. Specifically, neither Article 13 nor 14 GDPR requires disclosing processors' identity (except for extra EU data transfers based on 'suitable safeguards', e.g. EU model clauses, where disclosing the recipient's identity seems necessary as a part of describing specific 'suitable safeguards').

5 THE RIGHT TO ERASURE (RIGHT TO BE FORGOTTEN) (ARTICLE 17 GDPR)

5.1 History of the Right to Be Forgotten

The right to be forgotten introduced by the GDPR is not a completely new institution. It should be treated as a development and clarification of the current legal status and the case law of the CJEU. However, the new regulation needs to be carefully examined. It imposes far-reaching obligations on data controllers which will require insightful consideration, especially in terms of the technical aspects of implementing solutions that enable individuals to exercise their rights.

The Data Protection Directive (replaced by the GDPR), mentions the right to request the deletion of data not processed in accordance with the provisions of the Directive, especially due to incompleteness or inaccuracy of the data (Article 12 b of the Directive).

The most famous judgment of the CJEU regarding the right to be forgotten is the judgment of 13.05.14, C-131/12, Google Spain SL and Google Inc. vs. Agencia Española de Protección de Datos (AEPD) and Mario Costeja González, EU:C:2014:317. In this case, the Court examined the question of the processing of personal data by the internet search engine in the context of search capabilities based on the name of a given person. The Tribunal decided that the search engine operator should be considered as the data controller, and the data subject may request the discontinuation of processing so that the information in question would no longer be visible to searchers. The Tribunal derives this right from Articles 7 and 8 of the EU Charter of Fundamental Rights (OJ EU C 202, 2016, p. 389) – the right to respect for private and family life, home, and communication and the right to the protection of personal data. The wording: **'so that the information is no longer visible' reflects the functional meaning of the right to delete data.**

5.2 Principles of the Right to Be Forgotten

According to Article 17 GDPR, a person may request that a data controller immediately deletes data relating to them. The controller is obliged to:

(1) delete the data;
(2) if they have transferred the data to other recipients, they must inform the recipients about the deletion (Article 19 GDPR);
(3) if they have made public the data requiring deletion (especially online), they must request that other controllers who process this data also delete it, remove links to it, etc. and should take 'reasonable measures, including technical measures' towards this goal;
(4) at the request of the data subject, they must inform the data subject which recipients the data requiring deletion was transferred to.

5.3 Basis for Requesting the Deletion of Data

The data subject may request that their data be deleted by the controller in cases where:

(1) the data is no longer necessary for the purposes for which it was collected or otherwise processed;
(2) the data subject withdraws consent to the processing of their personal data, and there is no other legal basis for processing;
(3) the data subject objects to the processing of their data, and there are no overriding legal grounds for processing (Article 21 (1) GDPR), or they object to the processing of their data for direct marketing purposes;
(4) the data has been processed illegally;
(5) the data must be deleted in order to comply with a legal obligation stipulated by EU law or the law of the Member State governing the controller's activities;
(6) personal data has been collected in connection with offering information society services directly to children.

5.3.1 Necessity for the Purposes of Processing

The GDPR imposes the ability to request the deletion of data when this data is no longer necessary for the purpose for which it was collected or otherwise processed.

This requires the interpretation of the principle of purpose. For example, when data is no longer useful for performing a contract because the contract has already been executed, it will still be useful 'in case of claims' until the expiry of the limitation period. Therefore, the expiration of the primary purpose of data processing does not necessarily mean that the data has become unnecessary. The person requesting the deletion of their data has the right not to know this. Essentially, it is up to the controller to 'do their homework in assessing the life cycle' and usefulness of personal data by implementing the GDPR. The ability to request the deletion of data when it is no longer useful is a supplement to the principle of minimising the processing time of personal data (time restriction, retention).

5.3.2 Withdrawing Consent

A data subject may request the deletion of their data after withdrawing consent for its processing, provided there is no other legal ground for processing. As in the case of the purpose for which the data was collected no longer being relevant, this data should also be deleted on the controller's own initiative. Data processing may take place only in accordance with one of the legal grounds provided by the GDPR, so the lack of any such basis should be considered as exempting the possibility of further processing. A deletion request issued after the withdrawal of consent, or at the same time as withdrawal, should also be treated as an additional obligation of the controller.

Practical problems may arise when there is an alternative legal basis for data processing and consent has been withdrawn. To avoid ambiguity, the controller should clearly identify the legal basis for processing the data (e.g., it is a common mistake to request consent to process data when the data is needed to conclude or perform a contract), as well as the data life cycle and possible scenarios for its use.

Now let us make an observation that when processing took place based on consent (e.g., marketing communications were sent) data should be deleted from consent databases (a marketing database), but we believe the controller is not obliged to delete such communications or the initial consent from the data controller's systems as they serve to prove the legitimacy of such communications (principle of accountability). The legal basis for processing would be the controller's legitimate interest (Article 6(1)(f) GDPR).

5.3.3 *Objecting to Processing Data*

The controller is obliged to delete the data of a person who executes their right to object to the processing of their data. The right to object is discussed separately. This topic is quite complicated in itself, so it cannot be covered in full here, but we can give an example. Objecting to direct marketing does not require any justification. Therefore, if a person objects to direct marketing and requests the deletion of their data, their demand must be met. This example seems to be simple, but in reality it is not. In reality, the situation is identical to that described in a preceding paragraph concerning a withdrawal of a consent. A data controller is obliged to delete an objecting person's contact data from the data controller's marketing database but not to delete communications preceding filing an objection to processing. Moreover, if the data subject is at the same time the data controller's client, the data controller will not delete the contact details of that data subject from the data controller's CRM, but instead an objection to direct marketing has to be registered in the CRM system or otherwise if the CRM does not have such functionality.[20] As in the cases discussed so far, the obligation to delete data actually results from other regulations of the GDPR, so this provision should be treated as a supplement and, in principle, a description of the effects of objecting data processing.

5.3.4 *Illegal Processing*

The processing of personal data in accordance with the law is the guiding principle of data processing (legality). The failure to adapt data processing within the organisation to the requirements of the GDPR may lead to serious consequences – especially financial – for the controller.

If the controller refuses a request to delete data on claiming the processing is legal, it is likely that they will come into conflict with the data subject. The controller

20. If a CRM system does not support the right to object then it is time to think about upgrading to a CRM system supporting data subject's rights and other GDPR functionalities (if only such systems existed of course).

should be prepared for this eventuality and take into account the need to defend their position.

The burden of proving the legality of processing by demonstrating compliance with the requirements imposed by the GDPR lies with the controller, so the processes of data processing should be clear enough to be able to demonstrate the appropriateness of processing relatively easily. Data processing should be constantly monitored by the controller so that any irregularities can be detected immediately, and the controller should always be ready to demonstrate the legal compliance of the processing. Probably the best tool to map and monitor business processes involving data processing is an RDPA in most cases required anyway by Article 30 GDPR.

5.3.5 *Legal Obligation to Delete Data*

A request to delete data can also be made when the controller is faced with a direct legal obligation to delete it resulting from EU law or national law.

5.3.6 *Offering Information Society Services to Children*

One of the intentions of the GDPR is to facilitate the deletion of data posted by children online. Requesting the deletion of data makes it possible to 'fix' decisions taken during childhood. The GDPR has stricter requirements when it comes to the ability to process the personal data of children in terms of the use of information society services.

As set out in Recital 65 GDPR, even if the data subject is no longer a child, they have the right to request at any time the deletion of data they shared as a child.

5.4 Exceptions

The GDPR stipulates a number of exceptions which exempt the controller from having to comply with the right to be forgotten. Data does not have to be deleted if the processing is necessary for any of the following reasons:

(1) to exercise the right to freedom of expression and information;
(2) to comply with a legal obligation that requires the processing or performance of a task carried out in the public interest or in relation to public authority entrusted to the controller – the source of the legal obligation may be the law of the EU or the Member State governing the controller's activities;
(3) due to the public interest in the field of public health;
(4) for archival purposes in the public interest, for scientific or historical research purposes, or for statistical purposes;
(5) to establish, investigate, or defend claims.

5.4.1 Exercising the Right to Freedom of Expression and Information

This exception acknowledges the possibility of conflict between the rights of the individual regarding their data and the right to freedom of expression and information, which also belongs to the catalogue of fundamental freedoms described in the Charter of Fundamental Rights. The right to freedom of expression and information includes the right to obtain and transmit information.

When citing this exception, we need to take a balanced look at how these values clash in the case in point. Guidance comes from the above-mentioned judgment C-131/12, Google Spain, in which the Court noted that the removal of links to certain information might cause conflict with the interests of internet users trying to access this information. The interests of internet users may be strengthened, for example, by the data subject playing a particular role in public life (judgment C-131/12, Google Spain, point 81).

When refusing to delete data on the basis of this exception, the controller should not only consider the opposing interests but also justify their position in detail. The press will usually rely on this exception, though in most cases probably the Member States enacted specific provisions of their national laws to deal with a conflict of interest between the right to privacy and the freedom of expression and information.

5.4.2 Complying with Legal Obligations or Tasks Carried Out in the Public Interest or Due to Exercising Public Authority

Complying with the law or performing a task carried out in the public interest or exercising of official authority vested in the controller overrides the right to erasure.

The legal obligations regarding the processing of personal data will result from various provisions (e.g., the creation of medical records, employers keeping personal files), depending on the type of business. It is the responsibility of the controller to be familiar with these regulations and to keep track of any changes that may have consequences for the processing of personal data.

5.4.3 Public Interest in Protecting Public Health

The exception of public interest in the protection of public health may be invoked by a controller who processes data necessary for the purposes of preventive health or occupational medicine, to assess an employee's ability to work, for medical diagnosis, the provision of healthcare or social security, the treatment or management of healthcare systems and services or social security under the law of the EU or a Member State, or in accordance with a contract with a healthcare professional, provided this data is processed by a person obliged to observe professional confidentiality – in this case, doctor–patient confidentiality, nurse–patient confidentiality, etc.

In addition, the controller may refuse to delete data if its processing is necessary for reasons related to public interest in the field of public health – for example, protection against serious cross-border health threats, or ensuring high standards of quality and safety for healthcare, health products and medical devices.

This exception should be treated as an 'industry' exception, applicable to the medical and pharmaceutical sectors. In addition, the possibility of its use is limited by the issue of the existence of public interest in relation to the processing of data. The public health exception is sometimes abused in some countries as pharmaceutical and healthcare sectors are heavily lobbed.

5.4.4 *Archival Purposes, Scientific and Historical Research, Statistical Purposes*

Processing for these purposes may take place if it meets the conditions stipulated in Article 89 the GDPR. This means that such processing must be subject to the appropriate safeguards of the rights and freedoms of the data subject. These safeguards should involve the implementation of suitable technical and organisational measures to ensure that the principle of data minimisation is respected.

The wording of the provision indicates that the controller may invoke this exception if the processing complies with the terms of Article 89 and, at the same time, if exercising the right to be forgotten will prevent or seriously hinder the realisation of the goals of this processing.

The means by which the requirements of Article 89 GDPR can be met include: securing IT systems where data is located or processed, authorising access for people conducting research, and signing confidentiality agreements with people involved in the processing. The choice of resources should depend on the type of activities carried out. For example, if the data is used to extract statistics that refer exclusively to current trends within a certain group of people, without publishing their identities, then the controller should take measures to ensure that the identities of the people whose behaviour was studied do not become widely known.

5.4.5 *Establishing, Investigating, and Defending Claims*

This exception will apply mainly in cases where there are outstanding debts or other dispute proceedings between the controller and the data subject. It will allow the controller to pursue their claims pending the termination of enforcement of the obligation imposed on the data subject relative to the controller – for example, against a former client. This exception also allows for storing data for defensive purposes. When combined with the accountability principle it could actually lead a conclusion that storing data up to prescription deadlines which in some countries is up to twenty years (in relation to claims resulting from crimes) is justified. Of course, when further combined with the risk-based approach, the data controller might perform a risk assessment to counterweight risks resulting from storing data for a longer time (data breach mainly) against risks resulting from earlier deletion of data (mainly deletion of evidence). A practical issue most of the controllers encounter is though how to separate data outdated from 'usable data'. Dealing with the latter requires adopting the privacy by design approach and redesigning a data storage logic and systems which is a major challenge to any organisation.

5.5 Scope of Data Deletion

The controller should immediately delete data for which a valid request for deletion is received. This applies to all places where the data of the person exercising their right to be forgotten is located. This usually means the servers used by the controller, including email servers (though an exception from Article 11 GDPR may apply), documents in the organisation's resources, and contact details – both digitised and paper copies. The data should be deleted in such a way as to exclude any access to it in the future, especially access that enables the identification of the data subject. One of the proposed ways of deleting personal data from paper copies is blacking out the relevant data in paper documents and replacing identification data with meaningless data in computer databases entries (to avoid decomposing of a database).

However, we should keep in mind the basic issues that can be determined by residual or technical purposes of data processing, particularly two of them:

(1) processing data in order to implement the right to be forgotten and the right to delete data,
(2) processing data in order to ensure data security (which according to the Recital 49 GDPR constitutes a legitimate interest of the controller).

We should also be aware that deleting data in a way that is understood explicitly as completely forgetting about the data and the person goes against the principle of accountability. In the field of accounting, where the principle of accountability prevails, there is no such thing as deleting data. There is only the addition of a negative state (contra entry, red-ink entry).[21] The question of how to effectively achieve the purpose of the right to delete data without exposing all personal data to an unacceptable level of risk forms the axis of the problem and the dispute over the right to delete data.

Another area of potential conflict is unstructured data (Article 11 GDPR). As a rule, the controller is not required to search all of their information resources to find and delete data. Where the controller does not know the identity of the people whose data is being processed (including the content of the data being processed), it is generally not necessary to search this kind of unstructured data only to erase the data of the person requesting the data deletion.

21. According to Wikipedia, a contra entry (reversing entry) is an entry cancelling an erroneous accounting operation, a way of correcting accounting errors by removing their impact on the final balance of the account, and in some cases also on the turnover. This means that the erroneous entry is not deleted (based on the double-entry rule).

5.6 Processing in Order to Exercise the Right to Delete Data and the Right to Be Forgotten

The implementation of the right to be forgotten should be documented in case of a potential dispute and to facilitate accountability. This makes it hard to imagine the complete erasure of a person from a company's memory. In this case, like the lead singer of Chumbawamba's hit song Amnesia, we would not remember whether we were meant to forget something.[22]

From a functional perspective, the right to be forgotten serves to ensure that a company or other organisation does not perform certain activities with regards to the concerned party or does not spread certain information about them. Erasing information from a company's systems does not protect us completely from the company 'assimilating' this information again, in particular when information is exchanged between different controllers (hence the obligation to inform other controllers about the deletion). Therefore, it is possible that, in addition to deleting all information from the company's 'production' systems and resources, it will be necessary to add the person to a list of exceptions (people whose data is subject to processing restrictions), such as a Robinson list (people who do not wish to be contacted, etc.). Moreover, different business units may collect deleted and then 'prohibited' data separately, so there need to be a mechanism in place allowing to identify data 'forgotten'. Specialists point to a mathematical hashing function as a method of marking specific data without knowing their contents. Theoretically, that can be used to recognise and ban data forgotten in result of a specific data subject request. However such solutions need to be developed to achieve market maturity; their developing probably will not be cheap, and they will not be error-free, especially taken into consideration variations of the natural language and required multilanguage capabilities.

5.7 Processing to Ensure Security: Backup and Archive Problems

5.7.1 *Everything Means Everything*

The supervisory authorities take the position that everything should be deleted, including backup copies and archives.[23] The UK Information Commissioners Office as well as the Polish Ministry of Digitalisation recommend to delete data from backups and logs, by manually 'reheating' the backup, deleting the data and then 'refreezing' the copy. We do not advocate this approach if backups are made on magnetic tape. It might make sense if online storage is used for backup.

22. The song's chorus goes: 'Do you suffer from long-term memory loss? I don't remember.'
23. Likewise, the NSA judgment of 03.07.09, I OSK 633/08, LEX No 552323.

5.7.2 *The Problem of Security and Business Continuity*

Deleting or changing individual data from a backup copy deprives the copy of integrity, may impede or prevent its subsequent reproduction, and thus compromises the security of the information. It increases the threat to the integrity and availability of all personal data in the backup. Therefore, deleting data from backups as a rule contradicts the data security principle.

5.7.3 *The Problem of Accountability*

In fact, tampering with backup copies generates a problem with accountability, hinders or prevents the use of the copy as evidence, and opens up routes to abuse.

5.7.4 *Practical Problems: Resources and Processes*

Single or multiple interferences with backup copies can be difficult to handle from a resource and backup process perspective. The concept of 'rewriting' backups creates an organisational problem.

Example

Let us assume that a small company has five critical systems that process personal data and a backup policy as follows: seven daily copies and fifty-two weekly copies, giving a total of fifty-nine backup copies for each system. Personal data which was subject to deletion resided for a year in three of the systems subject to this backup policy. In this situation, it was necessary to launch the copy, make the changes, recopy and verify (restart) for 177 data carriers. If the act of modifying one backup copy took one computer technician 3 hours for each copy of data, we get 531 man-hours – that is, three months of work for one person (one man-month = 176 man-hours), or one month of work for one computer technician for each IT system. In addition, there is the issue of the infrastructure within which you can run a backup to change its content. Of course, the technicians are able to check the input data and change the parameters, but it is doubtful that this would lower our estimates. To make it more difficult, three of these five systems can actually be outsourced – operated by an external provider or even located in the cloud.

In theory, it is possible to imagine the development of this process. However, this will generate significant costs, and – even worse – in the long run, it will lead to the centralisation of personal data processing, therefore increasing the threat to privacy.[24]

5.7.5 *The Solution*

The rationale, terms, and scope of data deletion can be reconciled at the level of the GDPR with information security and common sense:

(1) in principle, the obligation to delete data is limited by the existence of a different processing basis or a balance of interests; even in the case of the obligation to delete data which has been processed illegally, this cannot be understood as an encouragement to destroy evidence;
(2) the security of information (personal data) processed by the controller as a legitimate interest of the controller is a good basis for the processing of personal data;
(3) data to be deleted should be removed from the production systems (systems for running the business);
(4) if, due to complications or for some other reason, deleting data from backups would threaten data security, a procedure should be introduced to force the re-deletion of the relevant data from the production systems when using a backup (restoring data/a system from a backup); to this end, an appropriate list (register) of exceptions should be kept, including a description of data which is subject to deletion or rectifying (e.g., by stating only a specific category of data which cannot be processed).

There are technical possibilities for appropriate re-deletion without coming into contact with the content of the data to be deleted. The record subject to deletion (which can also be done by overwriting with generic data, if we use some kind of anonymisation to delete the personal data) can be marked with a unique identifier. Then, when performing the original deletion, all you have to do is record the ID on the exceptions list and, if you restore the backup, automatically delete or overwrite the identified data with the original replacement content. Companies to which we have recommended this approach have highlighted the option of using a compound key. This may consist, for example, of the system ID and the client's personal ID number. As a result, if necessary, we are able to reach and identify the data in the backup so that it can be automatically deleted on the restored copy. If the system will not mark a record with a unique identifier by itself, you can use a different method of identifying the 'forbidden' content, such as a checksum.

24. A careful observer will notice that the huge volume of obligations flowing from the GDPR generally encourage the centralisation of personal data processing, which in turn increases and generates systemic risks to privacy.

5.8 The Problem of Unstructured Data

The right to delete data creates another problem of interpretation, which can be seen when compared to a stance of the Polish Ministry of Digitization: 'The controller must ensure appropriate technical and organizational measures enabling the complete deletion of the data of a person who is exercising the right to be forgotten. It is necessary to delete the data from all places, including: servers, email, Word and Excel files, external and portable disks, and paper copies. The storage of the data by the controller alone still qualifies as personal data processing.'[25]

The Ministry refers to the necessity of also deleting the personal data of specific people from resources where the content is not really known – that is, from resources containing unstructured data (e.g., the content of emails and Word files). However, according to Article 11 GDPR, we do not need to implement the rights of an individual with respect to these resources until the data subject identifies themselves.

On receiving a data deletion request from Joe Bloggs, do we need to search all our resources, check through emails, documents, and so on, to determine all the places where he may have been mentioned and from where he will have to be erased? There is no clear answer at present. A literal interpretation of the GDPR would indicate that we actually need to delete all information about Joe Bloggs from our systems and therefore from emails, as well as from content developed by us or located in our documentary check. Does this mean that we need to change the content of previously written documents or delete them? Do we have to search all our information resources to identify occurrences of Joe Bloggs' data and erase them completely?

It seems that the scope of data deletion is limited to the data in relation to which Joe Bloggs identifies himself – it is not enough simply to present himself; he must also indicate the data (information resources) where he might appear. However, this is not a trivial interpretation, and it requires some deliberation.

Another problem – once Joe Bloggs has defined the scope of the data, we need to try to resolve the issue of deleting it from our documents on the grounds of the data processing purposes.

Example

In a divorce case, a wife threatens to provide evidence that her husband is an alcoholic. The parties come to an agreement, the divorce is conciliatory, a civil settlement is reached out of court, and as part of the arrangements, the wife confirms the husband's moral standing. The husband then applies to his wife's lawyer with a request for the deletion of his personal data indicating that he is allegedly an alcoholic. Will the lawyer anonymise or delete the reports written for the wife?

25. Ministry of Digitization, *The GDPR – an information source*, p. 6, https://www.gov.pl/cyfryzacja/rodo-informator (last accessed on 8 March 2018).

We could probably find a good basis for our lawyer's data processing (e.g., overriding legitimate grounds), but this is the kind of dilemma we face after GDPR.

5.9 Informing Other Controllers

According to Article 17(2) GDPR if the controller 'make published' the data which should be erased, the controller should inform controllers which are processing data subject to erasure about the request to erase the data made by the data subject, taking account of available technology and the cost of implementation, shall take reasonable steps, including technical measures. These are mostly quotations from the letter of law, which we repeat here as they require a few words of explanation.

The duty to inform other controllers in case data subject to erasure were published (made public) by the controller overlaps with the general duty to inform recipients of data about that fact that they were erased in result of application of the right to erasure provided by Article 19 GDPR. That duty applies to every recipient of data to whom the personal data have been disclosed unless this proves impossible or involves a disproportionate effort. Article 17(2) GDPR concerns specifically data published (e.g., in the internet, social media) and should be understood as making it clear that not knowing who actually reached to the data subject to erasure does not relieve the data subject from taking steps aimed at 'withdrawing' the erased data from the public space.

Reasonable steps to inform other data controllers about erasing the data previously 'made public' can be, for example, announcing it on the website where they were first published and directly notifying those who can be traced to delete all links, copies, and replications of this data. The data controller should approach that duty in a sensible manner, in particular consulting the way of acting with the data subject, in order not to achieve unintended results (e.g., the data subject might not be interested in publishing an announcement referring to incorrect data).

Based on Article 19 GDPR, the data controller is also obliged to notify the data subject about recipients of deleted data, should the data subject requests. We discuss understanding the notion of 'data recipient' in the context of Article 19 and how to comply with duties to notify in a relevant chapter below.

5.10 Limitation of the Obligation to Inform

This obligation is subject to the following restrictions:

(1) available technology;
(2) cost of implementation;
(3) actions limited to reasonable actions.

In short: you should do what is possible, and not disproportionately expensive, under the circumstances to inform everyone who should know that the data has been deleted.

5.11 Checklists

5.11.1 Preparing for the GDPR: Implementing the Right to Be Forgotten Within the Organisation

- Identify places where our organisation is keeping personal data.
- Understand how our organisation processes data and how our employees use this data.
- Set up a procedure for the data deletion process; appoint people to be responsible for verifying and handling requests.
- Train employees.
- Consider how the controller will be able to demonstrate the deletion of data once it has been deleted.
- Implement technical measures to facilitate data deletion.

5.11.2 Processing Requests for the Deletion of Data

(1) Receive the request.
(2) Authenticate the person making the request.
(3) Analyse whether the controller can invoke one of the exceptions:
  - YES – the person who made the request should receive a justification explaining why the controller is invoking the exception,
  - NO – see next steps.
(4) Carry out an inventory of data held – it is worth blocking the internal use of data at this stage so that it is not subject to further processing.
(5) Delete the data to the greatest extent possible.
(6) Inform other controllers about the need to delete the data.
(7) Inform the data subject about the deletion.
(8) Inform the data subject about recipients of the data, if they have requested to be informed.

The above checklists should be treated purely as examples and indications of what directions to take. When planning activities, the controller should take into account the specific operating conditions.

6 RIGHT TO RESTRICTION OF PROCESSING (ARTICLE 18 GDPR)

6.1 Restriction of Processing

According to the definition given in Article 4(3) GDPR, the term 'restriction of processing' means 'the marking of stored personal data with the aim of limiting their processing in the future'. Of course this is not the complete definition. The missing element can be found in Article 18(2) GDPR:

> Where processing of data has been restricted, such personal data shall, with the exception of storage, only be processed with the data subject's consent or for the establishment, exercise or defence of legal claims or for the protection of the rights of another natural or legal person or for reasons of important public interest of the Union or of a member state.

As a result of restriction of processing, a controller can hold (store) data and only perform those operations (i) where the data subject has given consent, (ii) where the data are necessary for disputes or to protect another person's or organisation's rights, and (iii) where there is an important public interest.

6.2 Right to Restriction of Processing

Under Article 18(1) GDPR, an individual can demand the restriction of processing of data concerning him/her in the following situations:

(a) the accuracy of the personal data is contested by the data subject – for a period enabling the controller to verify the accuracy of the personal data;
(b) the processing is unlawful, and the data subject opposes the erasure of the personal data and requests the restriction of their use instead;
(c) the controller no longer needs the personal data for the purposes of the processing, but they are required by the data subject for the establishment, exercise, or defence of legal claims;
(d) the data subject has objected to processing pursuant to Article 21(1) GDPR pending the verification of whether the controller has legitimate grounds and whether those grounds override those of the data subject.

The right to request the restriction of data processing means that a boundary can be drawn between the disputed data processing (dispute concerning accuracy of data, restriction of use of data, dispute over legitimacy of the objection to processing) and the areas about which there is no conflict between the data subject and the controller. It also enables the data subject to retain evidence for court proceedings.

The right to restriction of processing is a kind of a temporary measure helping to execute other rights of the data subject. If the data subject demands to restrict processing of data, initially the data controller should comply – for the time required to process a particular underlying demand or for a longer period of time if the data subject demands the preservation of evidence (Article 18(1)(c) GDPR).

6.2.1 *Restriction in the Case of a Dispute Concerning Accuracy*

Where a dispute arises, the controller can probably no longer present the data subject with the option of 'all or nothing'. If the individual requests restriction of processing of their data, the controller can only perform those operations that are not a subject of dispute between the parties.

Example

A telecommunications operator is mistakenly seeking recovery of outstanding payments from the wrong John Smith (unlawful processing/inaccuracy of data) and is threatening to disconnect his telephone. Mr Smith can refer to restriction of processing to defend against mistaken debt recovery or to have it postponed (he does not have to take court action straightaway) and can continue to make calls, in the expectation that in the meantime the debt recovery department will resolve the issues with the subscription department.

6.2.2 Restriction in Cases of Unlawful Processing

In cases of unlawful processing, the controller is required to cease the processing and erase the data. The data subject might, however, be considering, for example, making use of the controller's services and prefers the controller to have the data but not perform any operations on the data for the time being. The data subject might also prefer to exercise the right of data restriction rather than erasure, especially if the controller completely erases the data and then starts processing the data again because it has forgotten that it erased the data. According to this logic, the data subject prefers the controller to have certain data concerning the data subject in its systems merely so that the data is marked in red as 'do not touch' (so-called Robinson lists).

6.2.3 Restriction for the Purpose of Legal Claims

Data may serve as evidence. In such a case, the data subject may request that the controller retain the data (even if, and especially if the data are needed for a dispute with the controller) even if the controller no longer needs the data (and in fact would rather dispose of the data).

In case a car is left at a monitored parking of a shopping mall and then found damaged, the driver may demand the shopping mall to hand over a video recording of a situation. If the shopping mall is afraid of handing over the recording directly to the driver because there are other people's personal data, the shopping mall may suggest the driver to use the right to restriction of data to request the shopping mall to keep the recording for the police.

6.2.4 *Restriction in the Case of Objection Due to a Special Situation*

Objecting (Article 21(1) GDPR) to processing someone's data due to the special situation of that person (the data subject) which overrides the legitimate grounds for the controller to process data leads directly to a dispute with the data controller.

> **Example**
>
> Ms Chrząszczyńska may come to the conclusion that her personal data, which are part of employee data, should not be transferred to the parent company in France, because not only will the French make fun of her name, she is also patriotic and has four children at school, and so there is no chance of her moving and having a career at the headquarters in France, and when they pester her with proposals it depresses her, and what is worse refusal may give the impression that she does not like the company, and that will ruin her chances of being promoted locally.

A creditor frequently calls a debtor's mobile nudging a debtor to pay her/his debt. A debtor objects to constant calling (so-called soft enforcement) and demands restriction of processing (i.e., not calling) until her/his objection is processed by a creditor.

6.3 How to Restrict Processing

Under Recital 67 GDPR, the means by which a request from a data subject can be fulfilled that are applicable include:

(1) temporarily moving the selected personal data to another processing system;
(2) making the selected data unavailable to users or temporarily removing published data from a website;
(3) in automated filing systems, restricting processing in principle by technical means in such a manner that the processed data are not subject to further processing operations and cannot be changed;
(4) clearly indicating in the system that the processing of personal data is restricted.

The GDPR thus states that the controller is required to take real measures and take the appropriate technical measures to prevent processing of the restricted data.

Restriction of personal data processing can also be handled mainly in a procedural manner – for example, by drawing up a list of persons to whom the restriction applies, by flagging a particular person/record, indicating that the list of persons subject to the restriction has to be reviewed.

7 OBLIGATION TO NOTIFY ABOUT RECTIFYING, ERASING, OR RESTRICTING OF PROCESSING OF DATA (ARTICLE 19 GDPR)

7.1 Duty to Follow Your Data

The controller should remember about the obligation provided for in Article 19 GDPR to notify about the restriction of data processing to 'each recipient to whom the personal data have been disclosed, unless this proves impossible or involves disproportionate effort'.

The controller is also required to inform the person exercising the right to restriction of processing about the recipients subject to the restriction if the data subject so requests.

Both of these obligations will be a subject examined during a supervisory authority inspection and therefore should be taken seriously.

Article 19 GDPR in practice requests from the data controller to follow their data. The data controller should know who they make data available to, to be able to inform those entities about data rectification/restriction/erasure as well as to let the data subject know who has received hose 'faulty data' of those.

7.2 'Recipient' of Data under Article 19 GDPR

We believe that 'recipient' of data referred to in Article 19 GDPR is not the same 'recipient' as defined in Article 4(9) GDPR. The definition of 'recipient' contained in Article 4(9) GDPR is very broad, covering data processors, though excluding public authorities when they request data for specific proceedings.

If we would apply the definition of 'recipient' from Article 4(9) GDPR strictly to Article 19 GDPR, the data controller would have to inform the data subject about the identity of data processors (subcontractors of the data controller – which makes no sense and which would lead to disclosing trade secrets). At the same time, the data controller would not have to inform the Police about changes to the data previously passed to the Police on a specific request (which makes even less sense).

Therefore, we believe Article 19 GDPR does not require the data controller to inform the data subject about data processors but at the same time requires the data subject to inform public authorities which obtained data subject to rectification/erasure/restriction (that does not mean that public authorities would be under the duty to comply with rectification/erasure/restriction requests).

8 RIGHT TO DATA PORTABILITY, I.E. HOW TO TRANSFER DATA FROM ONE CONTROLLER TO ANOTHER (ARTICLE 20 GDPR)

8.1 Preliminary Remarks

The right to data portability is a new right that has never existed before in personal data protection laws. It was implemented into the legal system in GDPR. This is a right that had to be granted to data subjects due to the rapid development of services based on new technologies, in particular those that use automated personal data processing.

The right to data portability **is intended to prevent technological dependence on the services of a particular provider by reducing the cost of discontinuing one service in order to move data to another service or receive transferred data (so-called vendor lock-in)**. It is aiming to be practical in nature from the point of view of those who make use of everyday services, as it helps when changing service providers. Instead of rewriting data into a new system, it will be sufficient to submit a request to the current service provider (controller) to transfer the personal data to another, specified, service provider. This was, in fact, the aim of EU lawmakers, who wished to increase competitiveness on the market by introducing the right to data portability. This is a consumer-friendly right, and there are rights similar in nature and purpose in other industry regulations, whether they are payment services, where accounts can be transferred between banks, or telecommunications services, where telephone numbers can be moved between various providers.

Executing the right of data portability entails a number of practical issues.

8.2 What Exactly Does the Right of Data Portability Entail?

There are two elements to the right to data portability:

(1) right of the data subject to obtain the personal data concerning them in a structured, commonly used and machine-readable format, and then;
(2) right of the data subject to request the data controller to transfer the data subject's personal data directly to another controller 'without hindrance from the controller to which the personal data have been provided'.

This means that the data subject can not only request that they be provided with data that they provided previously, which can be demanded in connection with the right to copies of data, but also request that the data be transferred directly to another specified controller.

The difference between the right to copies of data and the right of data portability is that the right of data portability includes the right to receive the data in a format that can be uploaded, i.e. automatic insertion into the new provider's system or the organisation's IT system.

8.3 When the Right of Data Portability Can Be Exercised?

The right of data portability is not a general right and does not apply in each case or to each method of processing personal data. The data subject can exercise this right where personal data are processed upon prior consent or on the basis of a contract. Also, the data must be processed in an automated fashion. This means that where personal data are processed on paper or on a basis other than consent or contract (e.g., based directly on law – legal obligation, public duty, public authority), the data subject is not entitled to request that the controller move the data to another controller. Automatic personal data processing also occurs where data are sent on paper and then digitally converted and saved in the form of files (though a structure of such digitalised data strictly depends on a degree of automation of their processing).

8.4 The Scope of Data to Be Transferred

Under Article 20(1) GDPR, an individual is entitled to be provided with 'data concerning him or her, which he or she has provided to a controller'.

'Data provided by the data subject' include data provided by an individual directly, such as contact details and identifying data, or their CV, and content concerning that person (even if including data of other persons), which the person placed in the controller's resources in performance of an agreement with the controller or on the basis of consent granted to the controller for the processing of that information.

As the author (Maciej Gawronski)[26] intended, inclusion of the right of data portability in personal data protection laws was not aimed at limiting the scope to data that are *stricte* personal data. It was intended to apply to all data placed in the controller's system (and systems of the controller's subcontractors) by the individual. This is the way EU lawmakers interpret and defined this right in the GDPR.

Example

In 2017, there was a much-publicised case in which a journalist at the Guardian exercised the right to copies of data with respect to the dating site Tinder. Under Article 20 GDPR, the journalist would be formally entitled not only to be provided with a copy of his 'dating' data but also to move those data to a different dating site.[27] A defined list of recipients of bank transfers can certainly be transferred from one bank to another, as can a list of contacts in online mail.

The Article 29 Working Party's view is that the right of data portability also includes data with which the controller is provided through the actions (behaviour) of the data subject, for example electricity consumption history (meter readings), or readings of smart wearable fitness bands – say 'data observed/data registered'. The guidelines on the right of data portability state that the data provided should also

26. In 2014 when acting as a consultant on standard ad hoc contractual clauses on 'Processor in the EU to another processor engaged outside of the EU' (WP214), M. Gawroński made a proposal to the European Commission to provide for the data portability right in the drafted contractual clauses (a kind of repeat of the data portability right discussed within the European Commission Expert Group on Cloud Computing Contracts). This proposal was well received at the time, and as it transpired was implemented in a manner beyond that expected by the person who proposed it.
27. For the time being in practice there would probably be technical obstacles, in particular the lack of a standard for sharing data.

include 'personal data resulting from observation of activities of users, such as raw data processed by a smart meters or other types of connected objects, activity logs, history of website usage or search activities'.[28] This concept is in line with the EC's intentions behind the introduction of the right of data portability.[29]

Execution of the right of data portability should, therefore, include data generated by the data subject's actions, for example loan repayment history, account history, electricity consumption history, and information placed in a customer relationship management system.

In this situation, a right that is apparently quite clear and simple to execute becomes a challenge for the controller, as the controller has to collect and then transfer a much broader range of data.

The scope of data transferred in machine-readable form does not have to include data generated by the controller as a result of its own analyses, for example a certain profile or internal rating attributed to a customer. This may be deceptive, however. An individual can obtain data of this kind through the right to copies of data (for which there is no limitation to data provided solely by the data subject). Moreover, in case of profiling resulting in material consequences for the data subject (legal effects or similarly significantly affecting the data subject – Article 22 GDPR), the controller is obliged by Article 13(2)(f) and Article 14(2)(g) GDPR) to provide to the data subject meaningful information about the logic involved in such automated processes. Those GDPR provisions create the 'right to know why' which corresponds to a recently articulated[30] right to understand the logic underlying artificial intelligence decisions.

Meanwhile, the issue of the mandatory scope of data subject to transfer is not entirely clear. The EC is experimenting by introducing Article 20 GDPR and is well aware of this.[31]

8.5 How the Right of Data Portability Should Be Executed?

Another task faced by a controller when executing the data portability right is the manner and form in which it should happen. Article 20 GDPR states as follows:

> The data subject shall have the right to receive the personal data concerning him or her in a structured, commonly used and machine-readable format.

The Article 29 Working Party has also formulated guidelines on this provision, stating that in addition to formats usually used in a particular sector, 'controllers

28. Article 29 Working Party Guidelines on the right to data portability, adopted 12 December 2016, recently amended and adopted 5 April 2017 (WP 242 rew. 01), p. 10, http://www.giodo.gov.pl/pl/1520296/10055 (last accessed on 23 January 2018).
29. Based on M. Gawroński's and A.P. Czarnowski's experience and information when working in the European Commission Expert Group on Cloud Computing Contracts.
30. For example, https://christophm.github.io/interpretable-ml-book/?fbclid=IwAR3T-ED8IdBWdRbcQ5e51JBHGrPXIR9YsD-X_t6UTdaCxnHDLATS8aoP_e4 (last accessed on 12 January 2019).
31. Information from the European Commission when working in the European Commission Expert Group on Cloud Computing Contracts.

should provide personal data using commonly used formats (e.g. XML, JSON, CSV) along with useful metadata at the best possible level of granularity'.[32] This means that this right cannot be executed using the popular PDF format.[33] It will be sufficient however to save data in XML format and transfer the data to the specified controller. One can imagine various scenarios for the procedure: starting with the now somewhat old school method of saving data on a CD or other type of data carrier and then sending them by courier service to the specified recipient, through sending an encoded file by email, to using an application programming interface (API). The choice of the manner in which the right of data portability is executed will depend on the industry sector in which the controller operates and the scale of requests from customers (data subjects). Sometimes a regulator may enforce full automating of data portability (i.e., creating proper APIs) like in case of account information services and payment initiation services introduced by the so-called second EU Payment Services Directive requiring banks to open their systems to providers of such services.

The data must be suitable for import via a different system or application, using a simple 'open file' or 'import data' option. The controllers exporting data should not impose unnecessary restrictions on the controller importing data or the data subject. Article 20(1) GDPR states clearly that data is transferred 'without hindrance from the controller'. Hindrance can take various forms, from charging extra fees, implementing an unclear and complicated procedure for execution of the right, imposing discriminatory security requirements, to simply delaying its execution.

Finally referring to the receipt of data (or import of data in the IT meaning), the Article 29 Working Party says that controllers transferring data are not responsible for the processing of data by the data subject or by the controller to which the data are transferred.[34] A controller transferring data is also not required to review and verify the quality of the data before sending them.

8.5.1 Exceptions

There are limitations on the right to portability of data.

Above all, to reiterate, transfer of data can be requested if the data have been made available to the controller on the basis of consent or a contract. Therefore, data portability does not apply to data processed to perform a task carried out in the public interest or in the exercise of official authority vested in the controller, for compliance with a legal obligation, processed to protect a vital interest, and when the controller collects and processes data for the purpose of legitimate interests pursued by the controller or by a third party. These 'limitations' follow from the function and envisaged purpose of the right of data portability, which is to enable transfer of data between various service providers – thereby reducing dependence on a particular

32. Article 29 Working Party Guidelines ..., p. 19.
33. Some IT experts are appalled by this statement, but because within the EC there is a belief that PDF format is not suitable for data transfer, it is best not to try this if there is no need.
34. Article 29 Working Party Guidelines ..., p. 6.

service provider (often called 'vendor lock-in') due to the costs and effort involved in moving ('exit costs').

8.5.2 *Third-Party Rights*

An exception *sensu stricto* preventing the execution of the right of data portability, under Article 20(4) GDPR, is the adverse effect of transferring data from one controller to another on the rights and freedoms of 'others'. The same exception is provided for in Article 15(4) GDPR with respect to the right to copies of data. The right to copies of data cannot have an adverse effect on the rights and freedoms of persons or entities other than the data subject. Release of copies of data (including machine-readable) should therefore be refused where they also cover:

- data of third parties, if release of the data would be a breach of the law;
- court, disciplinary, or criminal proceedings, if release of copies of data would disrupt those proceedings;
- information covered by exclusive rights – copyright, related rights, patents – if release of copies of data would breach these rights;
- information subject to professional privilege, trade secrets, or other legally protected secrets of a third party, if release of copies of these data would be a breach of those secrets;
- data that breach personality rights of persons other than the data subject.

Of course, there is also a question if and when the controller learns of a situation of this kind and how a controller intends to resolve it. A controller is not under an obligation to have information of that kind and in particular is not required to monitor the content of the data (as a rule it should not do this, in fact, to avoid unnecessary liability). If the controller does, in fact, learn in a reliable manner of this problem (potential breach of rights of 'others'), it should not hand over the data. The situation is similar to the so-called notice and takedown procedure resulting from the EU E-Commerce Directive.

8.5.3 *Transfer of Data Concerning at the Same Time the Requesting Person and Another Person*

Some authors claim that as a rule a data controller is not allowed to hand over copies of data or transfer data containing third-party personal data (such as lists of contacts in an email system, lists of recipients of bank money transfers). This is incorrect and distorts the very essence of the right to copies of data. When processing data for household purposes, a natural person is not subject to the GDPR and is entitled to do so. Contact details or other data processed by a person exercising the data portability right are 'theirs', and as a rule the controller cannot contest this right.

But even if processing (possession) of certain third party personal data by a data subject falls under GDPR (such data subject being a controller or even a processor of such data) there is no reason to reject that data subject's request to transfer data to another services provider (another controller) simply because the requested data include other people too.

8.6 Who Is Affected the Most by Data Transfer?

In practice, the data portability right will probably be the most commonly exercised right with respect to providers of online services, for example banks, social networking sites, online stores, providers of electronic payment services, providers of email services and space for data storage, music websites, and other cloud service providers.

8.6.1 Security

The data export service must have the appropriate safeguards, like any other data processing operation. For example, during C2C data transmission, an assessment must be conducted of the need for encryption and, where applicable, other safeguards. The differences in safeguards between one controller and another may be one of the causes preventing the transfer of data not involving the data subject (e.g., the requirement for separate authentication of the individual by the transferring controller and the receiving controller). These processes will definitely be more automated as certification becomes more common – then organisations in a single industry who are signatories to the same code of conduct will have the same security standards. This will still take some time to come about.

8.6.2 Technicalities

A controller is required to transfer data in a 'structured, commonly used, and machine-readable format'; that is, the controller is required to employ some kind of generally accepted format for a file/data transmission. A controller is not required however to transfer data in an exotic format if the data recipient uses a format of that kind. The data portability right is technologically neutral. The aim is to facilitate the transfer of data between digital service providers, but there is no aspiration to introduce full interoperability standards in a single move.

9 THE RIGHT TO OBJECT (ARTICLE 21 GDPR)

9.1 The Right to Object

GDPR provides that a person may object to the processing of his or her data by a controller. An effective objection to data processing should result in the data covered by the objection no longer being processed.

But we cannot object to the processing of our personal data in every situation. There are two types of objection:

(1) an objection due to one's particular situation, or
(2) an objection against direct marketing (an objection 'at will', since it requires neither a justification nor conditions of effectiveness).

Upon receiving an objection based on a particular situation, a controller should no longer process the data, unless it can show that:

(1) compelling legitimate grounds exist for the processing that override the interests, rights, and freedoms of the data subject, or
(2) grounds exist for establishing, pursuing (exercising), or defending claims, or
(3) the processing is necessary in order to perform duties in the public interest – if the objection refers to processing for the purposes of scientific or historical research, or for statistical purposes (pursuant to Article 89(1) GDPR).

If an objection refers to direct marketing, the controller must simply cease the processing covered by the objection.

If, however, what the objection concerns is unknown, then, based on Article 12 GDPR, the controller is obliged to facilitate the person's right to object. The controller has no right to ignore an objection that has been expressed incompletely. The controller must ask the data subject exactly what he or she is objecting to and what the justification is. The right to object is always contextual – in order to determine the basis and scope of an objection, the circumstances associated with it must be specified.

Example

For about ten years I [M.G.] have been objecting to the processing of my personal data for direct marketing purposes by a certain bank, where I have an account, almost every time the bank calls me up with an offer. One could say, to paraphrase Oscar Wilde, that up to now, filing an objection has been as easy as giving up smoking – I have done it many times. Let us hope the GDPR improves this situation somewhat.

If a controller receives an objection and wants to continue running its business in peace with the minimum effort, it should comply with the objection and document this (the principle of accountability).

Alternatively, the controller may begin proceedings to assess the justifiability of the objection and the grounds for complying with it.

9.2 Objecting Due to a Particular Situation of the Data Subject

Depending on a person's particular situation, he or she may object to the processing of data when that processing is based mainly on the following legal grounds:

(1) a justified interest of the data controller,
(2) the public interest or interest of public authorities,
(3) scientific or historical research purposes, or statistical purposes, pursuant to Article 89(1) GDPR.

What constitutes a 'particular situation' is any factual circumstances which differ from the situation of other people whose data are being processed. An example is a threat to the personal safety of a particular person or a state of grief or even a mental health condition. It is also vital that the particular situation affects the data processing such that there is an imbalance between the interests of the data subject and the data controller.[35]

In principle, whether a particular situation exists should be determined individually. In reality, it will normally be an extraordinary situation of a person that differs from the general group of people 'processed' by the controller. But it need not always be so, especially when the processing itself is exceptional. It will then be a simple matter of weighing the particular circumstances of the data subject against the interest of the controller (or a third party).

A particular situation will also depend on the processing context – the purpose of the processing and the interest of the controller (or third party) the processing serves.

A controller can dismiss an objection that does not concern direct marketing if it can show the existence of:

(1) compelling legitimate grounds exist for the processing that override the interests, rights, and freedoms of the data subject, or
(2) grounds exist for establishing, exercising, or defending claims.

9.2.1 Compelling Legitimate Grounds

In accordance with what is set out in Recital 69, as well as in light of the principle of accountability, it is up to the controller to prove that it (or a third party) has a compelling legitimate ground for processing that overrides the interests or basic rights and freedoms of the data subject.

If the personal data processing is based on a justified interest (as indicated in Article 6(1)(f) GDPR), then even at the initial stage (before the data processing begins) the data controller should weigh the interests of the data subject against its own (or those of another entity in whose interest it intends to process the data). An objection also requires that such interests be weighed, but here this takes place in a situation where the controller has already collected the data and is processing them on an ongoing basis and only then does the data subject file an objection; the weighting of interests, therefore, is done individually.

35. P. Litwiński, P. Barta, M. Kawecki [w:] *Rozporządzenie UE ...* 2018, p. 426.

Example

A conflict of interests between a natural person and a controller (or third party) may occur. For example, if our data are being processed by an association or other institution whose world view we do not share (e.g., a specific Church or religious organisation, or a butcher's association if we are vegetarian); if we believe that our data are being processed unjustifiably, e.g., by the City of Warsaw when it requires us to enter our vehicle registration number to use a parking meter; if we find out we have been entered on someone's 'blacklist'; if we do not want a former employer using our personal data because this could cause us harm.

Example

As we saw when commenting on the right to limit data, a particular situation could arise where Ms Chrząszczyńska, the director of a project management office in a Polish subsidiary of a French company, decides that her personal data contained in the company's employee data should not be sent to the parent company in France, because: for one thing, the people in France will be making fun of her name; for another, she is a Polish patriot and has four school-aged children, so there is no chance at all of her leaving the country to make a big career at the head office and it will only upset her to be receiving job offers – constantly turning them down could give out the impression she does not like her company, harming her chance of advancing locally.

Example

We can submit an objection if we are flooded with telephone calls from a debt collection company pursuing an expired debt (not only the debt of the deceased mother of a former brother-in-law, as happened to me [M.G.] for three years until I threatened the chairman that I would write about it).

9.2.2 Claims and Disputes

The second basis for refusing to comply with an objection would seem to be quite obvious. The EU legislator stipulated that processing may take place in spite of an objection if grounds exist for establishing, pursuing, or defending claims. In truth, the GDPR does not specify what claims this concerns, but, taking account of the general prohibition on destroying evidence, it must concern claims by anyone – as long as the controller is able to show that the personal data concerned are genuinely needed for the purposes of pursuing a specific claim.

When determining whether there is an exception that permits data processing despite an objection, remember that this also is contextual – that is, it must be seen in the context of the purpose. It is permissible to process data despite an objection if the data are needed to process a claim, but then they can be processed only for the purposes of the claim, and not, e.g., for direct marketing purposes.

9.2.3 The Public Interest or Interest of Public Authorities

The general regulation on data protection also permits objections to the processing of data based on a person's particular situation when the processing is based on the public interest or the interest of a public authority. Since such an exception exists, it must mean that it is not enough for a controller to simply say that a public interest or interest of a public authority exists in order to dismiss an objection. The controller must either show that the objection to processing is not grounded because the personal situation of a data subject is not so peculiar or that the public interest or need to exercise public authority outweighs the specific situation of the person objecting to the processing. Such assessments are very fluid, and one can expect that 'public' controllers will tend to overrule objections. This does not mean, though, that we should immediately condemn such a tendency, since within certain limits the public interest usually does override individual interests, and public authority is also exercised in the public interest.

Example

It is hard to find a specific example of the particular situation of a natural person overriding the public interest or the interest of a public authority concerning data processing. However, in reference to arguments raised elsewhere as to the constitutionality of the mandatory collection of all data on all the medical procedures of all the people in Poland, we can say, for example, that a woman who has an intrauterine device (International *Classification of Disease and Related Health Problems ICD-10* code Z97.5) demand that data concerning her device could not be processed due to a justifiable fear of her being ostracised by some members of society or facing aggression from health services personnel having a different world view.

A somewhat similar situation also occurs in the context of the right to object when data are processed for the purposes of scientific or historical research, or for statistical purposes pursuant to Article 89(1) GDPR. Here as well, an applicant must show his or her particular situation, but the data controller may refuse to comply with the demand to cease processing if the processing is necessary in order to carry out a duty in the public interest.

9.3 Data Processing for the Needs of Direct Marketing

Where data are being processed for the needs of direct marketing, the data controller must simply comply with an objection from a data subject.

Filing an objection to the processing of data for direct marketing purposes is not the same as the deletion of data. The controller will still be able to process the data – but only for other purposes, e.g., in relation to conducting mandatory financial reporting.

9.3.1 Objection to Direct Marketing and Withdrawal of Consent to Processing

Functionally, an objection to direct marketing directly corresponds to a withdrawal of consent to processing. In both cases, no conditions need to be stated in order to eliminate the basis for processing. For example, the supervisory authority in Great Britain (the Information Commissioner's Office) lists a marketing objection alongside a withdrawal of consent.

9.3.2 Objection to Direct Marketing and Consent to Remote Marketing Communications

The law makes it difficult to understand the rules governing direct marketing because it regulates the issue of the right to process data for direct marketing purposes separately from the issue of the permissibility of contacting a person for direct marketing purposes. Pursuant to the GDPR (unchanged in relation to the old provisions), direct marketing is deemed to be a justifiable legal interest of a data controller constituting grounds for data processing. Hence, the GDPR does not require consent to data processing for direct marketing purposes; it only makes it possible to object to that activity (an opt-out approach). Except that the E-Privacy Directive requires prior consent to the use of electronic or telephone communication for direct marketing purposes. The EU is planning to regulate this issue in a uniform manner in an e-privacy regulation, which is currently on its way through the EU legislative process.

9.4 Effective Submission of an Objection to Data Processing

As already indicated, when faced with an objection to processing data for direct marketing purposes, a controller is obliged to comply with the demand. The same applies in other cases, provided there are no circumstances that permit the controller to dismiss the objection.

Of course, one can imagine a situation in which a data controller decides that the data subject is not in a particular situation that justifies their exercising the right to object. Such a case may then be considered by the supervisory authority (on the basis of a complaint by the data subject), which may order compliance with the objection (*see* Article 58(2)(c) GDPR, where the authorisation granted by the EU legislator to supervisory authorities includes that of ordering a data controller to comply with demands by data subjects that result from the rights they enjoy under the GDPR).

9.5 How an Objection Should Be Submitted

In theory, a data subject can exercise their right to object in any form, provided it is authenticated other than verbally (Article 12(1) GDPR). An objection may be articulated in a written email or a phone conversation (during which a PIN electronic authentication is used), etc. This interpretation is supported by the content of Recital 59 GDPR, in which it is stated that a data controller implements procedures that make it easier for data subjects to exercise their rights under the GDPR, including the right to object. A controller should ensure that it is also possible to submit demands electronically, particularly if the personal data are processed electronically.

In practice, apart from the need to authenticate, the accountability requirements also mean that objections must be documented at some stage. If an objection is submitted by phone or face-to-face at a branch, the controller's personnel must document the situation, e.g., by immediately sending an email describing the content of the demand to the data subject, getting a data subject to sign an objection form, etc. In this way, both the demand itself and the date and time it was submitted are recorded in order to meet the service level requirements (response time) contained in Article 12 GDPR.

10 PROFILING AND AUTOMATED DECISION-MAKING (ARTICLE 22 GDPR)

10.1 Preliminary Remarks

We live in an information society. Information (including to a large extent that concerning natural persons) is becoming more valuable than material goods (with value assessed not only quantitatively but also qualitatively). For this reason, it has long been accepted that what counts is not collecting the greatest number of data possible, but selecting them appropriately and having them available for use.[36] To this end, profiling is conducted.

Put simply, profiling is a process of collecting unrelated data and extracting patterns and correlations from them using mathematical and statistical models.[37] In the case of the profiling of personal data, the goal of the profiling is to place an individual the data concern in a specific category and to predict or evaluate:

(1) capabilities of a person,
(2) his or her interests,

36. Cf. FIDIS report, D7.2: *Descriptive analysis and inventory of profiling practices*, 29 June 2005, http://www.fidis.net/fileadmin/fidis/deliverables/fidis-wp7-del7.2.profiling_practices.pdf (last accessed on 27 January 2018).
37. Cf. FIDIS report, D7.2: *Descriptive …*, pt. 1.

(3) how he or she is likely to behave.[38]

From a processing perspective, profiling is divided into three stages:

(1) text and data mining,
(2) profile building, and
(3) profile analysis in terms of decision-making in individual matters.[39]

Because the creation of a profile requires the processing of very large amounts of data, the process involves the use of computer algorithms and new technologies that make it possible to both collect more data and build profiles effectively. During **automated profiling,**[40] a human or an algorithm makes a specific decision on the basis of a profile prepared by another algorithm. The development of automated profiling is greatly affected by the development of techniques of big data analytics, machine learning, and of the Internet of Things, which provide different data on the people for whom the profile is being created.

In practice, profiling is used: to create better-tailored advertising (**behavioural marketing**); in the financial and banking industry where, on the basis of credit card data, bank account use and debt registers a **credit rating** is generated; in the insurance industry where, on the basis of data collected on insurance risk, **total risk and optimal insurance premiums** are calculated; in the transport and services industry where, on the basis of data on consumption and browsing history, **dynamic tariff systems** are constructed; and to analyse the movements of individuals in order to evaluate their purchasing habits, manner of using their car or the popularity of particular business locations, broken down by individual visitors (and their characteristics, such as age and wealth). For several years now, precise data obtained by profiling have been used, for example, to prepare election campaign promises better suited to voter preferences[41] leading to the Cambridge Analytica scandal.

In the public sector profiling is used: to detect terrorism by analysing information on to and from where and how often a given person travels;[42] to detect financial abuse by monitoring transactions and building account owner profiles; to identify cases of human trafficking; and to suit job offers to the unemployed.

38. Article 29 Working Party, Guidelines on automated individual decision-making and profiling for the purposes of Regulation 2016/679, adopted on 3 October 2017 (WP251), p. 5, http://ec.europa.eu/newsroom/just/document.cfm?doc_id=47963 (last accessed on 27 January 2018).
39. In academic studies, one comes across a more comprehensive division into: (1) data collection and registration, (2) data aggregation or preparation in databases, (3) data exploration or start-up of algorithms using databases, (4) interpretation of patterns arising, (5) decision-making on the basis of the profiles obtained, (6) multiplication of those profile in appropriate social contexts; *see* FIDIS report, D7.2: *Descriptive* ... .
40. Article 29 Working Party, Guidelines on Automated ... .
41. Including the Facebook Elections project run by the portal facebook.com (https://politics.fb.com).
42. To this end, a PNR system was created, introduced by Directive of the European Parliament and of the Council (EU) 2016/681 of 27 April 2016 on the use of passenger name record (PNR) data for the prevention, detection, investigation and prosecution of terrorist offences and serious crime (OFEU L 119, p. 132).

Even though profiling makes it possible to enhance the security and effectiveness of an organisation, as well as to reduce costs, its automated nature also makes it very controversial. Alarms have gone out that automated profiling may constitute a universal threat to the rights and freedoms of individuals. The main reservations expressed about profiling include:

(1) a lack of transparency in the algorithms used to create profiles and to build relations between a profile and, e.g., a service offered;
(2) potential breaches of privacy (by collecting data without the data subject's knowledge);
(3) a lack of understanding about what may result from profiling;
(4) the perpetuation of existing stereotypes and social segregation;
(5) the possibility of a person being permanently assigned to a specific category and having specific preferences attributed to him or her that may constitute a source of discrimination.[43]

As pointed out by the Chairwoman of the American Federal Trade Commission, Edith Ramirez, with automated and autonomous profiling, 'Individuals may be judged not because of what they've done, or what they will do in the future, but because inferences or correlations drawn by algorithms suggest they may behave in ways that make them poor credit or insurance risks, unsuitable candidates for employment or admission to schools or other institutions, or unlikely to carry out certain functions.'[44]

Even more serious doubts are raised by **automated decision-making systems**. In the case of classic automated profile, one may have doubts as to how a profile was created, yet we can assume that even if certain important circumstances were omitted by the system (because of how the algorithm was built), these could still be taken into account when a human being makes a final decision. In totally automated systems based on algorithms, machine learning and artificial intelligence, decisions are not subject to any human control, meaning all we can do is hope that all important circumstances were taken into account by the system (and, as everyone knows, there is no perfect system).

In the face of such a threat, the EC decided to comprehensively regulate through the GDPR:

(1) when we can profile,
(2) what obligations we bear in connection with profiling,
(3) what the rights of profiled people are, and

43. J. Niklas, *Profilowanie w kontekście ochrony danych osobowych i zakazu dyskryminacji*, http://ptpa.org.pl/site/assets/files/publikacje/opinie/Opinia_profilowanie_w_kontekscie_ochrony_danych_osobowych_i_zakazu_dyskryminacji.pdf (last accessed on 27 January 2018).
44. Speech by E. Ramirez, *The Privacy Challenges of Big Data: A View from the Lifeguard's Chair*, https://www.ftc.gov/sites/default/files/documents/public_statements/privacy-challenges-big-data-view-lifeguard's-chair/130819bigdataaspen.pdf (last accessed on: 27 January 2018).

(4) in what cases particularly sensitive automated decision-making systems can be applied, including systems that make decisions on the basis of earlier profiling.

Just how important it was for the EC to regulate profiling issues in detail is shown by the fact that the concept of profiling appears in the GDPR, in different contexts, more than twenty times.

10.2 Definition of Profiling in the GDPR

For the purposes of the GDPR, profiling is defined as:

> 'any **form of automated** processing of **personal data consisting of the use of personal data to evaluate** certain personal aspects relating to a natural person, in particular to analyse or predict aspects concerning that natural person's performance at work, economic situation, health, personal preferences, interests, reliability, behaviour, location or movements' (Art. 4(4) GDPR).

As emphasised, in order to qualify as profiling in the meaning of the GDPR, it is key that:

(1) the processing (profiling) is automated (not entirely performed by a human),
(2) the processing (profiling) is performed on personal data,
(3) the result of the processing (profiling) is an evaluation of personal aspects (traits) of a natural person for given needs of the processor.

Other forms of data processing (non-automated or performed on data other than personal data or involving the use of personal data for a purpose other than evaluating personal aspects) do not constitute profiling under the GDPR, while in certain conditions they may qualify as automated decision-making.

It is also important to consider Recital 75 GDPR, pursuant to which:

> 'where personal aspects are evaluated, particularly if analyses or forecasts are made of aspects concerning job performance, economic condition, health, personal preferences or interests, reliability, behaviour, location or travel – in order to create or use personal profiles', – a risk may arise of individual rights and freedoms being violated. The passage of the GDPR evidently concerns profiling, and there is no word on the subject of automation.

10.2.1 Automation

For the needs of profiling under the GDPR, the concept of 'automation' should be understood as the use of computer algorithms or systems for profiling. Automation may take place at the stage of:

(1) text and data mining,
(2) profile building,
(3) profile analysis in terms of decision-making in individual matters.

In contrast to Article 22 GDPR, the definition of profiling does not require profiling to be completely automated; that is, it does not rule out the presence of the human element in the profiling process.

Profiling may be as simple as segregating a database in Excel according to the criteria contained in one column.

10.2.2 Personal Data

Collecting data on a group of natural persons without the possibility of extracting individuals from the group is not profiling in the meaning of the GDPR. Nor is collecting data on a group of customers in shopping centres without extracting the movement of particular natural person profiling or preparing energy tariffs for particular user groups on the basis of power consumption in particular hours without verifying the power consumption of individual persons.

10.2.3 Impact

For processing to be profiling, the impact of the processing must be in the form of an assessment of certain personal factors. As the provision indicates, this involves, in particular, analyses and prognoses (drawing conclusions about the future) regarding aspects of a person's behaviour. Put simply, this means that personal data are used to assess or predict a given person's behaviour and assign him or her to some kind of category (e.g., bad debtors with a zero credit rating, or persons who, encouraged by a dynamic tariff dependent on energy consumption, will remain loyal customers of a power company).

10.2.4 Activities Treated as Profiling

Table 2.1 shows examples of profiling versus corresponding actions that are not profiling.

Table 2.1 Examples of Profiling Based on Personal Data

Profiling	*Not Profiling*
Introducing dynamic tariffs based on the actual power consumption of a given user	Introducing dynamic tariffs based on actual power consumption in a given city/district (no connection with personal data of a particular person)

Profiling	*Not Profiling*
Building a credit rating based on Credit Information Bureau (CIB) data, credit card use, and bank account funds use	Processing data concerning credit card use and funds use without reference to decisions concerning individual customers (no processing impact)
Pricing car insurance based on an analysis of driving habits	Pricing car insurance based on car age and amount of use (no personal data processing)
Issuing fines after a system pre-analyses too frequently exceeding the speed limit during bad weather conditions	Issuing fines automatically after radar detects speeding (**no profiling**); in such a case, although there is no profiling, there is an automated issuance of a decision, to which the restrictions of Article 22 GDPR apply.
Basing a bonus system on statistics on late arrivals at work	Electronically recording employee presence at work (no profiling)
Using data on social media use to address advertisements to individual users	Collecting data on social media use (no profile, no processing impact)

Source: own study.

10.3 Obligations of a Personal Data Controller in Connection with Profiling, Automated Decision-Making, or Decisions Made on the Basis of Profiling

GDPR foresees several important obligations related to three situations: profiling, automated decision-making, and making decisions on the basis of profiling:

(1) **notification of an automated decision based on profiling** – both decision-making based on profiling and automated decision-making require informing the data subject of how the process works and what it means for that person. Information should be provided when the data are collected, within a month from obtaining data indirectly (from other sources than the data subject) and when exercising a request for data access (Article 13(2)(f), Article 14(2)(g), Article 15(1)(h) GDPR). If profiling is made through artificial intelligence or more accurately machine learning mechanisms, it may be difficult to identify and apply deadlines for providing such information to a data subject;

(2) **the right to human intervention** – Article 22 GDPR introduces the right not to be subjected to a decision based solely on automated processing, including profiling, which produces legal or other similar effects. However, such a decision can be made solely automatically or solely on the basis of profiling if consent is expressly granted as necessary to the conclusion or performance of

an agreement;[45] in such a situation, though, there must be a complaint procedure in place that involves a competent, authorised person;

(3) **impact assessment** – Article 35 GDPR requires an assessment to be made of the impact on personal data if systematic, comprehensive profiling is conducted in order to make decisions that cause legal or similar effects.

10.3.1 General Obligations of a Controller

10.3.1.1 Notification of Automated Decision-Making and Decision-Making Based on Profiling

As we have shown, both making decisions based on profiling and automated decision-making require notification to the data subject of how the process works and what it means for that person. Notice should be sent when the data are collected and when exercising a request for data access (Article 13(2)(f), Article 14(2)(g), Article 15(1)(h) GDPR).

10.3.1.2 How Often to Notify

Given that profiling is often conducted on the basis of many different data sources, the obligation to notify when profiling will often have to be fulfilled in two ways: once at the moment data are collected for profiling from the data subject the profiling concerns (at the moment data are obtained or when collection begins, e.g. at the commencement of using the service in which the data are used for profiling) and a second time if the profiling is based on 'external' data not obtained from the person being profiled, within a month from when the data are obtained.

10.3.1.3 A Change of Purpose of Processing

Personal data controllers should remember that profiling is a purpose that differs from that of merely collecting and analysing data. If a data subject is not informed that his or her data will be profiled at the time when the data are collected, then that person must be promptly notified at the moment the profiling begins.

10.3.2 The Right to Object

The only provision of the GDPR that refers to every form of profiling – regardless of what the impact of the profiling is to be (whether a decision based thereon is to be issued by a person or automatically) – is that concerning the right to object.

45. The editing of Art. 21 GDPR is misleading. The understandable and not very controversial issue of profiling and automated decision-making is discussed in the Art. 29 Working Party Guidelines on automated decision-making and profiling (WP251).

The right to object applicable in case profiling is conducted based on public interest task or official authority (Article 6(1)(e) GDPR) or legitimate interest of a controller or a third party (Article 6(1)(f) GDPR) encompasses:

(1) the right to demand that profiling be stopped for reasons related to the data subject's particular situation (more on the conditions for submitting an objection and on a particular situation in the commentary to Article 21 GDPR); as we have indicated, good examples of a particular situation are when we do not fit a pattern (i.e., when the algorithm has made a mistake), when the profiling infringes our personal rights, or when it preys on our addictions;
(2) the unconditional right to demand that profiling be stopped if it is being conducted for the purposes of direct marketing (to the extent profiling is connected with such direct marketing[46]).

10.4 Profiling and Automated Decision-Making

As per Recital 71 GDPR, GDPR protects in particular persons who are subjected to automated decisions (e.g., electronic credit applications, electronic methods of recruiting without human intervention). This relates to the concerns discussed above over potential breaches of individual rights and freedoms, lack of transparency of profiling and automated decision-making as well as lack of accuracy and bias. The Regulation itself does not define directly what is to be understood by an automated decision. We can assume that it means all decisions made without human participation (as indicated by the use in Article 22 GDPR of the phrase 'based solely on automated processing'). Introducing an apparent human decision in the decision-making process (which is limited, e.g., to a single click on an 'accept' button) does not alter the automated nature of such a decision. For a decision to qualify as non-automated, it must be made by a human who is competent and professionally authorised to do so.

The Regulation restricts automated decisions, including profiling, that have legal or similar effects on the persons they concern. The concept of having legal effects would seem to be clear. Interpreting it in accordance with the GDPR recitals, it means any impact whatsoever on the legal situation of the person the decision concerns (inc. granting some kind of entitlement, granting or blocking access, concluding or terminating an agreement). Doubts arise, however, when analysing the phrase 'similarly significantly affects him or her'. The wording and sense of the provision indicate that this is a category of effects of decisions that, in fact, do not change the legal status of the individual (they do not affect his or her rights or obligations), yet which are significant enough to alter (mainly adversely) that person's situation (e.g., by depriving the person of access to goods or services of a given type). Examples of a significant impact on a person that does not cause any legal effects are: an automatic refusal to conclude

46. Also, the unconditional right to object to direct marketing itself.

a loan agreement (e.g., because of a customer's credit rating), or a customer being presented with an automated offer for services (e.g., to buy airline tickets) that, due to the algorithm employed, is at a level that makes it impossible to buy the ticket (e.g., in the case of a sudden blizzard to results in many flights being cancelled where the ticket price depends on the number of available flights and seats in planes). In commentaries, and especially in the Article 29 Working Party Guidelines, the example is also used of people who are particularly susceptible to the content of advertisements that urge them to purchase given goods or services (e.g., deliberately addressing online roulette ads to persons profiled as very susceptible to gambling read: addicted or children).

Automated decisions that do not involve profiling may be based on:

(1) data collected directly from data subjects (provided, e.g., by filling out a questionnaire);
(2) data collected from observations of a given person (e.g., data on travel recorded in an application or by a camera, monitoring location, monitoring physical activity);
(3) data resulting from a previously created profile (e.g., a credit rating).[47]

Examples of automated decisions that do not involve profiling are:

(1) a bank system imposing a debt collection charge on a customer who is in arrears with loan repayment instalments;
(2) a customer being sent an automated declaration of termination of an agreement due to the occurrence of circumstances set out in the agreement (e.g., a failure to pay bills);
(3) discount coupons being granted through a phone app for shops in a shopping centre the customer will pass by, where the customer's travels are analysed by an algorithm in a visual surveillance or geolocation system based on telephone tracking;
(4) ticket from a speed camera.

10.4.1 Security Measures

In accordance with the GDPR, a controller that uses systems for issuing automated decisions is obliged to employ:

(1) technical and organisational measures that ensure that irregularities that occur when issuing decisions are corrected and that the risk of errors is reduced as much as possible;
(2) measures for securing personal data in a way that takes account of risks to the interests and rights of the data subject and that prevents, among other potential problems, the effects of discrimination against natural persons due

47. Article 29 Working Party, Guidelines on Automated … .

to their racial or ethnic origin, political, religious views or convictions, trade union membership, state of health or genetic condition, or sexual orientation.

Given the serious penalties imposed for infringements of the GDPR, until binding guidelines on the provisions guaranteeing security and avoiding discrimination in data processing are issued, theoretically it is important to be diligent in striving to eliminate even unlikely errors or cases of discrimination when issuing automated decisions. When running tests, a data controller of a processor may think of engaging a group of persons to provoke system errors and effects of discrimination. From this perspective, the complaints mechanism with 'human intervention' required by Article 22(3) GDPR should be treated as an extremely important feedback channel for optimising an automated process.

In practice automated profiling and decision-making is present for a long time in various sectors, and in particular in the financial and insurance sector. Bank and insurers are often criticised over lack of transparency of their decision-making processes. Fintechs rely heavily on profiling and extensive access to personal data. GDPR, if taken seriously, should enforce much more clarity as to why such entities take specific decisions and allow question such decisions more effectively.

10.4.2 When Automated Decisions or Decisions Based Solely on Profiling Can Be Used?

Here we must cite the provision itself in order to clarify another editing inconsistency of the GDPR.

Pursuant to Article 22(1) GDPR:

> The data subject shall have the right not to be subject to a decision based solely on **[1]** automated processing, including **[2]** profiling, which produces legal effects concerning him or her or similarly significantly affects him or her.

Dissecting this sentence logically, we obtain two types of decisions: (i) decisions based solely on automated processing and (ii) decisions based solely on profiling. In the second case, a decision need not be automated at all, since profiling has automation built into it by definition. It is enough if the procedure obligates a person to comply with the results of profiling, or in practice there are no exceptions from the results of profiling.[48]

Regulation of automated decision-making, including profiling, starts with the general prohibition but foresees three exceptions to it. The right to automate a decision-making limited to:

48. Article 29 Working Party, Guidelines on Automated ... p. 10. Somewhat differently M. Czerniawsi [in]: *RODO. Ogólne rozporządzenie o ochronie danych. Komentarz*, ed. E. Bielak-Jomaa, D. Lubasz, Warsaw 2017, p. 566.

(1) 'need for a contract', when automated decision-making is necessary in order to conclude or perform an agreement between the data subject and the controller;
(2) 'law', when a provision of law can be applied under EU law or the domestic law to which the controller is subject, and which foresees due measures for protecting the rights, freedoms, and legitimate interests of the data subject; and
(3) 'express consent' of the person subject to automated decision.

The criterion of usefulness for a contract should be understood in a reasonably narrow manner taking into consideration the principle of minimisation. Thus, data useful for issuing an automated decision only include those data that are adequate, relevant, and necessary.

In turn, the criterion of a legal basis should be understood as a clear basis expressed in a provision of EU law (a regulation) or a domestic provision of an EU Member State. Such automated processing can, for example, happen when an obliged institution or a Member State authority processes financial data for the purpose of preventing money laundering and financing terrorism.

The criterion of consent requires as usual that consent is given completely freely and without coercion. In respect of profiling, all cases of economic encouragements (bonuses, discounts) to grant consent should be examined carefully, as pricing model may be structured in such a way that not granting consent results in exorbitant prices of a particular service, etc. Then freedom of consent is a fiction.

10.4.2.1 Right to Human Intervention

Where the issuance of an automated decision is based on the criterion of usefulness for an agreement, or on that of consent, the controller must implement measures for protecting the data subject's rights and freedoms. In particular, the controller must ensure that, in addition to the right to notification, the data subjects also have:

(1) the right to obtain human intervention during the decision-making process,
(2) the right to express their own views,
(3) the right to obtain an explanation regarding the decision resulting from the automatic evaluation,
(4) the right to question such a decision.

10.4.2.2 Complaints Procedure

In practice, the right to human intervention may be exercised through a complaints procedure.

A channel of communication with human participation should be provided. The person with whom the data subject communicates should respond in such a way that it is evident that he or she has become acquainted with and pre-analysed the data subject's position and is able to explain his or her evaluation.

Control mechanisms should be in place for confirming that human verification is being conducted reliably and with real decision-making power. The less overruled automated decision, the harder to prove that the human intervention is real. One should anticipate that the supervisory authority will ask data relating to complaints.

10.4.2.3 Automated Verification

A particular case of falling victim to an automated decision is when a data subject loses their digital identity, that is when such a person can no longer log in to their profile in a given service or application. Since the GDPR requires data controllers to provide a complaints procedure with human participation, this should also be the case within the scope of verification. Various complications arise, of course, but when designing verification methods in systems, applications and services, according to the rules of privacy by design one should remember to ensure there is a human channel for recovering identity, or at least a means of verifying system decisions.[49] At the same time, verification cannot be based on verbal methods of communication (pursuant to Article 12 GDPR[50]), so a compromise must be sought. Though data protection authorities usually do not like when data controllers copy identification documents of people (data subjects) this is a usual method of recovering digital identity in case of loss of credentials (e.g., login & password). In anti-money laundering procedures copying customers and beneficial owners IDs is a basic financial security measure, so it is not so rare.

10.4.3 Profiling of Children

Children should not be covered by automated decision-making (Recital 71 *in fine* GDPR). As the commentaries emphasise, children are much more susceptible to adults to behavioural advertising and to having their profiles created on the internet. They are not able to understand all the consequences of their personal data being processed. And so they should be given special protection. According to the GDPR, 'children' means anyone under 16 years of age, although GDPR allows Member States to reduce that age limit down to 13 years.

In practice, though, it will not be easy to ban the automated processing of children's data. To date, popular internet services have 'managed pretty well' with children by formally prohibiting persons below a certain age from using them. It remains to be seen whether this practice of forbidding and then turning a blind eye will continue to be approved.

---

49. How can I convince a system that I know my grandmother's maiden name? I actually had that problem.
50. And recently, a telecommunications operator was hit by an attack on customers of a bank through verbal verification.

10.4.4 Automated Decisions Concerning Sensitive Data

Apart from the regulations discussed above, the GDPR severely restricts automated decision-making based on sensitive data. Pursuant to the GDPR, such data may be processed solely:

(1) on the basis of the express consent of the data subject, or
(2) if the processing is related to the performance of an important public interest on the basis of EU or domestic law.

In both cases, the data controller must guarantee that proper measures exist for protecting the rights, freedoms, and legitimate interests of the data subject.

Taken the above, unless a specific provision of law exists, a data controller cannot enter into a valid contract with a data subject requiring automated decision-making based on special categories of data of the counterparty. In order to deal with the requirements for consent to be valid, a data controller should allow for a contractual process not requiring automated decision-making so that such automated decision-making becomes optional. Otherwise, a consent will not be freely given.

10.4.5 Conclusions

If you profile or use profiling - you should give notice of this.

If you base decisions on profiling - you should provide a human complaints procedure.

If you profile comprehensively - you should conduct a data protection impact assessment.

When creating a profile - you should consider whether you need to know the identity of the data subjects. Usually, this is not necessary.

CHAPTER 3

Security

Aleksander P. Czarnowski, Katarzyna Kloc, Katarzyna Kunda, Maciej Gawronski & Paweł Punda[*]

1 DATA SECURITY IN LIGHT OF THE GDPR: RISK ANALYSIS AND ADEQUACY OF SECURITY MEASURES

1.1 Security Appropriate to Risk

Pursuant to Article 32(1) GDPR:

> Taking into account **[1]** the state of the art, **[2]** the costs of implementation and the **[3.1]** nature, **[3.2]** scope, **[3.3]** context and **[3.4]** purposes of processing as well as **[4]** the risk of **[5]** varying likelihood and **[6]** severity for the rights and freedoms of natural persons, the controller and the processor shall implement **[7]** appropriate technical and organisational measures to ensure a level of security **[8]** appropriate to the risk, including inter alia as appropriate:
>
> a) the pseudonymisation and encryption of personal data;
> b) the ability to ensure the ongoing confidentiality, integrity, availability and resilience of processing systems and services;
> c) the ability to restore the availability and access to personal data in a timely manner in the event of a physical or technical incident;
> d) a process for regularly testing, assessing and evaluating the effectiveness of technical and organisational measures for ensuring the security of the processing.

Pursuant to Article 32(2) GDPR:

[*] Section 1 contributed by Aleksander P. Czarnowski and Maciej Gawronski. Section 2 contributed by Aleksander P. Czarnowski, Maciej Gawronski and Paweł Punda. Section 3 contributed by Maciej Gawronski and Katarzyna Kunda. Section 4 contributed by Maciej Gawronski and Katarzyna Kunda. Section 5 contributed by Katarzyna Kloc.

> In assessing if the level of security is appropriate account shall be taken in particular of the **risks that are presented by processing**, in particular from accidental or unlawful destruction, loss, alteration, unauthorised disclosure of, or access to personal data transmitted, stored or otherwise processed.

Article 32 GDPR is the fundamental, and in fact the only, provision that outlines the criteria to decide on the level of personal data security. Pursuant to this provision, both a controller and a data processor are obliged to ensure a degree of personal data security **appropriate to the risk** of a breach of the rights or freedoms of natural persons resulting from processing.

The requirement of employing appropriate (adequate) data protection is not new. Now, however, the General Data Protection Regulation (GDPR) puts much more weight on risk assessment. The requirement to adopt security measures adequate to the risk of processing does not set any material standard of data protection. It sets only a procedural standard of performing a risk analysis. That is deliberate as the GDPR intends to be 'technology neutral'. In practice, though it lefts in the dark data controllers and data processors, especially small and medium enterprises (SMEs), as they have limited resources and capabilities to conduct such knowledgeable risk assessment.

1.1.1 Risk

A security analysis should start with a risk analysis.

Pursuant to Recital 83 GDPR:

> In order to maintain security and to prevent processing in infringement of this Regulation, the controller or processor **should evaluate the risks inherent in the processing** and implement measures to mitigate those risks, such as encryption.

This recital also indicates a need to weigh the costs of implementing protective measures against the risk and the nature of the data involved.

Those measures should ensure an appropriate level of security, including confidentiality, taking into account the state of the art and the costs of implementation in relation to the risks and the nature of the personal data to be protected.

Further on, the recital states how risk should be evaluated.

In assessing data security risk, consideration should be given to the risks that are presented by personal data processing, such as the accidental or unlawful destruction, loss, alteration, unauthorised disclosure of, or access to personal data transmitted, stored or otherwise processed, which may lead in particular to physical, material, or non-material damage.

1.1.2 Risk of a Breach of Rights or Freedoms

The type of risk involved here is explained in Recital 75 GDPR, which specifies the following situations that threaten the rights or freedoms of data subjects:

- **harm** – where the processing may give rise to discrimination, identity theft or fraud, financial loss, damage to the reputation, loss of confidentiality of personal data protected by professional secrecy, unauthorised reversal of pseudonymisation, or any other significant economic or social disadvantage;
- **a loss of rights or control** – where data subjects might be deprived of their rights and freedoms or prevented from exercising control over their personal data;
- **sensitive data** – where personal data are processed which reveal racial or ethnic origin, political opinions, religion or philosophical beliefs, trade union membership, and the processing of genetic data, data concerning health or data concerning sex life or criminal convictions and offences or related security measures;
- **profiling** – where personal aspects are evaluated, in particular analysing or predicting aspects concerning performance at work, economic situation, health, personal preferences or interests, reliability or behaviour, location or movements, in order to create or use personal profiles; or
- **persons requiring special care** – where personal data of vulnerable natural persons, in particular of children, are processed;
- **large-scale processing** – where processing involves a large amount of personal data and affects a large number of data subjects.

1.1.3 Data Processing Risk Analysis

The GDPR repeats the word 'risk' seventy-six times. Risk analysis is found on the inspection list of the supervising authorities. Whether a data protection impact assessment (DPIA) (a formalised risk analysis) should be run depends on the degree of risk entailed by the data processing. Undoubtedly, from the perspective of the GDPR, every controller and every processor should begin evaluating data security by analysing and estimating the risks posed to the rights and freedoms of data subjects.

It seems that a risk analysis should be conducted in respect of data processing activities but taking account of the data processing operations that generate risk. This conclusion results from combining a functional analysis of the GDPR pertaining to data processing, the wording of Article 32(1) GDPR, which requires different likelihoods and weights of threats to be accounted for, and Article 35(1) sentence 2 GDPR, where, in the context of a DPIA, the GDPR speaks of 'processing operations'. We use here at once two terms that are not defined by the GDPR, but in our glossary, as well as when discussing the register of processing activities – we will try to clarify these. What is important is that every data processing activity should be preceded by a separate risk analysis.

The two basic dimensions of an analysis of risk are the likelihood of the risk and its impact, that is the (adverse) impact it can have on data subjects. An analysis is usually presented in the form of a two-dimensional, multilevelled grid. The CNIL proposes a grid having four levels (negligible, limited, significant, and maximal);[1] PUODO (Polish supervisory authority) suggests five levels (of likelihood: rare, unlikely, possible, likely, and almost certain; impact: very low, low, average, high, and very high).[2]

In practice, you have to anticipate what harm may result from processing data as part of a particular activity. Then you need to evaluate what the likelihood of each incident is, and to what extent it may adversely affect people's lives, and how many lives. You enter the findings in the grid, multiply, and a risk weighting results.[3] Next, you have to establish what level of risk is acceptable (including potential claims of compensation for harm caused) and then verify possible security measures and the costs involved. Do not forget that the GDPR does not permit a high risk of a breach of the rights or freedoms of natural persons; at the very least, these require consultation with the supervisory authority (Article 36(1) GDPR).

Further below we describe basic attributes of information security (confidentiality, integrity, availability) which should be taken into consideration in the risk analysis. We point out that usually measures taken to ensure confidentiality decrease availability. We also point out that performing a risk analysis according to existing ISO methodologies (ISO 27005, ISO 29134) is a time and resources consuming process. But we also give some hints on how to try to lower the required effort by taking some shortcuts.

1.2 Elements of Evaluating the Adequacy of Data Protection Measures

Article 32(1) GDPR mentions a total of eleven elements for analysing the adequacy of data protection measures:

- (1) the state of the art (current knowledge on cybersecurity and sector knowledge);
- (2) the costs of implementation;
- (3–6) the nature, scope, context and purpose of processing;
- (7–9) the risk, of varying likelihood and severity, of a breach of the rights and freedoms of natural persons;
- (10) appropriate technical and organisational measures;
- (11) the level of security appropriate to the risk.

1. Privacy Impact Assessment (PIA). Tools (templates and knowledge bases), June 2015 Edition.
2. A. Kaczmarek, M. Młotkiewicz, A. Łapińska, A. Miłocha, M. Mazur, consultant J. Zawiła-Niedźwiedzki, *Poradnik RODO. Podejście oparte na ryzyku*, part 2, *Jak stosować podejście oparte na ryzyku?*, GIODO 2017, http://giodo.gov.pl/pl/file/12932 (last accessed on 23 January 2018).
3. Instead of mechanically multiplying the values of the likelihood and seriousness of a breach of the rights and freedoms of natural persons, you can also use gradually increasing risk values that correspond to particular combinations of those factors. This is a question of what risk measurement convention you decide to use.

1.2.1 *The State of the Art*

In times of changing threats and knowledge of how to protect against them, you need to employ modern solutions that incorporate current thinking about cyberspace. In practice, if you do not have sufficient knowledge in this area yourself, you need to call on the services of cybersecurity professionals.

However, at least from the experience of authors of this book, not only it is hard to find knowledgeable cybersecurity specialists, but they usually recommend solutions which are not easy to implement, consuming time, and other resources of a particular organisation. Often they offer solutions which are difficult or impossible to implement, resulting in a so-called shadow IT user behaviour – which is using publicly available free resources for professional use.

Why is that so? Mostly because there is no such thing as cybersecurity [deliberate overstatement]. Due to the current nature of the grid, basic assumptions of modern information technology (IT) (and in particular due to the fact it is based on trust), and due to the rules of the market, creating truly secure IT systems does not seem possible at the moment. As an example – Polish Prosecution claims they have secure email, as an internal email is 'separated' from the public network. Let us even believe it is truly physically separated. However, I once assisted in an interrogation which had to be stopped because a prosecutor needed to send a document to another prosecutor's office. A fax machine was down, and the email quota was too low to accommodate a scan of that document (or the operators have not been trained to decrease a size of a scan). So what happened? Of course, eventually they sent that scan through a private email account of that prosecutor.

Another reason why achieving a state of cybersecurity is practically impossible is that cybersecurity experts usually do not offer complete solutions. The most common issue is requiring encryption and passwords for accessing specific resources. Why is it a problem? Because the market does not offer good solutions to devise and store those myriads of passwords. So, technically encrypting is good, but users are usually not offered with solutions allowing to manage all their digital credentials.

Finally, there will always be organisations ready to accept the risk (or not even carrying about it) and due to that being able to beat you on price. That is called unfair competition, and still security is mostly considered as a cost centre. For many reasons, supervisory authorities will not eliminate such organisations from the market, not even a small portion of them.

So, what to do? If you are small, look for ready to use solutions, rely on trustworthy cloud computing services and other out of the box solutions. If you are big, employ a competent team and see what happens.

However, there is hope. In February 2019, the German IT Security Association Germany (TeleTrusT) in association with ENISA issued guidelines on the notion of 'State of the art' in the meaning of the GDPR (as well as in the meaning of the German IT Security Act of 2015), relating to cybersecurity (and personal data security).[4,5] The

4. https://www.teletrust.de/en/publikationen/broschueren/state-of-the-art-in-it-security/ (last accessed on 11 February 2019).

guidelines to a certain extent can be understood by non-technical persons including lawyers, though for sure they cannot be questioned by non-experts. We must however remember that the guidelines describe 'state of the art' in cybersecurity which not always needs to be attained though in any case needs to be taken into consideration according to 'comply or explain' principle.

1.2.2 Cost

Liability for a leak or destruction of data is one thing; the obligation to provide appropriate security is another. You must ensure that the security in place is appropriate to the threats, but this does not mean that no incidents will ever occur. If one does, you may, and in general will, be liable for how a particular person is affected. But this does not mean that you have breached the general obligation to provide an adequate level of security. The GDPR acknowledges the fact that there is never 100% security.[6]

From this perspective, the cost of particular security measures and their effect on your activity can and should be taken into consideration when augmenting your level of security. It may not pay off to enhance security beyond a certain level; you accept a certain amount of risk along with the consequences (e.g., having to pay out compensation). The same is true in daily life where, for example, the risk of driving in traffic is high, but you are used to it. Of course, not every risk is acceptable, and apart from accepting risk or enhancing security, you can also cease processing that generates a high risk of a breach of the rights and freedoms of natural persons. Evaluating and deciding on how to deal with risk depends on who is doing the processing (whether as a controller or processor).

The logic of cost is a treacherous one, though. Even if you are a small organisation, you will not be able to rely on an argument that you could not have afforded a certain type of security measures if that led to a foreseeable severe adverse consequences for a particular person. Beware of relying directly on cost argumentation when resigning from certain TOMs (technical and organisational measures of data security). Neither supervisory authorities nor courts are very receptive to an argument that appropriate data security measures were too costly to implement.

Therefore, in reality, GDPR does not support the principle of proportionality as regards security measures. We may expect that proportionality will be manifested in practice by administrative (fines) and private (litigation) enforcement (focused on larger and wealthier entities) but purely due to practical reasons.

Moreover, despite the risk matrix is usually presented in the same units for likelihood and for severity, we believe that severity should be considered as a more

5. https://www.teletrust.de/fileadmin/docs/fachgruppen/2019-02_TeleTrusT_Guideline_State_of_the_art_in_IT_security_ENG.pdf (last accessed on 11 February 2019).
6. For example, it could happen that two bank employees agree among themselves to rob a customer. The bank will then be liable towards the customer for the harm the customer suffers at the hands of those employees. If, however, the bank had appropriately designed and implemented procedures in place, the incident should not give rise to any administrative liability of the bank for a breach of the GDPR. After all, certain situations simply cannot be ruled out entirely.

important dimension than likelihood. We believe that risk of minor adverse consequences can be easier accepted even despite it may affect much more people than accepting injury or death of a single person.

1.2.3 *Features of Processing Itself*

Obviously, in order to evaluate risk, you have to know the purpose of the processing, what the data are, what the scope of processing is, and in general what the context is.

The context of processing is what are you processing data for and what consequences your processing has or may have on the data subjects.

1.2.4 *Risk of a Breach of Rights or Freedoms*

Above we briefly discussed how to calculate risk, including how to anticipate any adverse consequences for natural persons. The CNIL provides sample adverse consequences (Table 3.1):

Table 3.1 Severity of Feared Events by CNIL

Levels	*Generic Description of Impacts (Direct and Indirect)*	*Examples of Physical Impacts*[7]	*Examples of Material Impacts*[8]	*Examples of Moral Impacts*[9]
1. Negligible	Data subjects either will not be affected or may encounter a few inconveniences, which they will overcome without any problem	– Lack of adequate care for a dependent person (minor, person under guardianship) – Transient headaches	– Loss of time in repeating formalities or waiting for them to be fulfilled – Receipt of unsolicited mail (e.g., spams) – Reuse of data published on websites for the purpose of targeted advertising (information to social networks, reuse for paper mailing) – Targeted advertising for common consumer products	– Mere annoyance caused by information received or requested – Fear of losing control over one's data – Feeling of invasion of privacy without real or objective harm (e.g., commercial intrusion) – Loss of time in configuring one's data – Lack of respect for the freedom of online movement due to the denial of access to a commercial site (e.g., alcohol because of the wrong age)

7. Loss of amenity, disfigurement, or economic loss related to physical integrity.
8. Loss incurred or lost revenue with respect to an individual's assets.
9. Physical or emotional suffering, disfigurement, or loss of amenity.

2. Limited	Data subjects may encounter significant inconveniences, which they will be able to overcome despite a few difficulties	– Minor physical ailments (e.g., minor illness due to disregard of contraindications) – Lack of care leading to a minor but real harm (e.g., disability) – Defamation resulting in physical or psychological retaliation	– Unanticipated payments (e.g., fines imposed erroneously), additional costs (e.g., bank charges, legal fees), payment defaults – Denial of access to administrative services or commercial services – Lost opportunities of comfort (i.e., cancellation of leisure, purchases, holiday, termination of an online account) – Missed career promotion – Blocked online services account (e.g., games, administration) – Receipt of unsolicited targeted mailings likely to damage the reputation of data subjects – Cost rise (e.g., increased insurance prices) – Non-updated data (e.g., position held previously) – Processing of incorrect data creating, for example accounts malfunctions (bank, customers, with social organisations, etc.)	– Refusal to continue using information systems (whistle-blowing, social networks) – Minor but objective psychological ailments (defamation, reputation) – Relationship problems with personal or professional acquaintances (e.g., image, tarnished reputation, loss of recognition) – Feeling of invasion of privacy without irreversible damage – Intimidation on social networks

Levels	*Generic Description of Impacts (Direct and Indirect)*	*Examples of Physical Impacts*[7]	*Examples of Material Impacts*[8]	*Examples of Moral Impacts*[9]
			– Targeted online advertising on a private aspect that the individual wanted to keep confidential (e.g., pregnancy advertising, drug treatment) – Inaccurate or inappropriate profiling	
3. Significant	Data subjects may encounter significant consequences, which they should be able to overcome albeit with real and serious difficulties	– Serious physical ailments causing long-term harm (e.g., worsening of health due to improper care or disregard of contraindications) – Alteration of physical integrity, for example following an assault, an accident at home, work	– Misappropriation of money not compensated – Non-temporary financial difficulties (e.g., obligation to take a loan) – Targeted, unique, and non-recurring, lost opportunities (e.g., home loan, refusal of studies, internships or employment, examination ban) – Prohibition on the holding of bank accounts – Damage to property – Loss of housing – Loss of employment – Separation or divorce – Financial loss as a result of a fraud (e.g., after an attempted phishing)	– Serious psychological ailments (e.g., depression, development of a phobia) – Feeling of invasion of privacy with irreversible damage – Feeling of vulnerability after a summons to court – Feeling of violation of fundamental rights (e.g., discrimination, freedom of expression) – Victim of blackmailing – Cyberbullying and harassment

			– Blocked abroad – Loss of customer data	
4. Maximum	Data subjects may encounter significant, or even irreversible, consequences, which they may not overcome	– Long-term or permanent physical ailments (e.g., due to disregard of contraindications) – Death (e.g., murder, suicide, fatal accident) – Permanent impairment of physical integrity	– Financial risk – Substantial debts – Inability to work – Inability to relocate – Loss of evidence in the context of litigation – Loss of access to vital infrastructure (water, electricity)	– Long-term or permanent psychological ailments – Criminal penalty – Abduction – Loss of family ties – Inability to sue – Change of administrative status and/or loss of legal autonomy (guardianship)

Source: Privacy Impact Assessment (PIA) Knowledge Bases, CNIL, February 2018.

The ISO 27005 standard mentions the following typical threats to information security:

Physical damage:

- Fire,
- Flooding,
- Pollution,
- Serious accident,
- Damage to equipment or media,
- Dust, corrosion, hypothermia.

Loss of basic services:

- Failure of an air conditioning system or water supply,
- Loss of power supply,
- Failure of telecommunications equipment.

Breach of information security:

- Interception of signals as a result of interference phenomena,
- Remote espionage,
- Wiretapping,
- Theft of media or documents,
- Theft of equipment,
- Access from reused or discarded media,
- Disclosure,
- Data from unreliable sources,
- Manipulation of devices,
- Falsification of software,
- Detection of location.

Technical failure:

- Failure of equipment,
- Improper functioning of equipment,
- IT system overload,
- Improper functioning of software,
- Breach of capacity to maintain IT system (lack of organisational and technical resources guaranteeing the proper functioning of the system).

Unauthorised activity:

- Unauthorised use of equipment,

- Unauthorised copying of software,
- Use of false or copied software,
- Deformation of data.

Breach of functional security:

- Unlawful data processing,
- User error,
- Breach of entitlements,
- Falsification of entitlements,
- Refusal to act,
- Breach of personnel access.

Personal breaches:

- Hacker (break-in to the system),
- Computer crime (cybernetic persecution, impersonation, data hijacking),
- Terrorism,
- Industrial espionage,
- Internal staff (badly trained, dissatisfied, angry, careless, dishonest, conducting themselves unethically or contrary to the law, dismissed employees).

Appropriate organisational and technical measures. Your palette of information and personal data protection measures can vary. It may consist of legal tools (e.g., confidentiality undertakings, provisions, agreements), organisational tools (procedures, levels of authorisation), physical tools (e.g., keys, safe envelopes, access control), and IT tools (e.g., levels of authorisation, firewalls, shared access, intrusion detection systems, antivirus tools, real-time cloud-based cybersecurity services). You should choose what best fits the risk determined.

Appropriate level of security. An organisation should manage its security through security levels. Of course, in theory you could just apply the highest level and forget about lower levels. But in practice it is usually more convenient to distinguish a number of levels so as not to hinder activity excessively. Further, when determining the most appropriate security level, attention should be also be paid to accessibility. Requirements that are too strict can hinder access to data, both within the organisation and among its customers.

1.3 Security Measures

Article 32(1) GDPR mentions the following categories of security measures:

(a) the **pseudonymisation** and **encryption** of personal data;
(b) the ability to ensure the ongoing confidentiality, integrity, availability, and resilience of processing systems and services – i.e., **cybersecurity**;

(c) the ability to restore the availability and access to personal data in a timely manner in the event of a physical or technical incident – i.e., **business continuity and disaster recovery**;
(d) a process for regularly testing, assessing, and evaluating the effectiveness of technical and organisational measures for ensuring the security of the processing – i.e., **testing**;

Article 28, the GDPR mentions such instruments as:

(e) agreements,
(f) confidentiality undertakings,

and, under various names, requires the application of the following principles:

(g) minimisation (of time, scope, amount, access, data used), as well as;
(h) particular security agreements concerning the export of data to third countries.

In an organisation, the personal data security system, which can be documented in a data security policy, should take account of at least the following control points:

(1) evaluating the usefulness and application of pseudonymisation;
(2) evaluating the usefulness and application of encryption (e.g., for mobile devices, media, and communications);
(3) IT system cybersecurity (including issues of scalability, redundancy, penetration defences, etc.);
(4) plans for business continuity and disaster recovery;
(5) plans for tests and testing (penetration tests, testing the disaster recovery plan);
(6) limiting personal data processing to the necessary minimum:
   - limiting the number of locations in which data are processed,
   - limiting the scope of data to the necessary minimum,
   - exercising control over access to personal data and establishing levels of access and authorisation,
   - limiting data storing time (retention).
(7) introducing data deletion/anonymisation mechanisms;
(8) introducing rules for safe communication;
(9) establishing rules for maintaining and developing IT systems;
(10) creating and using template agreements for entrusting data processing and establishing procedures for verifying the performance of these;
(11) selecting and training personnel (human resources security);
(12) creating and using temple confidentiality undertakings 'armed' with a list of provisions entailing sanctions for breaches of confidentiality;
(13) keeping an inventory of data processing resources and managing these;

(14) verifying SLAs (IT service level agreements) concluded in terms of the agreed levels of availability of services;
(15) verifying and deciding on the possible application of emergency procedures to ensure operational independence from suppliers;
(16) verifying the data export situations (together with appropriate obligations for processors in the template data entrustment agreement) and ensuring that appropriate data protection safeguards are in place;
(17) managing incidents (especially personal data breaches – Articles 33 and 34 GDPR).

When developing personal data security rules, you might wish to refer to a local implementation of the NIS Directive (European Union (EU) Network and Information Security Directive) – often called 'cybersecurity acts'.[10] Though primarily NIS Directive applies to large entities (operators of essential services), NIS cybersecurity systems standards will undoubtedly become best standards for evaluating data protection security (at a procedural level), especially that the GDPR in reality says nothing about data security (maybe except for something like this 'consider encryption and pseudonymisation, remember about backups and in general about business continuity, though we do not use words "backups" and "business continuity", because it would be too easy, so even Americans would know'). At the same time a relation between the NIS Directive (implementations) and the GDPR will become symbiotic; as though the NIS Directive does not provide for fines, breaching NIS' cybersecurity standards is easily penalised under the GDPR as violation of data protection security rules (not so easy applicable to operational technology, though).

Of course, if you intend to be EU-wide compliant, you need to develop a more holistic approach than relying on a local 'cybersecurity act'. That is where the TeleTrust and ENISA's guidelines on the state of the art in IT security might come in handy. Still, extracting a common denominator from all EU implementations of the NIS Directive seems to be the best approach.[11]

1.4 Shortcuts?

The CNIL (Commission nationale de l'informatique et des libertés), the French supervisory authority, has published an application on how to conduct a DPIA.[12] The application includes a predefined set of typical security measures. Using the CNIL's method in order to evaluate impact, you can conduct a risk analysis of your own data processing activities. Combined with security procedures, this should result in a data protection system that will stand up before the supervisory authority. The catch in

10. A link to a useful list of the NIS Directive implementations to be found here: https://eur-lex.europa.eu/legal-content/EN/NIM/?uri=uriserv:OJ.L_.2016.194.01.0001.01.ENG (last accessed on 27 February 2019).
11. Not that we tried so far. We are still chewing through the Polish Cybersecurity System Act and approaching the German, French, Irish, and Maltese implementations.
12. *See* https://www.cnil.fr/en/open-source-pia-software-helps-carry-out-data-protection-impact-assesment (last accessed on 10 March 2018).

using CNIL's PIA app is that it adopts a per-data processing activity approach, requiring an organisation to run it separately for each of their data processing activities (which one may have from several dozens to a couple hundred).

Other DPIA or PIA apps are being released to the market right now in different EU countries.

You may also employ a little less developed tools such as predefined spreadsheets which are less fancy than CNILs PIA, but they allow for a two or even three-dimensional perspective on an organisation, its resources, and risks associated.

Small organisations may try to approach risk analysis in a simplified manner, starting from defining their minimum security level set of 'TOMs' (technical and organisational (security) measures), from an increased security level TOMs up to maximum level TOMs (mostly moderated by an organisation's budget). Then within such defined range, an organisation may define its native level of risk in a few simple steps.

2 PSEUDONYMISATION AND ENCRYPTION: PREFERRED METHODS OF SECURING PERSONAL DATA?

2.1 Preliminary Remarks

The GDPR provisions refer to only two technical means of personal data protection: encryption and pseudonymisation. It does not necessarily mean that organisations are always forced to encrypt personal data or employ more sophisticated pseudonymisation technics. However, organisations should be able to explain in particular why they are not encrypting or pseudonymising personal data they process (e.g., due to specific risks to availability or integrity of data).

2.2 Encryption

The GDPR does not define encryption. The word makes us think of powerful encryption algorithms, that is cryptographic algorithms. By powerful algorithms we mean those that at a given moment are considered safe (e.g., due to key length or the strength of the algorithm itself). An encryption algorithm is nothing other than a mathematical function that deforms one item of information (which is public, in what is called open form) into another (non-public, encrypted, in what is called closed form). The reverse process, decryption, requires knowledge of specific, confidential (secret) data – this can be a password, a special key, or biometric data such as a fingerprint, the arrangement of veins in the hand, or the retina of the eye. The purpose of encryption is to protect information from being accessed by unauthorised third persons. It can have the added benefit of control over data quality since damaged encrypted data cannot be properly decrypted. Encryption can also be applied to data in transit, that is when the data are being sent, e.g. over the internet (or in a backpack in which we have a laptop, or a pen drive in an envelope sent by courier, or even in a smartphone), or when they are in what is known as state of rest, that is when they are recorded in files or a database. It does not matter where such a file is located – be it on our computer or somewhere in the cloud. Yet, so far there is no practical method of encrypting data while they are being processed by a computer in a RAM memory (since the file must be open).[13]

The GDPR refers to encryption four times – once in the recitals and three times in the provisions. This explains the 'popularity' of encryption, which is often presented as a panaceum for all problems concerning GDPR compliance. But it does not work that way. Encrypting everything everywhere in no way releases an organisation from the obligation to implement other security mechanisms. The basic requirements for GDPR security compliance are set out in Article 32 GDPR. The regulation also applies risk analysis and the principle of adequacy. Further, badly implemented encryption will not necessarily raise the level of security, and an organisation may continue to be exposed to penalties for lack of compliance with the GDPR if there is a breach of personal data security. Encryption increasing confidentiality decreases the availability of data. Associated risks may have technical nature – an accidental corruption of makes them impossible to decrypt (hence not accessible) or organisational nature – leaving users alone with passwords policy puzzle will result in the same – sooner or later inaccessibility of data. Nevertheless, since the GDPR refers directly to encryption, you cannot overlook encryption when assessing the adequacy of the personal data protection measures you have in place.

Risks associated with encryption are manifested well by an add of one of the tech giants promoting their encryption solution. What the add says is encryption can serve as a permanent data deletion measure – simply destroy (or loose) a data decryption key. Consequences are easy to imagine. We do not even need to imagine consequences of a partisan user encryption – probably every reader of this book received once via email an encrypted archive (ZIP, RAR, etc.). Who of us was able to decrypt it again after a certain period of time?

Encryption brings different organisational or technical problems. Let us look at email, while encryption of email in transit becomes standard (Transport Layer Security),[14] as well as encrypting data at rest (e.g., BitLocker native to Windows10) end-to-end or point-to-point encryption (S/MIME, PGP, GnuPG, etc.) is an organisational problem, portal encryption (secure webmail systems) is a UX (user experience) and durable medium problem, and user hand encryption is an organisational nightmare.

13. Although in theory it is possible to use what is known as homomorphic encryption.
14. For example Danish Personal Data Protection Supervisory Authority required email in transit encryption from public bodies and since 2019 requires the same from private entities. https://www.datatilsynet.dk/presse-og-nyheder/nyhedsarkiv/2018/jul/skaerpet-praksis-ift-krypteret-e-mail/ (last accessed on 12 February 2019).

2.3 Pseudonymisation

Pseudonymisation is a process of transforming data such that the data subject cannot be identified by anyone except for those who possess the key (a simplest example of a 'key' is a list of names corresponding to unique identifying numbers).

According to Article 4(5) GDPR, pseudonymisation means:

> the processing of personal data in such a manner that the personal data can no longer be attributed to a specific data subject without the use of additional information, provided that such additional information is kept separately and is subject to technical and organisational measures to ensure that the personal data are not attributed to an identified or identifiable natural person.

To simplify, pseudonymisation means replacing a given person's identifiers (such as first and last name, identity number, telephone number, email address) with pseudonyms – unique (unrepeatable) codes, figures, or images (within this scope there is some freedom) that have no real connection with that person. In this way, data that would give away the identity of specific people are changed into[15] meaningless data (pseudonyms, usually numbers, that connect the hidden personal identities with descriptions of those people's traits).[16]

Pseudonymisation is a reversible process, which means that the body carrying out the pseudonymisation can, in response to certain actions, ascertain that certain data concern, for example, John Smith. The reversibility of the process is crucial and distinguishes pseudonymisation from anonymisation.

The GDPR refers to pseudonymisation as many as fifteen times, including nine times in the recitals and six times in the provisions.

2.4 Anonymisation

Anonymisation is an irreversible process. Once data have been anonymised they can no longer be used to identify the person they concern. Anonymisation is used in order to prevent the identification of people whose data have been anonymised, and so it is not used when knowledge of identity is required.

The GDPR refers to anonymisation in Recital 26. Anonymisation is considered a method of deleting data. Anonymising records is a technically preferred way of deleting personal data, especially over deleting records, due to a risk of destroying the integrity of databases. Simply said, in case we delete a record (another words a row in a table) the database (a spreadsheet) may collapse and cells may no longer remain in their proper rows (records) making the whole database more or less useless. How at all would it be possible in a modern IT world? Simply it would be possible, and it happens every now and then, as IT is an erroneous technology by its nature. On a practical and

15. Display, print, etc.
16. A simple method of pseudonymisation would be to transfer columns with first and last names from one spreadsheet to another (provided that we first assigned a numerical order to the rows and also moved this to the new spreadsheet).

technical level, anonymisation may be more or less immune to reidentification. Proper anonymisation should be truly irreversible. However, poorly designed anonymisation may even retain directly identifying fields (cells). Therefore, it is important for a person responsible for data protection in a particular organisation what is understood by 'anonymisation' by persons responsible for specific IT systems or analogue data carriers (mostly – paper).

Anyway, anonymisation does not serve to protect personal data but to destroy personal data. Therefore we do not dig into it further.

2.5 Pseudonymisation or Encryption

A simple comparison of the number of occurrences of the words 'encryption' and 'pseudonymisation' in the GDPR leads to the conclusion that pseudonymisation is the favourite security technique of the authors of the regulation. In truth, pseudonymisation lends itself well in principle to minimisation, because it can be used to limit the amount of information on natural persons 'processed' by an organisation for business and other purposes and is therefore also suitable for limiting authorised access (graded access). Whereas encryption is 'only' a means of protecting against unauthorised access (on the principle of 'all or nothing').

In reality, both techniques usually serve different purposes. Encryption is more a technical measure of data security, simpler to implement. Pseudonymisation is more a means of minimising data processing (scope of data access) so more a means of privacy by default. While user-level implementation of encryption is not easy, implementing pseudonymisation is even more complicated. Though, we are not saying it is impossible, as, for example, in clinical trials 'double-blind trials' mechanism is a standard.

2.5.1 Security

The GDPR rightly recognises that encryption (Recital 83 GDPR) and pseudonymisation (Recital 28 GDPR) are means of minimising the risk of a breach of the rights and freedoms of data subjects.

Pursuant to Article 32(1)(a) GDPR, the following must be implemented:

> appropriate technical and organisational measures to ensure a level of security appropriate to the risk [of a breach of the rights and freedoms of natural persons], including inter alia as appropriate ... the pseudonymisation and encryption of personal data.

Since the first two examples of data protection measures specified in the GDPR are pseudonymisation and encryption, when actually evaluating the adequacy of and selecting data protection measures, one must not neglect to consider the usefulness of these two methods for a particular data processing operation or activity. This does not necessarily mean that you have to use either of them,[17] but (in accordance with the principle of accountability) you should at least be able to explain why you are not using them.

2.5.2 Risk Analysis

What specific data security measures are actually used should result from a prior analysis of the risk the data processing poses to the rights and freedoms of the data subjects.

Recital 76 GDPR states:

> The likelihood and severity of the risk to the rights and freedoms of the data subject should be determined by reference to the nature, scope, context and purposes of the processing. Risk should be evaluated on the basis of an objective assessment, by which it is established whether data processing operations involve a risk or a high risk.

An indication of how to decide what data protection measures to employ is provided by Recital 83 GDPR, which states:

> In order to maintain security and to prevent processing in infringement of this Regulation, the controller or processor should evaluate the risks inherent in the processing and implement measures to mitigate those risks, such as encryption.

Recital 83 also indicates a need to weigh the costs of implementing protective measures against the risk and the nature of the data involved:

> Those measures should ensure an appropriate level of security, including confidentiality, taking into account the state of the art and the costs of implementation in relation to the risks and the nature of the personal data to be protected.

Finally, the recital states how risk should be evaluated:

> In assessing data security risk, consideration should be given to the risks that are presented by personal data processing, such as the accidental or unlawful destruction, loss, alteration, unauthorised disclosure of, or access to personal data transmitted, stored or otherwise processed, which may lead in particular to physical, material or non-material damage.

Risks and threats are described broadly in Recital 75 GDPR, which primarily states when the type of risk is involved:

> 'The risk to the rights and freedoms of natural persons, of varying likelihood and severity, may result from personal data processing which could lead to physical, material or non-material damage', and then lists specific threats:

17. It may come as a surprise, but cybersecurity experts say that when they run a data protection impact assessment, it often turns out that other data protection measures are sufficient.

- 'where the processing may give rise to [1] discrimination, [2] identity theft or fraud, [3] financial loss, [4] damage to the reputation, [5] loss of confidentiality of personal data protected by professional secrecy, [6] unauthorised reversal of pseudonymisation, or [7] any other significant economic or social disadvantage;
- where data subjects might be [8] deprived of their rights and freedoms or [9] prevented from exercising control over their personal data;
- where personal data are processed which [10 – special category data] reveal racial or ethnic origin, political opinions, religion or philosophical beliefs, trade union membership, and the processing of genetic data, data concerning health or data concerning sex life or criminal convictions and offences or related security measures;
- if [11] personal aspects are evaluated, particularly if analyses or forecasts are made of aspects concerning job performance, economic condition, health, personal preferences or interests, reliability, behaviour, location or travel – in order to create or use personal profiles; or
- where personal data [12] of vulnerable natural persons, in particular [13] of children, are processed;
- where processing involves [14] a large amount of personal data and affects a large number of data subjects'.

Without much hesitation, we can say that wherever a risk exists of serious harm being caused to an individual or a large group of people, specific personal data protection measures should be employed, including encryption or pseudonymisation.

However, as mentioned above, at the same time organisations should bear in mind that both encryption and pseudonymisation affect the availability of data. Mandatory encrypting of all electric bills by an energy company would bring havoc to its customers, especially if strong passwords were required.

2.5.2.1 Data Protection Impact Assessment

Usually, a risk analysis is also needed to evaluate whether to conduct a more formalised risk analysis, known as a DPIA, as referred to in Article 35 GDPR. Article 35 states that a DPIA or PIA should be conducted where the risk associated with data processing is high. A DPIA is nothing other than a dedicated risk analysis of specific IT systems and data processing processes accompanied by additional verification of legality of processing and processing of data subject requests. Such an assessment should result in a list of threats to the IT system or a process. On that basis, appropriate security measures can be selected. Of course, it can happen that the cost, or technical or organisational limitations, do not permit one or more security measures to be implemented. In such a case, it may be possible to replace these measures with others, or with other control mechanisms. These would then be considered compensatory measures. However, such an approach is not always possible. It may turn out that the cost of implementation exceeds the cost of the loss entailed by the risk, or that the costs cannot be justified economically. This is why an impact assessment is so important. Where security is concerned, there is no upper-cost limit. It is easy then to end up in a situation where security costs are growing exponentially, data are still not safe, and GDPR compliance has not been achieved.

However, as already mentioned, we do not recommend relying directly on cost argumentation when deciding on appropriate technical and organisational measures of data protection.

2.5.2.2 Method of Risk Analysis

When it comes to running a risk analysis, theoretically there is no need to think up your own method – you can use one of those publicly available, such as from ISO 27005. In the opinion of one of the co-author's of this text, the ISO 27005 standard is ideal for both small and large organisations and is extraordinarily simple and concise. According to the other co-authors, who are attorneys, a standard that runs sixty-eight pages is not concise and cannot be simple. Therefore hopefully more ready to use methods emerge.

Because there is not always a high risk associated with personal data processing, not all processing systems and operations will require an impact assessment. Paradoxically, though, in order to find out where you stand, you have to first conduct a risk analysis.

Does this mean that in a system that does not generate a high risk of a breach of rights and freedoms you do not have to use pseudonymisation or encryption? Not necessarily. First, you should go by the principle that, when being transmitted through a public or third-party accessible network such as the internet, personal data should be encrypted. Second, if you grant anyone access to your personal data processing system, then, in accordance with the need-to-know principle, you may need to protect data and restrict access, e.g. through pseudonymisation. Pseudonymisation can also be an ideal solution if you process data for strictly statistical purposes, e.g. how many people in a given age bracket bought a certain product.

Remember, encryption and pseudonymisation have one common goal – to protect data from access by unauthorised third persons. Both processes are reversible, meaning that an authorised person should be able to recover the data (in the case of encryption) or identify the data subject (in the case of pseudonymisation). This property is extremely important and often misunderstood.

It is easier to discuss by way of example. Let us start with encryption: the personal data kept in the database are in encrypted form. If an unauthorised third person gains access to the database, they would not be able to retrieve them because they exist in closed form (encrypted). Only a decryption operation will render them open. This means that, in order to be processed, at some point, the data must be transformed from closed to open form. This makes the moment of transformation critical with respect to data protection.

In the case of pseudonymisation, however, we should imagine a system with two tiers: production and testing. Assuming that in the testing environment only test data, and not real data, are used,[18] there is no problem if those data are accessed by an external entity providing system support services (e.g., by the producer of the system). But when there is a need to fix an error at the production level where real personal data are stored, outside people cannot be granted access without additional formalities. This issue can be resolved by creating a three-tier system that contains data subjected to pseudonymisation. Pseudonymised data do not disclose information on the data subjects, thereby permitting an entity providing support services to fix the error. Afterwards, the process of pseudonymisation is reversed and the solution transferred from the third tier to the production tier. For example, there could be a problem with a person having ID 179923. The external entity cannot ascribe that ID to a specific person, but, thanks to the reversibility of the process, the system owner knows that the person in question in John Smith and can make changes in the relevant record in the production tier. Most important here is that, in terms of the GDPR, a proper pseudonymisation process is one that can be reversed only by the party authorised to do so.

2.6 Privacy by Design

Article 25(1) GDPR, which sets out the principle of data protection by design, refers to pseudonymisation. This is certainly because, up to now, pseudonymisation has been rarely used, even though it is a good method for implementing the basic principle of minimising data access. The authors of the GDPR recognised the value of including the use of pseudonymisation in new drafts that are to affect privacy in general.

2.7 Notification of Breaches of Data Protection

Article 34 GDPR releases a controller from the obligation to notify a data subject about a breach of data protection if 'the controller has implemented appropriate technical and organisational protection measures, and those measures were applied to the personal data affected by the personal data breach, in particular those that render the personal data unintelligible to any person who is not authorised to access it, such as encryption'.

You should keep in mind just how troublesome it can be on various levels to inform data subjects that there has been a leak of their data. Securing data by encryption during transmission or transport offers protection against the awkward, burdensome, and often costly obligation to notify data subjects of a breach.

2.8 Use of Business Pseudonymisation

Pseudonymisation is a good way to limit the impact of profiling on privacy. People are predictable, and with today's access to information we are able to create very detailed profiles for predicting or analysing behaviour based on our knowledge of the behaviour

18. From 'implementation' leaks, it seems that, in practice, integrity tests and user tests usually make use of production data (that is, full customer personal data). This is why testing is often used as a model example of the usefulness of pseudonymisation.

of people who are tracked (on the net, in ATMs, in places where they pay by card, using geolocation based on Wi-Fi, by means of monitoring, facial recognition, licence number plates, etc.). For privacy, it would be an unthinkable disaster (for now) if every business (and especially sellers) had access to a specific individual's full profile based on the work of a data analysis unit. How, then, can we avoid a situation where someone can establish on the basis of data that Smith is a drunk who beats his children? Profile building, whether for predictive or correlative purposes, should be undertaken without knowledge of the identity of particular persons - based on pseudonymised data. But that is not all. Profiles should certainly not be made available in their entirety to marketers. Rather, marketers should provide already-built marketing campaigns (where our Smith may find himself in an ad campaign for beer and separately in a campaign for books on self-help and anger management). Pseudonymisation relates somewhat to the problem of margin of error, that is improper profiling. Anyone who is not a terrorist or drug courier but has been chosen for an SSSS (secondary security screening selection) during a security check at the airport knows about this; so does anyone who has had their money frozen on their account under an anti-money laundering procedure even though the money was there legally.

Pseudonymisation is also used in 'trivial' cases, such as when data on remuneration are provided to trade unions or courts for the purpose of evaluating possible discrimination.

Double pseudonymisation (a double-blind sample) is standardly applied in clinical trials (where reversibility is obviously necessary, but for this two organisations must cooperate). Similarly, it is also applied in other studies where knowledge is required on various life circumstances of the people involved, but knowledge of their identity is not.

2.9 Summary

A data risk analysis should be conducted regardless of whether the process/system concerned is covered by an impact assessment pursuant to Article 35 GDPR. Based on the results of the risk analysis or DPIA, a decision should be made on whether to apply encryption, pseudonymisation, or other data protection methods.

An evaluation should be made of the justifiability of pseudonymisation in procedures for initiating and running new projects, new investments, and organisational changes (privacy by design).

Encryption during data transmission or when data are transported on physical media is recommended.

We recommend you specify encryption and pseudonymisation when describing the organisational and technical data protection measures in the RDPA.

3 PRIVACY BY DESIGN

3.1 Privacy by Design

Pursuant to Article 25(1) GDPR:

> Taking into account the state of the art, the cost of implementation and the nature, scope, context and purposes of processing as well as the risks of varying likelihood and severity for rights and freedoms of natural persons posed by the processing **[1 – corresponds to Art. 32(1) – processing security]**, the controller shall, both **[2]** at the time of the determination of the means for processing and **[3]** at the time of the processing itself, implement **[4]** appropriate technical and organisational measures, such as **[5]** pseudonymisation, which are designed to implement data-protection principles, such as **[6]** data minimisation **[*privacy by default*]**, in an effective manner and **[7]** to integrate the necessary safeguards into the processing in order to meet the requirements of this Regulation and protect the rights of data subjects.

Privacy by design requires you to think about personal data protection from the stage of designing procedures and IT systems, processes, and products. Accordingly, you must implement measures that guarantee the security of data processing from the design stage and not 'add' them later after a given solution has already been invented and designed. This makes it possible to avoid loopholes and inconsistent processes. Yet, it should be emphasised that the effects of privacy by design should be visible throughout the entire data processing procedure.

Important

New design activities also include modifying existing solutions.

The main advantages of the privacy by design approach are:

(1) identifying potential problems at the very beginning of the process;
(2) having a greater likelihood of meeting the GDPR requirements, and in particular embedding data subjects rights related functionalities into software systems;
(3) mitigating 'error in design' issues related to data processing and privacy;
(4) increasing awareness in the organisation of the personal data processing requirements.

Privacy by design is a consequence of one of the main assumptions of the GDPR – that of a preventive approach. But please note that the privacy by design concept is not entirely new – it was presented in the 1990s by Ann Cavoukian, the Ombudsman for Ontario.[19] Cavoukian's conception was based on seven pillars that included a

19. After D. Lubasz, K. Witkowska-Nowakowska [in:] *RODO. Ogólne rozporządzenie o ochronie danych. Komentarz*, ed. E. Bielak-Jomaa, D. Lubasz, Warsaw 2017, p. 601.

pro-active and preventive approach, privacy as the default setting, and data protection throughout the entire processing cycle.[20]

Privacy by design refers to minimisation, the latter in general corresponding to privacy by default. So you should probably start reading Article 25(1) GDPR from Article 25(2) GDPR.

3.1.1 *What Privacy by Design Consists In*

From the wording of the GDPR provision on privacy by design, three things can be distinguished: you must guarantee (1) security and (2) minimisation of access, and these must be taken account of (3) in advance, meaning that you must design whenever possible, that is for all new plans.

The provision itself is worth reading more or less from the end:

[7] in order to secure the processing and ensure its lawfulness, and
[6] in order to apply the principle of the minimisation of data,
[4] you must use technical and organisational measures appropriate
[1] to the risk of a breach of the rights and freedoms of persons as a result of the processing, and you must do this
[2] at the stage of selecting technologies, suppliers and processing procedure, as well as
[3] during the processing itself,
[5] including by using pseudonymisation, or at least by verifying its usefulness.

3.1.1.1 *Security*

The first part of the provisions is in effect a repetition of Article 32 GDPR on data processing security.

The factors that affect the scope of the privacy by design obligation are: the state of the art; the costs of implementation; the nature, scope, context, and goals of the processing; and the risk of a breach of the rights and freedoms of natural persons.

This means that in every case a controller should weigh those factors from the perspective of its own individual situation. Mind, however, that 'no considerations of an organisational or financial nature should be treated as a basis for the unlawful processing of personal data'.[21] A controller is not obliged to ensure that all security measures are used when processing data; it may limit itself just to those that are adequate and appropriate (whatever that means in light of the GDPR requirements. Actually, it means whatever comes out from a risk analysis and cannot be easily questioned).

20. More broadly: A. Cavoukian, *The 7 Foundational Principles*, https://www.ipc.on.ca/wp-content/uploads/Resources/7foundationalprinciples.pdf (last accessed on 28 December 2017).
21. Judgment of the Polish Supreme Administrative Court of 4.03.2002, II SA 3144/01 symptomatic for the general approach of courts and regulators.

3.1.1.2 *Pseudonymisation*

In respect of privacy by design, the GDPR directly specifies only one of the security measures available – the pseudonymisation of data. This does not mean, though, that you can neglect the other measures included in Article 32 GDPR or you are obliged to implement pseudonymisation. You should interpret things in this way – that you must not neglect pseudonymisation when analysing the adequacy of security measures or designing changes in data processing. In every case, you should verify whether pseudonymisation has a place in the solutions designed.

As shown above, when discussing pseudonymisation and encryption, pseudonymisation fits in with the principle of minimisation, because it can be used to limit the amount of information on natural persons processed by an organisation for business and other purposes and is therefore also suitable for limiting authorised access (graded access).

3.1.1.3 *Minimisation*

The concept of minimisation is discussed below in section 3.1.2 on privacy by default. Here we will just mention that it concerns minimising knowledge about a person in order to maximise that person's privacy and primarily involves minimising access to information (personal data) in the possession of an organisation.

3.1.2 *How to Implement Privacy by Design in an Organisation*

3.1.2.1 *Privacy by Design in a Specific Project*

Meeting the requirement of privacy by design in a specific instance involves conducting risk analyses and frequent DPIAs and then acting on the organisation and technical conclusions resulting from these. This can be by choosing a system that provides more diverse access procedures, purchasing access management tools having high organisational logic and intuitive screens that graphically organise supervision over authorised users in various systems, choosing suppliers that accept the most responsibility for personal data breaches or that offer certified solutions and tools that make it possible to force customers to go along with security policy in an integrated manner (cloud services often have a problem with this), etc.

3.1.2.2 *Rules of Privacy by Design*

As mentioned above, privacy by design involves taking care of personal data security in advance, minimising processing, and above all minimising data access. For this to take place, you must check when starting up a new project whether any other change in the organisation has taken privacy into consideration.

To this end, you should include the requirements for protecting privacy in your procedures for initiating new projects, new investments, seeking new suppliers, and making changes in the organisation. If your organisation has not yet worked out such procedures, it is high time to draw up a short checklist for those who make decisions on new outlays. That list should include questions on whether the impact of activity related to the outlay/investment on privacy has been verified, whether a risk analysis has been conducted concerning a potential breach of the rights and freedoms of people whose data the new project will affect, and whether privacy by design has been guaranteed – including through organisational or technical data protection measures and the principle of minimising data access as well as ensuring tools for executing data subject rights and allowing for accountability are in place. You should also make sure that new projects are reflected in the register of processing activities – by using appropriate connections between procedures or involving those persons responsible for the data processing activity record in the process of starting up new projects.

In practical terms, it may make more sense to perform a DPIA (DPIA – described in Chapter 5 below) for each new project initiated than to design an additional less detailed PIA procedure for a starter and then to check if a DPIA is needed and move to perform such DPIA.

3.1.2.3 When to Design Privacy

Privacy should be designed and implemented at once, that is, whenever there is to be an organisational, technological, process, or business change that could have an impact on data processing and that is completed after 25 May 2018. You must conduct a documented privacy analysis, make a decision on the requirements and activities needed to secure privacy, and implement those requirements and activities. Privacy by design programme might be a righteous response to legacy issues of existing personal data processing systems and processes in a particular organisation. Due to various practical reasons, you were probably not able to be truly GDPR compliant on 25 May 2018 or even by the end of 2019. And that may be even fine. However, you should achieve appropriate technical level of GDPR maturity in a definite time. And that is what a privacy by design programme may serve for.

3.2 Certification of Privacy by Design and Privacy by Default

Pursuant to Article 25(3) GDPR, you can demonstrate that you have met the obligations referred to in paragraphs 1 and 2 of the article by introducing an approved certification mechanism as described in Article 42 GDPR.

However, at the time we write this book, there are no existing certification mechanisms in place. So far only European Data Protection Board (EDPB) issued guidelines on certifications mechanisms,[22] not adding much to general rules already described in ISO standards.

22. Guidelines 1/2018 on certification and identifying certification criteria in accordance with Arts 42 and 43 of the Regulation 2016/679 Adopted on 23 January 2019.

4 PRIVACY BY DEFAULT: MINIMISATION

4.1 The Principle of Privacy by Default

'Privacy by default' is an unclear term, leading to a number of misconceptions. The term itself suggests it relates only to 'default settings' of computer systems and other procedures. Understanding it that way: in a situation where a data subject decides to make their data available, this should be within as limited a scope as possible, only to the extent necessary for the controller's purposes (e.g., when creating a social media account, the initial settings should guarantee the data subject as much privacy as possible; when registering in an application, a data subject should provide necessary data only). Only a data subject should decide whether they wish to reduce the level of protection of their privacy by making further data available, changing their privacy settings, etc.

However, reaching to the specific wording of Article 25(2) GDPR we end up with a different concept.

Pursuant to Article 25(2) GDPR, a controller 'shall implement appropriate technical and organisational measures for ensuring that, by default, only personal data which are necessary for each specific purpose of the processing are processed' [**minimisation of data**]. That obligation applies to the amount of personal data collected [**minimisation of data quantity**], the extent of their processing [**minimisation of data scope**], the period of their storage [**minimisation of data retention**] and their accessibility [**minimisation of data access**]. In particular, such measures shall ensure that by default personal data are not made accessible without the individual's intervention to an indefinite number of natural persons [**control of data access**].

As we see, in reality, the data controller should limit data processing in at least four dimensions (quantity, scope, retention, and access).

4.2 Privacy by Default, i.e. Minimisation

If we take a close look at Article 25(2) GDPR, we can see that privacy by design is, in fact, the principle of minimisation. Minimisation is a multidimensional principle and one quite difficult to put into practice.

We see the following dimensions of data processing minimisation:

(1) minimisation of data quantity;
(2) minimisation of data processing scope;
(3) minimisation of data retention periods;
(4) minimisation of data access, hence;
(5) regulation of data access;
(6) minimisation of data control.

The principle of minimisation derives from the need-to-know principle of information and systems security. Explained simply, it means that a controller or even more accurately a particular member of a controller's personnel knows only what is necessary for only as long as necessary and that access to the data processed is suitably regulated within the controller's organisation.

The most important pillar of the principle of minimisation is the minimisation of access, directed both without and within the organisation. To this end, apart from introducing mechanisms that secure systems against external attacks, a controller should also analyse in advance how processing looks internally and then limit the access of new employees in lower positions to information, divide users into classes and resources into thematic groups that can be accessed only by specific classes (e.g., general resources, ascribed to a particular organisational unit, for the purposes of marketing, customers or other purposes on whose basis profiling is performed – here access should be the most restricted).

4.3 Attributes of Privacy by Default

Guarantee privacy by design means implementing at least three of the following measures:

(1) controlling access to personal data (and the possibility of verifying who accessed data and when);
(2) protecting personal data against access by unauthorised persons or data leaks, e.g. by means of pseudonymisation (named directly as an example of security in Article 25(1) GDPR) or encryption;
(3) restricting the scope of data processing, i.e. processing only those personal data that are necessary to achieve a given processing goal, e.g. using email to send information about a new promotion in an online shop requires only an email address, and so the database need not contain any other personal data.

4.4 Practical Guidelines

To meet the above attributes of privacy by default in practice, you should begin by:

(1) developing information architecture within your organisation. By 'information architecture' we mean not only IT but also a general design of storing, processing, naming, and indexing information;
(2) developing access management rules, including default entitlements for particular user groups to particular resources within the IT architecture and rules for privileged access management;
(3) employing appropriate tools – basic tools for managing logical access can be found in computer operating systems, while managing physical access usually involves keys and access cards;
(4) using such IT services (including cloud computing) and purchasing IT systems that provide access management and accountability;

(5) granting appropriate access rights and obligating personnel to use only those resources necessary for particular employees;
(6) designing appropriate office infrastructure.

While the last point above may not seem key, in practice, the absence of a well thought out infrastructure can result in a high risk of data leakage. For example, we suggest having dedicated printers available to departments that process employee data, including payroll (of course, you should treat this remark as applying also to other departments that handle specific categories of data). A leak can occur if such data are printed out on a printer to which everyone has access.

Moreover, the principle of minimisation is reflected in other principles foreseen in the GDPR:

(1) the principle of adequacy, based on restricting the scope of data collected;
(2) the principles of limiting the duration of data processing.

We will discuss the basic principles of personal data processing individually.

4.5 Access by an Indefinite Number of Persons

The last issue worth taking a look at with respect to privacy by default is that of data being made accessible 'to an indefinite number of natural persons'. In our view, this issue should not be treated strictly quantitatively (although when data are made accessible to a larger number of persons, great caution should obviously be exercised).

It seems that as long as we are able to precisely specify the circle of recipients who are natural persons, we meet the requirements of privacy by default. It may turn out, though, that such a precise specification of addresses is problematic, even when it seems that the circle is closed.

Example

If we make resources available to all employees, then, as a result of employee turnover (particularly at lower levels, training programmes, etc.), this apparently closed circle may be deemed to be open and to contain an indefinite number of natural persons. Therefore, privacy by default should be taken to mean a limited group having data access, from which it follows that it would not be GDPR compliant for every new employee (or newly established company systems user) to immediately have access to all resources.

4.6 Certification of Privacy by Design and Privacy by Default

Pursuant to Article 25(3) GDPR, you can demonstrate that you have met the obligations referred to in paragraphs 1 and 2 of the article by introducing an approved certification mechanism as described in Article 42 GDPR.

In accordance with the above provision, a controller can fully meet its obligation to apply privacy by design and privacy and default by introducing an approved certification mechanism in its organisation. Even if a controller decides not to introduce such a mechanism, it is advisable to possess complete documentation confirming that the requirements have been met.

4.7 Privacy by Design and Privacy by Default and Software

The GDPR imposes privacy by design duties on data controllers and data processors. Formally software developers are out of the scope of the Regulations. In practice, however, complying with privacy by design principles requires operating compliant and capable software. Which makes software developers indirectly but very tightly affected by Article 25(1) GDPR.

The Norwegian data protection supervisory body issued Guidelines on Software development with Data Protection by Design and by Default.[23] The Guidelines refer to ISO 27001 standard, to the ISF Standard of Good Practice for Information Security, Microsoft Security Development Lifecycle and OWASP methodologies.

When we look directly at GDPR's, we come up with a set of conclusions for developing GDPR compliant software.

Principles of processing. It seems not all principles of personal data processing defined in Article 5 GDPR translate into software requirements. Going systematically through the whole list of data processing principles:

- legality of processing – not relevant unless software allows for capturing basis for processing;
- fairness of processing – mostly not software relevant, even if software developers are asked to build in potentially excessive functionalities;
- transparency – software related – proper design, technical and user documentation of software, including describing decisive algorithms;
- minimisation (adequacy of processing)– software related, e.g. relating specific data retention to specific goals of processing (e.g., why and where a system performs certain data dumps), functionalities allowing for user per-data access and other rights micromanagement (regarding records, cells, etc.);
- data accuracy – software related – how to ensure data consistency, deduplication, synchronisation;
- data retention – software related – software tools for management of data retention;

23. https://www.datatilsynet.no/en/regulations-and-tools/guidelines/data-protection-by-design-and-by-default/ (last accessed on 15 February 2019).

- security (integrity and confidentiality) - software related - how to ensure software quality and security;
- accountability - software related - how to ensure user accountability (capture user activities) and non-repudiation.

Privacy by design and by default software potential control points:

- does a system process personal data: system processes data about persons (personal data), system processes other data than personal data (what other data?), it is an operational technology system (can it affect processing of personal data?);
- what is personal data: 'regular personal data', content (potential personal data), encrypted (potential personal data), pseudonymised, hashed, geolocation data, IP, cookie/Facebook pixel/other internet and other tracking data (personally attributable RFID, IMEI, etc.), if sensitive data are processed (special categories data, 'criminal' data, vulnerable persons notably children data);
- transparency - documentation: data flows mapping including data storage, synchronisation, documenting algorithms, documenting functionalities;
- purpose limitation: what is software business purpose, what is a scope of collected data, what data are automatically retained, if no other data are intercepted;
- minimisation and data subjects' rights: retrievability, selective data deletion, restriction of access, specific types of flagging, automatic data deletion (though dangerous) or other mechanisms allowing for limiting data retention (e.g., multiversioning);
- data accuracy: consistency, deduplication, synchronisation mechanisms, 360 data view;[24]
- accountability: logging user access and actions;
- data micromanagement (is it possible?) managing specific consents (for data processing, for marketing communication), objections, specific data cells, deleting specific data cells (fields), deleting whole records, defining appropriate data field statuses (restricted, updated by a data subject, objected, consent withdrawn, etc.);
- minimisation - user management - user rights management, user rights micromanagement, managing privileged access, responding to external user management;
- data access and data copy: formats of data reports, aggregating data from different systems and profiles, automation of review of 'rights of others' (Articles 15.4 and 20.4 GDPR);

24. (Un)surprisingly and ironically it seems that the best way of fulfilling data accuracy principle and data access and data copy right would be to create a single unified database of individuals (data subjects) across the whole organisation, allowing to capture all information about a specific person within control of an organisation.

- data recipients: registering data recipients (Article 19 GDPR) – registering data transfer;
- data portability – automation of data export, automation of review of 'rights of others' (Articles 15.4 and 20.4 GDPR);
- automated decision-making – identification and description automated decision-making and decision-making algorithms, designing human intervention functionalities;
- risk assessment: performing basic personal data processing risk assessment for software, awareness of internal (taken care of) and external (to be taken care by a client) data protection control points, verifying (to the extent possible) necessity of DPIA (including providing default input when required);
- pseudonymisation, encryption, anonymisation – ensuring internal encryption in transit, verifying user communication encryption, verifying potential and methods of pseudonymisation, verifying use and strength of hashing and salting, verifying usability of differential privacy, verifying risks of non-availability or losing integrity (loss of passwords or decrypting keys, mixing pseudonymised patients etc);
- business continuity and disaster recovery – checking resilience and restorability of software;
- international data transfers: ability of maintaining multiple instances (EU and non EU), ability to maintain EU located data warehouse combined with processing pseudonymised[25] data).

Apart from the above which is a result of our own thinking, the Norwegian data protection supervisory authority Datatilsynet issued their own guidelines on software development with Data Protection by Design and by Default.[26] The Norwegian Guidelines are not very concrete though they include some hints as to designing software. Also, the European Data Protection Supervisor issued on 31 May 2018 the Opinion 5/2018 Preliminary Opinion on privacy by design.[27] That document is, however, even far less specific than the Norwegian Guidelines.

5 DATA PROTECTION IMPACT ASSESSMENT

5.1 Preliminary Remarks

A DPIA is a new obligation of data controllers not foreseen in the Personal Data Protection Directive.

Pursuant to Article 35(1) GDPR:

25. As already mentioned homomorphic encryption so far is not practically available.
26. https://www.datatilsynet.no/en/regulations-and-tools/guidelines/data-protection-by-design-and-by-default/?id=7733 (last accessed on 17 February 2019).
27. https://edps.europa.eu/sites/edp/files/publication/18-05-31_preliminary_opinion_on_privacy_by_design_en_0.pdf (last accessed on 17 February 2019).

> Where a **[1]** type of processing – **[2]** in particular using new technologies, and taking into account the **[3]** nature, **[4]** scope, **[5]** context and **[6]** purposes of the processing, **[7]** is likely to result in a high risk to the rights and freedoms of natural persons, the controller shall, **[8]** prior to the processing, carry out an **assessment of the impact of the envisaged processing operations on the protection of personal data**. A single assessment may address **[9]** a set of similar processing operations that present similar high risks.

5.2 'Qualified' Risk Analysis and Accountability

What is hidden within the mysterious name 'DPIA'? The GDPR does not introduce any legal definition of a DPIA, nor does it contain clear indications of when and how a company must conduct such an assessment.

Nevertheless, a DPIA is one of the key elements for ensuring GDPR compliance, and in practice is nothing other than **a 'qualified' form of risk analysis and prior evaluation of the adequacy of the data protection measures for the processes planned** accompanied by additional verification of legality of processing and verification of the way data subject rights are being serviced within a specific data processing set of operations.

In its guidelines on DPIAs, the Article 29 Working Party stated that a DPIA is a process to describe processing, assess the necessity and proportionality of processing, and help in managing the risk of a breach of the rights or freedoms of natural persons resulting from the processing of personal data by assessing existing risk and determining means of managing it. A DPIA is thus a further element of the GDPR that deals with protection and security using a risk-based approach and requires organisations to introduce risk management rules that are as clear and specific as possible, taking account of personal data processing procedures.

The Article 29 Working Party emphasises that the DPIA is an important tool for accountability because it facilitates for a controller not only to comply with the requirements of the GDPR but also to show that it has taken appropriate measures to comply. A DPIA, then, makes it possible to build and demonstrate GDPR compliance.[28] It is a process that should be implemented according to the method accepted within an organisation and appropriately documented.

Apart from a 'data protection impact assessment' another term exists: 'privacy impact assessment'. DPIA differs from PIA though in reality nobody precisely defines that difference – experts differ as to differences between both terms. Probably the simplest explanation would be that PIA is a general term – not having a legal definition, while DPIA is formally defined in the GDPR. Though the difference between the two is to that level unclear that the CNIL named their software tool designed to support manifesting GDPR compliance 'PIA Tool'.

28. The Art. 29 Working Party Guidelines concerning data protection impact assessments and helping to determine whether process 'may cause a high risk' against the goals of Regulation 2016/679, approved on 4 April 2017, amended and again approved on 4 October 2017.

Dissecting Article 35(1) GDPR on the general obligation of the DPIA, we find the following elements:

(1) a DPIA concerns **planned** personal data processing operations; that is, a DPIA should take place prior to beginning processing, e.g. prior to offering new services;
(2) the obligation to conduct a DPIA should be considered if the planned operations will involve **new technologies** such as cloud computing;
(3) when evaluating whether there is a need to run a DPIA, the controller must consider the **nature, scope, context, and purposes** of the data processing in the planned process and, as a result, whether the data processing **will entail a high risk** of a breach of the rights or freedoms of the data subjects;
(4) similar data processing operations may be covered by a single DPIA.

5.3 Similar Processes, One DPIA

A data processing impact assessment may concern a single data processing operation or may cover a number of similar operations. Recital 92 GDPR adds that:

> There are circumstances under which it may be reasonable and economical for the subject of a data protection impact assessment to be broader than a single project, for example where public authorities or bodies intend to establish a common application or processing platform or where several controllers plan to introduce a common application or processing environment across an industry sector or segment or for a widely used horizontal activity.

This means that data processing operations can be grouped together, and that, where necessary, a DPIA can be conducted in respect of a specific group of processes in order not to replicate activities within this scope.

5.3.1 Risk Analysis

How can a controller know whether the operations it is planning may entail a risk of a breach of the rights or freedoms of natural persons?

In practice, for every data processing operation, a controller must evaluate whether and to what extent it poses a risk to the rights and freedoms of data subjects. There is no simple checklist in the GDPR of security measures that allow you to say with certainty that you are processing data safely and in compliance with the law. This is why a risk approach entails conducting a 'first-degree' risk analysis for every data processing procedure (activity). We mention this as part of our discussion on how to approach data security. The GDPR imposes a change in how we approach the issue of data protection, and how we think about processing security.

If such a 'first-degree risk analysis' shows that a given type of process may cause a high risk of a breach of the rights or freedoms of data subjects, then you should conduct a further, more formalised 'second-degree risk analysis' – a DPIA – that is systematic and documented.

'Both an overall risk analysis and a data protection impact assessment involve the multiple (periodic) repetitions of four basic stages (context, control mechanisms, risk estimate, risk management)'.[29]

Without an initial evaluation of every data processing operation in terms of the possibility of the occurrence of a risk of a breach of rights or freedoms, even given the large number of guidelines from supervisory and consultancy authorities such as the EDPB or your local friendly data protection supervisory authority, you cannot know for sure when a DPIA should be conducted in your organisation.

5.3.2 *In Practice, How Can I Conduct a First-Degree Risk Analysis and Have an Initial Overview of What Operations Require a DPIA?*

The basic tool of accountability is helpful here – the RDPA (records of data processing activities). It covers the purposes of processing, a description of data categories and data recipients, and 'where possible, a general description of the technical and organisational security measures as referred to in Art. 32(1) GDPR'. In an RDPA you can make an initial assessment of whether there exists a likelihood of a high risk occurring and identify operations (activities) that may require a DPIA.

5.4 When Is a DPIA Necessary?

Theoretically, an organisation need not conduct a DPIA for every processing operation that may cause a risk of a breach of the rights or freedoms of natural persons. A DPIA is compulsory only when the processing '**may cause a high risk of a breach of the rights or freedoms of natural persons**', especially when introducing new data processing technologies.

How should the logic of the GDPR be understood as to the need to conduct a DPIA? There must be a situation where, **first, a)** we may know too much or **b)** a data leak may occur, **and second**, there is a serious risk that, as a result of these circumstances, serious harm may be caused to data subjects.

The GDPR does not specify all the possible situations in which a high risk of a breach of rights and freedoms may arise and in which a DPIA must be conducted. It only gives certain indications of what direction to proceed in, providing a catalogue of operations that may require a DPIA, that is, of 'high-risk' processes.

Article 35(3) GDPR states:

> A data protection impact assessment referred to in paragraph 1 shall in particular be required in the case of:
>
> a) a systematic and extensive evaluation of personal aspects relating to natural persons which is based on automated processing, including profiling, and on

29. GIODO, *Poradnik RODO. Podejście oparte na ryzyku*, part 2 ..., 2017, p. 27.

which decisions are based that produce legal effects concerning the natural person or similarly significantly affect the natural person;

b) processing on a large scale of special categories of data referred to in Article 9(1), or of personal data relating to criminal convictions and offences referred to in Article 10;

c) or a systematic monitoring of a publicly accessible area on a large scale.

Thus, the GDPR only gives very general examples of operations that can cause a high risk of a breach of the rights and freedoms of data subjects.

5.4.1 Large Scale

Large-scale processing is probably the most debated GDPR term. There is a strong dissent among supervisory authorities what and if there should be generally applicable quantitative thresholds for large-scale processing. The problem is not easy, because the Union legislator did not provide quantitative (countable) criteria, even though the figure of 5,000 records came up in the legislative work on the GDPR.

The Article 29 Working Party also avoided giving figures. It counts the following (unhelpful) examples of 'processing on a large scale':

(1) a hospital processing data of patients as part of its activities;
(2) processing data concerning the movements of people who use public transport (e.g., tracking by means of city cards);
(3) a specialist entity processing geolocation data of customers in real time on behalf of an international fast food chain for statistical purposes;
(4) a bank or insurance company processing data of customers as part of their activities;
(5) a search engine processing data for behavioural advertising purposes;
(6) telephone or internet service providers processing data (concerning content, traffic, or location).

The Article 29 Working Party Guidelines do not, however, consider the processing of patients' data by individual doctors,[30] or of data on rulings by an attorney, as 'large scale'.

When discussing the obligation to appoint a data protection officer (DPO), we mentioned that the legislator had considered introducing an obligation to have a DPO when more than 5,000 records were processed annually.[31] Ultimately, though, no quantitative threshold was agreed.

Initial debates within EDPB have not resulted in agreeing what is large-scale processing. In the meantime Viljar Peep head of the Estonian supervisory authority in

30. This is interesting, because a dentist can easily treat 3,000 patients in a year. And this affects what 'large scale' means, since the threshold of 5,000 records was discussed during the legislative work.
31. *See* https://iapp.org/news/a/gdpr-conundrums-the-data-protection-officer-requirement/ (last accessed on 26 January 2018).

his LinkedIn post suggested: 5,000 records for special category as well as 'criminal' data, 10,000 for other high-risk data (e.g., financial data, e-signatures, real-time geolocation) 50,000 for other data (Viljar has not managed to indicate conditions for large-scale monitoring at the time). The Dutch supervisory authority indicated 10,000 records for health data. Those numbers have not been so far accepted by the EDPB. EDPB specifically requests supervisory bodies to remove numbers from their compulsory DPIA lists. We find EDPB's approach counterproductive.

The figure of 5,000 remains, though, as a kind of mental anchor for monitoring. Yet, the non-invasive monitoring of unknown persons is one thing, but monitoring a fixed group of people or tracking and profiling unknown persons is another. This is why we propose using a number of quantitative parameters:

- For video and other monitoring of employees, we propose a threshold of **500 employees**, based on the following logic: with less than 250 employees, an employer is 'small' from the GDPR perspective; with 250–500 employees, an employer is considered medium-sized; with above 500, it is a large employer, and so the video monitoring of employees is monitoring on a 'large scale'. Mind, however, that EDPB seems to consider each case of monitoring of employees as requiring DPIA (which does not seem workable at all).
- For monitoring special category data, we suggest a threshold of 6,000 persons calculated as four doctors examining 1,500 patients per year.
- For monitoring persons other than employees (e.g., energy consumers) known from their first and last name, and for tracking people based on electronic tags (e.g., cookies) or other tracking that makes it possible to build personality profiles, we propose a threshold of **10,000 persons**.
- For monitoring other data we recommend threshold of 50,000 persons/records in line with the optics of Viljar Peep.

You do not have to stick with these figures and can question them for a particular industry, but the logic behind them at least provide a starting point for considering your own calculations.

5.4.2 Article 29 Working Party

Apart from these situations, there are others in which processing may involve a high risk of a breach of the rights and freedoms of data subjects. Some of these have been taken into consideration in the Article 29 Working Party Guidelines; they recommend considering nine criteria when deciding whether a DPIA is necessary. Based on the Article 29 Working Party Guidelines, the following are examples of processing that requires a DPIA to be conducted:

- evaluating or scoring. A business creating behavioural or marketing profiles based on the scope of use of a website and on that basis addressing advertisements (ratings or scores, including profiling and forecasting);

- systematic monitoring. Monitoring a shopping centre, street, market, railway station, or public library (systematic monitoring of public spaces);
- innovative technological or organisational solutions. Processing data using innovative technological solutions (cloud computing, blockchain, data analytics, machine learning, etc.) (use of new technologies);
- processing sensitive or highly personal data. A hospital processing data contained in medical records), a private detective processing data of a highly personal nature, processing data from personal identity documents, email messages, online diaries (including using applications of the nutrition log or pregnancy calendar type), notes from e-books **equipped** with a notes function, or highly personal data contained in applications that automatically record daily activity - step measurements, heart rate, GPS location, collecting public data from social media in order to generate a profile (sensitive or highly personal data, large scale, ratings, or scores).

Examples

Even with the Article 29 Working Party Guidelines concerning DPIA criteria at our disposal, it is difficult to be sure in advance when exactly a DPIA will be necessary and when it can be dispensed with. For example, in 2016 there was a leak of data from Uber. Even though it involved data of millions of people, the risk of anyone being harmed as a result was small, since no cases of individuals suffering harm were voiced. The information processed by Uber that fell into the wrong hands included the names, email addresses, and telephone numbers of people who used the mobile app for ordering transport services. The conclusion is that, even when data are processed on a large scale and an enormous amount of data are leaked, it may turn out that no real damage is caused.[32]

But a leak from a dating application such as Tinder may prove catastrophic in terms of the scope of harm suffered by users if data is published on who they arranged to meet, how often, the content of their conversations, or their sexual preferences. The same goes for when users (or their computers) are tracked using cookies, and data on their sexual preferences are obtained and then published (anonymously - this is possible) for the marketing purposes of a sex shop. A tracked user or tracked computer may then be targeted with sex-related ads beyond their control, which can lead to

32. Incidentally, it seems that, in the long run, data leaks do not impair the value of companies who fall victim to them; *see* M.C. Arcuri, M. Brogi, G. Gandolfi, *How Does Cyber Crime Affect Firms? The Effect of Information Security Breaches on Stock Returns*, https://www.researchgate.net/publication/322274957_How_does_cyber_crime_affect_firms_The_effect_of_information_security_breaches_on_stock_returns (last accessed on 26 January 2018).

awkward situations for such people, e.g. when ads pop up on a tracked computer at work.[33]

Another example of an operation that will probably require a DPIA is what is known as anti-fraud processing. Of course, you have to verify potential frauds, but at the same time, you have to be very careful about the circle of people who have access to the results of such analyses, because these are often not accurate and reliable, and cross into an area reserved for the judicial authorities. In the event of a leak of such data, the risk of harm being caused to the data subjects is very high. That risk relates to both the type of data processed and the nature and scope of the processing.

Out of interest, it is worth considering that another serious risk is the possibility of someone (usually an IT administrator) destroying large amounts of data in revenge against a company. Such incidents occur now and then around the world. This type of problem can be abated using a mechanism we call a 'double nuclear key'[34] – that is, a requirement of two-person authorisation for any operation having a large impact on data (the problem being that current IT systems do not generally support 'countersignatures').

The conclusion: in 'sensitive' cases, you need to conduct a DPIA because the risk of harm being caused by a data leak is very high. When evaluating whether to run a DPIA, you should consider absolutely all of the factors that could affect the risk of harm being caused, including not only the nature of the processing but also the activities you are engaged in and the level of awareness of your employees. Even at this stage, one can say with a high degree of certainty that e-commerce, banks, insurers, telecommunications companies, and producers of 'tracking' applications have no escape from the obligation to conduct DPIAs.

5.5 How Can I Determine Whether I Need to Run a DPIA in My Company and for What Processes?

Taking account of (a) the provisions of the GDPR, (b) the Article 29 Working Party Guidelines setting out criteria for evaluating the justifiability of conducting a DPIA, (c) having a properly maintained RDPA, and (d) those factors that are completely individual for your company, we recommend you develop your own, tailor-made criteria for determining whether or not to conduct a DPIA. Or instead, perhaps you can rely on the DPIA screening list prepared by the Information Commissioner's Office – UK supervising authority (ICO),[35] according to which:

> you should **consider** carrying out a DPIA if you plan

33. One example of this is a well-known journalist who posted on Twitter that on his work portal an ad for 'Ukrainian girls' popped up as a result of his lack of knowledge of how internet advertising works (i.e., tracking).
34. Coined by Maciej Gawronski from the two-person authorisation needed to launch nuclear rockets.
35. https://ico.org.uk/for-organisations/guide-to-data-protection/guide-to-the-general-data-protection-regulation-gdpr/accountability-and-governance/data-protection-impact-assessments/ (last accessed on 17 February 2019).

- any major project involving the use of personal data;
- evaluation or scoring;
- automated decision-making with significant effects (legal or similar);
- systematic monitoring;
- processing of sensitive data or data of a highly personal nature;
- processing on a large scale;
- processing of data concerning vulnerable data subjects;
- innovative technological or organisational solutions;
- processing that involves preventing data subjects from exercising a right or using a service or contract;

you should **carry out** a DPIA if you plan to:

- use systematic and extensive profiling or automated decision-making to make significant decisions about people;
- process special-category data or criminal-offence data on a large scale;
- systematically monitor a publicly accessible place on a large scale;
- use innovative technology in combination with any of the criteria in the European guidelines;
- use profiling, automated decision-making or special category data to help make decisions on someone's access to a service, opportunity or benefit;
- carry out profiling on a large scale;
- process biometric or genetic data in combination with any of the criteria in the European guidelines;
- combine, compare or match data from multiple sources;
- process personal data without providing a privacy notice directly to the individual in combination with any of the criteria in the European guidelines;
- process personal data in a way that involves tracking individuals' online or offline location or behaviour, in combination with any of the criteria in the European guidelines;
- process children's personal data for profiling or automated decision-making or for marketing purposes, or offer online services directly to them;
- process personal data that could result in a risk of physical harm in the event of a security breach.

5.5.1 Regulatory Catalogue of DPIA Operations

Pursuant to Article 32(4) GDPR:

> The supervisory authority shall establish and make public a **list of the kind of processing operations which are subject to the requirement for a data protection impact assessment** ... The supervisory authority shall communicate those lists to the [European Data Protection] Board referred to in Article 68.

In practice, this means that an authority must create a catalogue of processing operations subject to a compulsory DPIA as a supplement to the situations set out directly in the GDPR.

EU supervisory authorities created DPIA lists and delivered them to the EDPB. EDPB opined on those lists in the fourth quarter of 2018. At the time we write this book there is no general pan-EU list of compulsory DPIA processing operations, as EDPB seems to be at an early stage of working out consensus.

If you are a controller operating in one Member State, you should check a DPIA list issued by your local supervisory authority as well as a respective opinion of EDPB. And if you operate in more.

5.6 When Do I Not Need to Conduct a DPIA?

A DPIA is not required:[36]

(1) when it is unlikely that the processing operation 'could cause a high risk of a breach of the rights and freedoms of natural persons';
(2) when the nature, scope, context, and purposes of the processing are very similar to processing operations for which a DPIA has already been conducted. In such a case, you can use the results of the DPIA conducted for similar processing operations;
(3) when the processing operations were checked by the supervisory authority before May 2018 in respect of particular conditions that have not since changed;
(4) if, pursuant to Article 6(1)(c) GDPR, the processing operation has a legal basis in EU law or the law of a Member State, which regulates a given processing operation, and if a DPIA has already been conducted in connection with the acceptance of that legal basis – unless the Member State has decided that it is necessary to perform a DPIA before the processing activities are commenced (Article 35(10) GDPR);
(5) if the processing operations have been placed on an optional list (created by a supervisory authority) of processing operations not subject to the requirement to conduct a DPIA.

5.7 DPIA Step by Step

5.7.1 *General Remarks*

It will probably come as no surprise to learn that the generally-worded and unclear GDPR does not say how to conduct a DPIA. Organisations will have to work out their own methodology for this, taking account of the specific nature of their activities, their data processing procedures, the security measures they are able to apply, their available resources, organisational structure, and so on. You can draw, though, on certain theoretical studies that have arisen, including:

(1) the Article 29 Working Party Guidelines concerning DPIAs;
(2) ISO standards, particularly on risk management (ISO/IEC 27005) and on the PIA (ISO/IEC 29134);

36. Article 29 Working Party Guidelines on data protection impact assessments … .

(3) a publication by the French supervisory authority, the CNIL[37] *Privacy Impact Assessment – Methodology (How to Carry Out a PIA)* and *Tools (Templates and Knowledge Bases)* from June 2015;
(4) an open source application 'CNIL PIA tool' for conducting DPIA, published by the CNIL.[38]

When? Before commencing processing.[39] This is in line with the principles of taking data protection into account during the design phase and of privacy by default. When planning any business process, you should always take account of the possible need to perform a DPIA and to document it appropriately. If there is a data processing process already in place, DPIAs should be conducted before any change to the process impacting personal data processing.

Who? The data controller is responsible for conducting a DPIA. If you have a DPO appointed in your company, you must consult the DPIA process with the DPO (Article 35(2) GDPR). The company must document the results of the consultation and the decisions taken. A DPO's obligations also include monitoring the performance of the DPIA, though for any non-compliance with the GDPR it is the controller that is responsible. Despite it is the data controller who is ultimately responsible for conducting a DPIA, in many cases the controller will be unable to perform their DPIA without an input from a data processor. Therefore in practical terms, a data processor will be responsible as well for performing their DPIA.

How? Drawing on the above publications, a company should develop its own method of conducting a DPIA, adjusted to its own needs. Based on the logic applied by the French supervisory authority, the CNIL, the methodology for running a DPIA should take account of the following elements:

(1) **processing activities** – identifying processing activities that give rise to a high processing risk and identifying who is responsible for those processes (whether a change will result in a change in how data are processed, with a consequent increase in risk);
(2) **determining the stakeholders** – including any representatives of data subjects and experts; contact with the DPO;
(3) **data types** – identifying what data are processed as part of a given activity (in particular, whether these are ordinary, sensitive, or 'highly sensitive' data);
(4) **determining the processing context** – verifying the purpose of the processing for the organisation;
(5) **legality** – verifying the legality of the processing activities (e.g., whether appropriate consents are in place, whether the data are being processed for the original purpose);

37. Commission nationale de l'informatique et des libertés.
38. *See* https://www.cnil.fr/en/open-source-pia-software-helps-carry-out-data-protection-impact-assesment (last accessed on 17 February 2019).
39. Article 35(1) and (10) GDPR, Recitals 90 and 93.

(6) **adequacy** – verifying the adequacy of the data (whether you possess more than is necessary);
(7) **verifying the means of safeguarding personal rights** (information, consents, demands);
(8) **protection measures** – identifying existing protection measures;
(9) **threat 1**: identifying potential threats to data subjects as a result of unauthorised access, modifications or destruction (e.g., the inability to punctually treat a patient as a result of a loss of all medical records in a hospital – the risk of death);
(10) **threat 2**: identifying situations that may cause a breach of data protection, and the source thereof (e.g., technology – an obsolete computer; human – poorly trained employees; event – a hacker attack);
(11) **evaluating the likelihood and seriousness** of potential threats;
(12) **reaction plan – identifying and implementing adequate security measures;**
(13) **evaluating residual risk** – i.e., the risk that remains even after the application of what you believe to be adequate security measures;
(14) **determining how to measure risk during the processing;**
(15) **consulting with the supervisory authority** when residual risk remains high;
(16) **the DPIA report.**

In short, DPIA consists of (regulatory elements underlined):

(1) describing the process, the data and their meaning (context) – (Article 35(7)(a) GDPR description);
(2) confirming legality (Article 35(7)(b) GDPR – necessity and proportionality);
(3) verifying data subject rights;
(4) enlisting current TOMs (technical and organisational measures of data protection);
(5) assessing threats and their impact on the risk of processing under existing TOMs (Article 35(7)(c) GDPR – risk assessment);
(6) drafting reaction plan/additional TOMs – if risk assessed is considerable (higher than low) – (Article 35(7)(d) GDPR – reaction plan);
(7) reassessing and documenting all the above. And if the reassessment indicates high risk – consulting the supervisory authority what to do.

5.7.2 Data Protection Officer

A DPIA must be consulted with the DPO. In practice often this is a DPO who conducts a DPIA. This is not in line with the GDPR of course.

5.7.3 *Experts*

Resorting to outside experts is recommended. The EU legislator is aware of the size of the challenge it has imposed, and of how difficult it can be for organisations to meet that challenge on their own. That is why Article 29 Working Party Guidelines recommend turning to specialists, which we as experts wholeheartedly endorse.

5.7.4 *Representatives of Target Groups*

In model DPIA methodologies, a data controller is encouraged to consult with representatives of data subjects. It is hard to say what would need to be a minimum cost threshold to conduct a meaningful representative group test. Even more questionable how meaningful such tests are. Therefore, unless you are a multinational corporation, you may start with testing your privacy ideas on an unprepared colleague or any other layperson. That is what we refer to as the 'John or Jane Doe test' (not to mix with the 'Jerry of the Day test').

5.7.5 *Prior Consultations with the Supervisory Authority*

When should you consult the supervisory authority?

Article 36(1) GDPR is worded somewhat mysteriously:

> The controller shall consult the supervisory authority prior to processing where a data protection impact assessment under Article 35 indicates that the processing **would result in a high risk** in the absence of measures taken by the controller to mitigate the risk.

Given that Article 35(1) GDPR says that a DPIA must be conducted:

> Where a type of processing ... is likely to result in a high risk ...', When put together, the whole forms a tautology: 'if the risk could be high, it could turn out that the risk is indeed high ...'.

The more foolish the law, the more power we put in the hands of bureaucrats. As you can see, the GDPR is a perfect example of this. But fortunately, this time the bureaucrats have come to our aid and are trying to give some kind of sensible explanation of Article 36 GDPR.

In accordance with those explanations, a DPIA must be consulted with the supervisory authority if the residual risk is high; in other words, when a controller cannot eliminate the risk identified to a sufficient degree (the residual risk remains high), it must consult the supervisory authority.

The GDPR leaves certain procedural loopholes concerning such consultations. There is no need to go into the details here; it is enough to take a look at the last sentence of Article 36(2):

> Those periods may be suspended until the supervisory authority has obtained information it has requested for the purposes of the consultation.

It results from this provision that the supervisory authority has an unlimited amount of time to evaluate the problematic processing in a consultation procedure and that this provision was introduced for that very purpose. We are not questioning the sense of that solution (at least officially), although it does leave a lot to be desired in terms of the principles of reliability and clarity. It would be more honest to write: 'The authority can think about it until it comes up with something.'

Being realistic, knowing that the supervisory authority may tell you not to initiate processing, to stop processing and may initiate investigation against you and fine you, how inclined you are to address the supervisory authority with your concerns about the security of processing?

CHAPTER 4

Data Processing

Maciej Gawronski, Aleksander P. Czarnowski & Patrycja Naklicka

1 DATA ENTRUSTMENT AND ELEMENTS OF THE NEW DATA PROCESSING CONTRACT

1.1 Introductory Remarks

The entrustment of data was regulated directly by the ten paragraphs of Article 28 GDPR, which established a large number of requirements concerning the relations between a controller and a processor. Pending publication by the European Commission of a template data processing contract (under the prerogative of Article 28 paragraph 7 GDPR), below we provide a comprehensive checklist for a data processing contract.

1.2 Sufficient Guarantees of Compliance

A data processing contract (or another document) should describe a processor's guarantees that it will implement technical and organisational measures that ensure its processing meets the requirements of the General Data Protection Regulation (GDPR) and protect the rights of data subjects. Article 28 paragraph 1 GDPR, this requirement stems from, allows for a very broad range of interpretations as to what should be required of a processor. The technical and organisational measures referred to in Article 32 GDPR, for example, concern the protection of data, but Article 28 paragraph 1 GDPR speaks about guaranteeing that the requirements of the GDPR itself are met; in principle, this could cover all of the obligations of both the controller and the processor, not only personal data security. Such guarantees can be set out in a preamble to a contract or in declarations and warranties of the data processor to do the processing, or may also comprise a description or attachment of references, or a description of the processor's experience in providing services that are GDPR compliant. The data controller may also require the data processor to complete a survey on technical and organisational measures of protection of personal data and other aspects of personal data protection compliance. The controller may even wish to perform an audit of the data processor. Recital 81 of the GDPR specifies that this concerns such guarantees as: expert knowledge, reliability and resources. According to it, the processor can demonstrate compliance by means of an approved code of conduct or approved mechanism of certification.

1.3 Written Contract

Pursuant to Article 28 paragraph 9 GDPR, the entrustment of data processing or subprocessing must be in the form of a written (including electronic)[1] contract or other legal act[2] entered into by the controller and the processor. In short, a data processing agreement should be documented.

1.4 Consent to Subprocessing

According to Article 28 paragraph 2 GDPR, a data processor is obliged to obtain the consent of the controller if it wishes to make use of the services of another processor. That authorisation may be initially general, but then the processor must notify the controller of the 'intended' addition or replacement of any subprocessor so that the controller has an opportunity to object to the changes (right of objection). So, at the end of the day, the controller should be notified in advance about each subprocessor (including sub-subprocessor and so on, as it stems from Article 28(4) GDPR – explained below).

1.5 'Cloning' of Obligations onto Subprocessors

Pursuant to Article 28 paragraph 4 GDPR, a processor when engaging a subprocessor should impose on a subprocessor the same data protection obligations as set out in the processor's agreement with the controller (at least within the scope defined in Article 28 paragraph 3 GDPR, but also concerning 'providing sufficient guarantees to implement appropriate technical and organisational measures in such a manner that the processing will meet the requirements of' GDPR[3]).

1. Most likely the phrase 'including electronic' was introduced to the GDPR by the EU legislator in connection with the problem of how to interpret a written data processing contract in Poland. Maciej Gawronski brought that issue to the attention of the EU regulator during consultations of draft subprocessing contractual clauses. The similar interpretation problems of 'written form' exist in relation to national interpretations of the EIDAS Regulation in several countries including Poland.
2. Though 'other legal act' sounds somewhat mysterious, it may refer to a regulation, administrative understanding, some kind of act of law or binding corporate regulations.
3. Something is amiss here in the editing of the GDPR: reference is made to Art. 28 para. 3 GDPR, but the content of the reference also covers Art. 28 para. 1 GDPR.

1.6 Ban on 'Empty Shells'

Article 28 paragraph 4 GDPR permits yet another conclusion to be drawn: it states that 'a processor engages another processor for carrying out **specific** processing activities on behalf of the controller'. This would seem to indicate that the GDPR provides only for specific activities to be subcontracted out, and not data processing as a whole. The wording of the GDPR requires interpretation, but certainly it will be in the interest of the controller to ensure that its direct contractual partner (the processor) is not a mere shell acting to save entities hiding on the lower levels of liability (a structure often implemented by global vendors acting through their 'partners').[4]

1.7 Subject Matter of the Processing

A contract should set out the subject matter and duration of the processing, its nature and purpose, the categories of personal data involved, and the types of data subjects the data concern.[5] And so, the subject of the contract should not only take account of the data processing itself (i.e., the technical measures to be taken by the processor) but also define the purpose for which the controller wishes to process the data, the categories of persons whose data will be processed, and the scope of data processing (categories of personal data). Providers of IT solutions and services have commonly defended themselves against taking on any conscious responsibility for their 'clients' business'. Clearly, this approach should not pass muster under the GDPR.

1.8 'Written' (i.e., Documented) form of Controllers' Instructions

A processor may process personal data solely on the basis of a documented instruction from a personal data controller. An exception to this is when the processor is obliged to do so by law, in which case it must inform the controller about the processing unless the law forbids this. This is a classic contractual solution (Article 28 paragraph 3 letter a GDPR).

1.9 Confidentiality Obligation

A processor is obliged to obtain an undertaking from persons involved in the processing (i.e., from its personnel assigned to perform a contract between the processor and the subprocessor) that they will maintain the secrecy of the data concerned, unless those persons are subject to a statutory duty to maintain secrecy

4. It seems Art. 82 GDPR imposes liability for data processing not only on data controllers and direct data processors but also on data subprocessors of any level. Still legal risk mitigation tactics encourage processors to place themselves as low in the supply chain of processing as possible.
5. Article 28 para. 3 GDPR also mentions the need to determine the rights and obligations of the controller, but this is an unnecessary addition, since by its very nature a contract should set out the rights and obligations of every party. Perhaps the authors of the GDPR wanted to make sure that a controller would not forget about its own obligations.

(e.g., legal counsel). In practice, it is more manageable to require non-disclosure agreements from all persons having access to personal data than to deliberate who is covered by professional secrecy and who is not. The GDPR does not directly state how a controller is to hold a processor accountable for that obligation, or specifically: does a controller have the right to demand a list of personnel together with access to their confidentiality undertakings. Yet, in the meaning of Article 28 paragraph 3 letter h GDPR, a processor must make available to the controller 'all information necessary to demonstrate compliance with the obligations laid down in this Article', which no doubt means that information on confidentiality undertakings should also be provided (Article 28 paragraph 3 letter b GDPR).

1.10 Data Security

Processing must guarantee data security as set out in Article 32 GDPR (security of processing). This is a primary duty of a processor. The controller and processor should agree what they understand by appropriate measures of data protection. The data security standard in place at a processor may be more strict or less strict than that at the controller. If the processing is selective or occasional, the standard may even be lower (still adequate to processing), but if the processor performs the same duties for a number of entities (e.g., acting as an infrastructural provider, cloud computing provider), then the standard of data protection must probably be higher (Article 28 paragraph 3 letter c GDPR).

1.11 Response to Data Subject Rights

A processor is obliged to help the controller respond to data subject requests exercising their rights. It should do this 'by appropriate technical and organisational measures' – in this way the GDPR emphasises that processors should take steps to automate or properly staff their responses to requests from data subjects exercising their rights (Article 28 paragraph 3 letter e GDPR).

1.12 Support for the Controller's Security Obligations

A processor should work together with the controller when analysing data security risk and determining appropriate data protection measures, when evaluating the consequences for data protection and in consultations with the supervisory authority, when reporting data breaches, and when notifying persons affected by a breach of personal data.

1.13 Notification of a Suspected Personal Data Breach

Apart from the obligation to support the PDC with security, a processor has a separate obligation to notify the controller of any breach of personal data, without undue delay.

This issue is addressed in Article 33 paragraph 2 GDPR and, given its importance, a separate contractual clause should be devoted to it. It is important to consider what is meant by 'without undue delay'. The guidelines concerning reporting personal data breaches[6] say that a processor should report a breach to the controller quickly enough to allow the controller to report it to the authority within seventy-two hours after having been informed of the breach by ... the processor. Such approach is controversial as it omits the operational aspects of notification. Still it is how the European Union (EU) regulator perceives the case. The operational problem can be avoided to some extent if the processor immediately reports its suspicion of a breach to the controller, thereby allowing the controller to take part in its efforts to clarify the situation prior to a moment that breach is confirmed and seventy-two-hour notification deadline starts. The solution suggested in the WP29 Guidelines consisting of empowering a data processor to notify a breach on behalf of a controller does not seem feasible, or more precisely it does not address an operational issue of allowing a data controller to understand a situation (not even to be in control of the situation). In any case, until the Working Party Guidelines are updated after supervisory authorities are flooded with data breach notifications, we recommend taking account of Article 29 and proceeding as set out above.

1.14 Deletion and Return of Data

A processor 'deletes or returns all the personal data to the controller after the end of the provision of services relating to processing, and deletes existing copies unless Union or Member State law requires storage of the personal data' (Article 28 paragraph 3 letter g GDPR). The requirement to return data must be agreed in detail between the controller and the processor, because data may reside in various systems and locations, including, for example, email. We are far from suggesting email deletion; to the contrary, we believe storing emails is essential to accountability and each organisation is a controller in relation to its email correspondence. But as data deletion is a complicated and multilevel issue, a data processing agreement should be reasonably detailed in that regard. Of course, from the opposite perspective, being vague and general allows to adjourn deciding on uncertain and doubtful details hoping that before they need to be decided proper market standards and interpretations are developed.

Technically, probably deleting data of a particular data controller corresponds to the problem of deleting data at the request of a data subject. The GDPR does not rule out agreeing a certain extended period during which a processor may store data. To avoid legal disputes it would be better to formulate such period as a 'deletion period', 'data expiration period' or similarly, and not as a period 'after the end of the provision of services relating to processing'.[7]

6. Article 29 Working Party, Guidelines on personal data breach notification under Regulation 2016/679, adopted on 3 October 2017 r. (WP250), https://www.poradyodo.pl/pobierz-zalacznik/8302/322 (last accessed on 24 January 2018).
7. For example 'A supplier stores client data to the end of the year following the conclusion of the basic period of services.'

What about keeping data for know-how purposes or defence from claims?

As for know-how purposes, if a data processor properly anonymised data (ensuring reidentification is impossible), they would fall out of the scope of GDPR. Not that a data controller would always be happy to allow for such use of their data but that would be a trade secret issue.

Keeping data by a data processor for legal claims is an interesting situation. Storing data 'just in case' for some extra time after a termination of a data processing agreement would turn a data processor into a data controller, and it would most likely be against the data processing agreement (Article 28(3)(g) GDPR). But what if a termination of a data processing agreement is connected with a dispute related to the way entrusted data were being processed, or if a supervisory authority initiated administrative proceedings against a data processor? Should that data processor still delete entrusted data or should it keep the data? The GDPR does not provide a direct simple answer to such – quite likely – situations. We believe that a data processor deciding to keep entrusted data turns into a data controller. We also believe that if data kept are truly needed for dealing with 'legal claims' keeping those data would not infringe the GDPR (despite the general rule of Article 28(10) GDPR). And we believe that a data processor (turned into a data controller) could often rely on the exception to the information duty contained in Article 14(5)(b) GDPR, as (and when) informing data subjects about the fact that their data have been retained by a data processor 'is likely to [...] seriously impair the achievement of the objectives of that processing'. The objective of processing would then be allowing to decide the legal dispute with the least collateral damage to the parties involved. Informing data subjects about that dispute could be detrimental to the reputation of involved parties no matter what the outcome would be. Unless the dispute concerns or impacts rights or freedoms of data subjects, it would not make sense to let them know about such dispute. From the other perspective, say a data processor decides to file as evidence with a court a copy of the whole database containing personal data. Should persons involved be informed about it? We would probably find a good exception in Article 14(5)(c) GDPR which allows to refrain from completing the information obligation if 'obtaining or disclosure is expressly laid down by Union or Member State law to which the controller is subject' – such law being rules of respective civil, administrative, or criminal procedure.

1.15 Obligation to Demonstrate Compliance with the Contract

A processor is obliged to provide the controller with whatever information is necessary to demonstrate the processor's compliance with the contract (Article 28 paragraph 3 letter h GDPR). Under that obligation, the processor should *inter alia*, in our opinion, grant the controller access to the part of its data processing register concerning that specific controller.

1.16 Subjection to Audits

A processor must 'allow for and contribute to audits, including inspections, conducted by the controller or another auditor mandated by the controller'[8] (obligation to cooperate) (Article 28 paragraph 3 letter h RODO).

The problem of simultaneous audits is well known for cloud computing providers, but solutions to that problem are also reasonably developed (mostly independent third-party audits).

1.17 Additional Payment

It is not stated that a processor's obligations that are 'auxiliary' in nature must be performed within the basic service price. Certainly, a contract should contain some sort of basic package, but extraordinary work performed beyond that package may be settled separately.

1.18 Information on the Legality of Instructions

The processor is obliged to promptly inform the controller about any doubts it has regarding the legality of a controller's instruction. Call centres are already requiring that their clients demonstrate they have consents to communications for the purposes of direct marketing[9] (Article 28 paragraph 3 section 2 GDPR). We see no legal basis, however, for a processor being entitled to notify the supervising authority in each case about a 'suspected breach of the GDPR'.

1.19 Procedure for Determining Legality

The issue of the legality of a controller's instructions can often lead to dispute, which is why the GDPR provides that the parties institute an escalation procedure and rules for resolving doubts (e.g., by seeking a legal opinion from an agreed law firm, the costs to be shared equally).

1.20 Rules of Responsibility

A data processing contract will usually contain provisions on responsibility. It makes sense to include provisions on cooperation in the event of proceedings before the supervisory authority or litigation brought by a data subject. Both the processor and the controller may be directly held responsible for a data processing breach. Article 82 paragraph 2 sentence 2 GDPR states that: 'A processor shall be liable for the damage

8. With this provision, the GDPR seeks to 'settle a score' with global cloud data processing service providers, who in the past have been extremely reluctant to agree to external inspections.
9. Remember, though, that the requirement of obtaining consent for electronic or telemarketing is not a requirement of the GDPR but of the e-Privacy Directive.

caused by processing only where it has not complied with obligations of this Regulation specifically directed to processors or where it has acted outside or contrary to lawful instructions of the controller.' We discuss liability separately.

1.21 Designation of a Data Protection Officer

The Regulation requires this in specific cases (Article 37 GDPR).

2 NEW CHALLENGES FOR CONTROLLER AND PROCESSOR

(1) **Definition of channels of communication** – verbal, unwritten instructions seem to be out of the question in important matters (a practical solution would be to send a written/email/etc. confirmation note). A *call centre* has the right to demand, among other things, the provision of third-party consents to marketing and electronic communications.
(2) **Division of responsibility** – in practice, division of responsibility may become a big problem. The GDPR does not leave much freedom in this regard; however, the GDPR does not regulate remuneration for basic or extra data processor's services and more importantly, as data processors before the GDPR were out of scope of data protection liability, they may be not prepared to provide proper compliance maturity soon.
(3) **Choice of external suppliers** – when choosing service providers, a controller will look for an extensive support of data subject requests, proof of appropriate security measures, and support during inspections by the supervisory authority. For processors, this will entail new obligations (and, in practice, increased fees for services).

3 RECOMMENDATIONS

In order to regulate the area of data entrustment in accordance with the GDPR, the following steps should be taken:

(1) Create a new data processing contract or use a ready-made template (an extensive one such as the one we propose – developed on the basis of the GDPR and a proposal by the CNIL, the French supervisory authority, or a simplified version similar to what the leading cloud suppliers provide).
(2) Update request for offer templates.
(3) Ensure mechanisms are in place for verifying a processor to the subprocessor transfer of obligations.
(4) Ensure mechanisms are in place for verifying basic obligations, e.g. signing confidentiality undertakings, verifying the controller's consent to further data entrustment, and for reporting objections to subprocessing by the controller.

(5) Create a record of categories of processing activities carried out on behalf of a controller.
(6) Verify whether the processor is obliged to appoint a DPO.
(7) Follow the activities of the European Commission, European Data Protection Board, and supervisory authorities.

CHAPTER 5

Managing Incidents and Data Breaches

*Maciej Gawronski, Witold Chomiczewski, Zuzanna Piotrowska & Katarzyna Kloc**

1 NOTIFICATION OF A PERSONAL DATA BREACH TO THE SUPERVISORY AUTHORITY (ARTICLE 33 GDPR)

1.1 The Provision

Pursuant to Article 33(1) GDPR:

> In the case of **[1]** a personal data breach, the controller shall **[2]** without undue delay and, where feasible, not later than **[3]** 72 hours after **[4]** having become aware of it, **[5]** notify the personal data breach to the supervisory authority competent in accordance with Article 55, unless the personal data breach **[6]** is unlikely to result in a risk to the rights and freedoms of natural persons. **[7]** Where the notification to the supervisory authority is not made within 72 hours, it shall be accompanied by reasons for the delay.

Pursuant to Article 33(2) GDPR, a similar obligation weighs on the processor, which:

> shall notify the controller without undue delay after becoming aware of a personal data breach.

1.2 What Is a Breach of Personal Data Protection?

Pursuant to Article 4(12) GDPR:

* Section 1 contributed by Maciej Gawronski, Witold Chomiczewski and Zuzanna Piotrowska. Section 2 contributed by Katarzyna Kloc and Maciej Gawronski.

> personal data breach' means [1] a breach of security leading to the accidental or unlawful [2] destruction, [3] loss, [4] alteration, unauthorised [5] disclosure of, or [6] access to, personal data transmitted, stored or otherwise processed.

In line with that definition, a personal data protection breach is **a 'consequential' breach of the security of information** concerning personal data, i.e. a breach of security resulting in adverse irreversible effects.

This definition focuses on a breach of the integrity and confidentiality of data, but mistakenly omits the idea of a breach of data availability.[1] In its guidelines concerning the notification of data breaches, the Article 29 Working Party[2] European Data Protection Board (EDPB) states directly that a breach of access to data is also a data protection breach if it results in the risk of a breach of rights and freedoms. Whether the letter of the law or the views of the European Union (EU) Regulator are most important is open to discussion. Let us take a closer look at this issue.

If we break down the definition of a data protection breach into parts, we can identify the following elements:

- **destruction of personal data** – a situation where data cease to exist in a form usable by the controller.

Example

A document archive catches fire; files are erased from a computer memory; backup copies are physically destroyed; an archive of personal data processing consents is flooded.

- **alteration of personal data** – damage (accidental or unlawful) to data as a result of which the data are altered or spoiled, becoming incomplete, partially illegible or defective.

Example

An unauthorised person makes changes in a database such that the data become defective, e.g., by changing names, mixing up telephone numbers, altering the content of files. An old version of a cv is kept instead a new one sent in by a candidate.

1. That is, three aspects of information security from the CIA triad, i.e. Confidentiality, Integrity and Availability.
2. The Art. 29 Working Party Guidelines on Personal data breach notification under Regulation 2016/679, adopted on 3 October 2017. (WP 250), https://www.poradyodo.pl/pobierz-zalacznik/8302/322 (last accessed on 24 January 2018).

- **loss of personal data** – a situation where data continue to exist, but the controller loses control over them or access to them or is no longer in possession of them.

> **Example**
>
> The theft of an office computer containing a large amount of personal data; the loss of a smartphone that contains emails from the past month.

Unauthorised or unlawful processing includes cases where personal data are disclosed or made available to recipients **not authorised** to obtain them or obtain access to them, as well as all other forms of processing in breach of the provisions of the General Data Protection Regulation (GDPR).

Note that the definition of a personal data protection breach does not include a temporary loss of data availability, from which even the principle of data protection is given the name 'integrity and confidentiality' rather than just 'data security'. But let us not be deceived by this omission of inaccessibility in the definition of a personal data protection breach. As we show below, the Article 29 Working Party Guidelines also refer to such a situation (e.g., a momentary loss in the availability of medical data when there is a need to conduct surgery).

1.2.1 Data Protection Breach According to the Article 29 Working Party

In the opinion of the Article 29 Working Party (to which we subscribe), there are three types of personal data protection breaches,[3] one for each of the three fundamental aspects of information security. These are breaches of: confidentiality, integrity and availability.

1.2.1.1 Breach of Confidentiality

A breach of confidentiality involves the disclosure of personal data to an unauthorised person, often including loss of unsecured data (e.g., loss of an unencrypted pen drive).

> **Example**
>
> Sending email messages concerning a specific person to the wrong department or company, or to a another not intended addressee.[4]

3. Article 29 Working Party, Opinion 03/2014 on notifying cases of personal data breach, adopted on 25 March 2014 (WP213), http://www.giodo.gov.pl/pl/file/6336 (last accessed on 24 January 2018).
4. Or sending data covered by client–attorney privilege to a *New York Times* journalist who has the same first and last name as the lawyer representing the defendant in a case.

If the controller is in a relationship with the recipient, knows the recipient's procedures and other important details that indicate it is trustworthy, the controller can ask it to return or safely destroy the data it has obtained. In other words, this means a situation where the controller has justifiable certainty as to the recipient and can expect that the recipient will not read or use the improperly sent data but will follow instructions concerning the return thereof.

1.2.1.2 Breach of Availability

Article 4(12), Article 5(1)(f), Article 32(2) GDPR refer to a breach of availability, and as usual for GDPR wording of these provisions may be misleading. Article 4(12) and Article 5(1)(f) GDPR refer to 'accidental loss, destruction'. Article 32(2) GDPR refers to 'accidental or unlawful destruction, loss'. Neither of those provisions refers to 'temporary inaccessibility'.

Example

The loss of an encryption key in the case of encrypted data amounts to the loss of availability of data.

Despite those ambiguities, breach of availability of personal data in the meaning of GDPR must be understood in line with general principles of information security knowledge, and it is understood that way. The fact that Article 5(1)(f) misses 'unlawful destruction or loss' referred to in Article 32(2) GDPR is easily cured when we note that 'unlawful destruction or loss' amounts to 'unlawful or unauthorised processing' mentioned in Article 5(1)(f) GDPR. As for temporary loss of availability, Article 29 Working Party (EDPB) Guidelines on Personal data breach notification under Regulation 2016/679 (17/EN WP 250) rightly explain that 'If the lack of availability of personal data is likely to result in a risk to the rights and freedoms of natural persons, then the controller will need to notify' and support this view with the following example:

Example

'In the context of a hospital, if critical medical data about patients are unavailable, even temporarily, this could present a risk to individuals' rights and freedoms; for example, operations may be cancelled.' And we can add that for another example a healthy kidney may be amputated instead of the one attacked by cancer (real case).

1.2.1.3 Breach of Integrity

The third type of data protection breach is a breach of integrity, that is the unauthorised alteration of the content of personal data.

> **Example**
>
> Overwriting a new version of a client file with an older version, spelling mistakes in personal data, formatting and decoding issues, du-tri-multiplication of records, etc.

1.3 Must Every Breach Be Notified?

Losing a paper page containing personal data is a breach of personal data protection, and so is inadvertently allowing someone to look at someone's files on your laptop screen while reading in a train.

However, notification to a data supervisory authority is not necessary if the breach is 'unlikely to result in a risk to the rights and freedoms of natural persons'.

Taking into consideration that the definition of risk to the rights and freedoms of natural persons includes 'varying likelihood', it is not easy to decrypt what the EU legislator meant by the 'unlikely risk'. Does it refer to a low likelihood of any risk (which would practically cover any case except for resurrection) or to a low likelihood of any risk higher than low risk? We believe the second option is correct and that situations when a likelihood of a risk higher than low is low, there is no need to notify a breach to a data protection authority.

In our opinion, the GDPR's provision on data breach notification is one of the worst pieces of EU legislation known, requiring not only calculating likelihood of adverse effects of a breach but also multiplying it by the same likelihood and by severity of a breach.

In practical terms, however, let us try to assume that a notification to a supervisory authority is needed when unless it is unlikely that something wrong happens to a data subject's rights or freedoms.

Proving that despite a breach the risk to rights and freedoms of natural persons is low.

1.3.1 Notification Procedure

The GDPR provides specific, measurable time periods for notifying a breach of personal data.

1.3.1.1 *Time for Notification*

The time period for a controller is ‘without undue delay’, but:

(a) within seventy-two hours after becoming aware of the breach;
(b) after seventy-two hours, an explanation of the reasons for the delay must be attached.

Whether notification has been made without undue delay is determined theoretically taking account of: (i) the nature and severity of the personal data protection breach, (ii) the consequences thereof and (iii) its potential adverse effects on the data subjects. In practice, if a data controller fits into seventy-two hours that will certainly be without undue delay, as seventy-two-hour deadline is tight enough.

1.3.1.2 *Time Period for a Processor*

A processor must notify the personal data controller of a breach ‘without undue delay’. As we explain when discussing the entrustment of processing, the Article 29 Working Party Guidelines concerning notification of personal data breaches state that a processor should notify the controller of a breach soon enough to allow the controller to notify the supervisory authority within seventy-two hours of being made aware of the breach by the processor. This approach is hard to accept due to operational problems with communication and control. The operational problem can be overcome somewhat if the processor immediately notifies the controller that it ‘suspects’ there has been a breach and allows the controller to take part in its efforts to clarify the situation. Not that we believe all data processors will be eager to notify their clients about a suspicion of data breach until they are sure the milk is spilled. At any rate, until the guidelines are updated we recommend you take them into consideration and act as suggested above.

1.3.2 ***Determination of a Breach***

Allegedly, an organisation learns of an information security breach only after some time – three months on average, and from the press. The public disclosure of the most talked-about recent breaches was made after about a year, although the organisations involved knew about them much earlier, if not at once.

A controller is obliged to implement internal procedures that make it possible to detect and manage breaches. To this end, it may use available threat detection and prediction tools. It is also worth implementing tolerance for error in your organisational culture.

Here we need to specify exactly when we confirm a breach. According to the Article 29 Working Party, a controller determines there has been a breach at the moment when it has sufficient certainty that a security incident occurred that has resulted in a breach of personal data security. When no breach has yet been determined, but the event has already occurred, the controller’s most important task is to investigate the event and evaluate its effects in order to determine whether there has actually been a personal data security breach.

The Article 29 Working Party uses fuzzy terms such as 'a reasonable degree of certainty', 'not always immediately clear', 'on another occasion some time will be needed to determine that a personal data breach did occur' or 'a short investigation time'. It is hard to avoid getting the impression that the idea was not to give a precise answer.

In any case, the controller must act at once, making a quick evaluation and thinking it over later (after taking an initial decision on whether there was or was not a breach). Until better guidelines are available, it is better to assume that, from the time you receive information on a suspected breach (e.g., notification of a suspected breach), you have seventy-two hours to determine whether or not there really was a breach, and seventy-two hours to prepare a notification and submit it to the supervisory authority. Why not less or more time? The time cannot be shorter because, from the operational perspective, seventy-two hours is already very demanding, especially if the breach took place at the processor or subprocessor. Nor can it be longer because, since the EU legislator established seventy-two hours as the period for urgent notification, this is the measure we have to comply with.

An essential part of an action plan is to make an evaluation of the potential risk for natural persons that allows you to determine whether you are obliged to notify the breach. You should then make an additional evaluation, taking account of all the circumstances (a context of the breach). The importance of recognising a breach, of evaluating the risk for natural persons, and of notifying a breach where necessary are emphasised in Recital 87 GDPR. The faster you ascertain a breach, the faster you can react. It is possible for a controller to make an initial assessment of the risk that may be posed by a breach as part of a data protection impact assessment or within a risk analysis.

1.3.3 Notification: Content and Form

The GDPR does not introduce any requirement as to the form in which the supervisory authority is to be notified of a data protection breach or the results of not adhering to such form. Due to practical reasons, and especially the short seventy-two-hour deadline, a notification will be done electronically.

In a notification, a controller must include all the information specified in Article 33(1) sentence 2 and Article 33(3) GDPR. A notification must include, at least:

(1) a description of **the nature of the breach** of personal data protection, including, to the extent possible:
   (a) the categories and approximate numbers of data subjects concerned, and
   (b) the categories and approximate numbers of personal data entries the breach concerns.

Example

An archive containing the personal files of 200 employees catches fire.

(2) the first and last name and contact details of the **data protection officer**, or an indication of another contact point from which more information can be obtained;
(3) a description of the **possible consequences** of the personal data protection breach;

Example

The inability to access documents of former employees (lack of contact with them), causing a breach of the obligation under labour law to retain data for social security purposes, and difficulties in providing evidence if there is any litigation with a former employee.

(4) a description of the measures employed or proposed by the controller for handling any breach of personal data protection, including, where appropriate, measures for minimising any adverse effects of a breach.

Example

Notifying employees of an existing situation, requesting them to provide copies of whatever documents they have, appointing a recovery team to establish what is missing, search through different information resources to restore destroyed documents to the extent possible.

Under the GDPR, a submission need not immediately contain all of the elements specified in Article 33(3). These can be supplemented successively if all of the required information cannot be immediately included in the notification.

1.3.4 Delayed Notification

Pursuant to Article 33(1) GDPR, if a controller notified the supervisory authority later than with seventy-two hours, it must explain the delay. Let us note that GDPR acknowledges that there will be situations where 'without undue delay' means longer than seventy-two hours. This is indicated by the use in Article 33(1) of the formulation 'where feasible, not later than 72 hours'. This means that if, in a given situation, meeting the seventy-two-hour deadline is not possible, then providing notification later on will still fall within the basic expression of 'without undue delay'. Nevertheless, in each case, you exceed seventy-two hours for notifying a breach you should explain yourself.

1.3.5 Obligations of a Processor

Article 28(3) GDPR states:

> contract or other legal act shall stipulate, in particular, that the processor assists the controller in ensuring compliance with the obligations pursuant to Articles 32 to 36 taking into account the nature of processing and the information available to the processor.

In addition, Article 33(2) GDPR specifies that if a controller uses the services of a processor, the processor is obliged to notify the controller of any personal data protection breach 'without undue delay'.

The GDPR does not specify any deadline, but, in line with the Article 29 Working Party Guidelines, a processor should notify the controller immediately, and then successively send information on progress made. Here as well, the seventy-two-hour period for a controller to give notification is the point of reference. Above, we commented (unkindly) on the Article 29 Working Party's request that the controller's seventy-two hours starts running from the moment the processor learned about a breach.

1.4 When, in the Case of a Data Protection Breach, Is It Not Necessary to Notify the Supervisory Authority?

A data controller need not notify a data protection breach to the supervisory authority when:

> the personal data breach is unlikely to result in a risk to the rights and freedoms of natural person.

It is not totally unlikely that those who worded the GDPR knew what they exactly meant by 'unlikely risk to the rights and freedoms'; still it is hard to believe looking at the words used. It is likely they knew that the likelihood of the 'risk' in question refers to a risk of subsequent violation of rights or freedoms. Still, wording of respective provisions of the GDPR (Article 33(1) and 34(1) is a mastery of ambiguity.[5]

Let us start with an observation that a breach of confidentiality often equals to a breach of privacy – this when data fall into hands of an unauthorised person.[6] So, as to a breach of privacy there is no assessment of likelihood. Therefore we believe in such situations Article 33(1) GDPR requires a data controller to assess what subsequent negative consequences for rights and freedoms of a data subject could take place.

5. We are leaving aside a probable misuse of an operator 'AND' instead of 'OR' in 'risk to the rights and freedoms', in order not to get too technical here.
6. As opposed to a situation when we have lost unprotected data in a public place but we are not sure if they have fallen into unauthorised hands.

Then we need to ask ourselves that question what the GDPR means by 'unlikely risk'. Taking into consideration that 'risk' in the meaning of the GDPR is a result of a relationship between likelihood and severity of a breach,[7] we would end up calculating a result of multiplying [likelihood of likelihood of further negative consequences multiplied by severity of those potential negative consequences] by [likelihood of further negative consequences multiplied by severity of those potential negative consequences]. That sounds nonsensical. So, probably the EU legislator meant by 'likelihood of risk' simply likelihood of negative consequences.

At the end of the day, we believe that a data controller may resign from notifying a supervisory authority if further/subsequent (other than those which directly constitute a data breach) negative consequences (breach of rights or freedoms) for data subjects affected are 'unlikely', which should be true even for minor subsequent breaches of rights and freedoms. In plain words: if it is unlikely that something wrong happens, you do not need to notify your supervisory authority.

It is the controller itself that must evaluate whether there is a risk of a breach of human rights and freedoms. It should do so based on objective criteria (such as existing experience in connection with similar cases, knowledge about information security) and taking account of the circumstances (context) of the breach of personal data security.

Furthermore, please note that, although a loss of access to a controller's systems may be only temporary and may not entail any direct consequences for natural persons, the very fact that a network has been broken into should be seen as a potential breach of confidentiality that must be notified. A controller must always **consider all possible consequences of a breach**.

An example of a situation in which there is a small probability of a personal data protection breach, and in which notification to the authority is not required, is where personal data are deleted as a result of a telecommunications system error but are recovered immediately from a backup copy.

If there is a leak of data that are publicly available, e.g. on the company's website, this also causes no risk to natural persons and is not treated as a breach.

In Guidelines on Personal data breach notification under Regulation 2016/679 (17/EN WP 250), the Article 29 Working Party (EDPB), as usual in a complicated seemingly self-contradictory way, tackles the issue of losing control over encrypted data. Article 29 Working Party starts with stating 'a confidentiality breach of personal data that were encrypted with a state of the art algorithm is still a personal data breach, and has to be notified (our example: loss of an encrypted pen drive) but at least it does not need to be communicated to data subjects affected (because they are not really affected) unless there are no backups of data lost.' Straight from there the same Guidelines go to a more reasonable conclusion, contradicting the first quoted that 'if personal data have been made essentially unintelligible to unauthorised parties and where the data are a copy or a backup exists, a confidentiality breach involving

7. Risk is often presented as a multiplication of likelihood value and severity value.

properly encrypted personal data may not need to be notified to the supervisory authority.'

We do not agree with the first quote but we do agree with the second. Assuming an algorithm and a password are strong, a likelihood of decrypting is very small (unless we are discussing a targeted attack from a highly skilled private hacker or a national or foreign cyber-intelligence agency, likelihood of which needs to be assessed as well). Therefore in case we lose well protected encrypted data, we believe it is unlikely data are going to be compromised, so there would be no need to notify such breach to a supervisory authority and no need to inform data subjects.

At the same time, in line with our understanding, under the guidelines on notifying a personal data protection breach, if personal data become in principle impossible to be read by unauthorised persons, and if those data constitute a copy or another backup copy of them exists, then there is no obligation to notify the supervisory authority of a breach of availability of such data or confidentiality of appropriately encrypted personal data. Here there is only a small probability that such a breach could pose a risk to the rights and freedoms of natural persons. Of course, this also means that those natural persons need not be notified. The same guidelines insist on re-evaluation of the risk if new circumstances occur – e.g., a vulnerability of an encryption program/algorithm is disclosed. However, we believe only in case of a suspicion of a targeted attack that would really matter.

1.4.1 Practical Issues

The 'triggers' for notifying the authority and persons under Articles 33 and 34 GDPR are described using the words 'unless the personal data breach is unlikely to result in a risk' of a breach and 'a high risk of a breach'. The risk assessment methodology recommended by CNIL involves a four-level scale (negligible, low, high, maximal). A leak need not be notified to the supervisory authority only when the risk is negligible, while data subjects concerned need not be notified unless the risk is high.

1.4.2 Documentation of Breaches

Regardless of whether or not a breach requires notification, a controller should record every breach, in view of the GDPR principle of accountability.

While it is the controller that determines the manner and form of documenting breaches, there are certain rules for recording information that must be followed in every case. Pursuant to Article 33(5) GDPR, a controller must record information on a breach, encompassing the cause, the course of events and what personal data were compromised. A record should also include the effects and consequences of the breach, and what remedial action was taken by the controller.

The Article 29 Working Party also recommends documenting a justification of the decision taken in response to the breach. Specifically, this means documenting the reasons for a decision not to give notification of a breach. The controller must state the reasons why it deems that the risk of a breach of the rights and freedoms of natural persons is unlikely (Recital 85 GDPR). If the controller judges that one of the conditions described in Article 34(3) GDPR has been met, it should be able to provide relevant evidence that this is so.

Documentation must be kept in a way that, on the basis thereof, the supervisory authority can verify whether the obligations resulting from Article 33 GDPR have been duly met.

Despite the GDPR refers only to the term 'data protection breach' in reality controllers and processors need to record and control all 'incidents' (a term not defined by the GDPR for mysterious reasons) to demonstrate compliance with duties relating to data protection breaches.

Incidents, in plain words, are situations when data protection (information) security rules are broken, or data (information) security is compromised or exposed or (as for suspicions) we suspect that is the case. A simple example: someone left the office open for a night. Most likely it has not led to any data protection breach, but data protection security rules, of course, have been broken. Another example: someone at a telecom left their desk without blocking their computer and a journalist managed to copy billing information of a certain politician. It resulted in a country-wide data breach – that journalist published those billings, and they had been used in criminal investigations and commented widely in the press. In this case, an incident (leaving your working station without securing it) led to a personal data breach.

We recommend registering also 'suspected incidents'. In reality, we recommend to treat every internal notification of a breach as a notification of a suspicion of a breach. A competent person or competent body with a particular organisation should then confirm a breach and evaluate its potential consequences. It is not only about 'gaining time', a competent situation assessment requires expertise or at least proper training.

1.4.3 Administrative Sanctions

The GDPR provides for administrative liability for a breach of any of the provisions of Article 33 GDPR. For example, a failure to meet the obligations concerning documentation allows for imposing an administrative fine as referred to in Article 83(4)(a) GDPR, namely, in the amount of up to EUR 10 million, and in case of a business of over EUR 500 million global total annual turnover for the previous financial year in the amount of up to 2% of that turnover.

1.5 Elements of the Breach Notification System

To manage the whole process concerning the obligation to notify the supervisory authority of a personal data breach, you should have the following in place:

(1) a procedure for handling incidents, suspected breaches and breaches, including confirming breaches, assessing likelihood and severity of consequential

breaches, notifying supervisory authority, informing data subjects, documenting (register of personal data protection breaches);
(2) responsible persons and a business continuity plan;
(3) instructions on how to proceed when there is a suspicion of a breach – for all personnel and processors;
(4) training for personnel on what a breach of personal data protection is and on how to proceed when there is a suspicion of a breach;
(5) an understanding with processors, expressed in a data processing agreement, on how to proceed when there is a suspicion of a data protection breach at the processor (to avoid any delay in notifying the breach on the part of the processor, or to at least expressly attribute responsibility for such a delay to the processor).
(6) documenting incidents, suspected breaches and breaches, possibly in a record of personal data breaches;
(7) instruction on notifying breaches to the supervisory authority and informing data subjects.

2 NOTIFYING DATA SUBJECTS ABOUT A DATA PROTECTION BREACH (ARTICLE 34 GDPR)

2.1 Preliminary Remarks

Pursuant to Article 34(1 and 2) GDPR:

> (1) When the **[1]** personal data breach is likely to result in **[2]** a high risk to the rights and freedoms of natural persons, the controller shall **[3]** communicate the personal data breach to the data subject **[4]** without undue delay.
> (2) The communication to the data subject referred to in paragraph 1 of this Article shall describe **[5]** in clear and plain language **[6 – elements of the notification]** the nature of the personal data breach and contain at least the information and measures referred to in points (b), (c) and (d) of Article 33(3) **[7 – elements of a notification of a breach of personal data protection to the supervisory authority]**.

The obligation to notify data subjects about incidents such as a data leak is a very uncomfortable duty for a controller. Similar to the obligation to notify the supervisory authority of a data protection breach under Article 33 GDPR, this is something new that organisations must face. It is not just that notifying 'victims' of a leak or other data security-related incident is yet another organisational and procedural hurdle for companies; fulfilling that obligation can also entail consequences, from the need to deal with difficult customers having a lot of time on their hands to the loss of reputation.

2.2 High Risk of a Breach of Rights and Freedoms

A controller is obliged to notify data subjects if a personal data breach is 'likely to result in a high risk to rights and freedoms of natural persons'.

Similarly as in Article 33(1) GDPR, we need to understand what 'likely to result in a high risk' means. Let us note once again that 'risk' in the meaning of GDPR already includes 'likelihood'; therefore, 'likely to result in a high risk' should translate to 'likely to result in likelihood and severity of potential consequences constituting high risk'. Does not get clearer though. It is even less clear when we note that Article 34(1) GDPR refers to 'high risk to rights and freedoms of natural **persons**' and not to 'a natural person' instead. Does it mean that we need to inform a data subject if there is high risk to that particular data subject or if we get to a conclusion that overall a breach in question generates a secondary high risk (e.g., where consequences for one person affected would usually be not that bad but there is a lot of affected persons, making the overall risk score amounting to 'high')? Who writes these laws? I happened to propose a certain wording of data processing and cloud computing rules, but I am not at all responsible for the wording of commented provisions.

Using common sense as a rule of thumb, you should inform a person about a breach in case you establish considerable likelihood (if something is likely it means that its likelihood is considerable) of severe consequences to that person. You should also inform persons about a breach (or make a public announcement) if a scale of persons affected is such that an overall assessment of a risk resulting from a breach is 'high' according to your methodology. I usually use an example of wrong addressing of an electrical bill (already mentioned in this book in another context). If an electricity company addresses wrongly one bill, the risk most likely will be negligible. However, if 10,000 bills go out to wrong addressees, one may concern a power delivery point unknown to one's wife, leading her to a conclusion that her husband is renting another apartment and not telling her about it and draw further conclusions. And in result, an electricity company becomes co-responsible for a divorce. Which seems to be a pretty severe consequence for persons affected. There is, however, an interesting and more common variation of the same example. The same electric bill may be wrongly dispatched to an address of residence of a buyer instead of an address for delivery indicated in the power supply agreement, leading to a higher likelihood of similar consequences.

When a controller becomes aware that a breach has taken place, **it must evaluate the likelihood of high risk**. It should consider criteria similar to those used when notifying a breach to the supervisory authority under Article 33 GDPR. But it is easier to avoid notifying natural persons than the authority.

2.2.1 Rights and Freedoms

The rights and freedoms of data subjects that can be breached as a result of an incident are the fundamental rights and freedoms granted on the basis of European law (e.g., the Charter of Fundamental Rights of the EU and the European Convention on Human Rights), e.g.:

- the prohibition on discrimination on the basis of sex, race, colour, language, religion or political or other opinion (Article 14 ECHR);
- human dignity (Article 1 CFR);
- personal data protection (Article 8 CFR);
- the right to legal protection of one's private and family life, honour and good reputation;
- privacy of correspondence;
- ownership.

Recital 75 GDPR describes situations where a breach of the rights or freedoms of data subjects may arise.

Example

If there is a data leak in your company (a breach of data protection) from a database containing, e.g., financial data on customers, due to a theft perpetrated by a group of hackers knows for such activity, it is highly likely (based on knowledge of previous incidents) that those data will be used in a way that will breach the rights of your customers; e.g., in the future they may be robbed or at least their ID will be stolen (there is a high risk of a breach of the rights or freedoms of natural persons). You must promptly notify the 'victims' of the leak.

Example

In a company, there is a leak of the contents of email inboxes and correspondence between two employees holding key positions who are having an affair. The correspondence is private and of an intimate nature and was intercepted by an employee who had been dismissed for some other reason and may wish to take revenge on the company or their former superiors. There is a high risk that the dismissed employee will want to publish the stolen correspondence in the press, in social media or otherwise make it available to undesirable recipients (e.g., the lovers). In such a situation, the persons the data leak concerns must be notified about it immediately, because there is a very high risk that their rights (dignity, privacy of correspondence) will be breached further.

Example

An employee of a company leaves a briefcase with documents containing personal data in a tram. The following morning, however, the briefcase and documents are recovered; they were found by the tram driver. The briefcase seems untouched. In such a situation, the risk of a breach of the rights or freedoms of the data subjects concerned does not seem high, and the company does not have to notify those customers about the lost briefcase.

2.3 Exceptions from the Obligation to Notify

Pursuant to Article 34(3) GDPR, no notification is required in situations where:

a) the controller has implemented appropriate technical and organisational protection measures, and those measures were applied to the personal data affected by the personal data breach, in particular those that render the personal data unintelligible to any person who is not authorised to access it, such as encryption;
b) the controller has taken subsequent measures which ensure that the high risk to the rights and freedoms of data subjects referred to in paragraph 1 is no longer likely to materialise.

In practice, those provisions make it possible to avoid notifying data subjects about an incident, even if the theoretical risk of a breach of their rights or freedoms is high. A controller, then, may take preventive measures (i) before an incident happens, or corrective measures (ii) to deal with consequences of an incident post factum.

2.3.1 Preventive Measures

Preventive measures referred to in Article 34 GDPR are those which can secure data even after a breach. Mostly that would be encryption of data or data carriers (USB sticks, mobile phones, computer drives), location tracking solutions (e.g., find my Iphone IOs function) and enabling remote erasure solutions amount to preventive measures as well, though they, of course, require further corrective measures, i.e. tracking and finding lost data ASAP or enforcing a remote erasure. And let us not forget here about creating backups following a reasonable backup policy which constitutes preventive measure against loss of data availability of course.

2.3.2 Corrective Measures

Corrective measures that eliminate the need to notify data subjects include, e.g., remotely destroying data from lost media (remote erasure), concluding a confidentiality agreement with persons who became acquainted with personal data without authorisation, restoring destroyed data from backup copies.

2.4 Communicating a Breach to a Data Subject

2.4.1 Content of a Communication

An entity that has to inform a person about a breach should do so in a way that is clear, simple and easy for the recipient to understand. The scope of communication to a data subject about a breach of personal data protection is similar to that of a notification to the supervisory authority but need not contain information on the scale of the leak or on other 'injured parties'.

Such a communication should include:

- the nature of the breach,
- the contact details of the DPO or another contact point,
- the possible consequences of the breach,
- the measures employed or proposed by the controller in order to manage the breach and minimise any adverse effects it may have.

2.4.2 Form of Communication

The GDPR does not directly impose any form for informing data subjects about a breach of their personal data. Expressly, it states only that the communication must be expressed in clear, plain language and must describe certain elements in connection with the breach.

To the extent possible a communication must be documented (in writing, email, text message, instant message) so that the data subject has the opportunity to read the content multiple times. In its guidelines concerning notification of personal data breaches, the Article 29 Working Party [8]permits other documented forms of communication, including text messages, electronic communicator messages and banners published on a website (for more on an announcement instead of a communication, *see* section 2.4.3).

The time in which an entity is obliged to give communication of a breach means that the most convenient way of doing so, for both the data controller and the recipient, is in electronic form. This guarantees quick communication and allows the data subject concerned to become thoroughly familiar with the content of the communication.

2.4.3 An Announcement Instead of a Direct Communication

Article 34(3)(c) GDPR introduces an additional, supposed exemption from the obligation to inform data subjects directly about a breach. If the communication:

8. The Art. 29 Working Party Guidelines on Personal data breach notification under Regulation 2016/679, adopted on 3 October 2017. (WP 250), https://www.poradyodo.pl/pobierz-zalacznik/8302/322 (last accessed on 26 January 2018).

> would involve disproportionate effort … there shall instead be a **public communication** or similar measure whereby the data subjects are informed in an equally effective manner.

A decision on whether to replace direct communication with an announcement should be documented and justified both in principle and by the type of announcement you choose to make. The guidelines on notifying breaches permit announcements on prominent websites or in newspapers.

A mere note in the press or information in the company's website news or corporate blog would not be sufficient in most circumstances. However, if, for example, a breach affects only employees, a data controller may choose to place an announcement at the entrance to the place of work (assuming a controller does not maintain email accounts for all employees).

2.4.4 Time for Informing about a Breach

A communication should be sent 'without undue delay', that is as fast as is reasonably possible. Communication must be made when the risk of a breach of rights and freedoms is high. If the possible consequences of that risk to natural persons are not severe, it is possible to work during normal business hours and in that way perform all the actions needed to issue the communication. If, however, the consequences could be very serious, you must act at once, regardless of whether it is after hours or a weekend. Remember, Article 33 GDPR places a 'mental anchor' for counting a deadline around '72 hours after having become aware of' a breach.

Should you first notify a breach to a supervisory authority or inform data subjects? Taking into consideration that Article 33(3)(d) GDPR requires a data controller to describe measures to mitigate adverse effects of a breach, you should probably start by informing affected persons or at least explain in the notification to the supervisory authority whether you are going to do it and why it requires more time.

2.5 Cooperation with the Supervisory Authority

The guidelines on notifying breaches indicate that, in line with Recital 86 GDPR, communication to data subjects should be made in cooperation with the supervisory authority. This is how it is in practice since persons affected by a breach are usually notified after the controller has notified the supervisory authority. It would be imprudent not to take advantage up the opportunity to agree on the communication with the authority, or at least to try to do so (e.g., you can immediately include your proposals in the notification sent to the authority).

In certain cases, where the harm to natural persons could be serious and occur at once, those persons should be notified even before notification is sent to the authority. In any case, you should not delay informing data subjects hoping to get instructions from a supervisory authority. First, you will not be able to rely on the lack of reaction of a supervisory authority to justify your delay. Second, it will be hard for you to contest a supervisory authority's instructions even if they are hysterical if you let them come in before you act.

> **Example**
>
> If customer passwords in your system are leaked, you should immediately inform the persons concerned so they can change their passwords in other systems as well. After all, everyone knows that people use the same two passwords everywhere.

2.6 Closing Remarks: How to Calculate Consequential Data Breach Risk Assessment

Simplifying, if consequential risk resulting from a data breach is low, you do not need to notify a supervisory authority and if the risk is high, you need to not only notify a supervisory authority but also inform data subjects affected.

So, how to calculate the consequential risk to the rights and freedoms of data subjects resulting from a data breach?

EU Agency for Network and Information Security issued in 2013 Recommendations for a methodology of the assessment of the severity of personal data breaches.[9] The Recommendation is often referred to when discussing notification and information duties under the GDPR. We are not big fans of the Recommendation, though we acknowledge it is somehow helpful especially because it grades specific types of data from the perspective of consequences of the severity of a breach. However, the Recommendation does not at all tackle the other dimension of the risk to rights and freedoms the GDPR requires us to calculate, which is likelihood. So, how to calculate likelihood and how to combine severity with likelihood?

Targeted attacks. If we have reasons to believe that a breach resulted from a targeted attack we notify a supervisory authority. Targeted attacks are done for purpose. Plus we are very cautious in establishing if that breach created high risk to rights and freedoms of affected or potentially affected persons.

Accidental breaches. In case of (assumed) accidental breaches we rely more on calculating probabilities.

How to calculate likelihood. We would calculate likelihood of specific consequences of a breach using Bernoulli Trials. We would calculate separate likelihood for consequences of a specific severity. However, we would not be calculating separately every likelihood of every possible adverse consequences of a breach for a data subject affected. We would focus on answering two questions: First, if high risk to rights and freedoms of affected persons exist, we need to inform them about a breach. Second, if

9. https://www.enisa.europa.eu/topics/data-protection/personal-data-breaches/personal-data-breach-notification-tool (last accessed on 1 March 2019.

any negative consequence to persons affected is more than unlikely, we need to notify a supervisory authority.

How to combine severity with likelihood. We would start combining both dimensions of risk to rights and freedoms by imagining and listing potential negative consequences of a specific breach. Second, we would group them into minimal, low, high, maximum severity consequences groups.

Then we would check which consequences have 'high-risk potential' and calculate their likelihood – to exclude of verify information duty (Article 34 GDPR). Again, we could rely on Bernoulli Trials to quantify the likelihood, if possible.

Then we would see if we are able to logically prove that any negative consequences of the breach for persons affected are unlikely, and if we fail to do so, we would notify a supervisory authority.

What you see above is bits and pieces from our practical experiences and works on risk assessment methodologies. Such approach would work for large organisations as long as they hire specialists capable of calculating probability. The same approach will not work at all for small and medium enterprises unless they outsource a ready to use solution (which will be a black box for them anyway). So, a much simpler way of calculating the consequential risk to rights and freedoms of data subjects needs to be developed for small and medium enterprises. We have developed such simplified, quantifiable and parameterised methodology built partially on ENISA's approach. We are planning to release it soon for public discussion.

CHAPTER 6
Data Protection Officer (DPO)

Michał Kibil & Maciej Gawronski

1 DATA PROTECTION OFFICER: APPOINTMENT AND STATUS

1.1 DPO: Evolution or Revolution?

The General Data Protection Regulation (GDPR) introduces a new formal role that of data protection officer (DPO), not known to the Directive 95/46/EC.

A DPO formally is not responsible for an organisation's compliance with the provisions on data protection. The responsibility for GDPR compliance rests upon the management of the organisation and cannot be ceded to the DPO. When a DPO is mentioned in the GDPR, their role is to consult, raise awareness, advise and inspect. Consequently, we advise against formally conferring responsibility for implementing the GDPR upon a DPO. It is better to appoint a different person to head up such a project or programme, while the DPO, where appointed),should be included as an essential participant in all activities.[1]

According to the GDPR, a DPO should act as an intermediary between the interested parties (e.g., the personal data protection authority and data subjects or individuals within a business) and a data controller. A DPO's role is therefore quite unique for anything we know before the GDPR (even for Member States where a similar function was foreseen by national legislations prior to the GDPR), unifying an in-house and external lawyer, a compliance officer, an information security specialist, a privacy advocate, an internal auditor, an adviser to the board, a consultant and a representative of a regulator within an organisation.

Moreover, there a popular misconception exists that a DPO is responsible for compliance with the GDPR and other data protection laws. To the contrary, a DPO is

1. Of course, reality does not match regulations on many levels. Often DPOs are in practice responsible for implementing data protection compliance.

NOT responsible for data protection compliance. A DPO should be treated more like an ombudsman of data protection in an organisation, but responsibility and liability remains with a management. 'It's not the responsibility of the DPO if there is an enforcement action,' WP29 Chairwoman Andrea Jelinek said. 'It's the responsibility of management. Our enforcement action won't be against DPOs, it will be against the company. The DPO must be independent.'[2]

1.2 Who Is Obliged to Appoint a DPO?

An entity is obliged to designate a DPO when:

(a) they are a public authority or another public body;[3]
(b) if their core activities consist of processing operations, which require regular and systematic monitoring of data subjects on a large scale, or where;
(c) if their core activities consist of processing on a large scale of special categories of data or personal data relating to criminal convictions and offences.

In any case, every entity must analyse (and document to comply with the principle of accountability) whether it is obliged to appoint a DPO.

Where an entity designates a DPO without being formally obliged to do so, none of the rules concerning the DPO's appointment, status or duties resulting from the GDPR apply.

Nothing stands in the way of an employer hiring an external consultant to facilitate GDPR compliance, regardless of whether a DPO has been designated. In such a case, though, the controller must take care to ensure that the consultant is not mistaken for a DPO. In particular, there should be nothing in that person's job title that could justify their being treated as a DPO. The role of a data protection specialist may be described similarly to the statutory role of a DPO, though specific points of distinction (e.g., 'under-executive' point of reporting, limited access rights) should be inserted to discourage anyone (and in particular the DP specialist her/himself) from trying to requalify themselves to a DPO upon dismissal.

As DPOs are formally difficult to terminate, they are often employed for a limited period of time.

1.2.1 Public Body or Entity

The GDPR does not define what is to be understood as a public body or entity. Even though the Article 29 Working Party says that the scope of public entities should result from domestic provisions of law, at the same time, it refers in its guidelines to

2. https://iapp.org/news/a/new-wp29-chair-talks-enforcement-role-of-the-dpo/ (last accessed on 3 March 2019).
3. Except for courts acting in their judicial capacity.

definitions contained in Directive 2003/98/EC of the European Parliament and of the Council of 17 November 2003 on the reuse of public sector information (OJEU C 345, p. 90). Therefore, domestic, regional and local authorities, as well as public law entities (such as ministries, central bodies of federal and provincial administration) should be treated as public entities.

Article 37 (1)(a) GDPR states that the obligation to appoint a DPO does not apply to courts 'acting in their judicial capacity'. And of course it means something opposite to what it seems. A court as a public entity must have a DPO, but a court DPO is not competent to assess how cases are considered and ruled on.

1.2.2 *Activity Requiring Systematic, Regular Monitoring and Processing on a Large Scale*

The two remaining cases when a DPO must be appointed are based on the criterion of the type of processing activity.

1.2.2.1 *Core Activity*

Under the GDPR, an entity's core activity is that which is key in terms of achieving the controller's or the processor's goals. For an insurance company, the core activity is analysing risk, selling insurance and handling claims. Auxiliary activities such as using information technology (IT) services or keeping payroll lists are not treated as main activities, even though they support the main activity.

1.2.2.2 *Monitoring of Persons*

You can find a basic definition of monitoring in the GDPR Recital 71:

> any form of automated processing of personal data evaluating the personal aspects relating to a natural person, in particular to analyse or predict aspects concerning the data subject's performance at work, economic situation, health, personal preferences or interests, reliability or behaviour, location or movements

and Article 4 point 4 GDPR:

> any form of automated processing of personal data consisting of the use of personal data to evaluate certain personal aspects relating to a natural person, in particular to analyse or predict aspects concerning that natural person's performance at work, economic situation, health, personal preferences, interests, reliability, behaviour, location or movements.

As usual for unknown reasons, the wording of both definitions differ slightly, and as usual for the GDPR that difference does not have any meaning.[4]

4. If it had that would be truly devastating.

To determine whether a processing activity can be considered 'monitoring of the behaviour' of data subjects, it must be established to what extent data subject's decisions and actions are being recorded and then analysed. For example, monitoring takes place when natural persons are tracked on the internet, 'including potential subsequent use of personal data processing techniques which consist of profiling a natural person, particularly in order to take decisions concerning her or him or for analysing or predicting her or his personal preferences, behaviours and attitudes'.

As the Article 29 Working Party points out, requirement for appointing a DPO does not cover all cases of monitoring, but only those that are regular and systematic.[5]

Regular monitoring is that which:

(1) is permanent or occurs at defined time intervals over a defined time period,
(2) is periodic or repeated throughout a defined time period,
(3) takes place permanently or periodically.

In turn, systematic monitoring is that which:

(1) takes place in accordance with a defined system,
(2) is arranged, organised and methodical,
(3) takes place as part of a general data collection plan,
(4) is conducted as part of a defined strategy.

The following are examples of activities that may constitute regular or systematic monitoring of natural persons: servicing a telecommunications network; providing telecommunications services; redirecting email; marketing activities based on data, profiling and evaluations for risk assessment purposes (e.g., to evaluate credit risk, determine insurance premiums, avoid fraud, detect money laundering); location tracking (e.g., by mobile apps); running loyalty programmes; behavioural advertising; monitoring personal data on health and physical conditions using portable devices; video monitoring or servicing communication devices (e.g., smart meters, smart cars, household automation).[6] One can say with complete confidence that the GDPR will make its mark in all key sectors of the economy.

The issue what constitutes a regular monitoring is a subject to a heated debate within the EDPB. For example, the EDPB seems to consider all electronic monitoring of employees as regular and systematic large-scale monitoring irrespective if it concerns twenty employees or twenty thousand employees. This results from a relative or subjective measure of 'large scale' (relative to a context in which the specific data controller operates). We strongly oppose to such approach as it promotes bigger (and better off) entities operating on a (namely) larger scale and as it directly opposes to the rule of proportionality and it seems against rules of competition. We recon that 'large

5. Article 29 Working Party Guidelines on the data protection office (DPO), approved on 13 December 2016, amended and approved on 5 April 2017. (WP243), p. 9, http://www.giodo.gov.pl/pl/file/12390 (last accessed on 27 January 2018).
6. Article 29 Working Party, Guidelines ..., pp. 10, 22.

scale processing of special categories data' is different from 'monitoring public spaces on a large scale'. But this is a totally different story.

1.2.2.3 Large-Scale Processing

Large-scale processing is that which is defined in Recital 91 GDPR. That recital refers to operations:

> which aim to process a considerable amount of personal data at regional, national or supranational level and which could affect a large number of data subjects and which are likely to result in a high risk,

and states further on that:

> The processing of personal data should not be considered to be on a large scale if the processing concerns personal data from patients or clients by an individual physician, other health care professional or lawyer.

It is not possible to say how many data must be processed for the activity to qualify as 'large-scale'. The Article 29 Working Party did not come up with any clear definition.

The Working Party count the following as examples of processing on a large scale:

(1) a hospital processing data of patients as part of its activities;
(2) processing data concerning the movements of people who use public transport (e.g., tracking by means of city cards);
(3) a specialist entity processing geolocation data of customers in real time on behalf of an international fast food chain for statistical purposes;
(4) a bank or insurance company processing data of customers as part of their activities;
(5) a search engine processing data for behavioural advertising purposes;
(6) telephone or internet service providers processing data (concerning content, traffic or location).

'Surprisingly' and to our relief the Article 29 Working Party Guidelines do not consider the processing of patients' data by individual doctors, or of data on rulings by an attorney, as large-scale processing.

Legislative discussions considered introducing an obligation to have a DPO when more than 5,000 records were processed annually.[7] Ultimately, though, no quantitative threshold was agreed. The figure of 5,000 remains, though, as a kind of mental anchor for monitoring. Yet, the non-invasive monitoring of unknown persons is one thing, but monitoring a fixed group of people or tracking and profiling unknown persons is another. This is why we propose using a number of quantitative parameters:

7. L. Moerel, *One for all ... Maybe?*, https://iapp.org/news/a/gdpr-conundrums-the-data-protection-officer-requirement/ (last accessed on 27 January 2018).

Employee monitoring. For video and other monitoring of employees, we propose a threshold of **500 employees**, based on the following logic: with less than 250 employees, an employer is small from the GDPR perspective; with 250–500 employees, an employer is considered medium-sized; with above 500, it is a large employer; and so then monitoring of employees is on a large scale.

Monitoring identified persons. For monitoring identified persons other than employees (e.g., energy consumers), and for tracking people based on electronic tags (e.g., cookies) or other tracking that makes it possible to build personality profiles, we propose a threshold of **6,000 persons** equal to the threshold of a number of records involving special categories of data we recon. We believe that monitoring identified persons generates an intimate knowledge about them comparable to knowing about what the GDPR calls special categories data. And yes, we believe most of the current e-commerce businesses actively profiling, retargeting, affiliating, etc. should appoint a DPO.

Special categories data. We have assumed that four physicians constitute a team and that they are capable of processing (examining) 1,500 patients per year each, resulting in 6,000 patients per year. And that is our threshold for large-scale processing of special category data. Vilijar Peep – head of the Estonian data protection authority – proposed 5,000[8] in his LinkedIn post, while the Dutch supervisory authority proposed 10,000 health records.[9]

Public spaces monitoring. Video monitoring of public spaces seems to be the hardest to quantify. We believe that in each case where there is at least a team of people (security team) constantly watching a public space, having to intervene frequently (maybe not once in a month but what if ten times per month) and watching people on a daily large scale, it amounts to large-scale monitoring. So, why not to apply the same threshold of 6,000 people as in case of special category data but per day instead of per year. We understand that it means a lot of organisations would have to appoint a DPO (and conduct a data protection impact assessment of their monitoring operations). But we believe that video surveillance can reveal a lot about people being monitored. As an example, a shopping mall security probably knows 'mall girls' and 'mall boys' operating in their establishment, as well as their clients. Such knowledge can be used in different ways, and it should be controlled.

You do not have to stick with these figures and can question them for a particular industry, but they and the logic behind them at least provide a starting point for considering your own circumstances and operations.

Alternatively, we recommend using qualitative (negative) criteria such as 'a little frequented location' or 'accessory monitoring' if the cameras covering a given building only 'catch' a public space incidentally.

8. https://www/linkedin.com/feed/update/urn:li:activity:6404572629235220480 (last accessed on 9 September 2018).
9. https://www.lexology.com/library/detail.aspx?g=1df77358-9313-4d21-b345-0c8c3aeb4101 (last accessed on 9 September 2018).

1.3 Acting Within a Group of Undertakings

Pursuant to Article 37(2) GDPR, a group of undertakings (businesses) may designate a single DPO. Recital 37 states that a group of undertakings covers a controlling undertaking and its controlled undertakings (a dominant relationship). A group of undertakings may extend beyond the borders of the European Union (EU).

According to the GDPR, a single DPO should be able to effectively perform their duties across the whole group of undertakings. If this is physically impossible due to the complexity of the structure of the business and the number of duties involved, the group should appoint more DPOs, dividing their duties into particular companies from the group. A group DPO may though have her/his supporting team.

When designating a single DPO for a group of businesses, you have to ensure that the DPO is able to communicate easily with the individual units of the organisation. The concept of ease of communication applies to a DPO's duties relating to communicating with data subjects, with the contact point of the supervisory authority, and within the organisation as well, taking account of the fact that one of the DPO's tasks is 'to inform and advise the controller or the processor and the employees who carry out processing of their obligations pursuant to this Regulation' (Article 39(1)(a) GDPR). In practice, such an international DPO must have a supporting team, and such a team should be able to speak in all the languages used by personnel and customers of the group of businesses.

Appointing a group DPO is just like appointing a DPO for a single organisation, except that the DPO is in charge of several companies rather than just one. This means that the process of appointing a group DPO does not differ from the standard process. Every member of a group of businesses appoints a DPO in accordance with the rules of representation and decision-making in force in a given company.

Article 37(4) GDPR suggests appointing a DPO even where it is not obligatory, particularly in the case of associations or other bodies representing specific categories of controllers or processors. The idea of an 'industry DPO' might be useful.

1.4 Qualifications of a DPO

Pursuant to Article 37(5) GDPR:

> The data protection officer shall be designated on the basis of professional qualities and, in particular, expert knowledge of data protection law and practices and the ability to fulfil the tasks referred to in Article 39.

Recital 97 GDPR states that the level of knowledge needed by a DPO should be determined by analysing the data processing operations they are to carry out.

A person holding a DPO post should have: a deep understanding of the GDPR; knowledge of European and domestic data protection law; knowledge of the industry of the controller and of the controller itself, including its IT systems and the security measures it employs and of its needs concerning data protection; and in the case of public entities and bodies, knowledge of administrative procedures and the principles according to which those establishments operate. A controller should apply these indications cautiously when formulating the requirements for a DPO position. They seem to require a DPO who not only is a one-man band but also has deep insight into the GDPR itself. In 2018 and 2019, wishing for a simultaneous a deep insight into the GDPR, law, IT and cybersecurity is wishful thinking. Probably in the next few years as well. To be realistic, there is probably not a single person among the personnel of supervisory authorities across the EU to meet these requirements.

1.5 Employing a DPO

The GDPR allows organisations to choose how they employ a DPO. The position may be performed on the basis of an employment contract or of an agreement on the provision of services – including outsourcing a DPO from a professional entity.

The GDPR does not make the rights and obligations of a DPO dependent on the form of their cooperation with an organisation; an outsourced DPO will also have to meet the criteria for independence and will need to be protected against termination.

Once a DPO is selected, the organisation must publish the DPO's contact details and notify the supervisory authority of the appointment. The DPO's contact details should enable data subjects and the supervisory authority to easily contact them. To this end, the contact details should include not only the DPO's correspondence address but also their telephone number and email address. When necessary due to the nature of the DPO's activities, they should also include other means of communication with the public, such as an infoline or contact form on the controller's or processor's website. When notifying the supervisory authority of a data protection breach, in addition to the DPO's contact details, their first and last name must also be provided.

1.6 Status of a Data Protection Officer

As indicated above, the GDPR protects the DPO and sets out their scope of duties quite clearly.

1.6.1 Obligations of the Controller Towards the DPO

An organisation must ensure:

> that the data protection officer is duly and promptly included in all matters concerning personal data protection (Art. 38(1) GDPR).

The DPO should be informed about all issues concerning data processing at the earliest possible stage.

In accordance with their role – regardless of the form of employment – the DPO should be treated by the appointing organisation as a discussion partner and not as an employee carrying out specific instructions. In accordance with the Article 29 Working Party Guidelines, an organisation should ensure, among other things, that:

(1) the DPO takes part in meetings of the upper and middle management of the organisation,
(2) the DPO takes part in decisions concerning the processing of personal data.

Moreover, the stance taken by the DPO should always be taken into consideration. It is recommended that cases and the causes of any actions taken that are contrary to the DPO's recommendations be documented. Where there has been a breach or other event related to personal data, the controller must immediately consult with the DPO.

For the DPO to carry out their duties, they must be granted access to personal data and data processing operations and must be supported by the management of the establishment.

One of the organisation's important obligations is to provide the DPO with the resources they need to carry out their duties, including:

(1) appropriate financial, infrastructural and staffing;
(2) enough time to do the job, including by assigning an appropriate amount of work (not assigning too much of other work if any);
(3) communication with staff so that they know of the DPO's existence and the duties they perform;
(4) access to other departments of the organisation, such as HR, legal, IT, security;
(5) continual training to update their knowledge;
(6) a team for the DPO if the scope of tasks cannot be handled by just one individual.

In principle, the more complex the data processing operations and the more data processed, the more resources should be allocated to the DPO.

1.6.2 Independence of the DPO

The general regulation grants a DPO an exceptional amount of formal independence.

In particular, a controller is obliged to ensure that:

(1) the DPO does not receive instructions on the performance of their duties (Article 38(3) GDPR);
(2) the DPO acts independently in performing their tasks;
(3) the DPO should report directly to the 'highest management level' (Article 38(3) GDPR);
(4) the DPO should not be dismissed or penalised for performing his tasks (Article 38(3) GDPR).

A controller cannot issue the DPO binding instructions on 'how to deal with a matter, for example, what result should be achieved, how to investigate a complaint or whether to consult the supervisory authority. Furthermore, they must not be instructed to take a certain view of an issue related to data protection law, for example, a particular interpretation of the law'.[10]

As in the case of legal counsel or a compliance officer, a DPO cannot be dismissed or penalised by the controller or processor for the performance of their duties, including for refusing to go along with the controller's instructions (pertaining to the DPO's tasks). An agreement with a DPO should expressly state that it cannot be terminated by the employer (or client in case of DPO outsourcing) if the DPO does not comply with the controller's instructions.

According to the Article 29 Working Party, the prohibition on penalties concerns not only direct penalties but also indirect ones, such as not giving or delaying promotion, hindering professional development or limiting access to benefits offered to other employees. It is a little intriguing what kind of promotion could the DPO be deprived of. Should an organisation foresee further positions to a regular DPO like a Senior DPO, Staff DPO, General DPO? We do not mean it seriously. Again, we are just a little critical here of a precision of Article 29 Working Party/EDPB guidelines.

However, hiring a DPO under an agreement for a defined period of time is allowed.

2 DUTIES OF A DATA PROTECTION OFFICER

2.1 Confidential Information and Avoiding Conflicts of Interests

Given the confidential nature of the information processed by a DPO, they are obliged to maintain the confidentiality of those data. Article 38(5) GDPR refers us here to relevant Member States or EU laws. For the avoidance of doubt, the issue of confidentiality must be addressed in any agreement with a DPO.

A DPO should also avoid conflicts of interests. This does not exactly mean that a DPO cannot be engaged in other work. But they cannot hold another position in the organisation that entails establishing data processing means and purposes. Particularly, they must not act as a member of the management board or any other director in the company in which they act as DPO.

According to the Article 29 Working Party, a conflict of interests arises in the case of managerial positions (general director, operations director, financial director, medical director, marketing director, HR director, IT director) and also lower positions where these take part in establishing data processing purposes and means. A conflict of interests may arise if a DPO is asked to represent the controller or processor before the courts in a case concerning personal data protection (in other words, a DPO should not do this).[11]

You should consider the following steps:

10. Article 29 Working Party Guidelines ..., p. 16.
11. Article 29 Working Party Guidelines ..., p. 17.

(1) identifying (in writing) positions that involve a conflict of interests with the role of the DPO in the organisation;
(2) developing internal rules and procedures that make it impossible for positions that involve a conflict of interests to be combined (there should at least be such a general clause in an agreement for the provision of DPO services, as a control);
(3) having the DPO declare they have no conflict of interests.

In practice, all of those three points can be covered by a proper template DPO agreement.

2.2 Duties of a Data Protection Officer

Under the GDPR, a DPO has the following duties:

(1) educating – to inform management and other personnel of the organisation about their duties resulting from the GDPR and other data protection related laws;
(2) monitoring – to monitor data protection compliance by:
    (a) gathering information on how the organisation (and its particular departments) processes data,
    (b) analysing and verifying the compliance of processing,
    (c) recommending specific actions to the organisation.
(3) consulting – to consult, on request, data protection related decisions of the organisation and data protection impact assessments performed by the organisation (remember, conducting a data protection impact assessment is an obligation of the controller – the DPO's acts as a consultant);[12]
(4) cooperating – to cooperate with the supervisory authority, including by acting as a contact point for the authority on issues related to processing, including for prior consultations and consultations on all other matters where appropriate;
(5) communicating – the DPO is also a point of contact for data subjects.

The above list describes the minimum duties of a DPO.

A DPO may be entrusted with other duties (e.g., keeping the RDPA) if these do not conflict with the nature of the DPO's work. However, you must consider the

12. The Art. 29 Working Party (Guidelines ..., p. 18) recommends that a controller consult with the DPO on the following issues: (1) whether a data protection impact assessment should be conducted; (2) the methodology for conducting a data protection impact assessment; (3) whether a data protection impact assessment should be conducted internally or outsourced; (4) the technical and organisational measures to apply in mitigating all threats to the rights and freedoms of data subjects; (5) the correctness of a data protection impact assessment conducted and the compliance of the results with data protection requirements (whether processing should continue and what measures should be applied).

need to provide the DPO with the resources and time needed to perform those duties.

All of the DPO's tasks must be performed with 'due regard to the risk associated with processing operations, taking into account the nature, scope, context and purposes of processing' (Article 39(2) GDPR). The activities of a DPO are also based on the principle of risk-based approach, in the sense that the DPO must assess where their involvement is most needed, and where less so since not everything can be done at once. This selective, pragmatic approach should make facilitate it easier to consult with the controller on what methodology to apply when conducting a data protection impact assessment, what areas should be audited internally or externally, what internal training to conduct for employees or managers responsible for data processing and what processing operations should be given more time and resources.[13]

2.3 DPO: GDPR Versus Reality

Applying the GDPR provisions on the DPO in practice will obviously look differently in larger organisations than in smaller ones. Small and medium enterprises might not be able to afford a full-time DPO, so they will either outsource or appoint an employee having other duties as well.

Organisations with undeveloped data protection culture usually expect their DPO to be fully responsible for data protection compliance. Acknowledging that a DPO might be the most data protection savvy person on board, we always recommend to formally appoint another person as 'responsible' for data protection compliance, even if then the organisation relies fully on the DPO.

According to Article 38(2) GDPR, the organisation should support their DPO by providing 'resources necessary to carry out those tasks and access to personal data and processing operations, and to maintain his or her expert knowledge'. At the same time according to Article 38(6) GDPR the DPO 'may fulfil other tasks and duties'. Providing resources necessary to carry tasks and maintaining expert knowledge while charging with other tasks seems slightly contradicting.

So, the principle of lack of conflict of interest as well as the risk-based approach need to account for limitations of the organisation.

13. Article 29 Working Party Guidelines ..., p. 19.

CHAPTER 7

The Regulator

Adrianna Michałowicz & Dominik Lubasz

1 THE SUPERVISORY AUTHORITY: STATUS, ROLE AND OBLIGATIONS

1.1 Preliminary Remarks

Article 51 of General Data Protection Regulation (GDPR) requires Member States to establish at least one supervisory authority in order to guarantee the proper functioning of data protection system in the European Union (EU). The legal source of this obligation may be found in Article 16(2) of the Treaty on the Functioning of the EU and Article 8(3) of Charter of Fundamental Rights of the EU which stipulate that compliance with data protection rules shall be subject to the control of independent authorities.

The obligation to establish independent supervisory authorities existed already under Directive 95/46/EC.[1] Provisions currently in force, however, enlarge the scope of powers given to supervisory authorities. This is because supervisory authorities are playing essential role in protecting natural persons with regard to the processing of their personal data.[2] According to Article 51(1) of GDPR, the basic task of supervisory authorities is to monitor the application of the regulation, which means that supervisory authorities are eligible to carry out control, inspection, audit and take every action necessary to ensure compliance with GDPR. They are required as well to contribute to the consistent application of GDPR throughout the Union (Article 51(2)).

Article 51(1) of GDPR leaves a choice for Member States to decide whether to establish one or more public authorities, depending on their constitutional, organisational and administrative structure. If a Member State chooses to set up more than one

1. *See*: Art. 28(1) of Directive 95/46/EC.
2. *See*: Preamble of Additional protocol to Convention 108 regarding supervisory authorities and transborder data flows; Recital 117 of GDPR.

public authority, it has to guarantee at the same time consistent application of GDPR, especially with regard to the execution of data subjects' rights. It should also establish by law mechanisms for ensuring the effective participation of those supervisory authorities in the consistency mechanism, particularly designate the supervisory authority that will act as a single contact point for the effective participation of those authorities in the mechanism and cooperation between them, the European Data Protection Board and the European Commission.[3]

1.2 Independence

2 INDEPENDENT STATUS

For the purpose of providing effective data protection, supervisory authorities must act with complete independence (Article 52(1)). Independence is essential to ensure the proper level of data protection in all EU countries and free data flow within the EU single market.

The requirement of independence is addressed both to the Member States and public authorities. It means that not only national legislators have to implement specific legal provisions that will guarantee the independence of supervisory authorities but also the organisational structure of the authority must demonstrate this quality.

Based on Article 52 of GDPR we can distinguish three different conditions of supervisory authority's independence:

(1) institutional independence which means no supervisory authority should be subject to any other public body, especially governmental, or could be held criminally liable or deprived of liberty;
(2) functional independence which excludes control of any other public authority within the scope of exercising its' tasks and powers;
(3) organisational independence, guaranteed by proper internal infrastructure, including financial and human resources.

The importance of supervisory authorities independence has been underlined by the Court of Justice of EU. The Court issued several rulings concerning this issue in which it stated that independence – yet within the meaning of Article 28(1) of Directive 95/46/EC – precludes not only any influence exercised by the supervised bodies but also any directions or any other external influence, whether direct or indirect, which could call into question the performance by those authorities of their task consisting of establishing a fair balance between the protection of the right to private life and the free movement of personal data.[4] Thus, supervisory authorities are considered as the

3. *See*: Recital 119 of GDPR.
4. The European Court of Justice judgment in Case C-518/07 European Commission vs. Federal Republic of Germany, pt 30.

guardians of fundamental rights and freedoms related to data protection, so they must act objectively and impartially.[5] In subsequent judgments, the Court explained that the independent status also precludes any indirect influence which is liable to have an effect on the supervisory authority's decisions.[6] The Court emphasised that any political influence, e.g., compelling to vacate the office without serving its full term is inadmissible.[7]

The independence of supervisory authorities is also perceived as a fundamental requirement by the Council of Europe. Article 15 of Modernised Convention 108 obliges each party to the Convention to provide for one or more public authorities to be responsible for ensuring compliance with the provisions of the Convention and which will act with complete independence and impartiality in performing their duties and exercising their powers and in doing so shall neither seek nor accept instructions.[8]

Article 52 of GDPR provides several conditions and criteria of complete independence of supervisory authority. To ensure compliance with this provision, members of each supervisory authority must remain free from external influence, whether direct or indirect, and shall neither seek nor take instructions from anybody while exercising their tasks and powers.[9] They must refrain from any action incompatible with their duties to prevent a potential conflict of interests.[10] Independence of members of the supervisory authority is a prerequisite to the independence of supervisory authority itself. Personal independence is also relevant in the light of Article 53 (4) of GDPR, as failure to comply with conflict of interest limitations may be considered as a serious misconduct and may lead to dismissal or compulsory retirement.

Certain obligations are imposed on Member States in order to satisfy the requirement of independence. The first and foremost duty of a Member State is to provide supervisory authority (or each of them if there are multiple supervisory authorities in a particular country – e.g., Germany) with proper resources, including human, technical and financial resources, premises and infrastructure that are necessary for the effective performance of their tasks and duties related to mutual assistance, cooperation and participation in the European Data Protection Board.[11] The supervisory authorities must be given the opportunity to freely choose – based on justified reasons and needs – their own staff that will not be subject to any external directions or instructions.[12] As regards financial control over supervisory authority, it cannot

5. The European Court of Justice judgment in Case C-518/07 European Commission vs. Federal Republic of Germany, pt 23, 25.
6. The European Court of Justice judgment in Case C-614/10 European Commission vs. Republic of Austria, pt 43.
7. The European Court of Justice judgment in Case C-288/12 European Commission vs. Hungary, pt 54.
8. Article 15(5) of the Modernised Convention 108.
9. Article 52(2) of GDPR.
10. Article 52(3) of GDPR.
11. Article 52(4) of GDPR.
12. Article 52(5) of GDPR.

affect its independence; therefore supervisory authorities are required to have separate and public annual budgets.[13]

The supervisory authority's independence is also systemic which means that actions or functions carried out by other national bodies should be of no relevance for the activity of supervisory authority. In particular, measures concerning the legislative process or binding interpretation of law, adopted by other authorities, should have no effect on the scope of competences and discretion of supervisory authority. Otherwise, it may affect its independence and adversely influence the role it plays in the data protection system.

Example

In January 2019, the Polish Ministry of Digital Affairs issued Guidelines on GDPR for entrepreneurs. The President of the Polish Personal Data Protection Office (PUODO) responded that PUODO is the only competent body, specialised in data protection matters in Poland.[14] Consequently, the President of the Personal Data Protection Office is the only authority legally authorised to issue guidelines and interpret legal provisions in this scope.

The Polish example brings out an interesting question. Does the principle of independence of supervisory bodies really mean that no other national authority of a particular Member State is allowed to opine on data protection? According to the stance of the Polish supervisory authority, PUODO supported by one of the authors of this chapter, no other national authority is competent to pronounce on data protection. According to another author of this book, though the supervisory authority's voice outweighs voices of other authorities until courts speak, any authority is competent to speak about data protection as long as local laws provide for such competence.

3 APPOINTMENT AND GENERAL CONDITIONS FOR THE MEMBERS OF THE SUPERVISORY AUTHORITY

The independence of supervisory authorities and their members should be reflected in the appointment procedure and general conditions regarding the performance of their duties. In this regard, Articles 53 and 54 of GDPR stipulate what kind of legal instruments Member States are required to provide for this purpose.

According to Article 53 of GDPR, the parliament, the government, the head of State or an independent body entrusted under Member State law are entitled to appoint, in a transparent procedure, each member of supervisory authorities. Member States should determine in their domestic law which national body is competent to

13. Article 52(6) of GDPR; cf. The European Court of Justice judgment in Case C-614/10 European Commission vs. Republic of Austria, pt 58.
14. *See*: https://uodo.gov.pl/pl/138/672 (last accessed on 1 March 2019).

appoint supervisory authorities' members (depending on the constitutional and political system of a particular Member State) and by which procedure.

Technicalities such as formal procedures in the event of the expiry of the term of office, resignation or compulsory retirement, the method of handing over the duties after termination, conditions for resignation, the exact moment of termination or expiration of the office or compulsory retirement are left to laws of particular Member States.

Article 53(4) of GDPR states that a supervisory authority member may be dismissed only in cases of serious misconduct or if s/he no longer fulfils the conditions required for the performance of the duties.

Article 54(1) of GDPR further clarifies that Member States are obliged to specify in their national laws following elements: the procedure of establishing a supervisory authority, qualification requirements and appointment procedure; the duration of the term of members of supervisory authorities and their reappointment; the conditions governing the obligations of members of supervisory authorities and their staff, including prohibitions on actions, occupations and benefits incompatible therewith during and after the term of office; and rules governing the cessation of employment.

4 COMPETENCE OF THE SUPERVISORY AUTHORITY

Article 55 GDPR, stemming from Article 28(6) of Directive 95/46/EC, specifies territorial jurisdiction, exclusive jurisdiction and limitation of material jurisdiction of a supervisory authority.

Each supervisory authority is competent for the performance of its tasks and powers on the territory of its Member State.[15] This principle may be modified according to Article 56 of GDPR which defines the competence of the authorities with respect to cross-border matters, as defined in Article 4 pt 23 of GDPR. I.

Article 55(3) of GDPR excludes the supervisory authorities' from supervising data processing by the courts when they are trying and deciding cases, to ensure the independence of the judiciary. At the same time, courts are subject to the supervisory body's authority regarding their internal processes such as employee or supplier relations.

EU legislator paid special attention to the regulation of the lead supervisory authority.[16] Article 56 of GDPR refers to the one-stop-shop mechanism that has been created in order to unify the rules governing the jurisdiction in transborder data processing operations and to eliminate the problem of choosing the competent supervisory authority in those cases or forum shopping.

The supervisory authority is competent to act in accordance with the procedure provided in Article 60 of GDPR as a lead supervisory authority for the cross-border processing carried out by a controller or processor. The lead supervisory authority is determined by specifying the 'main establishment' of the controller or processor as

15. Article 55(1) of GDPR.
16. Article 56 of GDPR.

defined in Article 4 pt 16.[17] It may also be established in relation to the controller or processor who does not have the 'main establishment' in different Member States but operates in one of them through a single establishment, and the data processing operations associated with that activity shall have cross-border nature. The notion of 'cross-border processing' is explained in Article 4 pt 23 of GDPR.[18]

Article 56(2) of GDPR provides a derogation from the general rule of the competence of the lead supervisory authority and states that each supervisory authority shall be competent to handle a complaint lodged with it or a possible infringement of GDPR, if the subject matter relates only to an establishment in its Member State or substantially affects data subjects only in its Member State. In such cases, the supervisory authority is required to inform without delay the lead supervisory authority on that matter. Then the latter should decide within three weeks whether or not it will handle the case.[19] When deciding whether or not to deal with the case, the lead supervisory authority should consider if there is an establishment of the controller or processor in a given Member State in order to ensure that the decision concerning the controller or processor could be effectively enforced. If the lead supervisory authority decides to handle the case, the supervisory authority which informed about the complaint lodged with it or a possible infringement of GDPR should be able to submit a draft decision. The leading supervisory authority should take utmost account of that draft when preparing its own draft decision.[20]

If the lead supervisory authority decides not to handle the case, the supervisory authority which informed the lead supervisory authority shall handle it according to procedures prescribed in Article 61 – 'Mutual assistance' and Article 62 – 'Joint operations of supervisory authorities'. Even though the lead supervisory authority remains the sole interlocutor of the controller or processor for the cross-border processing carried out by that controller or processor:[21]

17. As regards a controller having establishments in more than one Member State, a 'main establishment' means its central administration in the Union or another establishment of the controller in the Union where the decisions on the purposes and means of the processing of personal data are taken and which has the power to have such decisions implemented. As regards a processor with establishments in more than one Member State, a 'main establishment' means the place of its central administration in the Union or the establishment where the main processing activities in the context of the activities of an establishment of the processor take place to the extent that the processor is subject to specific obligations under this Regulation.
18. It stipulates that 'cross-border processing' means either (a) processing of personal data which takes place in the context of the activities of establishments in more than one Member State of a controller or processor in the Union where the controller or processor is established in more than one Member State; or (b) processing of personal data which takes place in the context of the activities of a single establishment of a controller or processor in the Union but which substantially affects or is likely to substantially affect data subjects in more than one Member State.
19. Article 56(2) of GDPR.
20. Article 56(3)(4) of GDPR.
21. Article 56(6) of GDPR.

Example

As we have mentioned before, the French National Data Protection Commission, CNIL, received two group complaints from the associations None Of Your Business and La Quadrature du Net against the company Google LLC, which was reproached for not having a valid legal basis to process the personal data of the users of its services.[22] Regardless the factual and substantive arguments put forward by Google LLC, Google pointed out that CNIL is not competent for handling the case, because the company has its main establishment in Ireland, so the complaints should be presented to the Irish supervisory authority. The CNIL emphasised that the Irish establishment does not have a decision-making power on the data processing operations and the services provided by Google LLC. For this reason, the one-stop-shop mechanism was not applicable, and the CNIL was competent to take any decision regarding processing operations carried out by Google LLC, as well as the other supervisory authorities in Member States.

5 TASKS OF THE SUPERVISORY AUTHORITY

Article 57 of GDPR defines primary tasks entrusted to the supervisory authorities. They could be divided into six main groups.

Informative and advisory tasks. The supervisory authorities may contribute to the creation of legal provisions in line with the data protection standards established by GDPR in order to ensure effective performance of right and obligations arising therefrom.

Advisory and information tasks include an obligation to promote both public awareness and understanding of the risks, rules, safeguards and rights in relation to processing, and the awareness of controllers and processors of their obligations under GDPR. Special attention has been paid to the promotion of awareness and understanding among children since a growing number of information society services are addressed directly to children and youth or heavily utilised by youngsters (even if their terms and conditions pretend not to be so), so it is essential to safeguard their rights and interests. It means also that supervisory authority activities should be understandable for children both on the level of content and form of a message. Supervisory authorities are required to advise public institutions and bodies on legislative and administrative measures relating to the protection of natural person rights and freedoms with regard to processing. They must provide, upon request, information to any data subject concerning the exercise of their rights under GDPR and, if appropriate, cooperate with the supervisory authorities in other Member States in this scope.

According to Article 57(1f) of GDPR, the authority investigates the subject matter of the complaint of a data subject and informs the data subject of the progress and the

22. The CNIL's decision regarding the case is available on site: https://www.cnil.fr/sites/default/files/atoms/files/san-2019-001_21-01-2019.pdf (last accessed on 27 February 2019).

outcome of the investigation within a reasonable period. It shall also facilitate the submission of such complaints, for e.g., by issuing a complaint submission form, including the possibility of electronic submission.[23]

Obligations stipulated in Article 57(1g)(1h) of GDPR intend to ensure consistent enforcement of the provisions of the GDPR with regard to the application of cooperation mechanisms. These obligations particularly concern the exchange of information, mutual assistance and cooperation with other authorities within the scope of proceedings.

Article 57(3) of GDPR indicates that the performance of the tasks of supervisory authorities shall be free of charge for data subjects and DPOs as a rule. This could be nonetheless limited where requests are manifestly unfounded, excessive or have repetitive character.[24]

6 POWERS OF THE SUPERVISORY AUTHORITY

GDPR unifies the scope and form of competences of supervisory authorities.

Recital 129 of GDPR explains that supervisory authorities should have in each Member State the same tasks and effective powers in order to ensure consistent monitoring and enforcement of GDPR throughout the Union, but Member States may specify additional tasks related to the protection of personal data. The powers of supervisory authorities should be exercised in accordance with appropriate procedural safeguards, impartially, fairly and within a reasonable time. Measures applied by supervisory authorities should be appropriate, necessary and proportionate; should take into account the circumstances of an individual case; respect the right of every person to be heard before any individual measure which would adversely affect them is adopted; and avoid superfluous costs and excessive inconveniences for the persons concerned. These measures should be in writing, be clear and unambiguous, and contain obligatory elements like: indication of the supervisory authority that has issued the measure, date, signature of the head or a member of the supervisory authority, reasons for the measure and information about the right of an effective remedy.

Taking into account the structure of Article 58 of GDPR, powers conferred on supervisory authorities may be divided into five categories:

(1) investigative powers,
(2) corrective powers,
(3) authorisation and advisory powers,
(4) powers related to judicial remedies,
(5) additional powers provided by national law of a Member State.

Article 58(1) of GDPR grants the supervisory authority investigative competences related to exercising control over data processing. Most of those powers refer to the

23. Article 57(2) of GDPR.
24. Article 57(4) of GDPR.

activities taken by controller and processor, who are the addressees of orders or requests and should satisfy them by, for e.g., providing information, or allowing access to personal data, information, premises and resources. Supervisory authorities are also authorised to carry out data protection audits and verify certifications issued pursuant to Article 42(7) of GDPR.

Corrective powers indicated in Article 58(2) of GDPR are various and depend on whether data processing operations are only planned or already in place. They may be exercised in the form of warnings, reprimands, orders, fines, limitation or ban on processing. As regards the certification procedure, the supervisory authority is entitled to withdraw a certification.

A wide range of authorisation and advisory powers has been conferred on supervisory authorities according to Article 58(3) of GDPR. These competences relate to specific obligations under GDPR and in particular refer to prior consultations, codes of conduct, certification, standard contractual clauses and binding corporate rules. They can take different forms like issuing permits, providing advice, opinions, accreditation or approvals.

Member States are required to provide by law the supervisory authority with the power to notify violations of GDPR to the judicial authorities, as well to commence or engage otherwise in legal proceedings, in order to enforce the provisions of GDPR. Supervisory authorities may be also attributed additional powers by national laws of Member States.

The activities of the supervisory authority indicated in Article 58 of GDPR are subject to control and appropriate safeguards. This is why Article 58(4) emphasises the need and obligation for Member States to grant effective judicial remedy and due process regarding the execution of powers by supervisory authorities.

7 ACTIVITY REPORTS

Supervisory authorities are obliged to report on how they exercise their supervisory powers and implement their priorities in order to preserve the transparency rule. For this purpose, each supervisory authority is required by Article 59 of GDPR to draw up an annual report on its activities. The report may include a list of types of infringement notified and types of measures taken in accordance with Article 58(2) of GDPR. The reports should be transmitted to the national parliament, the government and other authorities for the purpose of evaluation. They should be also made available to the public, to the Commission and to the European Data Protection Board.

8 THE ROLE OF THE SUPERVISORY AUTHORITY WITHIN THE COOPERATION AND CONSISTENCY MECHANISM

GDPR provisions impose on supervisory authorities obligations related to cooperation and consistency mechanism prescribed in Chapter VII. The introduction of a cooperation mechanism was one of the key elements of the data protection reform as it seeks to ensure the consistent application and enforcement of GDPR in the internal market.

Thus, Articles from 60 to 63 of GDPR entail obligations to cooperate with other authorities established in Member States, especially in situations referred to in Article 56 of GDPR when one-stop-shop mechanism may be applied, provide each other with relevant information and mutual assistance, conduct joint operations including joint investigations and joint enforcement measures and cooperate through the consistency mechanism.

CHAPTER 8

Legal Remedies, Liability, Administrative Sanctions

Maciej Gawronski

1 LEGAL REMEDIES: CIVIL AND ADMINISTRATIVE LIABILITY

1.1 Preliminary Remarks

General Data Protection Regulation (GDPR) contains many instruments of enforcement to effectively implement data protection across the European Union (EU). A data subject does not need to wait for a specific legal act of their Member State; they can claim legal protection directly under the GDPR. Breaching the GDPR may result in administrative and civil liability. Administrative liability can be pursued with by the supervisory authority, while a data subject may demand civil liability from a controller or a processor directly against the breaching party through the courts.

The GDPR provides the following legal remedies to a data subject:

(1) complaining to the supervisory authority (Article 77(1) GDPR),
(2) complaining to an administrative court against a decision or lack of decision by the supervisory authority (Article 78(1, 2) GDPR),
(3) suing the data controller or processor seeking an order or prohibition (Article 79(1) GDPR),
(4) suing the data controller or processor seeking compensation for material and non-material damage (Article 77(1) GDPR).

1.2 Complaint to the Supervisory Authority

A complaint to a supervisory authority is a basic measure of legal protection available to a data subject under the GDPR.

Pursuant to Article 77(1) GDPR:

> every data subject shall have the right to lodge a complaint with a supervisory authority, in particular in the Member State of his or her **[1]** habitual residence, **[2]** place of work or **[3]** place of the alleged infringement if the data subject considers that the processing of personal data relating to him or her infringes this Regulation.

Any natural person who believes that their personal data are being processed in breach of the GDPR is entitled to bring a complaint to a supervisory authority. A complaint can as well concern breaches of secondary legislation approved pursuant to the GDPR and the laws of Member States that specify how the GDPR is to be implemented.[1]

A complaint may be addressed, at the discretion of the data subject, to a supervisory authority competent for (venue):

(1) their habitual place of residence (where they actually live in a given territory),
(2) their place of work (resulting from an employment contract or self-employment contract),
(3) the place where the breach allegedly took place.

Example

If the data subject (person) lives or works in one Member State but the controller or processor against which the complaint is being made is located in another Member State, that data subject may address the complaint to whichever supervisory authority is most convenient for them.

When forming a complaint, bear in mind that the supervisory authority is bound by the content of the complaint (at least formally), and any proceedings must relate to a specific case. The supervisory authority should assist data subjects with filing complaints, e.g., by making a complaint form available, preferably one that can be completed in electronic form.

1. A useful list of implementing acts to be found here: https://iapp.org/resources/article/eu-member-state-gdpr-implementation-laws-and-drafts/ (last accessed on 26 February 2019).

1.3 Complaint to a Court Against a Supervisory Authority

According to Article 78(1, 2) GDPR, a data subject can file a complaint to the court against a decision by an authority or against a delay in informing on a progress of proceedings in three months.

Of course, a complaint should be filed with a court of a Member State where the supervisory authority is established.

As usual, a local (a Member State's) procedure applies to court proceedings initiated by a complaint against a supervisory authority. Laws 'implementing'[2] the GDPR across Member States will usually point to a specific local court competent to try complaints against their supervisory authorities.

Based on our practical experience from several EU Member States, we assume that a complaint on a delayed decision or information from a supervisory authority will not be a very useful remedy.

1.4 Civil Liability: Demand for Cessation or Preservation

1.4.1 The Right to Go to Court

Pursuant to Article 79 GDPR, a natural person (a data subject) is entitled to seek legal protection directly against a controller or processor (irrespective of a complaint to the supervisory authority) in case they believe their rights have been breached by a particular processing.

By this measure, a data subject can demand that the controller or administrator take certain actions or cease certain actions (mandatory or prohibitory judgment).

A proceeding may be started against a controller (co-controller), a processor or both jointly or a group of those, including so-called subprocessors.

A person (data subject) may sue to the court irrespective if they file a complaint with the supervisory authority in parallel. It brings interesting conflict issues. The supervisory authority's decision may collide with the court's decision, especially in case the court and the supervisory authority come from different EU Member States. The GDPR provides for a reconciliation mechanism between different supervisory authorities but not for a direct reconciliation mechanism for courts.[3] Therefore until the CJEU decides, the stance of supervisory authorities may in some cases differ to those of courts of the EU Member States.

2. The GDPR as an EU regulation, contrary to an EU directive, in a legal technical sense does not need 'implementation'. Though in practice local laws need to be adjusted to accommodate the GDPR. That is why we use the word 'implementation' here, in its natural meaning.
3. Probably that is why Andrea Jelinek (Head of the European Data Protection Board) says she does not care about judgments of local (Member States') courts.

1.4.2 Competent Court

The court before which legal protection can be sought against a controller or processor depends on the nature of the entity alleged to have breached the regulation:

(1) a public body – in each case the court having jurisdiction over the place where that body resides;
(2) private entity – the data subject can choose between the court of the Member State in which the controller or processor has its organisational unit and the court of the Member State in which the data subject has their habitual residence.

1.5 Compensatory Liability

According to Article 82 GDPR, in case the data subject suffers a material or non-material damage (financial damage, loss of property, loss of profits as well as a physical harm or moral harm) as a result of a breach of the GDPR by a controller or processor, that data subject may sue for compensation, independently from other legal remedies sought under the GDPR.

1.5.1 Controller and Processor

Liability for each breach caused by a breach of the GDPR will be borne by the controller, but in respect of the processor, Article 82(2) GDPR states that:

> A processor shall be liable for the damage caused by processing only where it has not complied with obligations of this Regulation specifically directed to processors or where it has acted outside or contrary to lawful instructions of the controller.

Given the long list of duties the GDPR requires of processors, a breach of the GDPR can be easily attributed to a processor.

1.5.2 Exemption from Liability

The GDPR sets the bar very high with regard to any exemption from liability if a number of entities take part in processing as controllers or processors.

Pursuant to Article 82(3) GDPR:

> A controller or processor shall be exempt from liability under paragraph 2 if it proves that it is not in any way responsible for the event giving rise to the damage.

According to the quoted provision, the burden of proving innocence lies with the defendant, and what is worse is that even the slightest contribution to a breach (e.g., a processor remaining silent on the subject of the legality of the controller's instructions) can mean full liability (which can later be shared regressively).

Natalia Zawadzka takes the view that the conditions for a controller or processor to be held liable are:[4]

(1) a data subject suffers material or non-material damage,
(2) a controller or processor breaches the provisions of the regulation,
(3) a causal relationship exists between the damage caused and the breach,
(4) the controller or processor is responsible and that these conditions must exist jointly in order for the controller or processor to be held liable.

A literal analysis of Article 82 GDPR seems to indicate not so much that 'is responsible' creates liability but that 'is not in any way responsible' excludes liability. This could be interpreted simply as a standard of extreme diligence, for it would mean 'did everything in its power'. We hope that case law will turn out to be more balanced and will soften the harsh wording of Article 82(3) GDPR.

1.5.3 *Presumption of Fault*

Theoretically, the burden of proof of a breach rests with a data subject who claims they have suffered damage. In practice, though, it is the controller who is obliged. In view of the existing principle of accountability (Article 5(2) GDPR), a controller must be able to show the correctness of its data processing and thus, in effect, the absence of any fault on its part in the incident. Article 82(3) GDPR also implies a presumption of fault on the part of the controller and processor. The burden of proof of the absence of any fault, therefore, rests with the controller or processor.

Note that neither a reduced degree of fault, nor the absence of wilfulness, nor a contribution to the occurrence of damage by the data subject eliminates liability.

1.5.4 *Joint and Several Liability*

If a number of entities – controllers and processors – take part in the processing, their liability is joint and several. This means that a natural person who has suffered damage as a result of improper processing of their data by several entities can choose to seek full compensation from all of them, or from any of them. The entity that pays full compensation then has recourse to the other 'guilty parties'. This solution is aimed at enabling a data subject whose data were processed contrary to the regulation to effectively obtain full compensation.

1.5.5 *Jurisdiction*

As we have mentioned above, the competent court in a case is determined in accordance with Article 79(2) GDPR. Where damage is caused by a public body, in

4. N. Zawadzka [in:] *RODO. Ogólne rozporządzenie o ochronie danych. Komentarz*, ed. E. Bielak-Jomaa, D. Lubasz, Warsaw 2017, p. 1049.

each case the competent court is the court having jurisdiction over the seat of that body. In other cases, the complainant can choose the court of the Member State in which the controller or processor has its organisational unit or the court of the Member State in which the data subject has their habitual residence.

1.6 Representation of Data Subjects by Specialised Entities

Article 80 GDPR provides the possibility of natural persons having an organisation or association lodge a complaint on their behalf, pursue their rights or seek compensation from a controller or processor. This means social organisations, foundations, etc., i.e. non-governmental organisations that are encouraged to support data subjects with their complaints and in their disputes concerning breaches of the GDPR.

2 ADMINISTRATIVE PENALTIES FOR BREACHES OF THE GDPR

2.1 Preliminary Remarks

Where a supervisory authority finds there has been a breach of the provisions of the GDPR, it may impose an administrative fine, regardless of other measures or actions taken by the data subjects involved.

2.2 Who May Be Fined?

Mainly, controllers and processors need to worry. Because the GDPR does not use the term 'subprocessor', but 'another processor', subprocessors can certainly also be fined. Additional penalties may be faced by entities that certify or monitor compliance with codes of procedure.

2.3 What Should the Fines Be?

Pursuant to Article 83(1) GDPR, fines should be 'effective, proportionate and dissuasive'.

In result of the realistic approach of supervisory bodies, until the early 2019 fines were very moderate, certainly not effective or proportionate.

2.4 Greater and Lesser Fines

The general regulation foresees two types of administrative fines:

(1) **up to EUR 10 million**, but in the case of a company or group of companies having a total global turnover of more than EUR 500 million, up to 2% of global annual turnover for the previous year;

(2) **up to EUR 20 million**, but in the case of a company or group of companies having a total global turnover of more than EUR 500 million, up to 4% of global annual turnover for the previous year.

A greater fine is imposed for a breach of:

(1) the basic processing rules, including conditions of consent (Articles 5, 6, 7, 9 GDPR);
(2) the rights of data subjects as referred to in Articles 12–22 GDPR (**delays in responding to demands**);
(3) the rules of data export – transmitting personal data to a recipient in a third country or to an international organisation;
(4) all obligations resulting from Member State law approved on the basis of Chapter IX GDPR, that is, a failure to comply with exceptions on data protection introduced by a Member State, e.g., in order to reconcile data protection with freedom of expression and information;
(5) a temporary order or final restriction on processing or a suspension of data transmission issued by the supervisory authority on the basis of Article 58(2) GDPR, or a failure to guarantee access resulting in a breach of Article 58(1) GDPR (hindering an inspection).

A lesser fine applies to other breaches of the GDPR, e.g. a breach of security obligations, the processing of unidentified data, a failure to appoint a DPO.

Remember! In practice, you can pay a heavy price for:

- **a breach of the data processing rules,**
- **a breach of the rights of individuals,**
- **unlawful data export.**

2.5 Recording Penalties

When imposing an administrative fine, the supervisory authority should take account of the individual nature of every case.

The criteria to be considered when imposing fines are listed in Article 83(2) GDPR. They include:

(a) the nature, weight and duration of the breach, taking account of the nature, scope and purpose of the processing, the number of data subjects harmed and the scale of the damage they have suffered;
(b) the intentional or unintentional nature of the breach;
(c) actions taken by the controller or processor in order to minimise the damage suffered by data subjects;

(d) the degree of liability of the controller or processor, taking account of their technical and organisational measures;
(e) all relevant previous breaches by the controller or processor;
(f) the degree of cooperation with the supervisory authority in order to remedy the breach and mitigate any adverse consequences of the breach;
(g) the categories of personal data the breach concerns;
(h) the way in which the supervisory authority learned about the breach, in particular whether and within what scope the controller or processor gave notification of the breach;
(i) if the same measures were applied to the controller or processor the case concerns;
(j) whether certification mechanisms approved under the regulation on codes of procedure were applied;
(k) any other aggravating or mitigating factors applicable to the circumstances of the case, such as whether in connection with the breach financial benefits or losses were incurred, directly or indirectly.

As you can see, Article 83(2) GDPR sets out nineteen criteria[5] in which a fine can be imposed, and it is not a closed catalogue. There is no point in going through them all in detail. The President of the Personal Data Protection Office will surely draw up a penalty grid in Excel and, like those entities obligated to calculate 'the risk of a risk' under Article 83(1) GDPR,[6] he will have to turn into a 'data protection accountant' when calculating fines.

2.6 Confiscation of Benefits from 'GDPR Crime'

At the end of Article 83(2) GDPR, under letter k) there are two criteria[7] of which the first is open and the second looks like an obligation of the Office to increase a fine by the amount of benefits obtained or losses avoided through 'GDPR crime':

> any other aggravating or mitigating factors applicable to the circumstances of the case, such as whether in connection with the breach financial benefits or losses were incurred, directly or indirectly.

In this light, benefits incurred by not complying with the rules of data protection may be confiscated by the supervisory authority by being 'added to the fine'. Similarly, savings achieved by not implementing the GDPR, as 'losses avoided', can also be taken away. And the entity penalised would then have to implement the GDPR anyway. Neglecting the GDPR, then, would seem to be risky, to say the least.

5. In Art. 83(2) GDPR there are eight criteria under letter a) alone.
6. 'Unless it is unlikely to result in a risk to the rights and freedoms of natural persons' (Art. 33(1) GDPR).
7. Letter k) contains, in essence, two criteria: the first is open-ended: 'any other aggravating or mitigating factor' and the second specific: 'financial benefits gained, or losses avoided, directly or indirectly, from the infringement'.

3 LIABILITY OF A PROCESSOR

The GDPR introduces direct liability of processors, as well as controllers, for breaches of the GDPR, with regard to both supervisory authorities and data subjects. This is indicated in the following provisions at least:

Article 82(1) GDPR:

> Any person who has suffered material or non-material damage as a result of an infringement of this Regulation shall have the right to receive compensation from the controller or processor for the damage suffered.

Article 83(3) GDPR:

> If a controller or processor intentionally or negligently, for the same or linked processing operations, infringes several provisions of this Regulation, the total amount of the administrative fine shall not exceed the amount specified for the gravest infringement.

In principle, a processor is responsible only for its own errors and omissions but is not responsible for the actions of the controller – but this is not the whole story.

From Article 82(2) GDPR it results that a processor is also responsible for the legality of the instructions of the controller. Pursuant to this provision:

> A processor shall be liable for the damage caused by processing only where it has not complied with obligations of this Regulation specifically directed to processors or **where it has acted outside or contrary to lawful instructions of the controller**.

Pursuant to the GDPR, the liability of a processor covers all aspects of the liability of the controller, though in a different way. The processor (and any other processors) is directly liable for data security, for processing data only for the controller and for refusing to carry out unlawful instructions. From Article 28 GDPR, and from an interpretation of Articles 13, 14 and 22, it results that a processor's obligation to use due diligence also extends to support in performing the obligations of the data controller (e.g., if the processor sends data outside the European Economic Area, it should notify the controller so that the controller can meet its information and other obligations. It is similar if a processor's services involve data profiling. The processor is also obliged to support the controller 'to the extent possible' in exercising the rights of individuals, etc.).

Finally, remember that liability does not rest solely with the entity directly doing the processing, but encompasses the entire chain of engagement and further data processing (subprocessing). The GDPR does not use the jargon term 'subprocessors' – only 'other processors' (Article 28(2, 4) GDPR). Thus, every entity that takes part in unlawful data processing will incur civil liability (unless it can show, as stated in Article 82(3) GDPR that 'it is not in any way responsible for the event giving rise to the damage'). It would not be possible to wriggle out of administrative liability by saying that you are just 'another cog in the data processing wheel' if you are the cog that failed.

Appendices

APPENDIX I

Personal Data Protection Policy

Maciej Gawronski & Katarzyna Kunda

PERSONAL DATA PROTECTION POLICY – A TEMPLATE

1. This "**Personal Data Protection Policy**" ("**Policy**") constitutes a map of requirements, rules and regulations concerning data protection in the Company. This Policy is a data protection policy as understood in the GDPR - Regulation (EU) 2016/679 of the European Parliament and of the Council of 27 April 2016 on the protection of natural persons with regard to the processing of personal data and on the free movement of such data, and repealing Directive 95/46/EC (General Data Protection Regulation).
2. This Policy consists of:
   a) the description of personal data protection rules in the Company;
   b) references to appendices and other documents specifying data protection rules in the Company;
3. Responsibility.

   Responsibility for implementing, executing, maintaining, reviewing and updating of this Policy relies
   (i) with the Board, within the Board:
   (ii) on a Member of the Board responsible for personal data protection; and on
   (iii) a manager appointed by the Board to ensure compliance with personal data protection;

   Responsibility for supervising and monitoring compliance with the Policy relies:
   (iv) on a Data Protection Officer, if appointed;
   (v) on internal audit department, if existing in the Company Responsibility for the application of this Policy relies on:

(vi) the Company;
(vii) the department responsible for information security;
(viii) departments processing special categories of data or criminal data;
(ix) departments processing data on a big scale;
(x) any other departments;
(xi) all personnel of the Company.

The Company ensures that recipients of personal data (including data processors) receiving data from the Company comply with this Policy to the extent adequate to the scope and nature of a particular data transfer in question.

4. **Abbreviations and definitions**

Policy means this Personal Data Protection Policy.

GDPR means Regulation (EU) 2016/679 of the European Parliament and of the Council of 27 April 2016 on the protection of natural persons with regard to the processing of personal data and on the free movement of such data, and repealing Directive 95/46/EC (General Data Protection Regulation).

data means personal data, unless other meaning is apparent from the context.

sensitive data means special category data and criminal data.

Special category data means data enlisted in the art. 9 of the GDPR, that is: data revealing racial or ethnic origin, political opinions, religious or philosophical beliefs, or trade union membership, genetic data, biometric data processed for the purpose of uniquely identifying a natural person, data concerning health or data concerning a natural person's sex life or sexual orientation.

Criminal data means data enlisted in the art.10 of the GDPR, that is data relating to criminal convictions and offences.

Children's data means data of persons under 16 years of age.

individual means a data subject, unless other meaning is apparent from the context.

Processor means an organisation to whom the Company has entrusted data processing (such as an IT support provider, outsourced accounting).

Profiling means any form of automated processing of data consisting of the use of data to evaluate certain personal aspects relating to a natural person, in particular to analyse or predict aspects concerning that natural person's performance at work, economic situation, health, personal preferences, interests, reliability, behaviour, location or movements.

Data Export means transfer of personal data outside of the European Economic Area (EEA) i.e. to third countries or international organisations

DPO or Officer means Data Protection Officer.

RPA or Record means a record of processing activities.

5. **PRINCIPLES OF DATA PROTECTION**

5.1. **Pillars:**

(1) The Company takes care of privacy protection and processes data in accordance to the law (**Lawfulness**).

(2) The Company takes adequate steps to ensure an appropriate level of data security (**Security**).

(3) The Company performs and facilitates data subjects requests (**Data subjects rights**).

5.2. **Foundations**

(4) The Company documents compliance and performance to be able to demonstrate compliance at any given time (**Accountability**).

(5) The Company assesses the risks it generates to individuals whose data it is processing and applies data security and compliance measures adequate to those risks (**Risk Based Approach**)

5.3. **Principles**

The Company processes data according to the following principles:

(1) based on a legal basis and in accordance with the law (lawfulness);

(2) fairly to individuals and with integrity (fairness);

(3) transparently, especially from the perspective of individuals (transparency);

(4) for specific purposes only and not "just in case" (purpose limitation, minimisation);

(5) no more than necessary (adequacy / data minimisation);

(6) taking care for data accuracy and updating (accuracy);

(7) no longer than necessary (storage limitation / retention);

(8) securely i.e. providing an adequate level of security (data security / integrity and confidentiality)

5.4. **System of data protection in the Company**

A Company's data protection system consists of the following elements:

1) **Data inventory.** The Company identifies its data resources, classifies data, identifies how data resources are used for data processing, including:
   a) when special categories data or criminal data are processed;
   b) when the Company processes data of individuals of identity unknown to the Company ("**unidentified data**" / "**UFO data**");
   c) when children's data or data of other persons requiring special attention are being processed;
   d) joint controllership
   e) significant parallel controllership (i.e. when in the same situation the Company and other entities are processing same data however with little influence on each other – e.g. corporate fan page on Facebook).

2) **Record of Processing.** The Company maintains the record of processing activities in the Company (Record of Processing). The Record

of Processing is a tool of accountability – demonstrating data protection compliance in the Company.

3) **Legal grounds.** The Company ensures, identifies and verifies legal grounds for processing and records them in the Record of Processing, as well as:
   a) systematically manages consents for data processing and for remote direct marketing communication (electronic and telephone);
   b) records and performs legitimate interest analysis for processing based on a legitimate interest of a Company or a third party.
4) **Data subjects rights**. The Company fulfils its information duties towards data subjects and timely processes data subjects' requests, and in particular:
   a) **Information duties**. The Company provides data subjects with information required by law while collecting data as and when required in other situations and documents fulfilment of this duty.
   b) **Ability to comply.** The Company ensures that each data subject right can be properly served by the Company and its processors.
   c) **Handling requests.** The Company ensures appropriate budget, other resources and procedures to timely process data subjects' requests and to document it.
   d) **Data breach communication.** The Company has a procedure in place to verify if a personal data breach needs to be communicated to affected data subjects.
5) **Minimisation.** The Company has appropriate minimisation (*privacy by default)* management procedures in place, including:
   a) data **adequacy** management
   b) data limitation management
   c) data **access** management
   d) data **retention** management
6) **Security.** The Company ensures an adequate level of data security, and in particular:
   a) performs risk analysis for processing operations or activities or categories thereof;
   b) performs data protection impact assessment, where a risk to the rights and freedoms of natural persons is high as well as a routine part of change management (privacy by design);
   c) adjusts technical and organisational data protection measures to the risk assessed;
   d) has an information security management system in place;
   e) has data breach management procedures in place allowing for identification of a data breach, assessment, response, and notification to the supervisory authority
7) **Processors** The Company has appropriate rules of data processors selection and verification, requirements for data processing (e.g.

template data processing agreement or checklist), rules on verification of the performance of processing agreements.

8) **Extra EU data transfer.** The Company has rules in place to identify if the Company transfers data to third countries (meaning outside the EU, Norway, Lichtenstein and Iceland) or to international organisations and to ensure the lawfulness of such transfer.
9) **Privacy by design.** The Company manages change impacting privacy or data protection. Procedures on initiating projects and investments in the Company take into account the necessity of assessing privacy and data protection impact, preferably in a form of a data protection impact assessment, allowing to ensure privacy (including compliance of purposes of data processing, security and data minimisation) at the stage of designing of a change, investment or a beginning of a new project.
10) **Cross-border processing.** The Company has rules in place to verify whether it processes data cross-border and rules on determining the lead authority and the main establishment as understood by the GDPR.

6. **Inventory**

6.1. **Sensitive data**

The Company identifies cases where it processes or may be processing special categories data or criminal data and maintains dedicated mechanisms that ensure compliance of such processing.

6.2. **Unidentified data**

The Company identifies cases where it processes or may be processing *unidentified* data and maintains mechanisms allowing the fulfilment of rights of data subjects concerned by such processing.

6.3. **Profiling**

The Company identifies cases where it uses data for profiling and maintains mechanisms that ensure compliance of this process with the law.

6.4. **Joint controllership and parallel controllership**

The Company identifies cases of joint controllership of data as well as situations where s parallel data controlling may take place.

7. **Record of Processing**

7.1. The Record of Processing documents processing activities in the Company, constitutes a map of data processing and is a crucial element to comply with the rule of accountability.

7.2. The Company maintains the Record of Processing, in which it records data processing activities and monitors the way it uses personal data.

7.3. Each data processing activity identified by the Company should be recorded with at least: (i) the name of the processing activity, (ii) the purpose of the processing, (iii) a description of categories of data subjects, (iv) a description of categories of data, (v) legal basis of processing along with a specification of a legitimate interests, if a legitimate interest is a basis for processing, (vi) ways of data collection, (vii) description of the categories of data recipients (including processors), (viii) information on an extra EU data transfer, (ix) a general description of the technical and organisational data security measures.

8. **Legal Basis**
    8.1. The Company records legal basis for data processing in the Record of Processing separately for every processing activity.
    8.2. While pointing to a particular legal basis (consent, contract, legal obligation, vital interests, public interests/official authority, legitimate interest of the Company), the Company provides a clarification when necessary. For instance, while relying on consent the Company demonstrates its scope, for legal obligation Company points to a specific legal provision, for vital interests – the Company describes categories of events, where such vital interests materialise, for legitimate interest – the Company points to a specific legitimate interest, such as self or third party marketing, claims handling, etc.
    8.3. The Company implements consent management methods enabling registration and verification of having consent of a data subject for processing hers/his data for specific purposes, for electronic communication (email, phone, text messages, others) and for registration of a consent refusal, withdrawal and other similar actions (objection, restriction request etc.)
    8.4. Each manager is obliged to understand legal basis on which her/his department processes data in each of the processing activities.
9. **Handling information duties and data subjects' requests**
    9.1. The Company ensures the clarity of the provided information and communication directed to data subjects.
    9.2. The Company facilitates performance of data subjects' rights, including: putting on the Company's website information and references (links) to the information on data subjects' rights and ways of performing them, including applicant's identification requirements, channels of communication with the Company, fees for "additional" requests, etc.
    9.3. The Company monitors meeting deadlines for handling data subjects' requests.
    9.4. The Company implements adequate methods of identification and authentication of data subjects when responding to data subjects' requests.
    9.5. The Company has appropriate procedures and mechanisms in place allowing to identify data of particular persons processed by the Company, integrate those data, correct them and erase in an integrated manner.
    9.6. The Company documents performing information obligations and processing data subject requests.
10. **Information duties**
    10.1. The Company determines effective and lawful ways of fulfilling information obligations, taking into consideration the duty to facilitate and

legibility, and applying the layered approach to information obligation respectively.

10.2. In case processing a data subject request requires more than one month the Company informs the applicant before the expiry of the one month deadline.

10.3. The Company performs the information obligation to a person at the time when data are obtained from that person. The Company accommodates to the extent reasonably possible preferences of data subjects regarding information obligation, for example by allowing to perform the information obligation via email even if data are collected by a phone, or by allowing to move the lengthy part of the information obligation to the end of the conversation/to a subpage.

10.4. The Company performs the information obligation to a person also when data are obtained from other sources than the data subject directly, unless it is not required according to Art. 14.5 GDPR (e.g. when data are collected from public registers and the purpose of processing corresponds to the purpose of such registers so that information obligation would require a disproportionate effort).

10.5. The Company determines way of informing data subjects when processing unidentified data, where feasible (for instance: notices on CCTV),

10.6. The Company informs the data subjects of a planned change of purpose of processing.

10.7. The Company informs the data subject before lifting the restriction of restriction.

10.8. The Company informs data recipients on any rectification, erasure or restriction of the processing (unless this requires disproportionate effort or proves impossible).

10.9. The Company informs the data subjects on their right to object to processing of data, at the latest at the time of the first communication with the data subject.

10.10. The Company communicates the data breach to the data subject without undue delay, if the breach is likely to result in a high risk to the rights and freedoms of this data subject.

11. **Data subjects requests**

11.1. While fulfilling data subjects' rights, the Company applies procedural guarantees protecting rights and freedoms of others. In particular, after obtaining a credible information that fulfilling the data subject request for a copy of data or a right to data portability may adversely affect the rights or freedoms of others (in particular rights connected with other people's data, intellectual property, trade secrets, personal rights etc.), the Company may request the data subject to explain or exercise other legal steps, including a refusal to fulfil the data subject's request.

11.2. **Not processing.** In response to a data subject's request the Company informs a data subject that their data are not being processed if that is the case. The Company may however require a data subject to provide a basic context of their request in order not to be considered manifestly excessive.

11.3. **Refusal.** The Company informs the data subject within a month of receiving a request on refusal to process their request and on related rights and remedies available.

11.4. **Right of access.** Upon a data subject's request, the Company informs the data subject whether or not it processes their data and informs the data subject on details of processing with accordance to the art. 15 of the GDPR (the scope of information corresponds with the scope of the information duty) and provides access to the data concerning the data subject.

11.5. **Copies of data.** Upon request, the Company provides data subject with a copy of data concerning the data subject and documents the provision of the first copy. The Company adopts and announces a data copy price list. The copy fee is calculated based on an estimated cost of handling of a copy request.

11.6. **Data rectification.** The Company rectifies incorrect data upon the data subjects request. The Company may refuse to correct data unless the data subject demonstrates incorrectness of data in a reasonable manner. In the case of data rectification, the Company informs the data subject on the recipients of data, upon the data subject's request.

11.7. **Data completion.** The Company completes and updates data upon data subject's request. The Company may refuse to complete data, if the completion should be against the processing purposes (i.e. the Company does not want to process data unnecessary for the Company). The Company may rely on data subject's statement concerning the completion of data unless it is not sufficient in the light of procedures adopted by the Company, the law or there are reasons to believe the data subject's statement is not credible.

11.8. **Data erasure.** Upon data subject's request, the Company erases data when:

1. data are no longer necessary for the purposes for which they were collected or otherwise processed,
2. the data subject withdraws consent on which the processing is based and there is no other legal ground for the processing,
3. the data subject successfully objects to the processing and there are no overriding legitimate grounds for the processing,
4. data have been unlawfully processed
5. data have to be erased to comply with a legal obligation
6. the erasure request refers to children data collected based on consent related to offering of information society services directly to a child (e.g. a child's profile in social media, participation in a contest on a website).

The Company determines a way of handling an erasure request in an efficient manner with respect to all data protection principles, including data security, and verifies whether any of exceptions of the art. 17.3 of the GDPR applies.

If data subject to erasure have been made public by the Company, the Company takes reasonable steps, including technical measures, to inform other controllers processing such data about the need to erase data and access to them.

In the case of data erasure, the Company informs the data subject on the recipients of data, upon the data subject's request.

11.9. **Restriction of processing.** The Company restricts processing upon data subject's request when:

a) the accuracy of data is contested by the data subject - for a period enabling to verify the accuracy of the personal data,
b) the processing is unlawful and the data subject opposes the erasure of data and requests the restriction of their use instead,
c) the Company no longer needs data for the purposes of the processing, but they are required by the data subject for the establishment, exercise or defence of legal claims,
d) the data subject has objected to processing on grounds relating to his or her particular situation - pending the verification whether the legitimate grounds of the Company override those of the data subject.

During the restriction of processing, the Company stores data, but does not process them (does not use or pass them on), without data subject's consent, unless for the purpose of the establishment, exercise or defence of legal claims or for the protection of the rights of another natural or legal person or for reasons of important public interest.

The Company informs the data subject before lifting of the processing restriction.

In the case of granting restriction of processing, the Company informs the data subject on the recipients of data, upon the data subject's request.

11.10. **Data portability.** Upon data subject's request, the Company provides data concerning her or him processed automatically (via IT systems) which he the data subject has provided to the Company, in a structured, commonly used and machine-readable format or (if possible) transfers data directly to another controller, where the processing is based on consent or on a contract.

11.11. **Objection on grounds relating to a particular situation.** If the data subject objects to processing of their data on grounds relating to their particular situation and data is processed by the Company on the grounds of the Company's legitimate interests or necessity for the performance of a task carried out in the public interest, the Company will **respect the objection** unless there are compelling legitimate grounds for the processing which override the interests, rights and freedoms of the data subject or there are basis for the establishment, exercise or defence of legal claims.

11.12. **Objection related to scientific or historical research purposes or statistical purposes.** If the Company process data for scientific or historical research purposes or statistical purposes, the data subject **may object** to such processing based on grounds relating to hers or his particular situation. The Company will respect the objection unless the processing is necessary for the performance of a task carried out for reasons of public interest.

11.13. **Objection related to direct marketing purposes.** If the data subjects objects to processing of hers or his data by the Company for the purposes of direct marketing, the Company will respect such objection and will cease to process data for that purpose.

11.14. **Right to a human intervention in the automated decision-making.** If the Company processes data automatically, in particular by profiling data subject's data, which results in decisions taken solely automatically producing legal effects or similarly significantly affecting a data subject (eg. depriving a person of their digital identity), the Company provides a communication channel for an appeal to a human intervention, unless the automated decision is directly authorised by the law.

12. **MINIMISATION**

The Company ensures data minimisation with respect to the (i) adequacy to purposes (amount and scope of processing) (ii) access to data, (iii) data retention period. In particular:

12.1. **Scope minimisation**

The Company, while implementing the GDPR, has verified the scope of obtained data, scope of processing and the amount of processed data taking into account their adequacy in the light of the purposes of processing.

The Company periodically analyses an amount and a scope of processed data, not less than once a year.

The Company verifies changes to the amount and scope of the processing as a part of a change management procedure (privacy by design).

12.2. **Scope minimisation**

The Company applies data access restrictions: legal (non-disclosure agreements, access authorisations), physical (access areas, door locking) and logical (access restrictions for data processing IT systems and network resources containing data).

The Company uses physical access control.

The Company updates access rights at the times of changes within personnel (changes in membership or positions) and among processors. The Company periodically verifies profiles of IT systems users and updates them, no less than once a year.

Detailed rules on physical and logical access control are enclosed in the Company's physical security and information security procedures.

12.3. **Time minimisation (retention)**

The Company applies data life-cycle control mechanisms, including verification of data further suitability with accordance to times and control-points indicated in the Record of Data Activities.

Data, which suitability decreases with time, are erased from production system as well as main and referential files. Such data may be subject to archiving or be present on backup copies of systems and information processed by the Company. Procedures on archiving and using archives, creating and using back-up copies take into account requirements of control over data life-cycle, including the erasure requirements.

13. **SECURITY**

The Company ensures level of security adequate to the risk to the rights and freedoms of natural persons resulting from processing data by the Company.

13.1. **Risks analysis and security measures adequacy**

The Company carries out and documents adequacy of data security measures analysis. For this purpose:

(1) The Company equips itself with an adequate level of knowledge on information security, cybersecurity and business continuity - internally or with a support of external specialized entities.

(2) The Company categorizes data and processing activities with respect to the risk posed by thereof.

(3) The Company carries out an analysis of risk to the rights and freedoms of natural persons of the processing activities or their categories. The Company analyses possible situations and scenarios of data protection breaches taking into account the nature, scope, context and purposes of the processing, risk to the rights and freedoms of natural persons of varying likelihood and severity.

(4) The Company determines organisational and technical measures possible to apply and assess cost of their implementation. This includes an assessment of suitability of measures and methods such as:

(i) pseudonymisation

(ii) data encryption

(iii) other cybersecurity measures providing the ongoing ability for providing confidentiality, integrity, availability and resilience of systems and processing services.

(iv) measures ensuring business continuity and preventing effects of catastrophes, meaning measures with the ability to restore the availability and access to data in a timely manner in the event of a physical or technical incident.

13.2. **Data protection impact assessment (DPIA)**

The Company carries out an assessment of the impact of the envisaged processing operations on the protection of data (data protection impact assessment), where according to the risk analysis, there is a high risk to the rights and freedoms of natural persons.

The Company uses methodology adopted in the Company.

To the extent possible the Company performs DPIA routinely as part of the organisational change control.

13.3. **Data security measures**

The Company applies data security measures (technical and organisational measures of data protection) as determined in the analysis of risk and security measures adequacy and data protection impact assessment.

Security measures are elements of information security and cybersecurity measures in the Company and are described in detail in appropriate procedures.

13.4. **Data breach notification**

The Company applies procedures enabling identification, assessment and notification of an identified data protection breach to the supervisory authority within 72 hours from the moment of identification of the breach.

14. **PROCESSOR**

The Company has rules on processors' selection and verification developed for the purpose of ensuring the provision of sufficient guarantees of implementing appropriate technical and organisational measures by the processors, in order to ensure security, fulfilment of data subject's rights and other duties relying on the Company.

The Company has adopted minimal requirements as to the processing agreement.

The Company accounts its processors for their use of subprocessor, as well as other requirements arising from the rules on entrusting data processing.

15. **DATA EXPORT**

The Company records in the Record of Processing cases of data transfers out of the of EEA (EU plus Iceland, Lichtenstein and Norway).

In order to avoid unauthorised Data Export, including the use of the publicly available cloud services (shadow IT), the Company periodically verifies users actions and provides equivalent solutions that are in line with data protection laws.

16. **PRIVACY BY DESIGN**

The Company manages changes that can influence data protection in a way that enables providing a suitable data security and minimisation of data processing.

In order to do so, procedures on starting new projects and investments in the Company refer to the principles of data security and minimisation and require assessment of an influence posed by a change on privacy and data protection as well as taking into account the necessity to design security and minimisation of the processing at the beginning of the project or an investment.

Unless unreasonable, the Company uses the methodology of data protection impact assessment.

17. **FINAL PROVISIONS**

This Data Protection Policy enters into force on 25 May 2018.

APPENDIX II

Data Processing Agreement

Maciej Gawronski, Pawel Punda & Katarzyna Kunda

Template

Agreement
on personal data processing
to the Agreement ....

concluded by between
.... as a Controller
and
.... as a Processor

Agreement
on personal data processing
supplementing the Agreement ....
concluded on ....
in ....,
by and between:

.... ("**Controller**")
and
.... ("**Processor**")
(hereinafter jointly referred to as "**Parties**")
As:

i. The Parties entered into the agreement .... ("**Main Agreement**") and in connection with the performance of the Main Agreement, the Controller entrusts processing of personal data with the Processor within the scope specified in the Agreement;

ii. The purpose of this Agreement is to set out the terms under which the Processor carries out data processing operations on behalf of the Controller;
iii. By entering into this Agreement, the contracting Parties intend to set out rules on personal data processing in accordance with the provisions of the Regulation (EU) 2016/679 of the European Parliament and of the Council of 27 April 2016 on the protection of natural persons with regard to the processing of personal data and on the free movement of such data, and repealing Directive 95/46/EC (General Data Protection Regulation) ("**GDPR**")

The Parties agreed to enter the following Agreement:

1. Description of the processing

1.1. **Subject matter. [GDPR.28.1]** Under the terms of this Agreement and the Main Agreement, the Controller vests processing (as defined in the GDPR) of further described Personal Data to the Processor.
1.2. **Duration. [GDPR.28.3]** Processing will be performed during the term of the Main Agreement.
1.3. **The nature and purpose of the processing. [GDPR.28.3]** The nature and purpose of the processing is provided in the Main Agreement. In particular:
  1.3.1. the nature of the processing is specified by the following task of the Processor [*example: providing accounting services for the Controller*], whereas
  1.3.2. the purpose of the processing is *[example: enabling the Controller to fulfil his obligations arising from the law connected to accounting management as well as financial management of the Controller]*
1.4. **Type of personal data. [GDPR.28.3]** The processing includes following types of personal data ("**Data**"):

Standard Data

(1) name and surname
(2) Personal Identity No.
(3) e-mail address
(4) IP address
(5) phone numbers
(6) address of residence
(7) date of birth
(8) Tax Identification Number
(9) ID series and number
(10) parent's names
(11) bank account number
(12) ....

Special categories Data and criminal Data:

(13) medical records
(14) ....

(15) ....

Children's data

(16) name and surname
(17) date of birth
(18) e-mail address
(19) alias
(20) ....

Unstructured data

(21) content potentially and probably consisting of personal data (entries, documents, pictures, footages, recordings)

1.5. **Categories of data subjects. [GDPR 28.3]** The processing of Data concerns following categories of data subjects:

(1) employees of the Controller and affiliated entities
(2) clients of the Controller's service/product as specified in the Main Agreement
(3) persons, with whom Controller's clients engage into social interactions
(4) contractors (recipients and suppliers) of Controller's clients
(5) recipients of the Controller's clients' electronic correspondence
(6) ....
(7) ....
(8) ....

2. Sub-processing

2.1. **Sub-processing. [GDPR.28.2]** The Processor may vest specific Data processing operations ("**sub-processing**") in form of a written sub-processing agreement ("**Sub-processing Agreement**") to another data processing entity ("**Sub-processor**"), provided the Controller does not object to such sub-processing.

2.2. **Accepted Sub-processors.** A list of Sub-processors accepted by the Controller constitutes **Annex no. 1 to the Agreement – "List of Accepted Sub-processors"**.

2.3. **Right to object.** Vesting data processing to Sub-processors not included on the List of Accepted Sub-processors requires prior notification to the Controller in order to enable him to object. The Controller may, due to compelling reasons, object in a documented way explaining the reasons to objecting to vesting data processing to a specific Sub-processor. If the objection is raised, the Processor is not authorized to entrust data with the objected Sub-processor, and if the objection concerns a current Sub-processor, the Processor must terminate entrusting data processing with the Sub-processor in question without undue delay. Any doubts about legitimacy of the objection and potential negative consequences must be reported by the Processor to the Controller in a time enabling the continuity of the processing.

2.4. **Transfer of obligations. [GDPR.28.4]** While further entrusting the processing of data, the Processor must oblige the Sub-processor to fulfil all of Processors' obligations arising from this Agreement, excluding those, which do not apply due to a nature of a specific sub-processing.
2.5. **Obligation towards the Controller.** The Processor ensures that the Sub-processor undertakes directly to the Controller to fulfil all of the obligations specified in the previous section. Such obligation may be performed by submitting a relevant statement, including a list of Sub-processor's obligations or a copy of a sub-processing agreement, addressed to the Controller, along with signing of the Sub-processing Agreement.
2.6. **Prohibition on subcontracting of the subject-matter of the Agreement. [GDPR.28.4]** The Processor is not authorized to subcontract the performance of the entirety of this Agreement to a Sub-processor.

3. The Processor's obligations

The Processor's obligations are as follows:

3.1. **Documented instructions. [GDPR.28.3.a]** The Processor processes Data only in accordance with documented instructions given by the Controller.
3.2. **No processing outside EEA. [GDPR 28.3.a]** The Processor declares that they do not transfer Data to a third country or an international organization (meaning outside of the European Economic Area ("**EEA**")). Processor also declares, that they are not using any subcontractors who transfer Data outside of the EEA.
3.3. **Intention of processing outside EEA. [GDRP 28.3]** Where the Processor intends or is obliged to transfer Data outside of the EEA, the Processor informs the Controller in advance, in order to enable the Controller to take a decision and relevant measures necessary to ensure compliance of the processing with the law or to terminate the processing.
3.4. **Confidentiality [GDPR.28.3.b.]** The Processor obtains documented non disclosure undertakings from persons authorised to process Data in the course of performance of this Agreement or makes sure that such persons are subjected to legal obligation of confidentiality.
3.5. **Security [GDPR.28.3.b]** The Processor ensures Data security and implements technical and organisational data security measures as described in the Article 32 GDPR, in accordance to further provisions of the Agreement.
3.6. **Sub-processing [GDPR.28.3.d]** The Processor fulfils the conditions of using another processor (Sub-processor).
3.7. **Data subjects' rights cooperation [GDPR.28.3e]** The Processor undertakes to the Controller to help the Controller to respond to the data subjects' requests described in the GDPR's chapter III ("**Rights of the data subject**"). In particular the Processor is responsible to the Controller for processing

data subjects' requests to the extent such requests refer to processing performed by the Processor.

3.8. **Support with security measures [GDPR 28.3.f]** The Processor supports the Controller with the fulfilment of the data security duties described in articles 32-36 of the GDPR (security of the processing, breach notification, communication of a breach to data subjects, data protection impact assessment, prior consultation with the supervisory authority).

3.9. **Legality of the Controller's instructions [GDPR.28.3.par2]** In the case the Processor has doubts about the legality of instructions given by the Controller, the Processor immediately informs the Controller on the doubts (in a documented way and with an explanation). If the Processor fails to timely inform the Controller about their doubts as to the legality of a particular instruction the Controller is relieved from liability to the Processor for the lack of legality of related instructions.

3.10. **Privacy by design [GDPR.25.1]** While planning a change in the processing of Data, the Processor is obliged to assess impact of the change on data protection and is obliged to inform the Controller on the planned changes and their privacy impact in advance in such a way and time, that the Controller has a real possibility to react, if the changes planned by the Processor endanger the agreed level of security of Data or increase the risk to the rights and freedoms of natural persons, posed by the processing of Data by the Processor.

3.11. **Data minimisation [GDPR.25.2]** The Processor undertakes to limit access to Data only to persons, whose access to Data is necessary for the performance of this Agreement, and who have an appropriate authorisation.

3.12. **RCPA [GDPR.30.2]** The Processor undertakes to keep the documentation describing means of data processing, including a record of categories of processing activities (Article 30 GDPR). The Processor, upon the Controller's request, makes the record of categories of processing activities available, excluding information containing business secrets of the Processor's other clients.

3.13. **Profiling and automated decision making [GDPR.13 and 14]** If the Processor uses an automated decision making for the performance of this Agreement, including profiling as described in articles 22.1 and 22.4 of the GDPR, the Processor informs the Controller on such processing in the scope necessary to enable the Controller to fulfil the information obligations.

3.14. **Personnel training.** The Processor undertakes to provide persons authorised to process Data with appropriate trainings in the scope of personal data protection.

4. The Controller's obligations

4.1. The Controller is obliged to cooperate with the Processor in the course of performance of the Data Processing Agreement, provide the Processor with explanations in case of any doubts as to the lawfulness of the Controller's instructions and to fulfil his detailed duties in a timely manner.

5. Data security

5.1. **Personal data security [GDPR.32]** The Processor has carried out a risk analysis of vested Data, provided it to the Controller and applies its result as to the organisational and technical security measures.
5.2. **Security measures.** The Parties agreed upon a level of security required of the Processor in a separate document.
5.3. **Security guarantees.** The Processor has provided the Controller with information and documents confirming that the Processor ensures sufficient guarantees of implementing appropriate technical and organisational measures. Both Parties retain copies of the provided documentation and proofs of providing information, for the purposes of accountability.

6. Data breach notification

6.1. **Data breach notification.** The Processor notifies the Controller of any suspicion of Data security breach no later than 24 hours from the first information on the suspicion, enables the Controller to participate in investigations, and informs the Controller about findings at the moment of their determination, in particular if the breach was found.
6.2. **Notification.** A breach notification should be provided with all the necessary documentation regarding the breach, so the Controller may fulfil the obligation of notifying of the supervisory authority.

7. Supervision

7.1. **Control [GDPR.28.3.h]** The Controller may audit means of Data processing after a prior notification about a planned control. The Controller or persons authorised by the Controller are allowed to (i) enter the rooms, where Data is processed and (ii) inspect the documentation connected to Data processing. The Controller is entitled to request information on the course of the processing from the Processor, as well as request access to the processing records.
7.2. The Processor:
(1) provides the Controller with any information necessary to demonstrate compliance of the Controller's conduct with the GDPR,

(2) enables the Controller or an authorised auditor to perform an audit or inspection. The Processor cooperates in the scope of a performance of audits or inspections.

8. Representations and Warranties

8.1. **The Controller.** The Controller hereby represents that he is the Data Controller and is authorised to process Data in the scope of entrusting of the processing to the Processor.

8.2. **The Processor.** The Processor herby represents that, in the scope of his business activities, he professionally processes data as described in this Agreement and the Main Agreement, holds the necessary knowledge in that scope, implements appropriate technical and organisational measures and warrants a proper performance of this Agreement.

8.3. **Letters of recommendation.** Upon the Controller's request, the Processor will present appropriate letters of recommendation, list of experience, financial information or other proofs, warranting the proper performance of this Agreement.

9. Liability

9.1. **The Processor's liability [GDPR.82.2]** The Processor is liable for the damage caused by his actions where he has not complied with the GDPR obligations specifically directed to the processors or where they have acted outside lawful instructions of the Controller or against such instructions. The Processor is liable for the damage caused by an incorrect implementation or lack of an implementation of appropriate security measures.

9.2. **Liability for Sub-processors [GDPR.28.4]** If the Sub-processor fails to comply with his data protection obligations, the Processor remains fully liable to the Controller for the performance of the Sub-processor's obligations.

10. Term of the Agreement

10.1. **[GDPR.28.3]** The Agreement has been concluded for the term of the Main Agreement.

11. Data erasure

11.1. **Data erasure [GDPR.28.3.g]** Upon termination of the Main Agreement, the Processor is no longer authorised to process Data and is obliged to:

(1) erase Data

(2) erase all of existing copies of Data or return Data, unless the Controller decides otherwise or EU or member state's law requires storage of the Data

11.2. **Grace period.** The Processor erases Data after 180 days from the termination of the Agreement, unless the Controller request the Processor to do so earlier.

11.3. **Declaration.** After erasing or returning of Data, the Processor submits to the Controller a written statement confirming a permanent erasure of all Data.

12. Final provisions

12.1. **Priority.** In the case of any discrepancies between provisions of this Agreement and the Main Agreement, the provision of this Agreement shall prevail. This means, that all matters regarding personal data processing between the Controller and the Processor should be regulated by amendments to this Agreement or by the performance of its provisions.

12.2. **Copies.** This Agreement has been drafted in two identical copies, one for each of the Parties.

12.3. **Governing law.** This Agreement is subject to the ....law and the GDPR.

APPENDIX III

Joint Controllership Agreement

Maciej Gawronski, Adrianna Gnatowska & Katarzyna Kunda

(„**Agreement**")
concluded on .... in ...., by and between:
.... („**Executive Controller**")
and
.... („**Joint-controller B**")
and
.... („**Joint-controller C**")
called also the "**Party**" and jointly called "**Joint-controllers**" or the "**Parties**".
Given that:

A. The Parties jointly determine purposes and means of processing relating to their joint activity [*i.e. joint compliance management in the group of companies, joint talent and personnel management in the group of companies, joint client acquisition, joint product offering, a consortium*], being joint personal data controllers in the meaning of Article 26 of the Regulation (EU) 2016/679 of the European Parliament and of the Council of 27 April 2016 on the protection of natural persons with regard to the processing of personal data and on the free movement of such data, and repealing Directive 95/46/EC (General Data Protection Regulation) ("**GDPR**").
B. Article 26 GDPR obliges the Parties as joint-controllers to comply with obligations regarding processing of personal data, including those connected with data subject rights and fulfilment of information duties as described in articles 13 and 14 of the GDPR.
C. The purpose of this Agreement is to jointly determine respective responsibilities of the Joint-controllers and to establish relation between the Joint-controllers and between the Joint-controllers and data subjects, including means of handling of data subjects' requests.

The Parties have decided to enter into the following Agreement:
§ 1 Description of joint-controllership

1.1. **Subject matter. [GDPR.26.1]** The Agreement determines the division of responsibilities of the Parties as joint controllers of personal data resulting from GDPR.

1.2. **Purpose and means. [GDPR.26.1]** Purpose and means of the processing of personal data covered by this Agreement (hereinafter called also just "data") by the Joint-controllers *is described in the Main Agreement/ is described in this Agreement.* In particular, the Parties decided that:

A joint purpose of the processing is:

Data are processed with the following means:

[*describe means of processing*]

1.3. **Type of data.** Processing by the Joint-controllers will cover types of data indicated in the ***Annex no. 1 to the Agreement – Types of processed data*** **OR LIST TYPES BELOW.**

1.4. **Data subject categories.** Processing of data by the Joint-controllers will cover the following categories of data subjects:

[for instance:

(1) *employees of the Joint-controllers and entities associated with the Joint-controllers*
(2) *Joint-controllers' service/product clients*
(3) *persons, with whom the Joint-controllers' clients engage into social interactions*
(4) *contractors' personnel (recipients and suppliers) of Joint-controllers*
(5) *recipients of Joint-controllers' clients' electronic correspondence*

§ 2 Joint-controllers' obligations

2.1. **Data subjects. I**nformation obligation and handling of data subjects' requests ("**Data subjects rights**") will be fulfilled by the Executive Controller. If a data subject addresses their request to another Joint-controller, the receiving Joint Controller will pass the data subject's request immediately (the closest working Friday or Monday, no later than within 5 working days) to the Executive Controller and will independently start actions necessary to process the request if the request concerns that Joint Controller directly.

2.2. The Parties determine roles and the scope of fulfilling GDPR duties as follows:

(1) **Complying with principles of data processing [GDPR.5]** The Joint-controllers undertake to process data in compliance with the principles of data processing set in Article 5 GDPR.

(2) **Accountability [GDPR.5.2]** The Executive Controller maintains all documentation relevant to the joint-controllership.

(3) **Lawfulness of processing [GDPR.6,9]** Joint-controllers undertake to process data only when one of the legal grounds for processing prescribed in articles 6 or 9 GDPR exists and only within the scope there allowed.

(4) **Processing outside of the EEA [GDPR 44].** The Joint-controllers do not transfer data outside of the EEA.

(5) **Privacy by design [GDPR.25.1]** While planning a change in the processing of data, the Parties are obliged to follow the privacy by design principle, as described in Article 25.1 GDPR, and are obliged to inform the other Parties on planned changes in such advance, that the Parties retain a real possibility to react, if changes planned by the Party, in opinion of at least one the other Parties, may adversely affect the appropriate level of security of data or increase the risk to the rights and freedoms of natural persons, posed by the processing of data by the Parties.

(6) **Data minimisation. [GDPR.25.2]** The Parties undertake to limit access to data only to persons whose access to data is necessary for the performance of goals of processing.

(7) **Confidentiality. [GDPR.29]** Only persons having a Party's authorisation and subject to a non-disclosure obligation may be allowed to access data on behalf of the Parties.

(8) **RPA. [GDPR.30.1]** Each of the Parties undertakes to keep documentation describing means of processing, including the Record of Processing Activities ("**RPA**") (as required in Article 30 GDPR). The Party makes their RPA available to other Parties in the scope of the processing activities covered by the joint-controllership.

(9) **Security. [GDPR.32]** Each of the Parties ensures appropriate data security and implements technical and organisational data protection measures as described in Article 32 GDPR and in further provisions of this Agreement.

(10) **Data Protection Officer. [GDPR.37]** *The Parties have appointed one Data Protection Officer ("**DPO**")./ The Executive Controller has appointed a Data Protection Officer ("**DPO**")./ .... carried out a documented analysis that points to the conclusion, that it is not obligatory to appoint a DPO, but the data protection specialist ("**DPS**") has been appointed. The Parties have exchanged DPO and DPS's data. / Each of the Joint-controllers has appointed a Data Protection Officer*

*("**DPO**") / data protection specialist ("**DPS**"). The Parties have exchanged their DPO and DPS's contact data.*

(11) **Trainings.** The Parties ensure that persons allowed to process data were provided with an appropriate training in the scope of personal data protection principles and regulations as well as consequences of breaching them, including in particular procedures on protecting personal data and their roles pursuant to those procedures.

(12) **Communicating the joint-controllership [GDPR.26]** The Joint-controllers inform data subjects on the fact of the joint-controllership and the essence of the arrangements made in this Agreement, in particular on the relation between the Parties, relation between the Parties and data subjects and the scope of duties of each of the Parties. Information on the joint-controllership and on the essence of the arrangements of the Joint-controllers should be disclosed at the time of collecting data for the joint-controllership purposes. Information on the joint-controllership might be included in the information obligation fulfilled in accordance with Articles 13, 14 and 26 GDPR. ***Information on the essence of arrangements made by the Joint-controllers with an information duty is enclosed in the Annex no. 2 hereto.***

(13) **Data protection breach notification [GDPR.33]** In case of a data protection breach, the Executive Controller is responsible for the notification of the breach to the supervisory authority. The Parties undertake to cooperate pursuant to further provisions of the Agreement.

(14) **Communication of a data breach to data subjects [GDPR.34.1]** If a data breach is likely to result in a high risk to the rights and freedoms of natural persons, the Executive Controller is responsible for communicating the data breach to the data subject without undue delay. The Parties undertake to cooperate pursuant to further provisions of the Agreement.

§ 3 Entrusting processing

3.1. **Entrusting processing. [GDPR.28.2]** Each of the Parties may entrust processing ("**Processing**") to another processor ("**Processor**") by a data processing agreement concluded in a documented form ("**Processing Agreement**") In such a case the entrusting Party is obliged to ensure the fulfilment of all duties related to entrusting of the personal data processing arising from the GDPR and inform the Parties of the Processor(s) identity.

3.2. A list of accepted Processors is enclosed in the ***Annex no. 3 hereto – A List of Accepted Processor.***

3.3. **Objection. [RODO.28.2 zd. 2]** Each of the Parties may, due to compelling reasons, object (in a documented form) to entrusting data processing to a specific Processor. Where the objection is raised, the entrusting Party is not

allowed use the Processor covered by the objection. In case an objection concerns a previously accepted Processor, the entrusting Party must terminate the processing that is covered by the objection. The entrusting Party and the objecting Party agree means and timelines allowing to sustain the processing continuity and agree on alternative solutions. If the Parties do not reach a mutually satisfactory conclusions, each Party may terminate this Agreement.

§ 4 Personal data security

4.1. **Risk analysis. [GDPR.32]** Each of the Joint-controllers have carried out a risk analysis and implements its results as to organisational and technical security measures that correspond to the established risk to the rights and freedoms of data subjects. The Parties update their risk analysis with accordance to their needs and inform the other Parties on the results of the update.

4.2. **Data security measures.** The Parties confirm that they implement a level of security measures appropriate to the risk established in the risk analysis described in the previous section. In particular, each of the Parties has decided, informed the other Parties and obliges to update information on adequacy and implemented technical and organisational measures including:

   4.2.1. the pseudonymisation and encryption of personal data;

   4.2.2. the ability to ensure the ongoing confidentiality, integrity, availability and resilience of processing systems and services;

   4.2.3. the ability to restore the availability and access to personal data in a timely manner in the event of a physical or technical incident;

   4.2.4. a process for regularly testing, assessing and evaluating the effectiveness of technical and organisational measures for ensuring the security of the processing.

4.3. **DPIA. [GDPR.35.1]** Where a planned type of processing covered by the joint-controllership - in particular using new technologies - taking into account the nature, scope, context and purposes of the processing - is likely to result in a high risk to the rights and freedoms of natural persons, the Parties will decide on the rules of the cooperation regarding the data protection impact assessment for the planned processing activities.

§ 5 Reaction times

5.1. **Notification of a data breach suspicion.** The Party notifies the other Parties on a data breach suspicion within 48 hours from when it has been first made aware of. If it is likely that a personal data breach took, the Party directly affected allows the other Parties to participate in investigations. Independently, the Party informs the other Parties on determining whether there has been a breach or no breach has been found within 4 hours from the moment of such determination.

5.2. **Breach notification.** Data breach notification should be done by the Executive Controller. If a notification concerns the Party that has found the breach, this Party draws up the contents of the notification immediately. The Executive Controller maintains a record of confirmed data protection breaches connected to the joint-controllership.

5.3. **Notification on the access request.** Each of the Joint-controllers notifies the Parties on each request to access data made by the authority of the State within 48 hours, unless law prohibits such a notification, in particular criminal law or anti-money laundering laws.

5.4. **Data subject's request notification.** Each of the Joint-controllers notifies the Parties on every data subject's request that the Party received within 48 hours. Additionally, all relevant parties supply the Executive Controller with all necessary documentation relating to the material data subject's request in order to enable the Executive Controller a performance of the request.

5.5. **Continuity.** The Joint-controllers will agree on means of communication between the Parties and will determine persons responsible for each of the Joint-controllers, so meeting of the deadlines' prescribed above will be ensured, in particular by establishing a requirement of receipt confirmation and redundancy of communication channels as well as appointed persons for each of the Joint-controllers.

§ 6 Contact persons

6.1. **Joint-controllers contact point.** DPOs should be the contact persons for the purposes of communication regarding personal data breaches and for data subjects.

6.2. **Joint-controllers' DPO's contact details.** *Joint-controllers appointed the DPO ...., phone number ...., e-mail .... / DPO appointed by each of the Joint-controllers is ...., phone number ...., e-mail ...., phone number ...., e-mail ....*

6.3. Entirety of the communication between the Parties made in connection to this Agreement should also be directed to contact points, with accordance to the section 5.5 of the Agreement.

§ 7 Liability

7.1. **Liability.** Each of the Joint-controllers is subject to legal measures and sanctions as described in articles 77-79 of the GDRP as well as articles 82-84 of the GDPR (joint and several liability). With respect to mutual settlements (recourse) the Parties rely on the principle of guilt. Where no Party is guilty or the degree of guilt is similar, the division of liability should be done proportionally to the turnover resulting from the joint controllership processing for each of responsible Parties, and if this is not possible to establish – in equal shares.

§ 8 Term of the Agreement

8.1. **Term of the Agreement.** *The Agreement is concluded for the infinite period / period of…. / term of the Main Agreement.*
8.2. **Termination.** The Agreement may be terminated upon a 3-months notice expiring at the end of the calendar quarter.

§ 9 Final provisions

9.1. **Annexes.** The Agreement has the following annexes:

Annex no. 1 – Types of processed data
Annex no. 2 – Information on the essence of arrangements made by the Joint-controllers with an information duty
Annex no. 3 – A List of Accepted Processor

9.2. **Entering into force.** The Agreement comes into force at the day of its signing by the Parties.
9.3. **Written form.** All modification or additions to the Agreement require a documented form under the pain of invalidity.
9.4. **Court's jurisdiction.** All disputes arising from the performance of this Agreement should be taken before the court of the Executive Controller's registered office.
9.5. **Copies.** One copy of this Agreement has been drawn up for each of the Parties.
9.6. **Governing law.** This Agreement is subject to the GDPR and Polish law, in particular the provision of civil code.

signatures:

Annex no. 1 ***Types of processed data***

Please indicate appropriate data categories covered by the joint-controllership or describe types of data in other way.

Basic identification data
Identification data assigned by government institutions
Electronic identification data
Electronic localization data
Biometrical identification data
Financial identification data

Financial means
Debts and expenditures
Solvency
Loans, mortgages, lines of credit
Financial assistance
Insurance policy details
Pension plan details
Financial transactions
Compensation
Professional activities
Agreements and settlements
Permits
Personal details
Military details
Immigrant status
Physical description
Private habits
Addictions
Lifestyle
Travel and movement details
Social contacts
Possessions
Public mandates
Complaints, incidents, or accidents
Distinctions
Media use
Psychological details
Marriage or current form of cohabitation
Marital history
Details regarding other family or household members
Leisure activities and interests
Memberships (other than professional, political, or in trade unions)
Legal data related to suspicions
Legal data regarding convictions and sentences
Legal data regarding judicial actions
Legal data regarding administrative penalties
Consumption habits
Residence data
Physical health data
Mental health data
Data regarding risk situations and risk behavior
Genetic data related to population studies, genetic research, etc.
Recuperation data
Education and training
Academic curriculum

Publications
Profession and employment
Current employment
Recruitment
Work termination
Career
Absenteeism and discipline
Occupational medicine
Wages
Assets in possession of the employee
Work organization
Review
Training for the position
Security data (authorizations)
Access levels
Use of technology
Racial or ethnic data
Data about the sex life
Political opinions
Political affiliation
Membership in an interest group or militant organization
Membership in a trade union
Philosophical or religious beliefs
Beliefs
Video recordings
Image
Sound recordings

ANNEX NO. 2 – INFORMATION OBLIGATION INCLUDING THE ESSENCE OF ARRANGEMENTS OF THE JOINT-CONTROLLERS

With accordance to articles 13, 26 and 28 of the Regulation (EU) 2016/679 of the European Parliament and of the Council of 27 April 2016 on the protection of natural persons with regard to the processing of personal data and on the free movement of such data, and repealing Directive 95/46/EC (General Data Protection Regulation) ("**GDPR**"), we inform you that we jointly process your data and hereby we present you with the essence of arrangements made between us as the Joint-controllers.

The Joint-controllers are:

.... with a registered office in ...., address ...., more information on ....*(website)*........

("**Executive Controller**")

.... with a registered office in ...., address ...., more information on ....*(website)*........

.... with a registered office in ...., address ...., more information on ....*(website)*........

I. The Executive Controller and other Joint-controllers jointly process your data for the following purposes:
   a. for the purpose of concluding an agreement with you and to jointly perform that agreement by providing you with a service......,
   b. for the purposes of direct marketing of our offer,
   c. for or the establishment, exercise or defence of legal claims between you and the Executive Controller and other Joint-controllers, which is based in the Executive Controller and other Joint-Controller's legitimate interest.

II. Processors of the Joint-controllers, in particular IT services provider, accountants etc., may be recipients of your data.

III. We plan to store your data for a 120 years after the end of our cooperation with you, in order to be able to establish, exercise or defend claims and its good chance by then that you are already dead so GDPR is no longer protecting you.

IV. You have the right to request access to, rectification or erasure of your data as well as restriction of processing of data concerning you.

V. Where the processing is based on the Executive Controller and other Joint-controller's legitimate interests, you have the right to object to such processing of your data.

VI. Where the processing is based on your consent, you have the right to withdraw consent at any time, without affecting the lawfulness of processing based on consent before its withdrawal.

VII. You have the right to data portability, where the processing is based on your consent or for the purpose of concluding and performing of an agreement.

VIII. You have the right to lodge a complaint with the supervisory authority.

IX. The provision of data is *voluntary/ voluntary but necessary for the performance of the ...... / a statutory requirement according to ....*

X. We also inform you that:
   a. The Executive Controller and other Joint-controllers hereby declare that they process your data with accordance to the data protection principles set by Article 5 GDPR.
   b. The Executive Controller maintains all documentation relevant to the joint-controllership.
   c. The Executive Controller and other Joint-controllers do not transfer data outside of the EEA.
   d. The Executive Controller and other Joint-controllers undertake to limit access to your data only to persons, whose access to data is necessary for the performance of the purposes described above. Additionally, the Executive Controller and other Joint-controllers ensure that only persons that have the Executive Controller's or the Joint-controller's

authorisation and are subject to a non-disclosure obligation may be allowed to process data. Such persons have been provided with an appropriate training in the scope of personal data protection principles and regulations.

e. The Executive Controller and other Joint-controllers ensure an appropriate level of data security. The Executive Controller and other Joint-controllers provide:
   - the ability to ensure the ongoing confidentiality, integrity, availability and resilience of processing systems and services;
   - the ability to restore the availability and access to personal data in a timely manner in the event of a physical or technical incident;
   - a process for regularly testing, assessing and evaluating the effectiveness of technical and organisational measures for ensuring the security of the processing
   - the Executive Controller and other Joint-controllers implement pseudonymisation and encryption of personal data when the risk of data processing requires so and benefits of implementing such data security measures overcome detriment to data availability for you and other persons affected.

f. The Executive Controller and other Joint-controllers may entrust the processing of your data to processors, given that the requirements of the GDPR, in particular those of the article 28 of the GDPR are met.

XI. In all cases regarding the protection of your personal data, you may contact the Executive Controller as well as the other Joint-Controllers, but we stress that it will be the Executive Controller, who is responsible for replying to you and looking after fulfilment of your data protection rights. Thus, it would be the easiest if you could direct your communication to:

Data Protection Officer, address: .... (adding "Data Protection Officer"), e-mail:....................., phone number:......................

Annex no. 3 – A List of Accepted Processors

Index

D

E

I

S

T

U

W

www.ingramcontent.com/pod-product-compliance
Ingram Content Group UK Ltd.
Pitfield, Milton Keynes, MK11 3LW, UK
UKHW020234290926
15470UKWH00002B/529